Rinse, Spin, Repeat

A graphic memoir of loss and survival

Edith Fassnidge

unbound

This edition first published in 2016

Unbound

6th Floor Mutual House, 70 Conduit Street, London W1S 2GF

www.unbound.co.uk

Text Design by Rich Carr

A CIP record for this book is available from the British Library

ISBN 978-1-78352-136-4 (trade hbk)
ISBN 978-1-78352-138-8 (ebook)
ISBN 978-1-78352-137-1 (limited edition)

Printed in UK by Bell and Bain Ltd, Glasgow

For Matt, and our dear Posy

With special thanks to

Catherine Holland

Dear Reader,

The book you are holding came about in a rather different way to most others. It was funded directly by readers through a new website: Unbound. Unbound is the creation of three writers. We started the company because we believed there had to be a better deal for both writers and readers. On the Unbound website, authors share the ideas for the books they want to write directly with readers. If enough of you support the book by pledging for it in advance, we produce a beautifully bound special subscribers' edition and distribute a regular edition and e-book wherever books are sold, in shops and online.

This new way of publishing is actually a very old idea (Samuel Johnson funded his dictionary this way). We're just using the internet to build each writer a network of patrons. Here, at the back of this book, you'll find the names of all the people who made it happen.

Publishing in this way means readers are no longer just passive consumers of the books they buy, and authors are free to write the books they really want. They get a much fairer return too – half the profits their books generate, rather than a tiny percentage of the cover price.

If you're not yet a subscriber, we hope that you'll want to join our publishing revolution and have your name listed in one of our books in the future. To get you started, here is a £5 discount on your first pledge. Just visit unbound.com, make your pledge and type **rinse** in the promo code box when you check out. Thank you for your support,

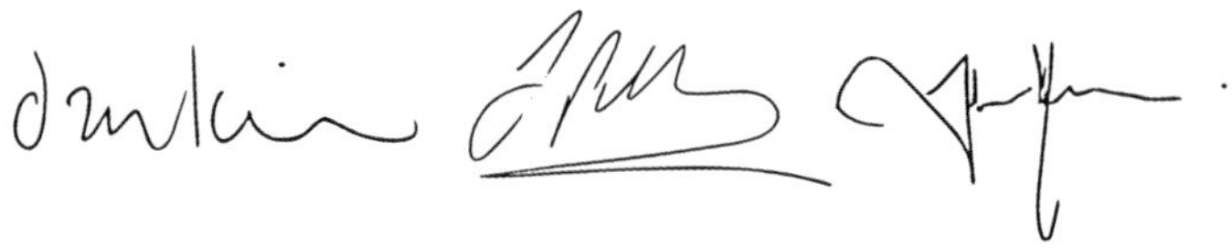

Dan, Justin and John
Founders, Unbound

Rinse, Spin, Repeat

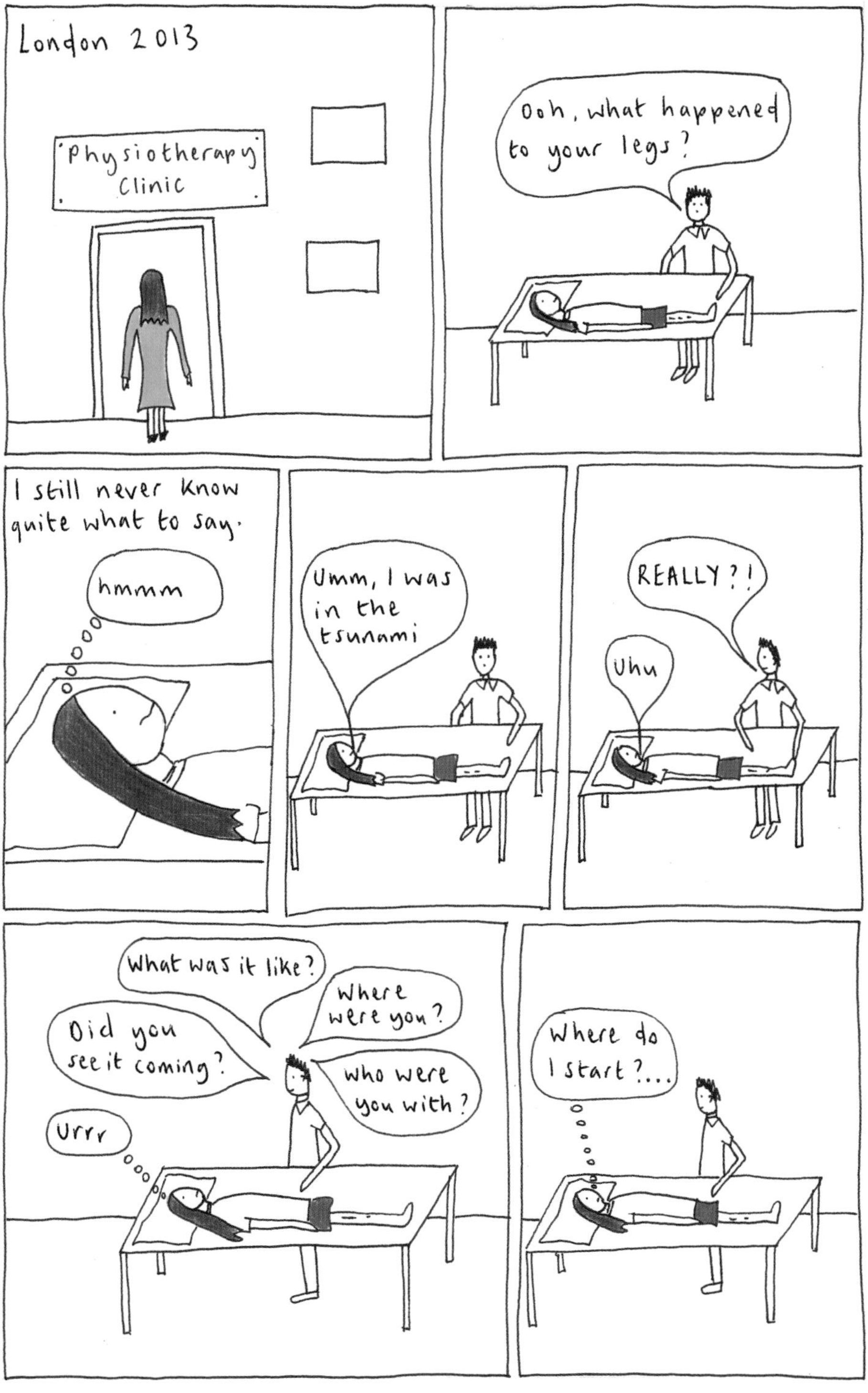
London 2013
Physiotherapy Clinic
Ooh, what happened to your legs?
I still never know quite what to say.
hmmm
Umm, I was in the tsunami
REALLY?!
Uhu
What was it like?
Where were you?
Did you see it coming?
Who were you with?
Urrr
Where do I start?...

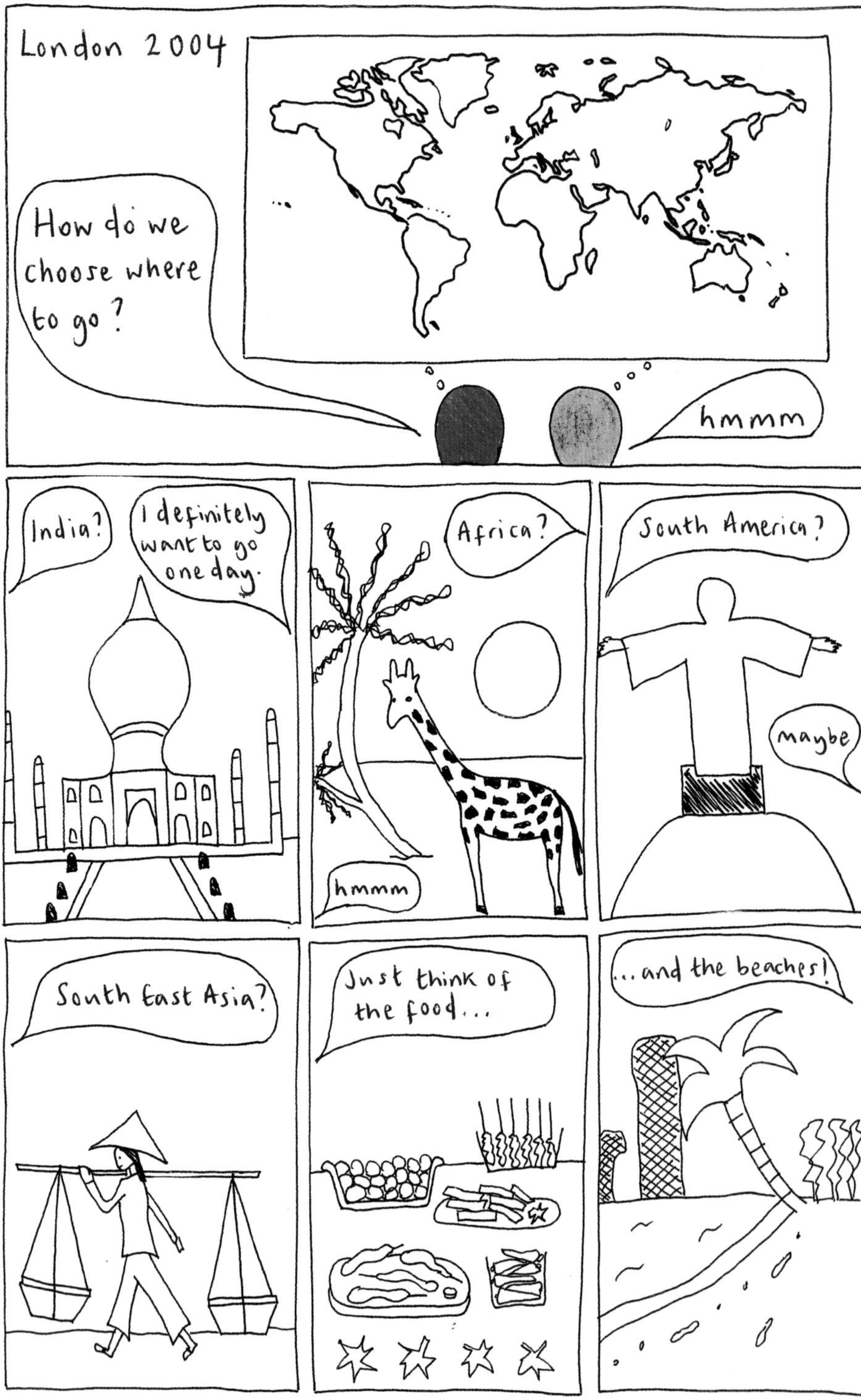
London 2004
How do we choose where to go?
hmmm
India?
I definitely want to go one day.
Africa?
hmmm
South America?
maybe
South East Asia?
Just think of the food...
...and the beaches!

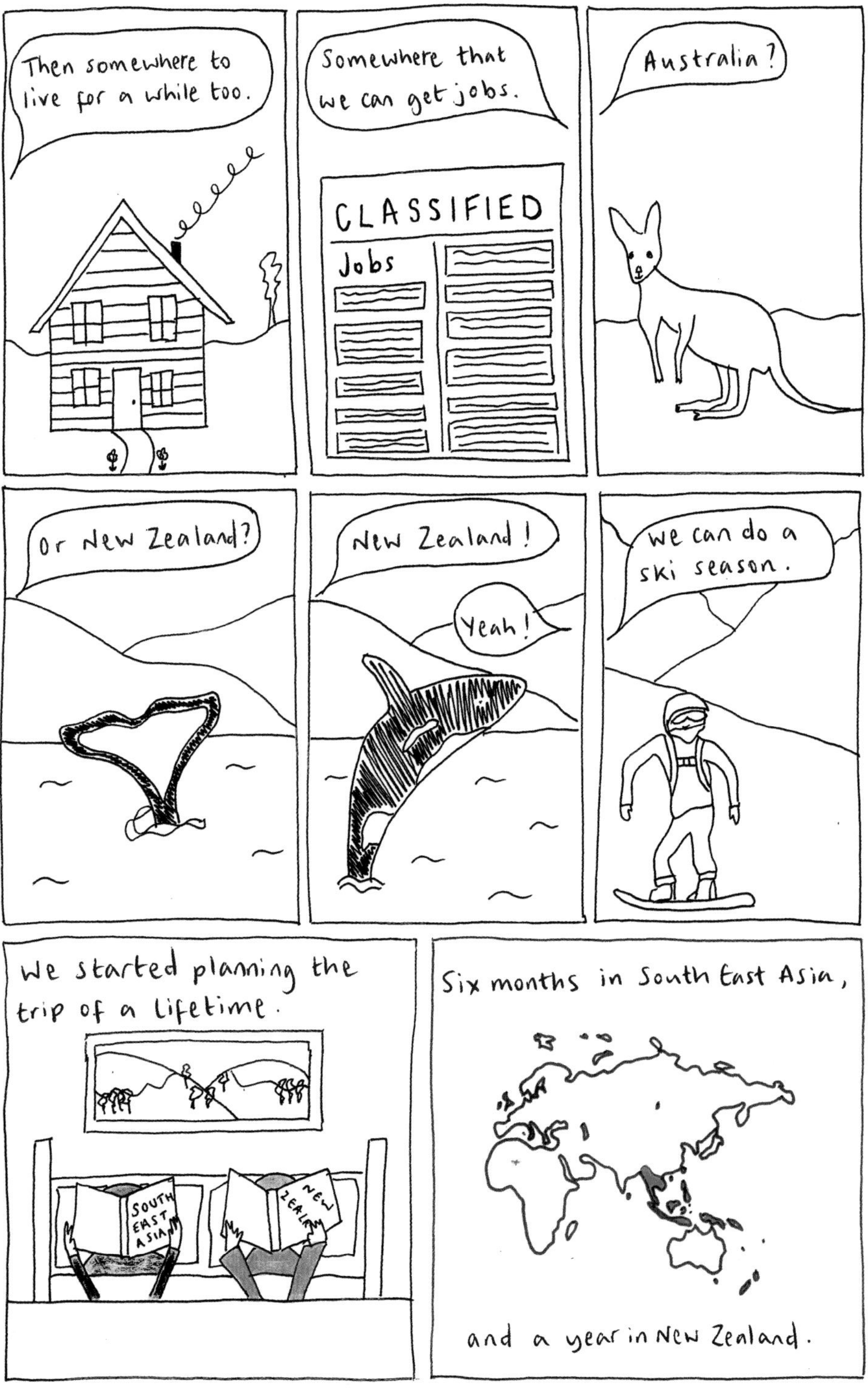
Then somewhere to live for a while too.
Somewhere that we can get jobs.
CLASSIFIED
Jobs
Australia?
Or New Zealand?
New Zealand!
Yeah!
We can do a ski season.
We started planning the trip of a lifetime.
SOUTH EAST ASIA
NEW ZEALAND
Six months in South East Asia,
and a year in New Zealand.

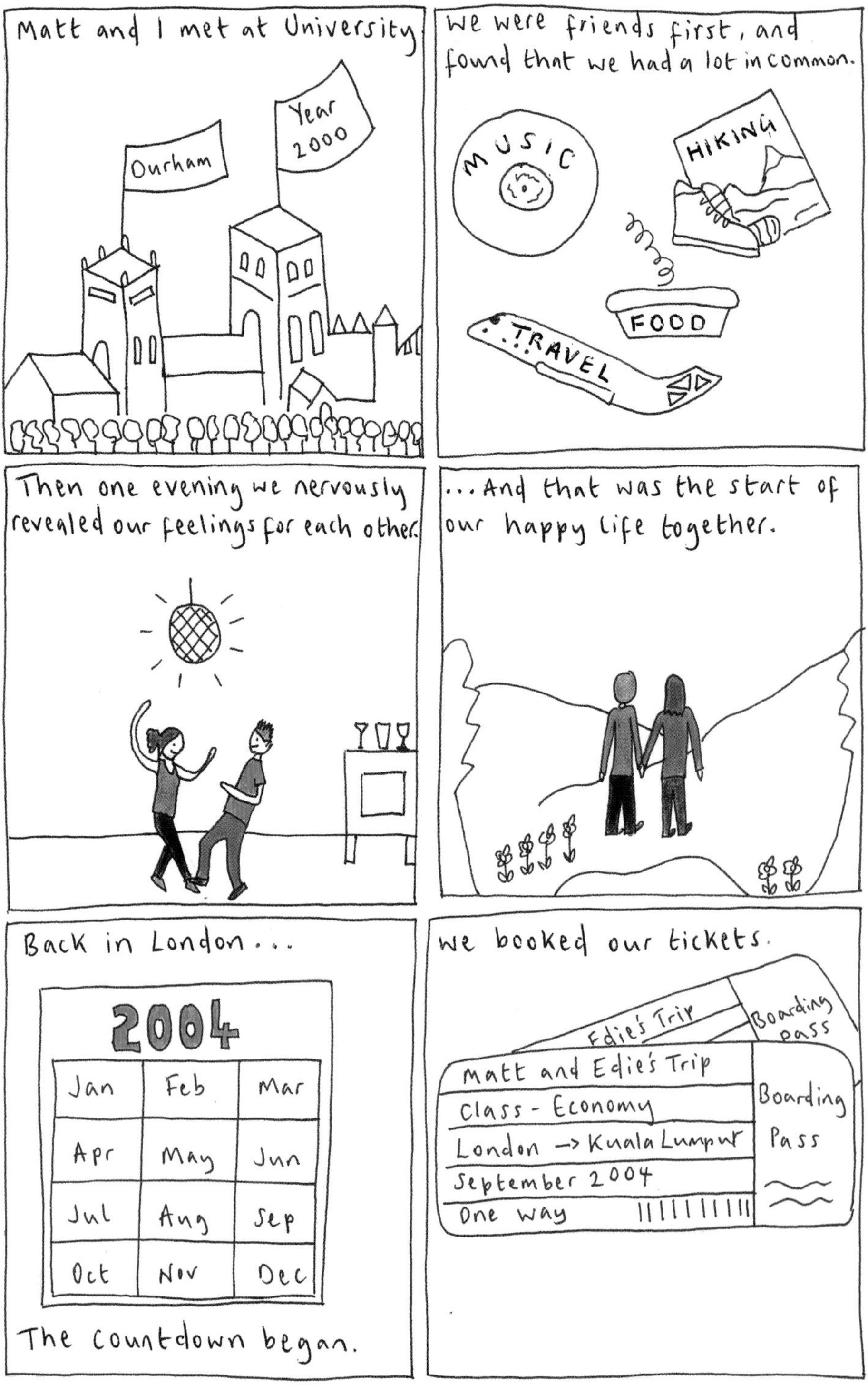
Matt and I met at University
Durham
Year 2000
We were friends first, and found that we had a lot in common.
MUSIC
HIKING
FOOD
TRAVEL
Then one evening we nervously revealed our feelings for each other.
...And that was the start of our happy life together.
Back in London...
2004
Jan Feb Mar
Apr May Jun
Jul Aug Sep
Oct Nov Dec
The countdown began.
We booked our tickets.
Edie's Trip
Boarding pass
Matt and Edie's Trip
Class - Economy
London -> Kuala Lumpur
September 2004
One way
Boarding Pass

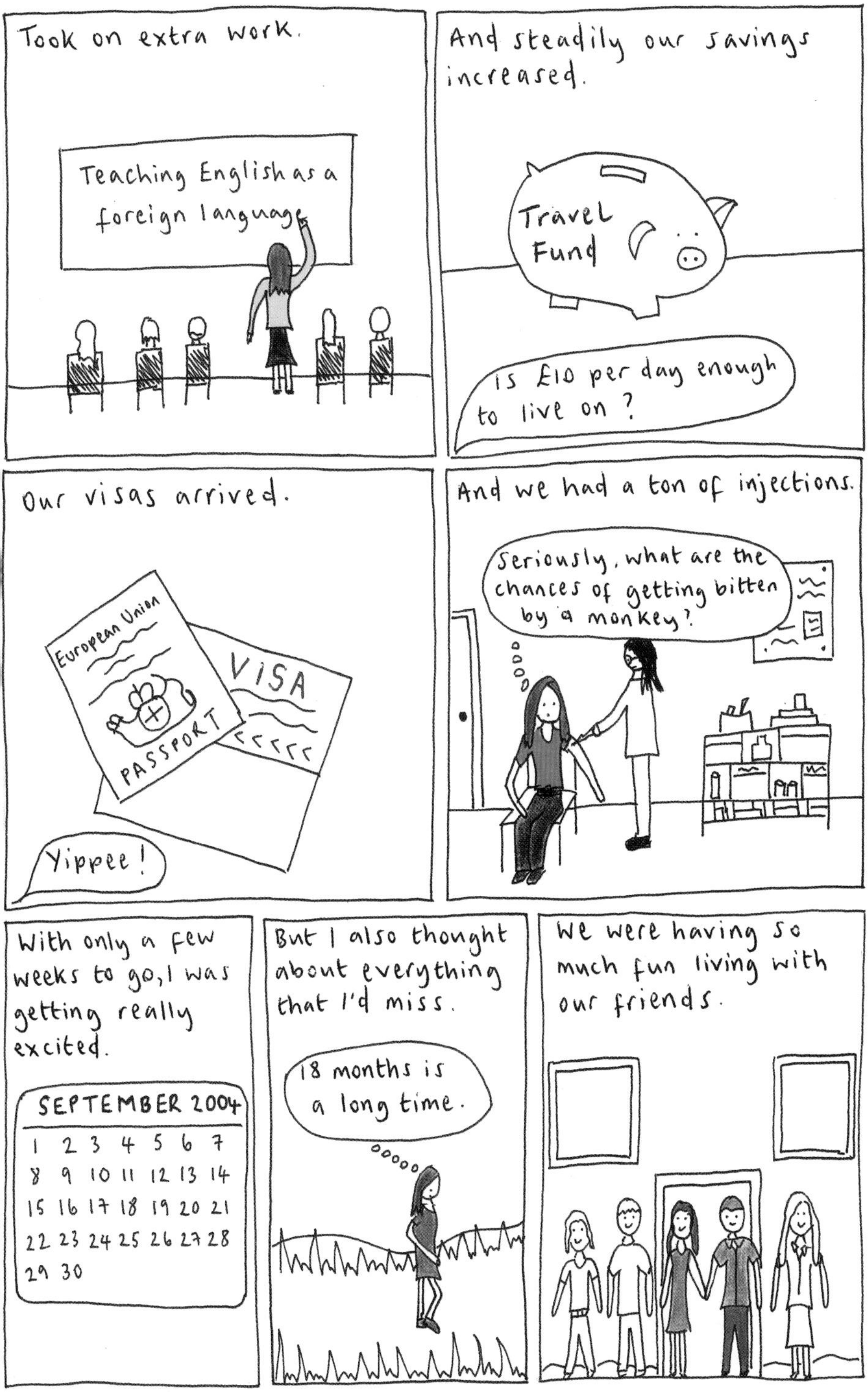
Took on extra work.
Teaching English as a foreign language
And steadily our savings increased.
Travel Fund
Is £10 per day enough to live on?
Our visas arrived.
European Union
PASSPORT
VISA
Yippee!
And we had a ton of injections.
Seriously, what are the chances of getting bitten by a monkey?
With only a few weeks to go, I was getting really excited.
SEPTEMBER 2004
1 2 3 4 5 6 7
8 9 10 11 12 13 14
15 16 17 18 19 20 21
22 23 24 25 26 27 28
29 30
But I also thought about everything that I'd miss.
18 months is a long time.
We were having so much fun living with our friends.

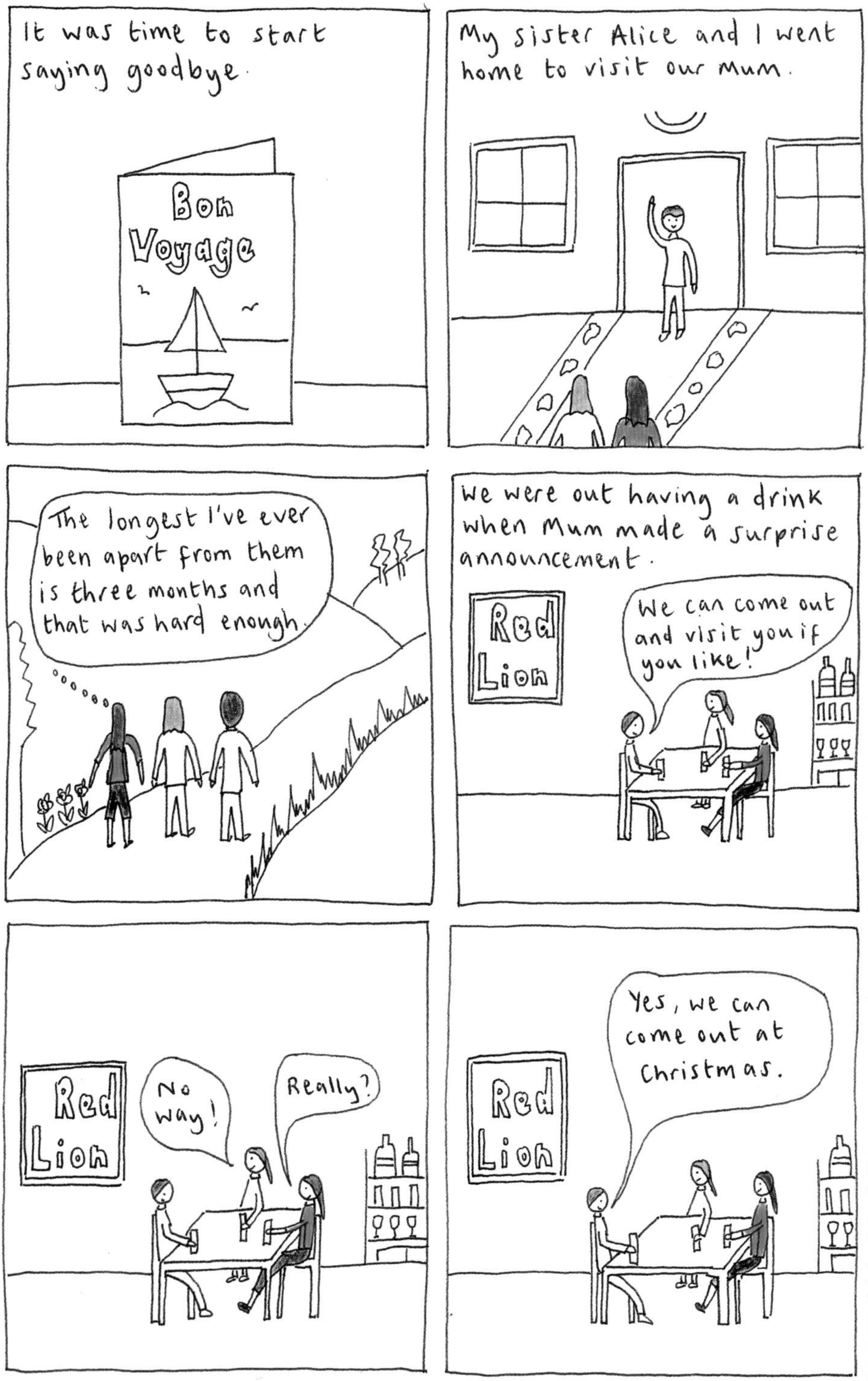

It was time to start saying goodbye.
Bon Voyage
My sister Alice and I went home to visit our Mum.
The longest I've ever been apart from them is three months and that was hard enough.
We were out having a drink when Mum made a surprise announcement.
Red Lion
We can come out and visit you if you like!
Red Lion
No way!
Really?
Red Lion
Yes, we can come out at Christmas.

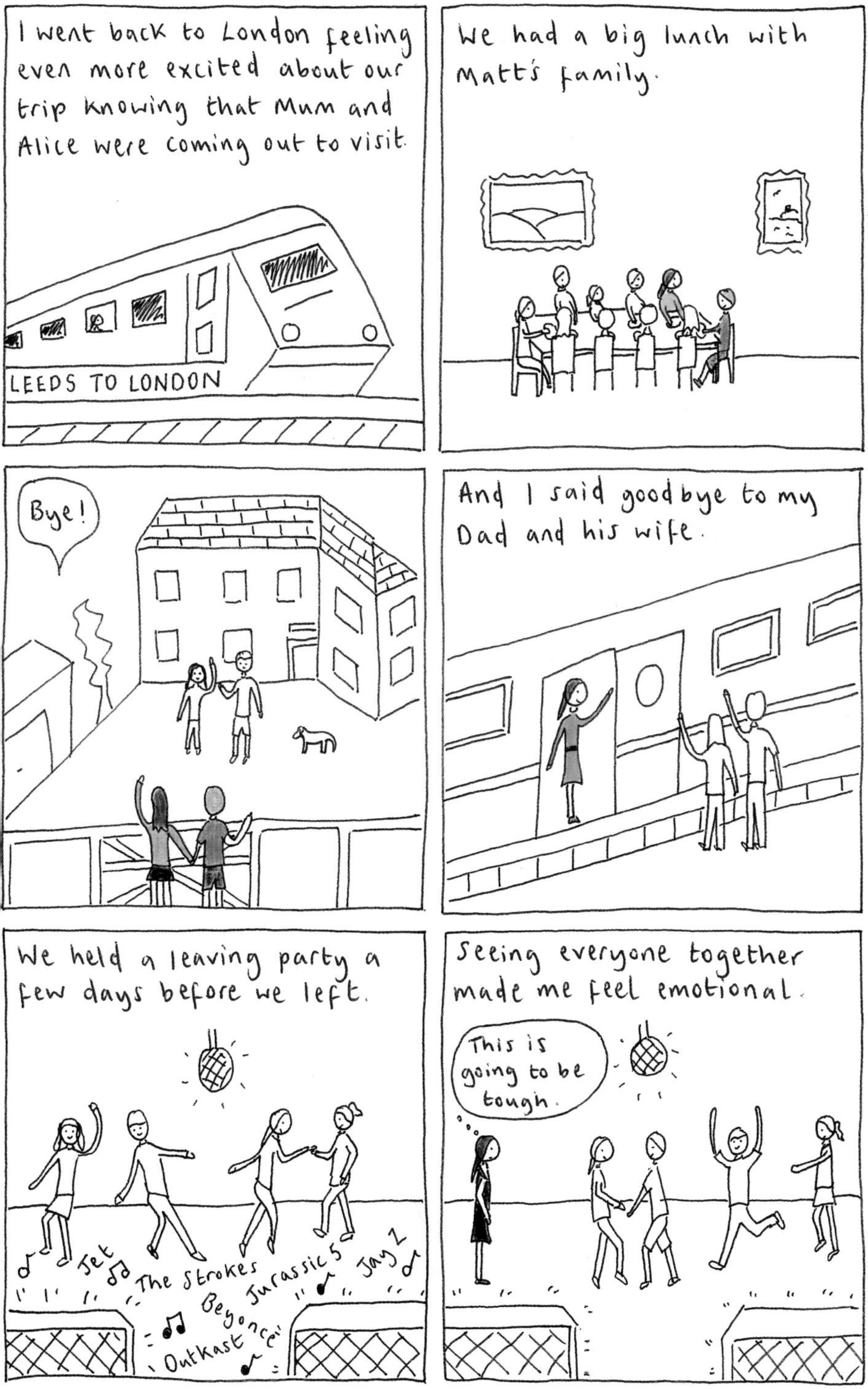
I went back to London feeling even more excited about our trip knowing that Mum and Alice were coming out to visit.
LEEDS TO LONDON
We had a big lunch with Matt's family.
Bye!
And I said goodbye to my Dad and his wife.
We held a leaving party a few days before we left.
Jet
The Strokes
Jurassic 5
Jay Z
Beyonce
Outkast
Seeing everyone together made me feel emotional.
This is going to be tough.

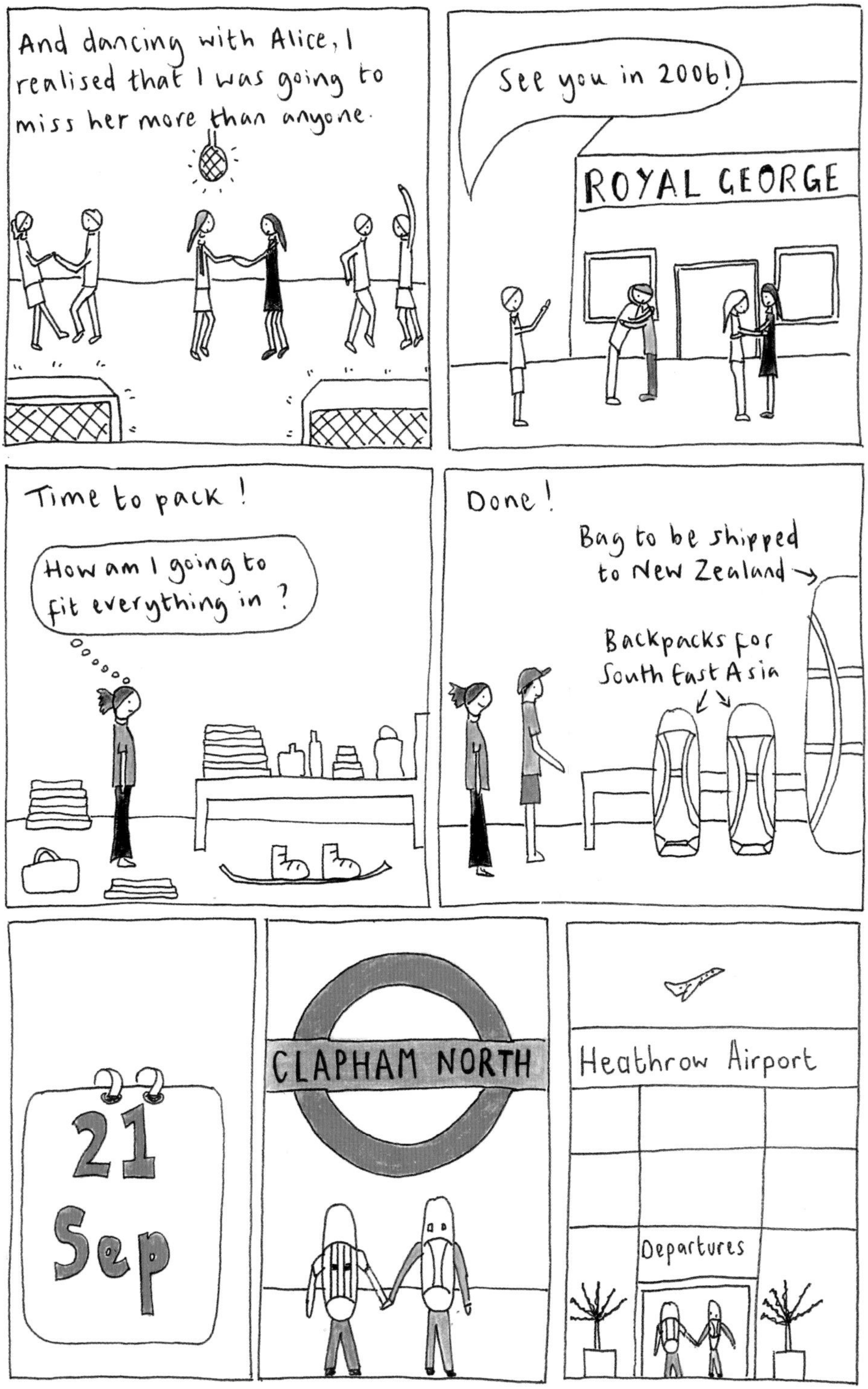
And dancing with Alice, I realised that I was going to miss her more than anyone.
See you in 2006!
ROYAL GEORGE
Time to pack!
How am I going to fit everything in?
Done!
Bag to be shipped to New Zealand
Backpacks for South East Asia
21 Sep
CLAPHAM NORTH
Heathrow Airport
Departures

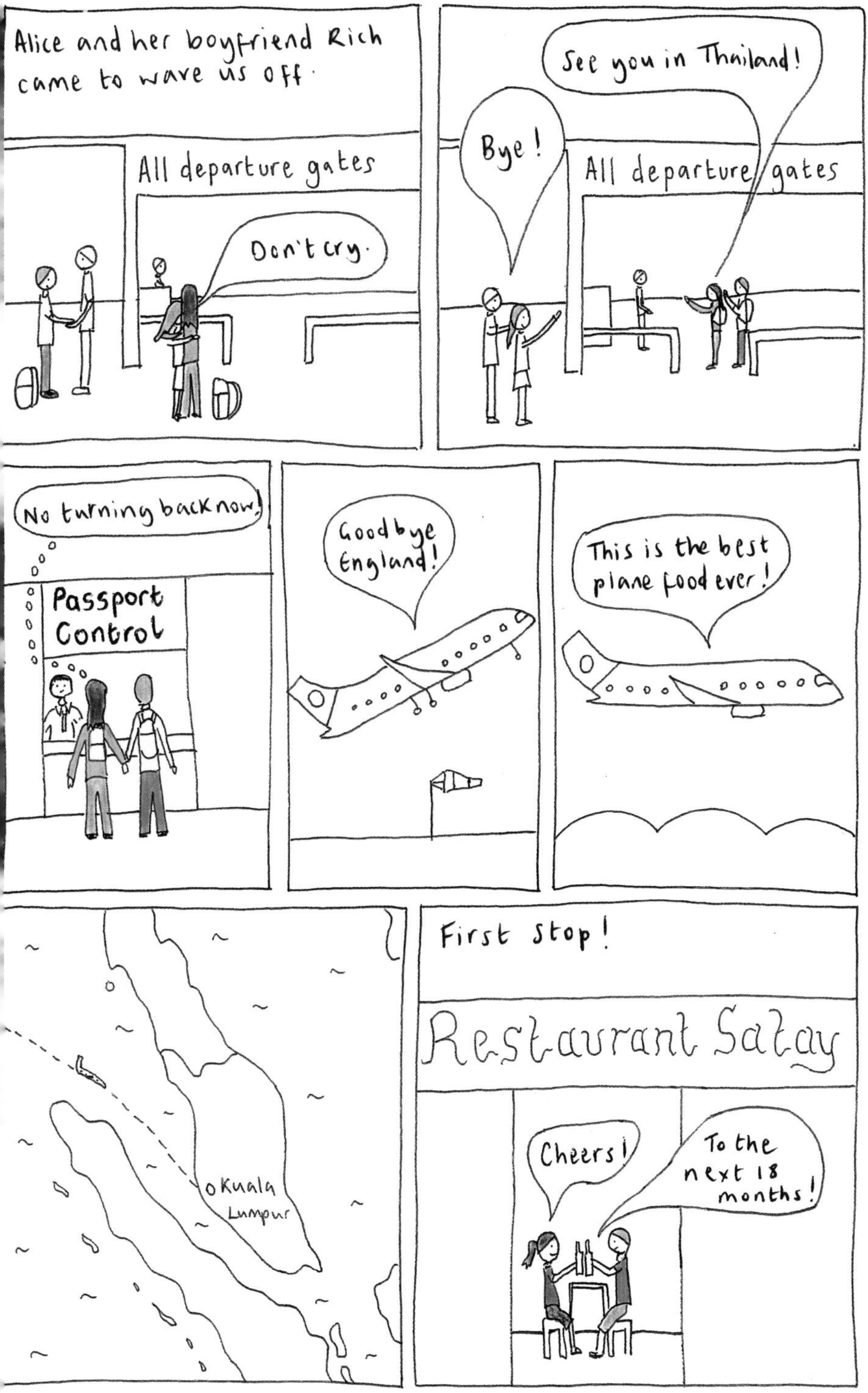
Alice and her boyfriend Rich came to wave us off.
All departure gates
Don't cry.
See you in Thailand!
Bye!
All departure gates
No turning back now!
Passport Control
Goodbye England!
This is the best plane food ever!
Kuala Lumpur
First stop!
Restaurant Satay
Cheers!
To the next 18 months!

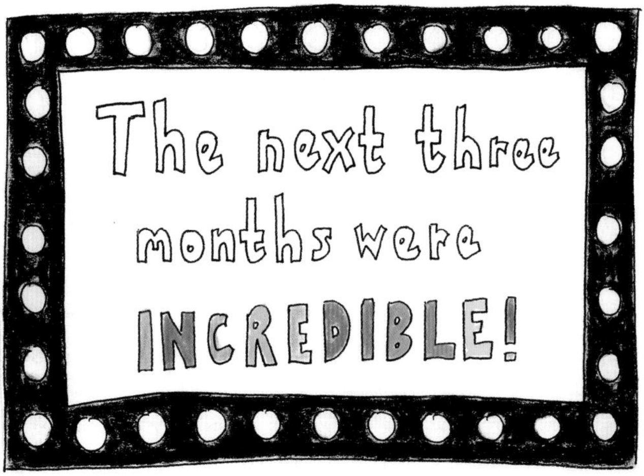
The next three months were INCREDIBLE!

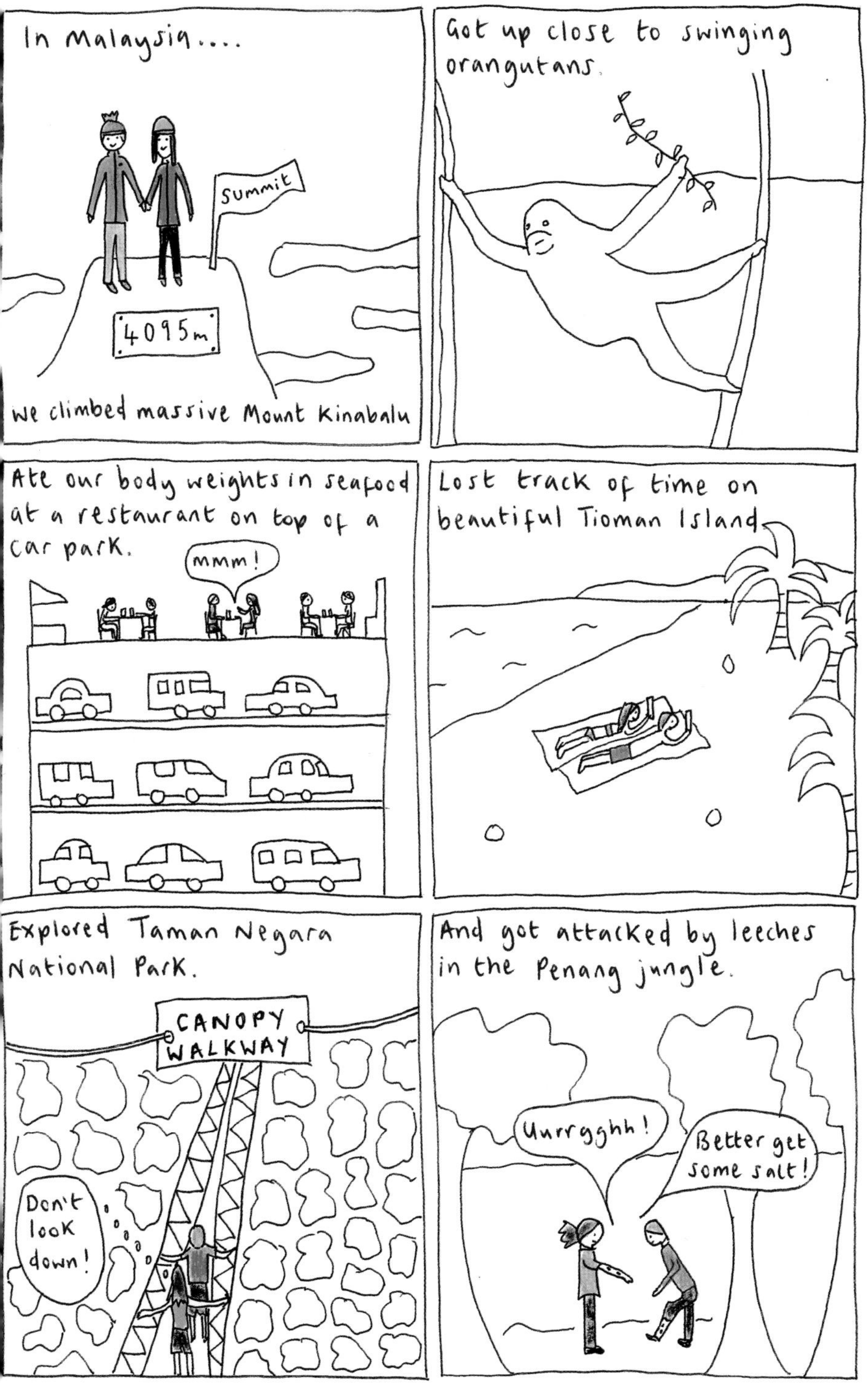
In Malaysia....
Summit
4095m
We climbed massive Mount Kinabalu
Got up close to swinging orangutans.
Ate our body weights in seafood at a restaurant on top of a car park.
mmm!
Lost track of time on beautiful Tioman Island.
Explored Taman Negara National Park.
CANOPY WALKWAY
Don't look down!
And got attacked by leeches in the Penang jungle.
Urrrgghh!
Better get some salt!

In Singapore....

HIGH TECH MALL

Say cheese!

We bought our first digital camera.

Dug out our smartest clothes for afternoon tea at Raffles Hotel.

Enjoyed delicious vegetarian food in Little India.

Happy Deepavali

Watched a mesmerising Taoist ceremony.

Stayed in an awesome hostel.

Free toast and marmite!

And discovered the incredible taste of laksa* watching bad karaoke

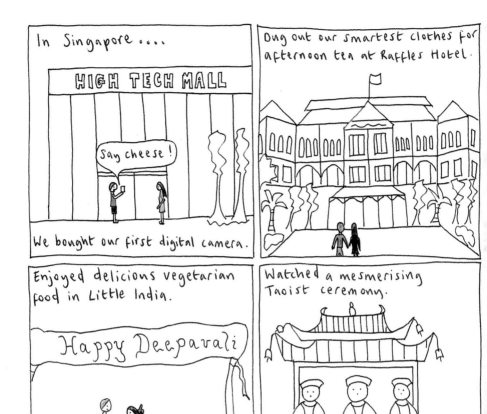

*spicy, coconut milk noodle soup

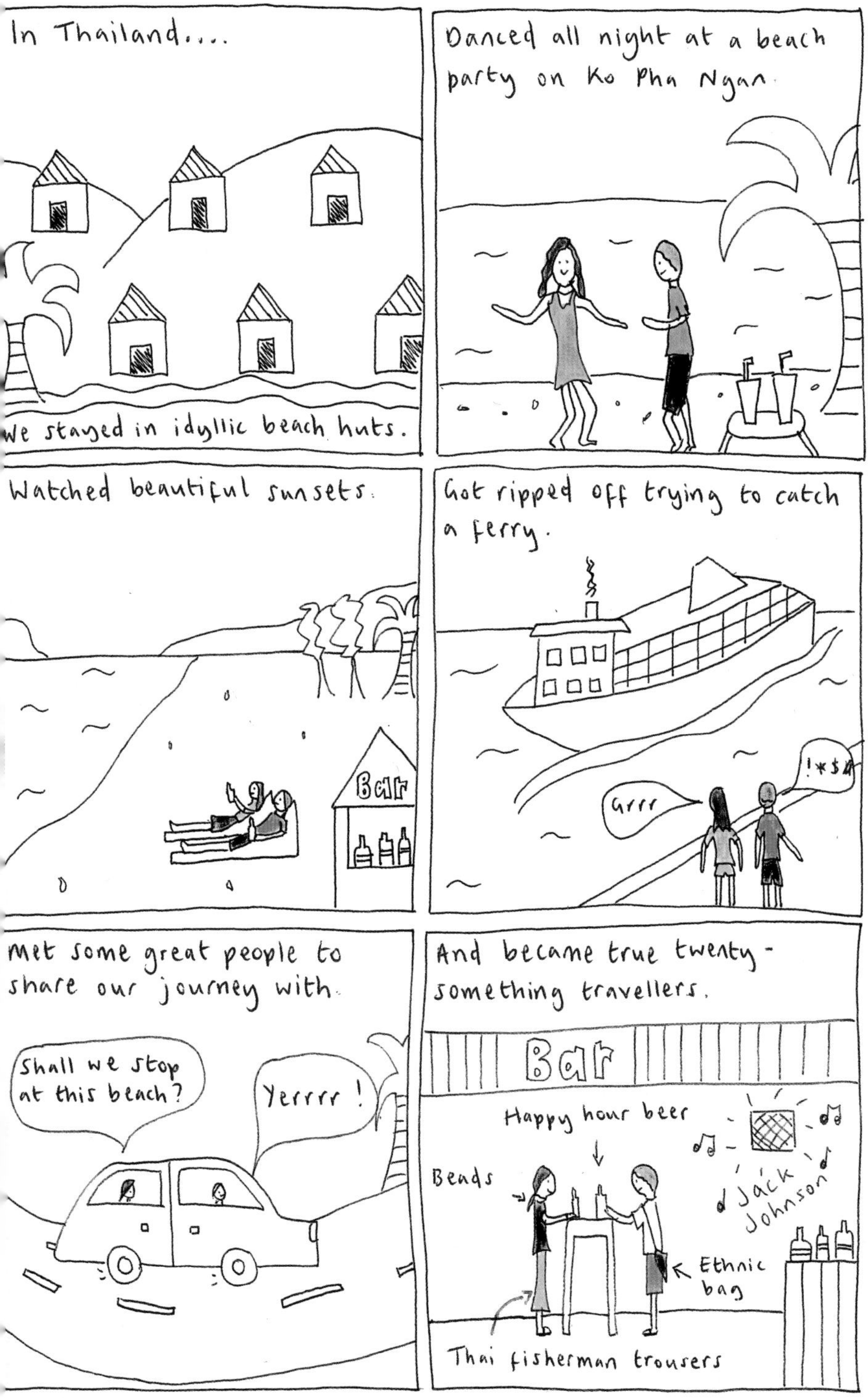
In Thailand....
We stayed in idyllic beach huts.
Danced all night at a beach party on Ko Pha Ngan.
Watched beautiful sunsets.
Bar
Got ripped off trying to catch a ferry.
Grrr
!*$
Met some great people to share our journey with.
Shall we stop at this beach?
Yerrrr!
And became true twenty-something travellers.
Bar
Happy hour beer
Beads
Jack Johnson
Ethnic bag
Thai fisherman trousers

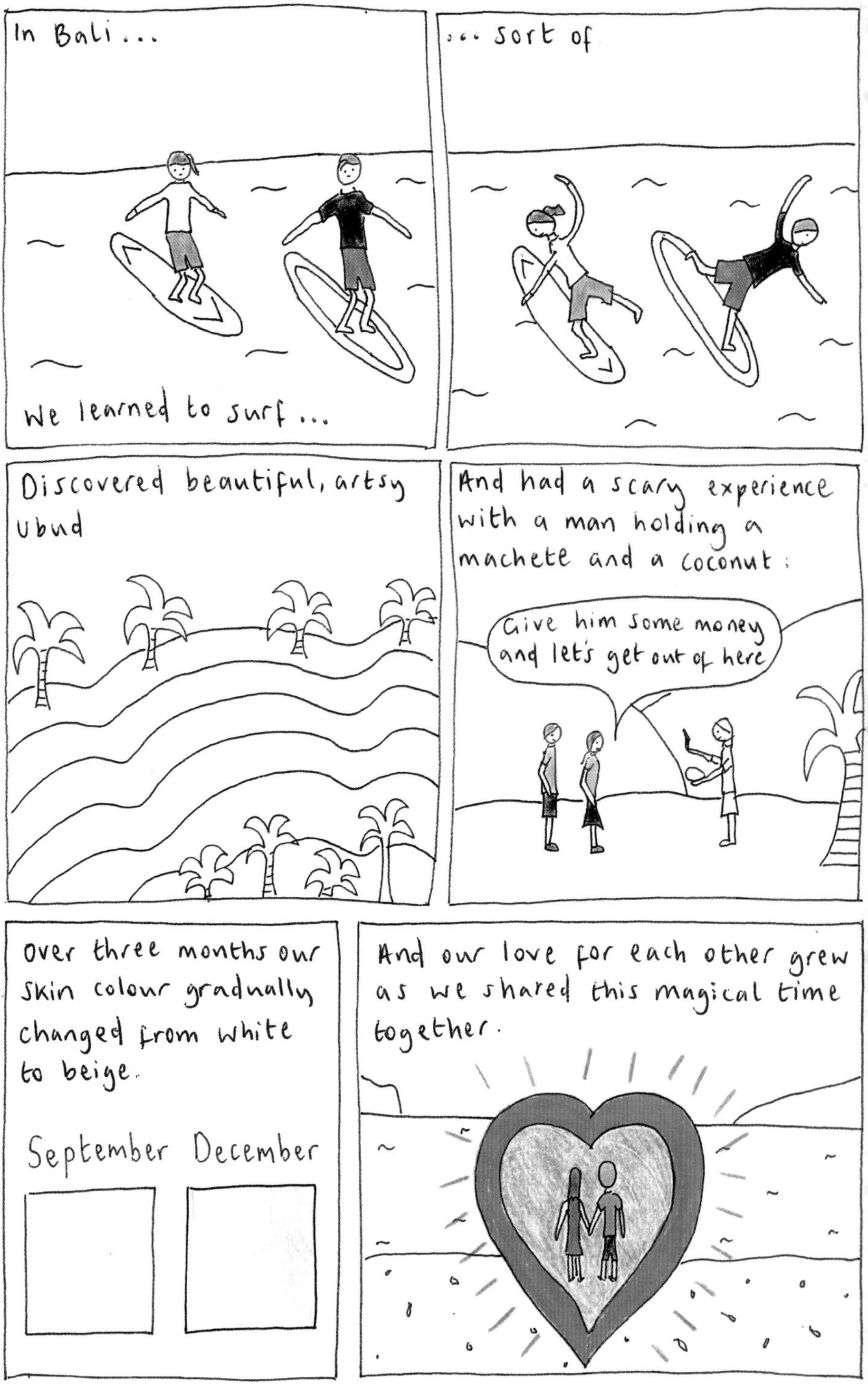

In Bali...
We learned to surf...
...sort of
Discovered beautiful, artsy Ubud
And had a scary experience with a man holding a machete and a coconut:
Give him some money and let's get out of here
Over three months our skin colour gradually changed from white to beige.
September
December
And our love for each other grew as we shared this magical time together.

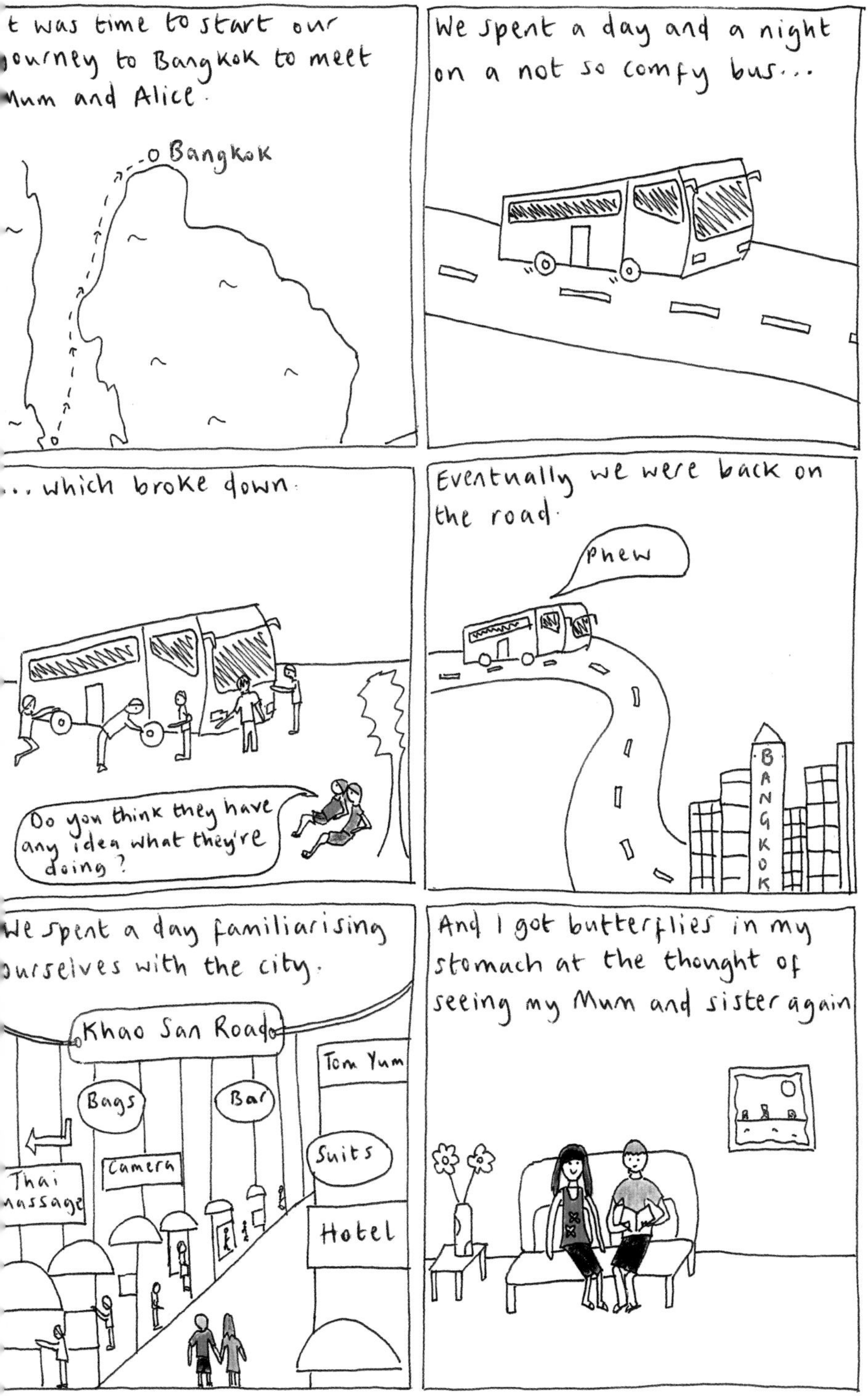
t was time to start our ourney to Bangkok to meet Mum and Alice.
Bangkok
We spent a day and a night on a not so comfy bus...
...which broke down.
Do you think they have any idea what they're doing?
Eventually we were back on the road.
Phew
BANGKOK
We spent a day familiarising ourselves with the city.
Khao San Road
Tom Yum
Bags
Bar
Suits
Camera
Thai massage
Hotel
And I got butterflies in my stomach at the thought of seeing my Mum and sister again

Bangkok Airport

ARRIVALS

Flight	From	Status
005	Sydney	Landed
762	New York JFK	Landed
185	Paris	Delayed
423	Beijing	Due 14:51
912	Tokyo	Landed
165	London	Landed
824	Amsterdam	Landed

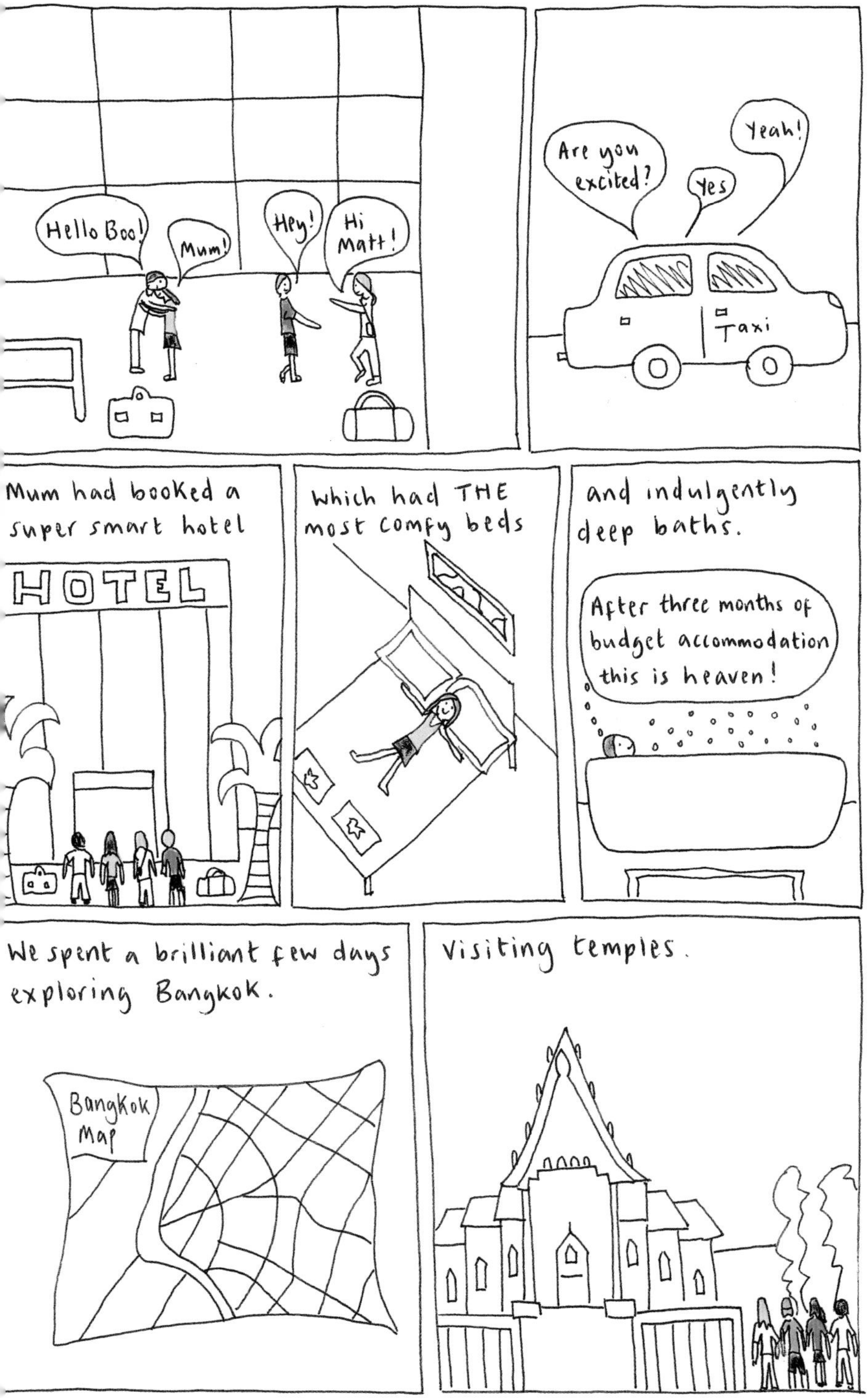
Hello Boo!
Mum!
Hey!
Hi Matt!
Are you excited?
Yes
Yeah!
Taxi
Mum had booked a super smart hotel
HOTEL
Which had THE most comfy beds
and indulgently deep baths.
After three months of budget accommodation this is heaven!
We spent a brilliant few days exploring Bangkok.
Bangkok Map
Visiting temples.

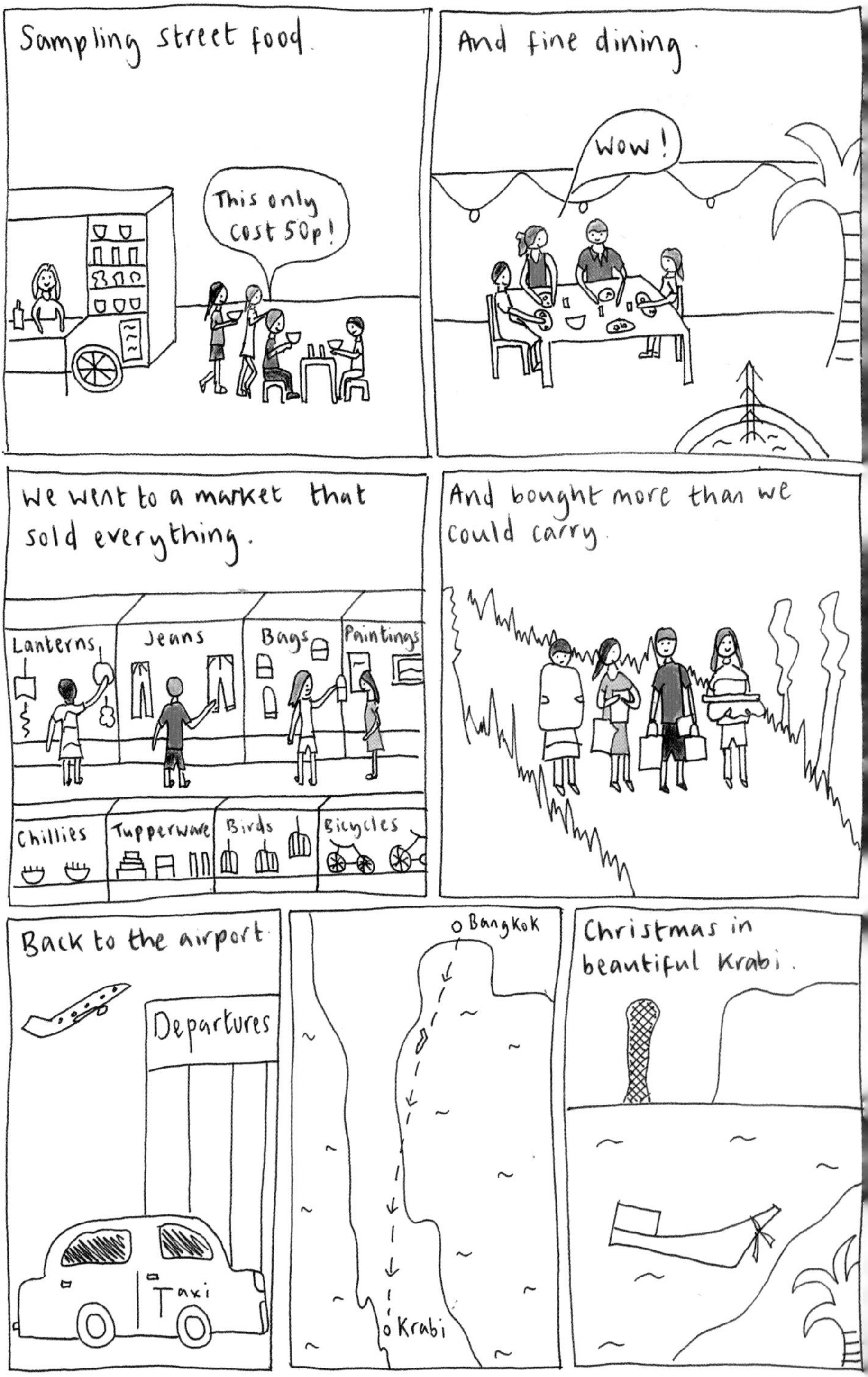
Sampling street food.
This only cost 50p!
And fine dining.
Wow!
We went to a market that sold everything.
Lanterns
Jeans
Bags
Paintings
Chillies
Tupperware
Birds
Bicycles
And bought more than we could carry.
Back to the airport.
Departures
Taxi
Bangkok
Krabi
Christmas in beautiful Krabi.

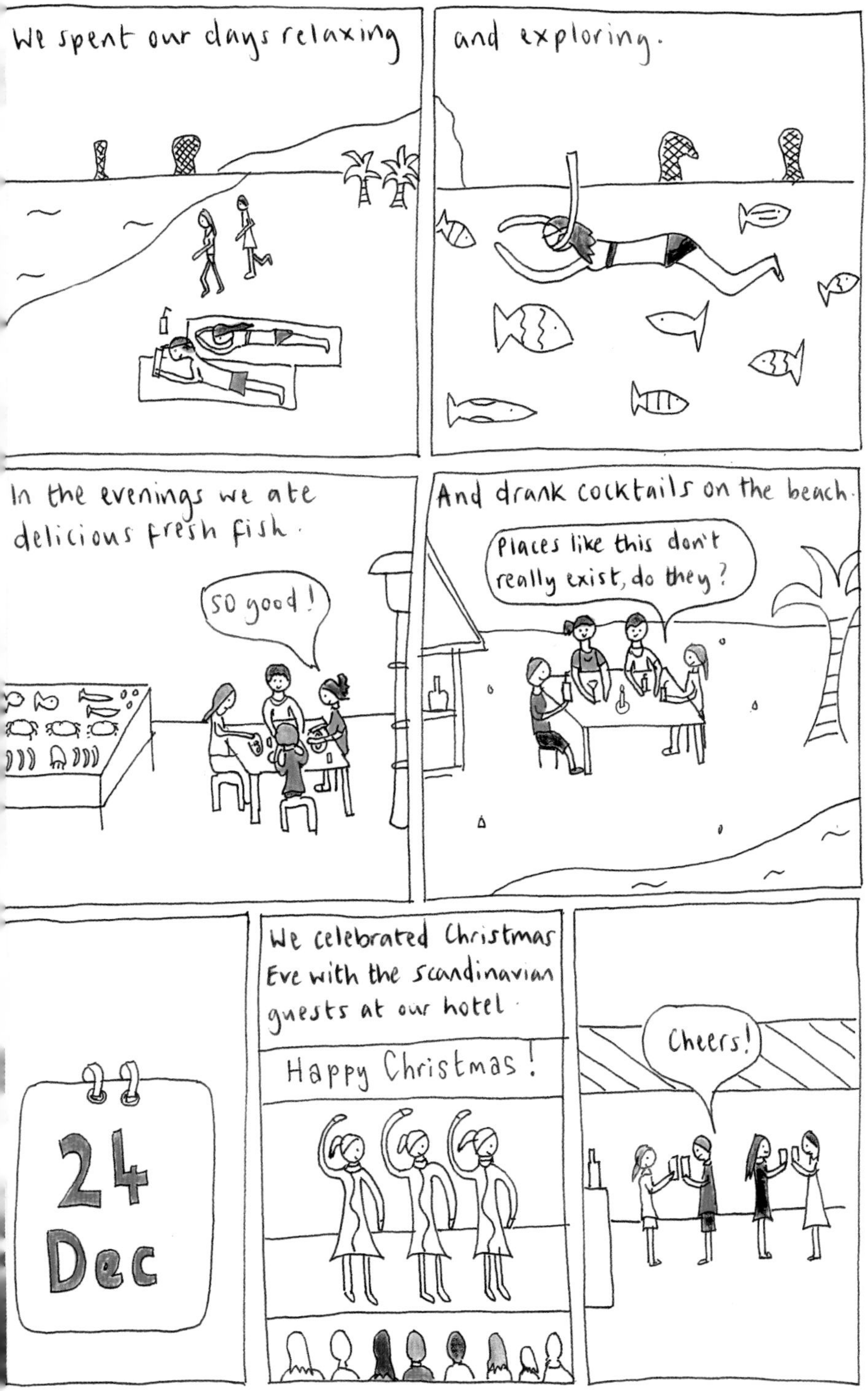
We spent our days relaxing
and exploring.
In the evenings we ate delicious fresh fish.
SO good!
And drank cocktails on the beach.
Places like this don't really exist, do they?
24 Dec
We celebrated Christmas Eve with the Scandinavian guests at our hotel.
Happy Christmas!
Cheers!

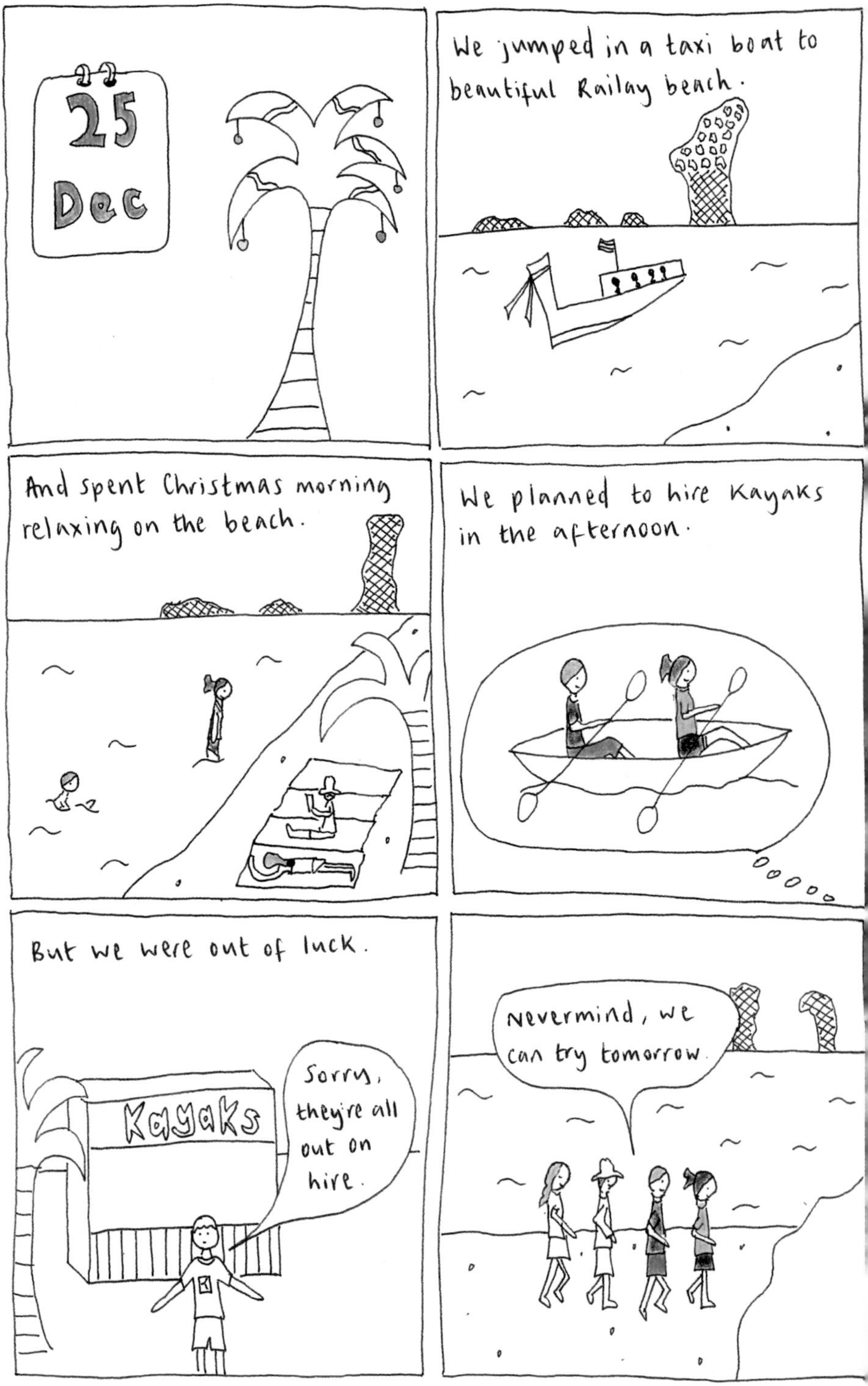
25
Dec
We jumped in a taxi boat to beautiful Railay beach.
And spent Christmas morning relaxing on the beach.
We planned to hire Kayaks in the afternoon.
But we were out of luck.
Kayaks
Sorry, they're all out on hire.
Nevermind, we can try tomorrow.

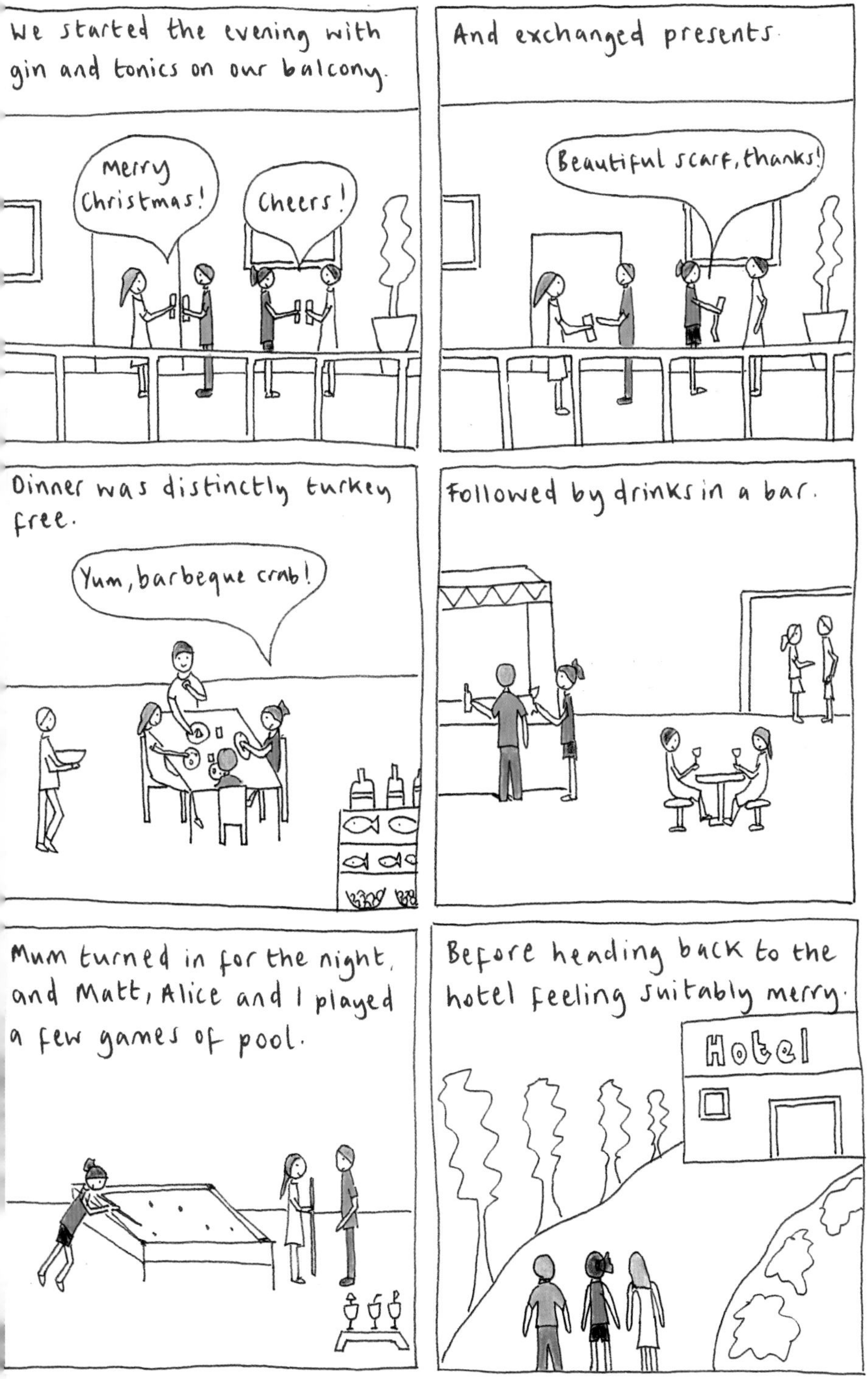
We started the evening with gin and tonics on our balcony.
Merry Christmas!
Cheers!
And exchanged presents.
Beautiful scarf, thanks!
Dinner was distinctly turkey free.
Yum, barbeque crab!
Followed by drinks in a bar.
Mum turned in for the night, and Matt, Alice and I played a few games of pool.
Before heading back to the hotel feeling suitably merry.
Hotel

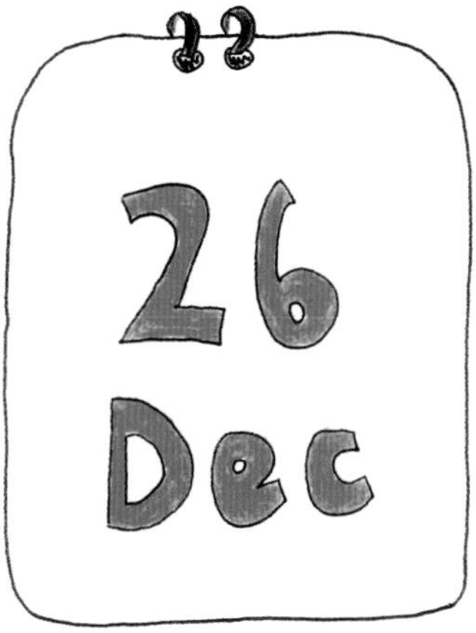
26
Dec

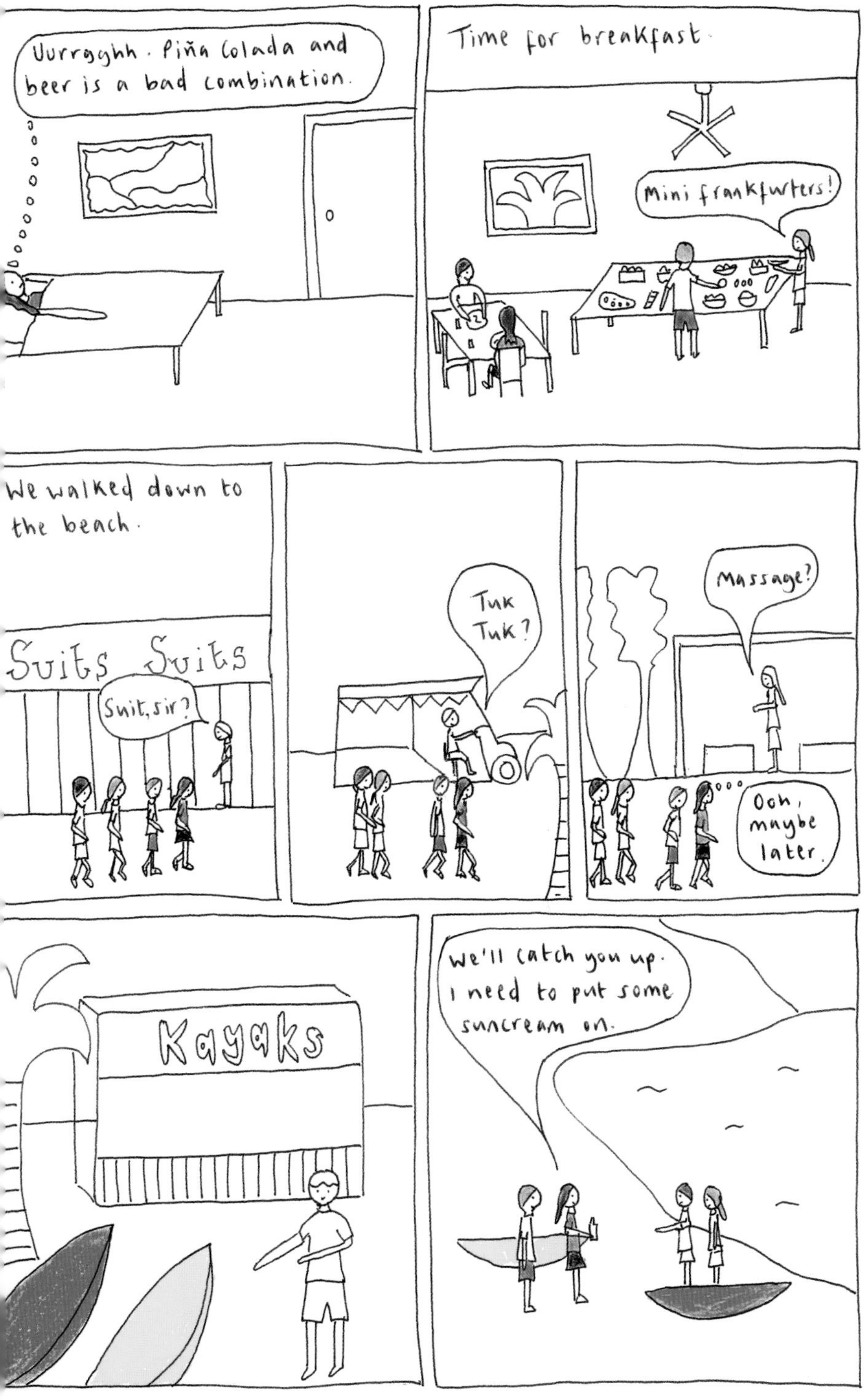
Uurrgghh. Piña Colada and beer is a bad combination.
Time for breakfast.
Mini frankfurters!
We walked down to the beach.
Suits Suits
Suit, sir?
Tuk Tuk?
Massage?
Ooh, maybe later.
Kayaks
We'll catch you up. I need to put some suncream on.

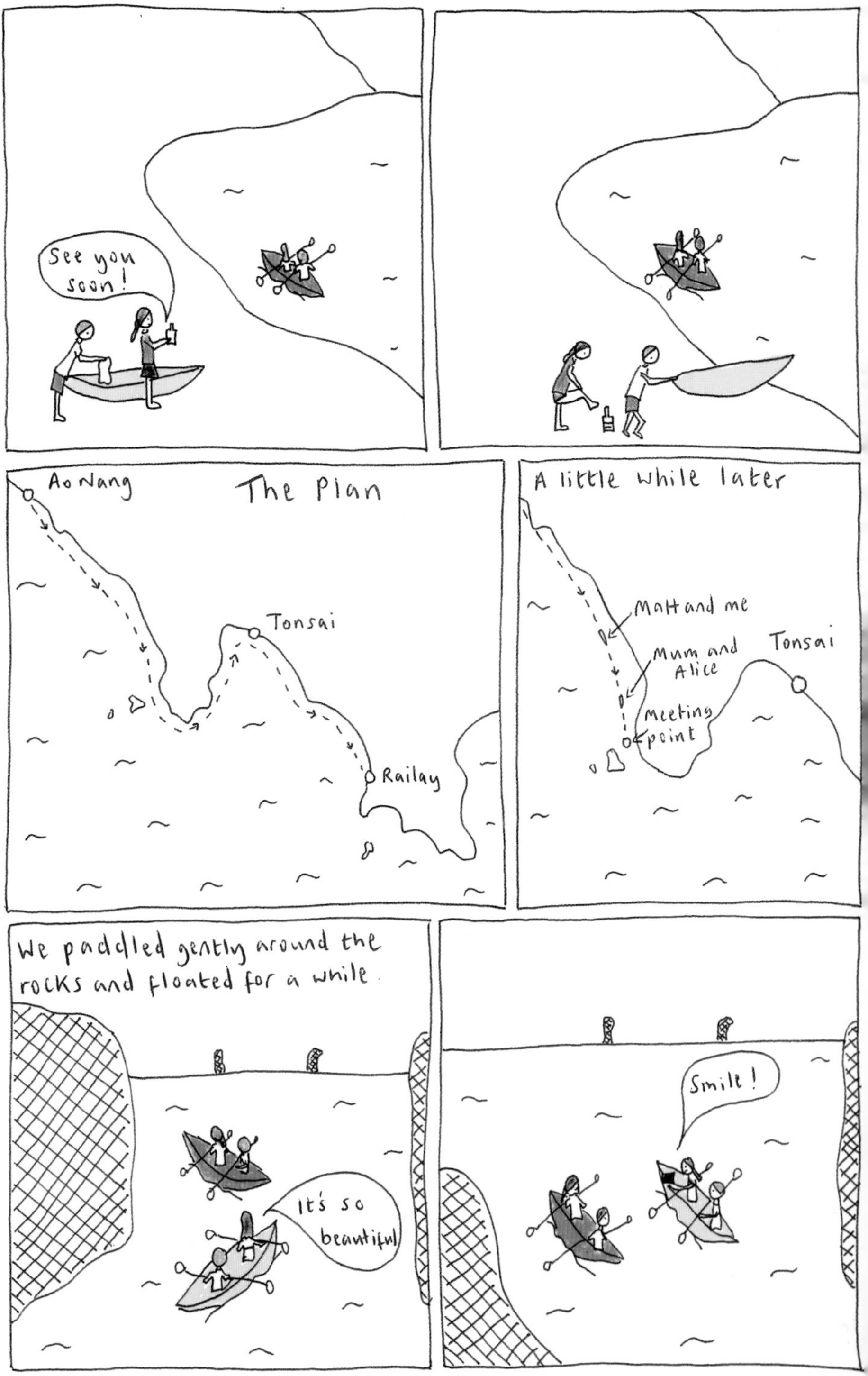

See you soon!
Ao Nang
The Plan
Tonsai
Railay
A little while later
Matt and me
Mum and Alice
Tonsai
Meeting point
We paddled gently around the rocks and floated for a while
It's so beautiful
Smile!

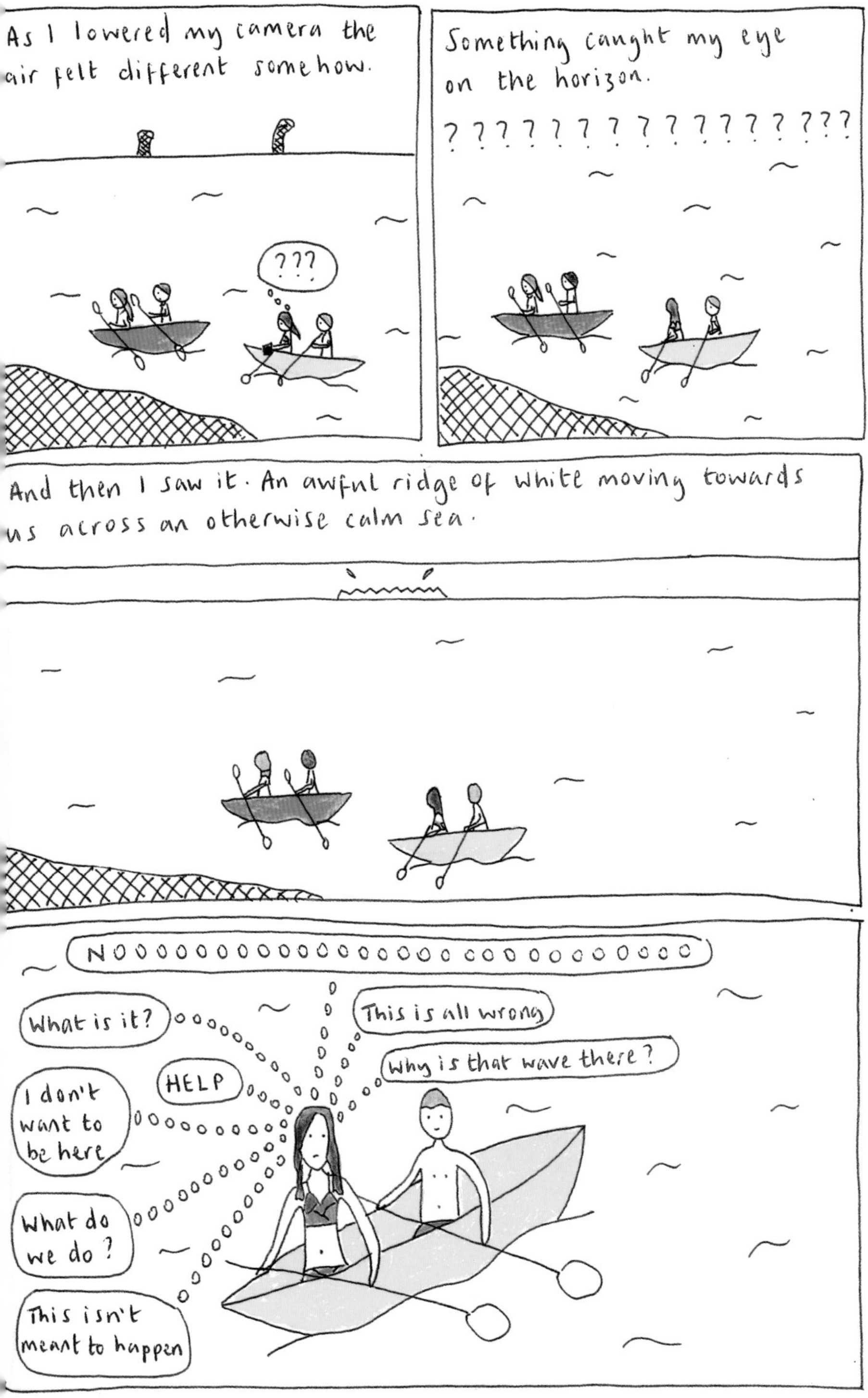

As I lowered my camera the air felt different somehow.
???
Something caught my eye on the horizon.
?????????????????
And then I saw it. An awful ridge of white moving towards us across an otherwise calm sea.
NOOOOOOOOOOOOOOOOOOOOOOOOOOOOO
What is it?
This is all wrong
Why is that wave there?
HELP
I don't want to be here
What do we do?
This isn't meant to happen

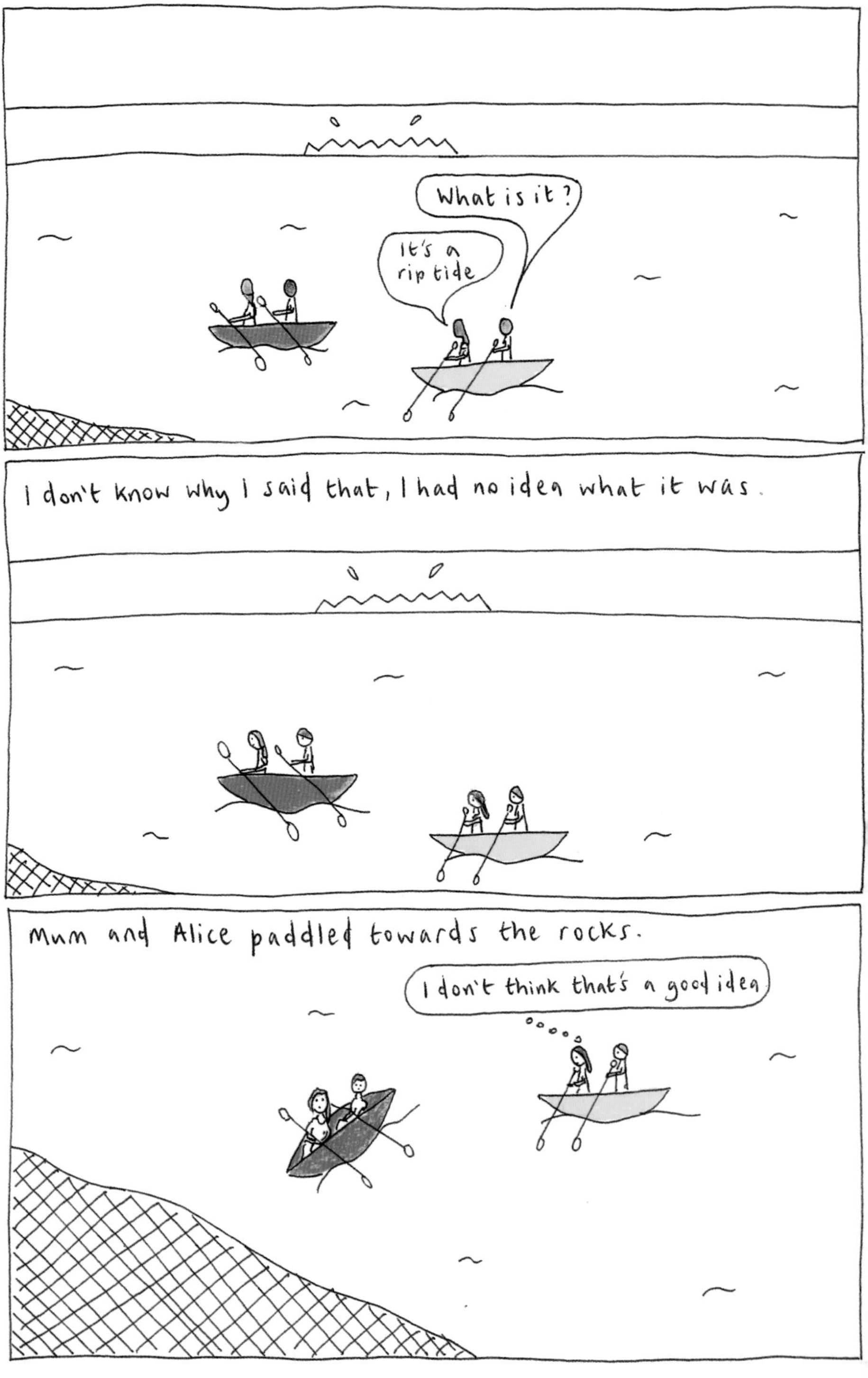
What is it?
It's a rip tide
I don't know why I said that, I had no idea what it was.
Mum and Alice paddled towards the rocks.
I don't think that's a good idea

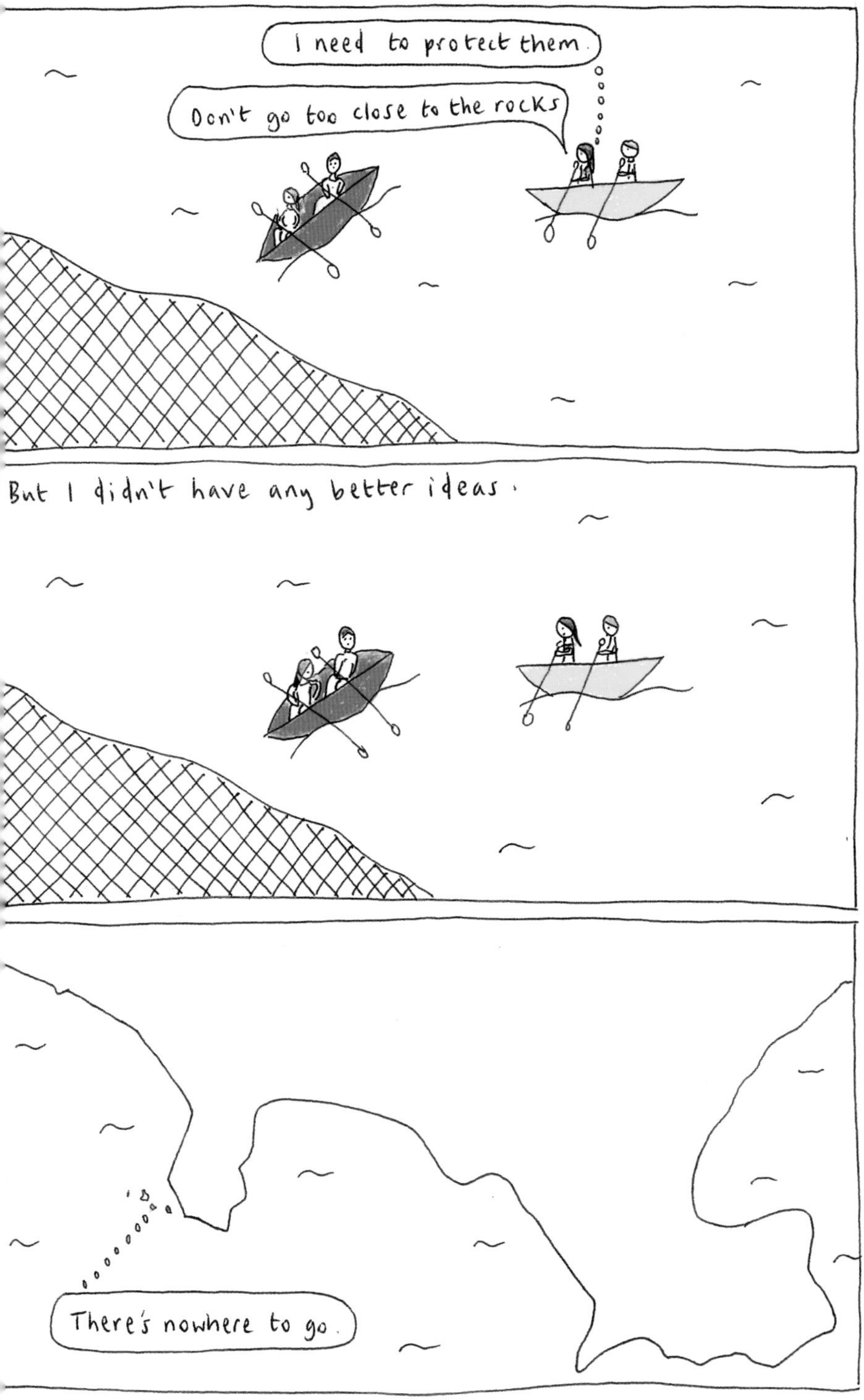
I need to protect them.
Don't go too close to the rocks
But I didn't have any better ideas.
There's nowhere to go.

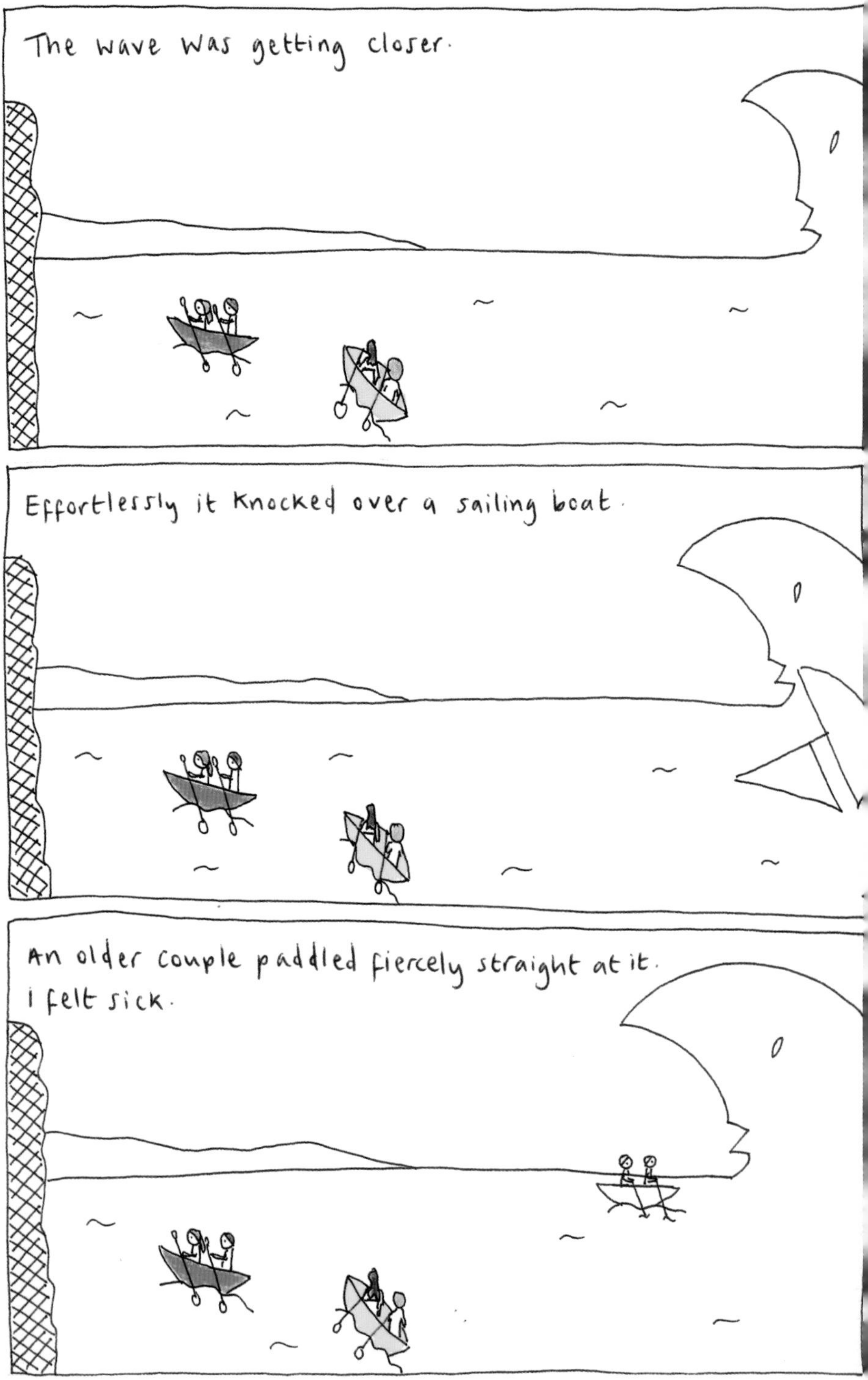
The wave was getting closer.
Effortlessly it knocked over a sailing boat.
An older couple paddled fiercely straight at it.
I felt sick.

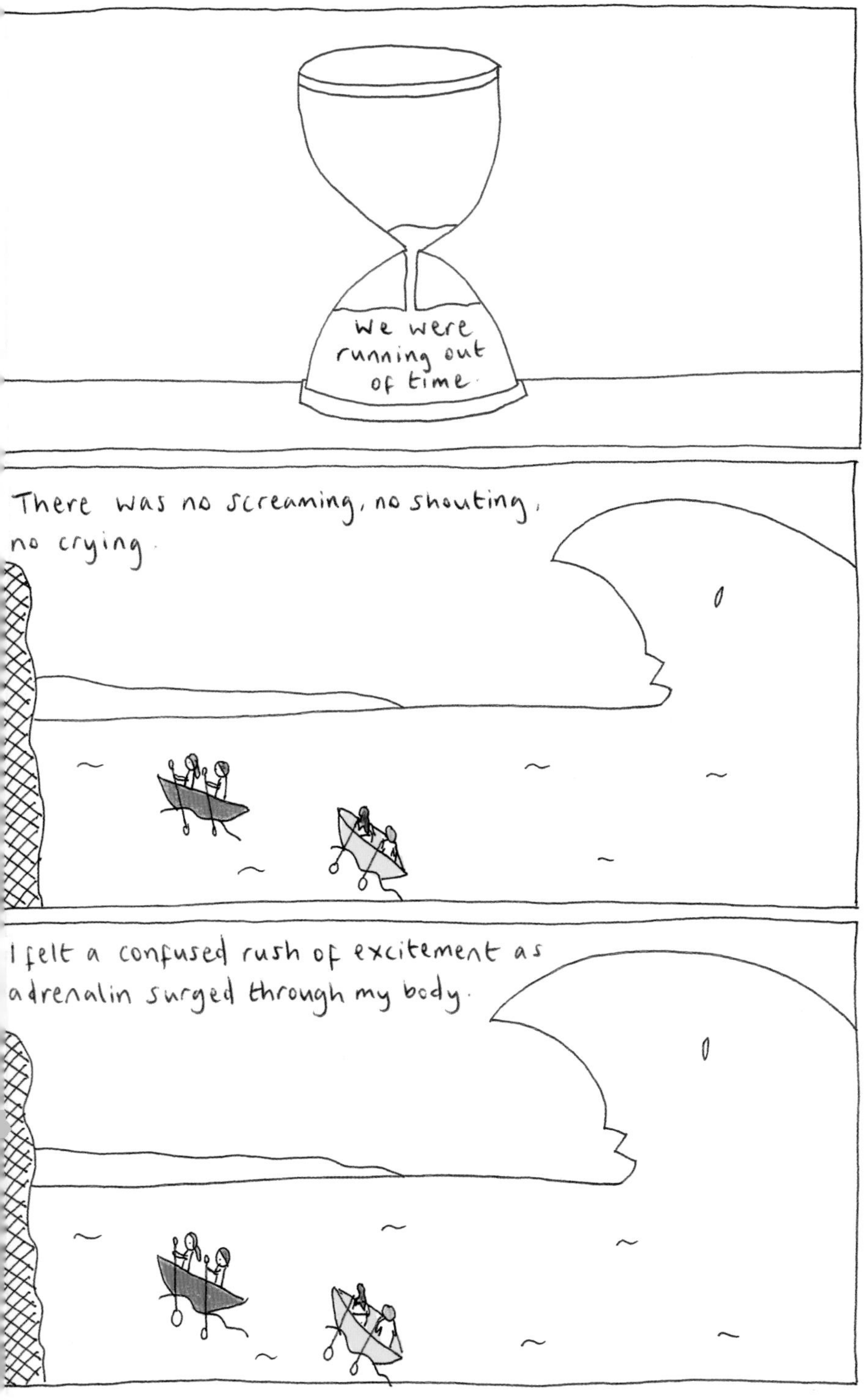
We were running out of time.
There was no screaming, no shouting, no crying.
I felt a confused rush of excitement as adrenalin surged through my body.

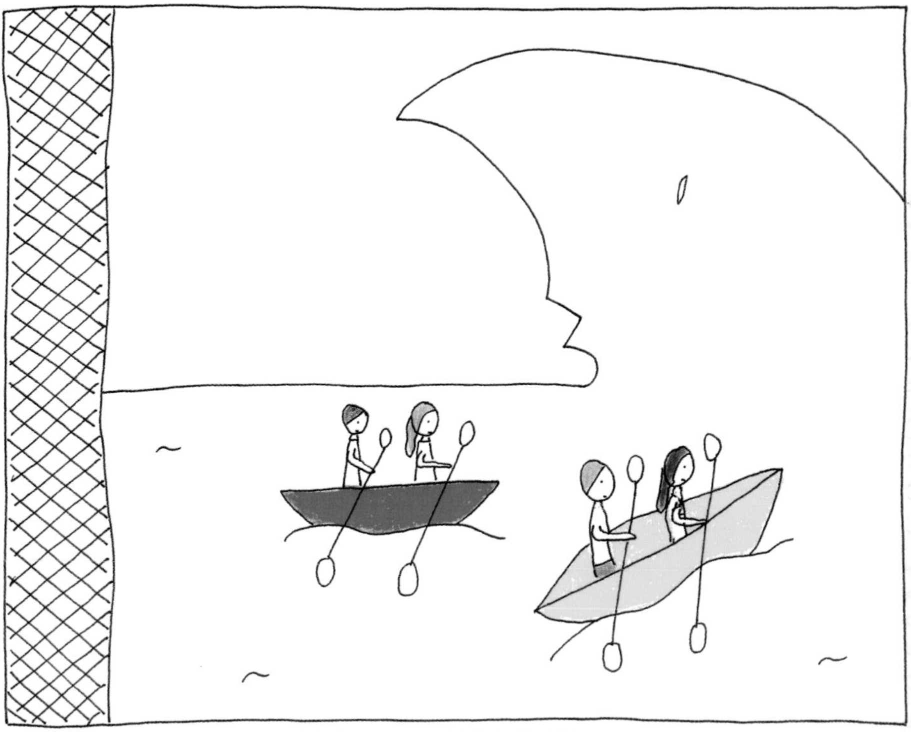

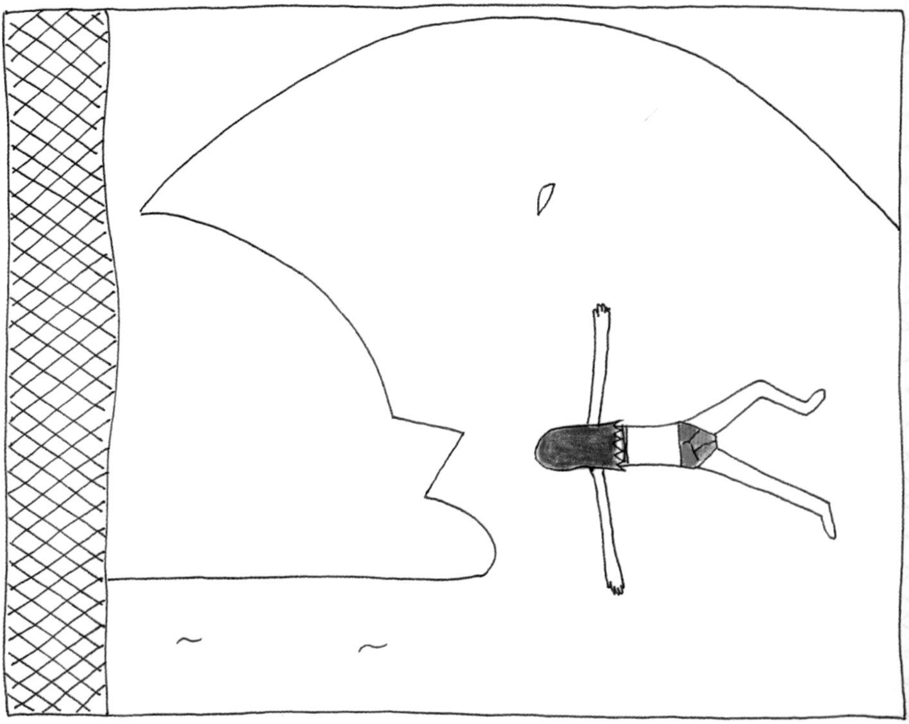

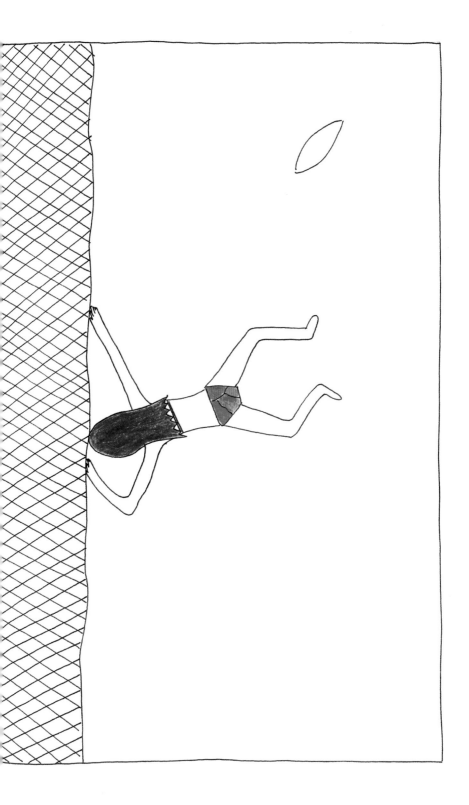

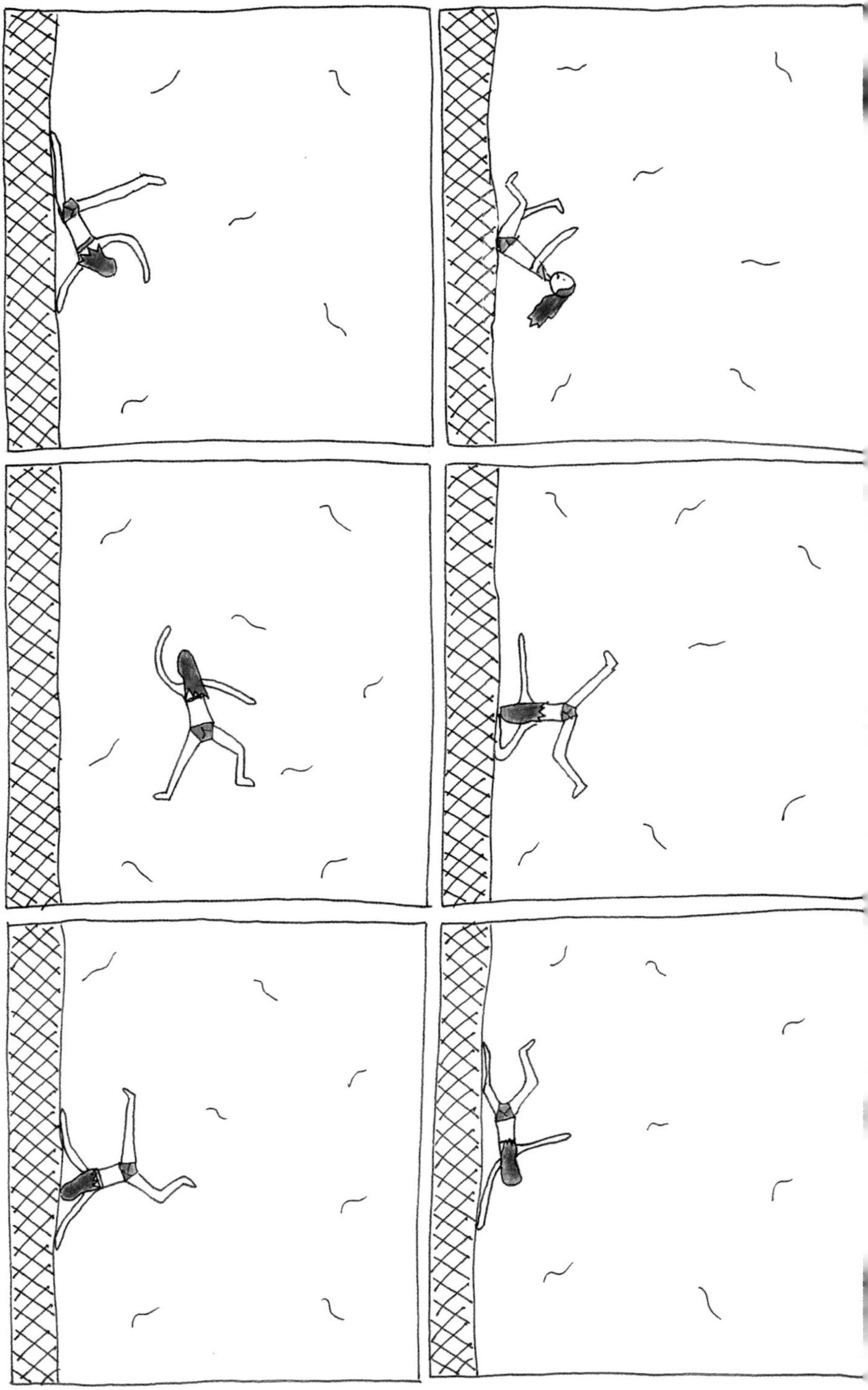

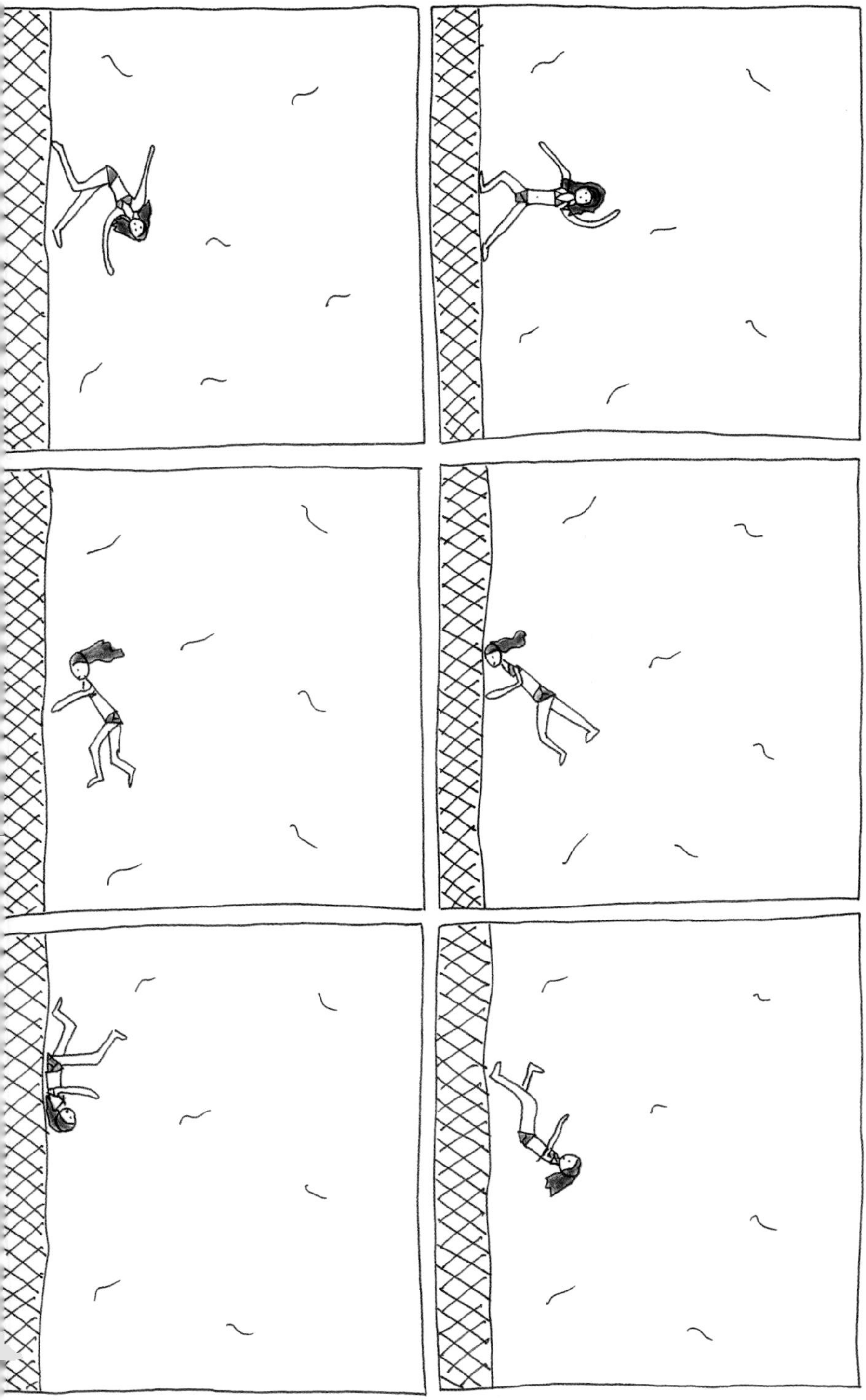

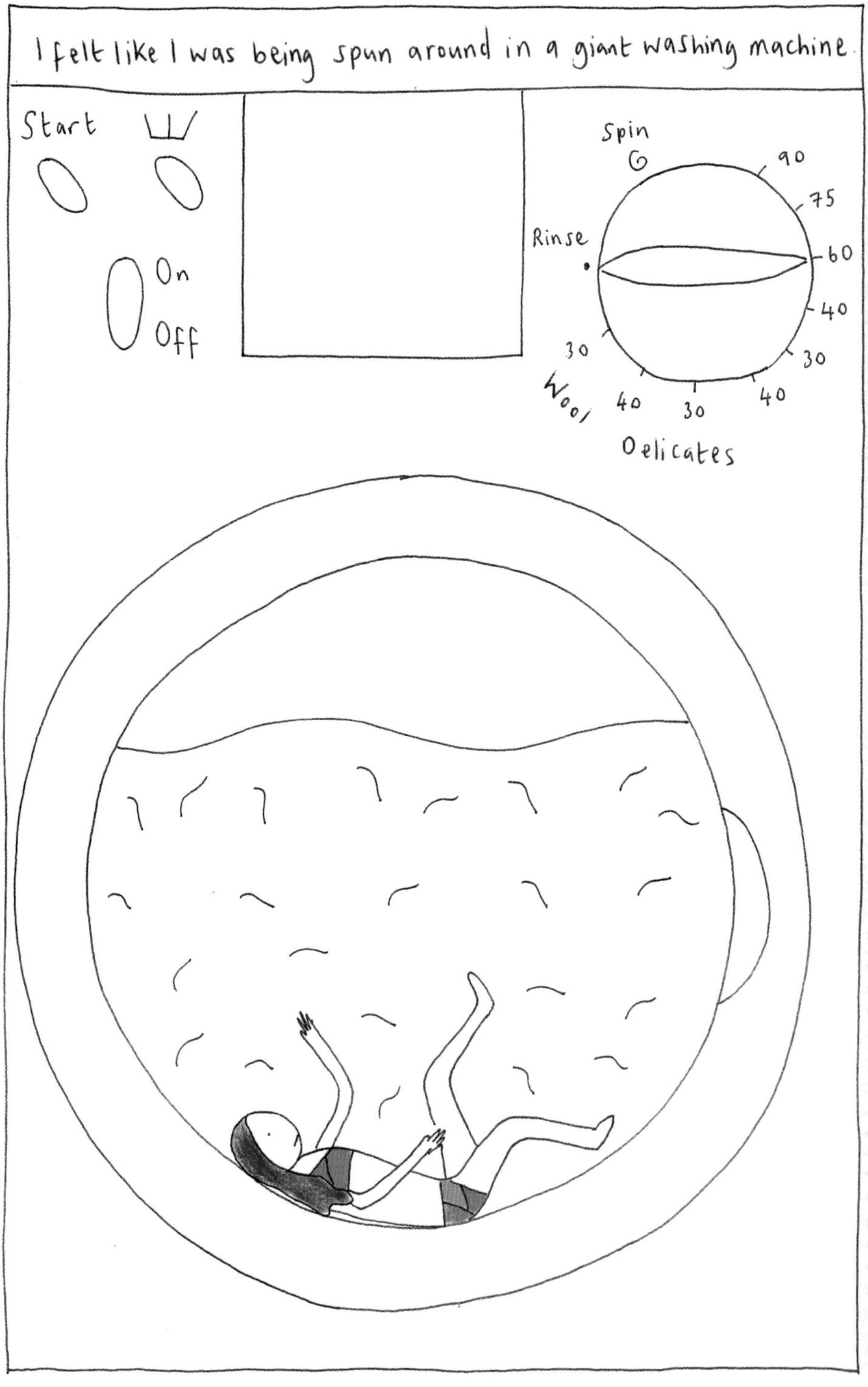
I felt like I was being spun around in a giant washing machine.
Start
On
Off
Spin
90
75
Rinse
60
40
30
30
Wool
40
30
40
Delicates

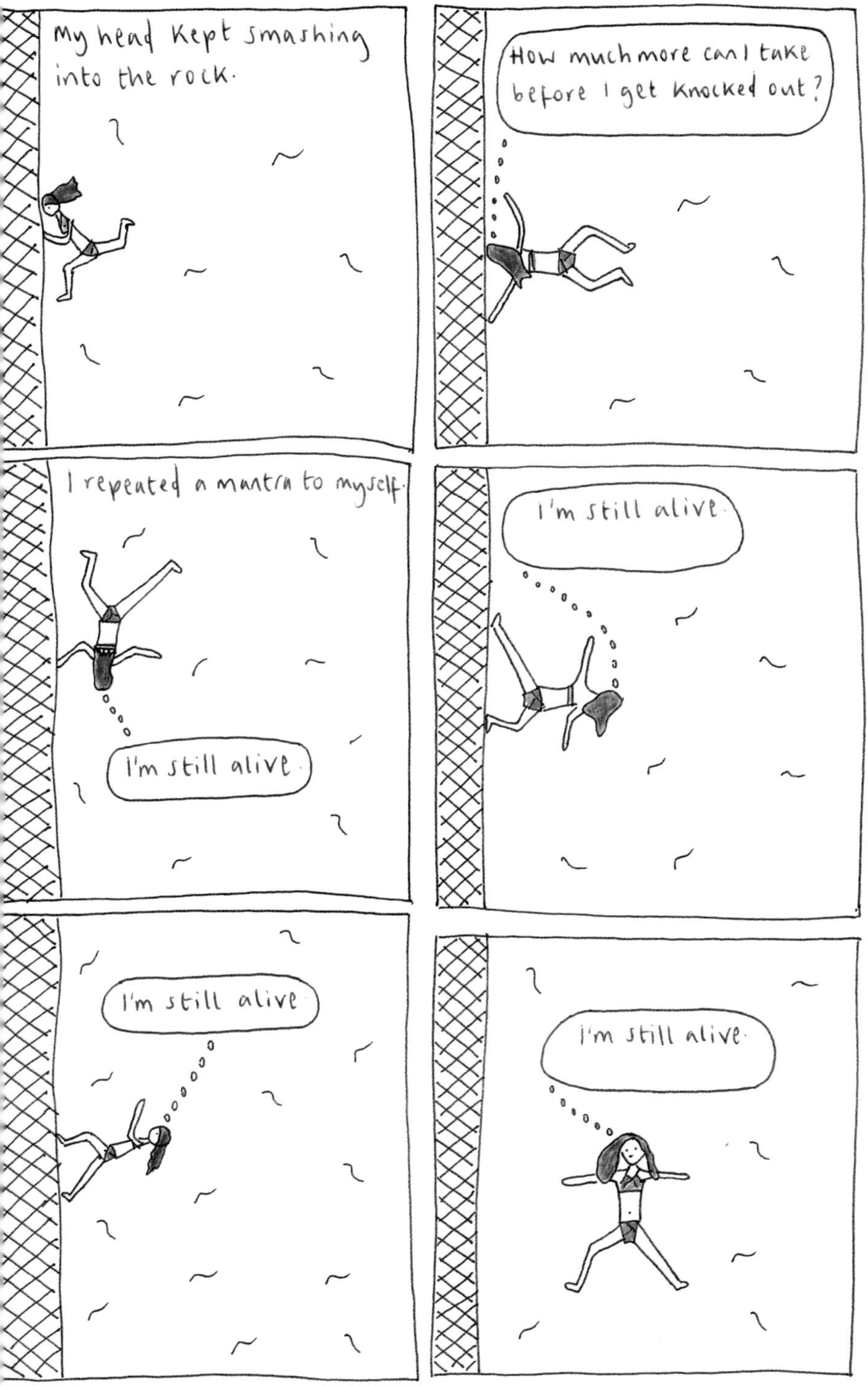
My head kept smashing into the rock.
How much more can I take before I get knocked out?
I repeated a mantra to myself.
I'm still alive.
I'm still alive.
I'm still alive.
I'm still alive.

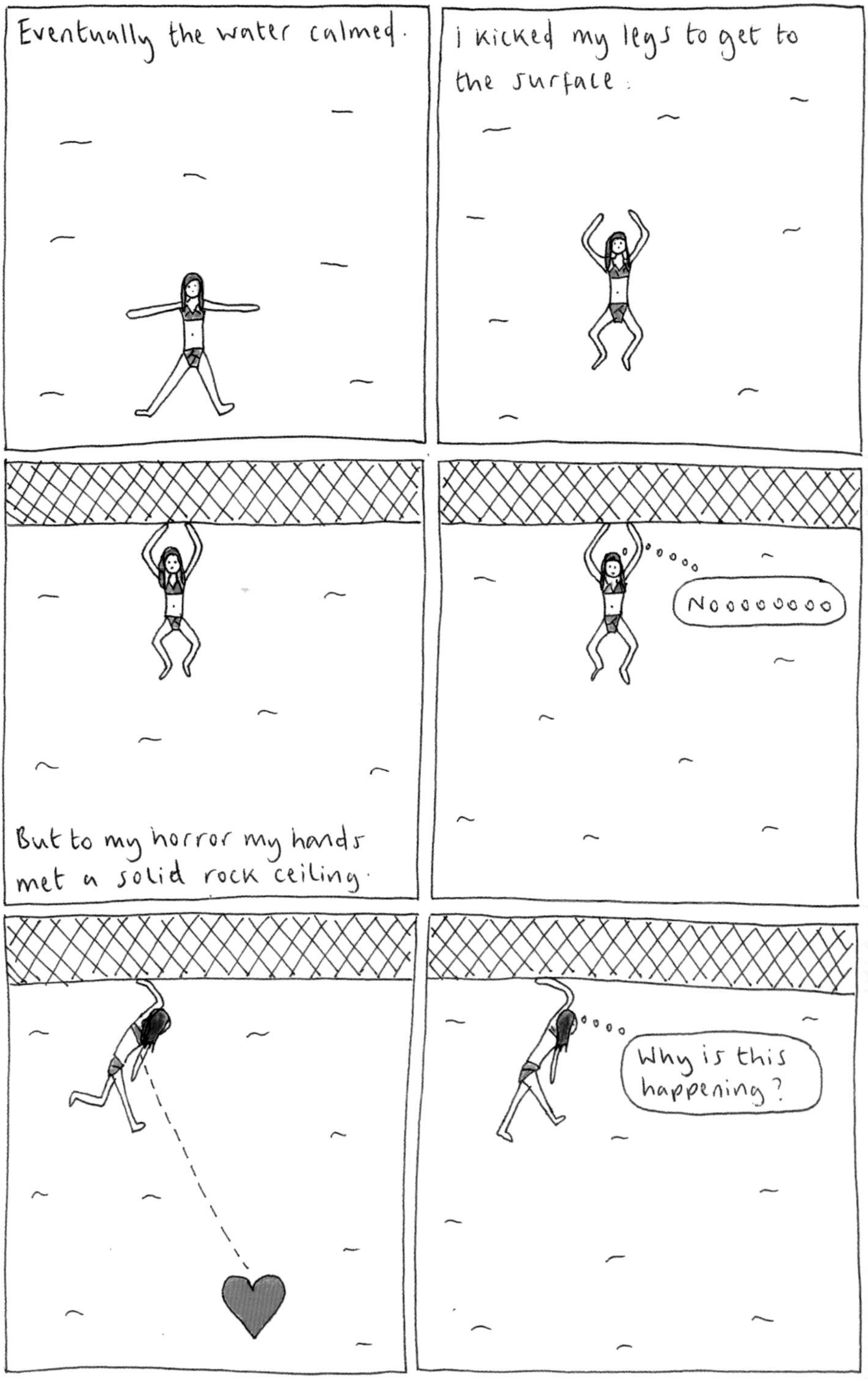

Eventually the water calmed.
I kicked my legs to get to the surface.
But to my horror my hands met a solid rock ceiling.
Nooooooooo
Why is this happening?

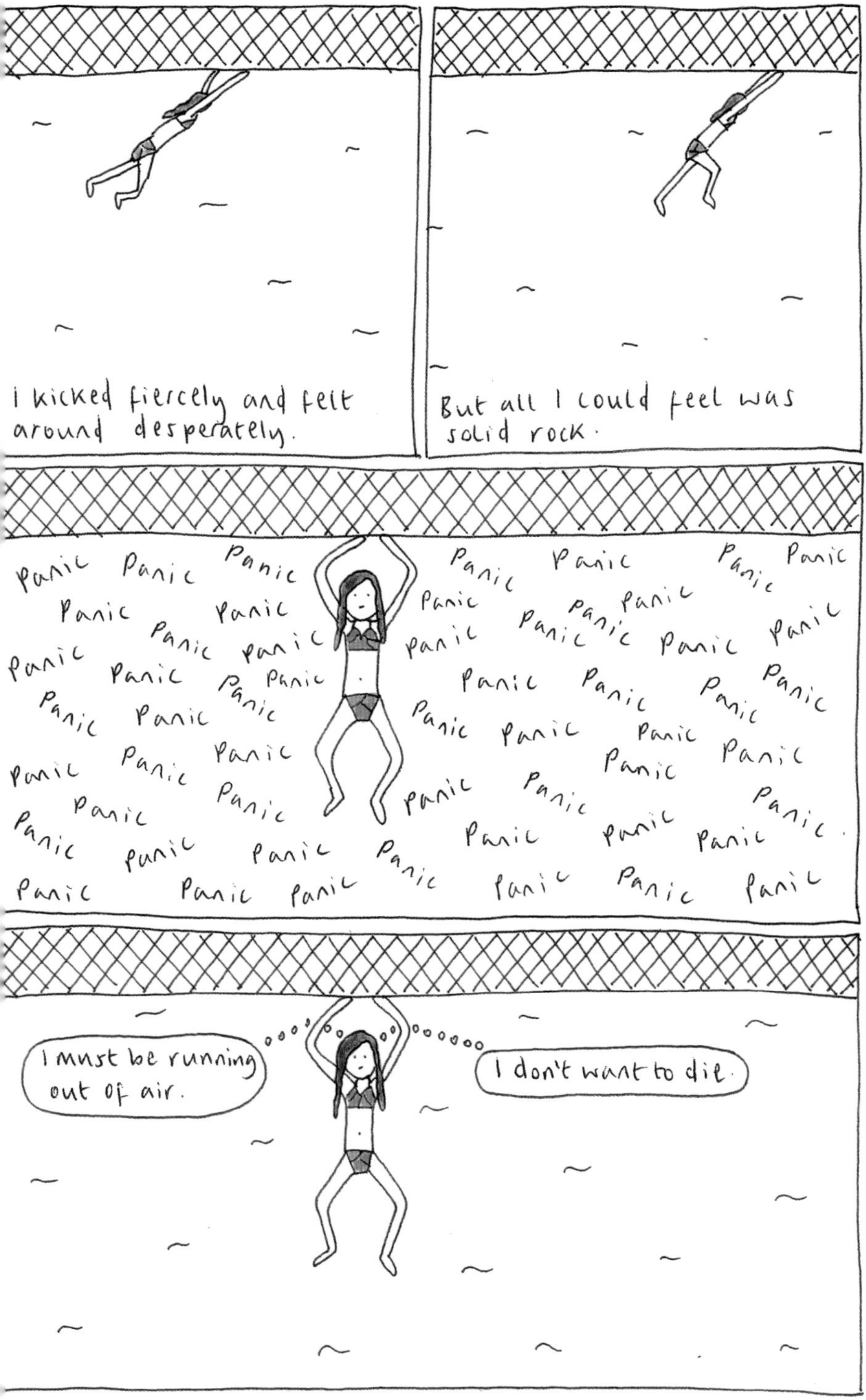
I kicked fiercely and felt around desperately.
But all I could feel was solid rock.
Panic Panic Panic Panic Panic Panic Panic Panic Panic Panic Panic Panic Panic Panic Panic Panic Panic Panic
Panic Panic Panic Panic Panic Panic Panic Panic Panic Panic Panic Panic Panic Panic Panic Panic Panic Panic
Panic Panic Panic Panic Panic Panic Panic Panic Panic Panic Panic Panic Panic Panic Panic Panic Panic Panic
I must be running out of air.
I don't want to die.

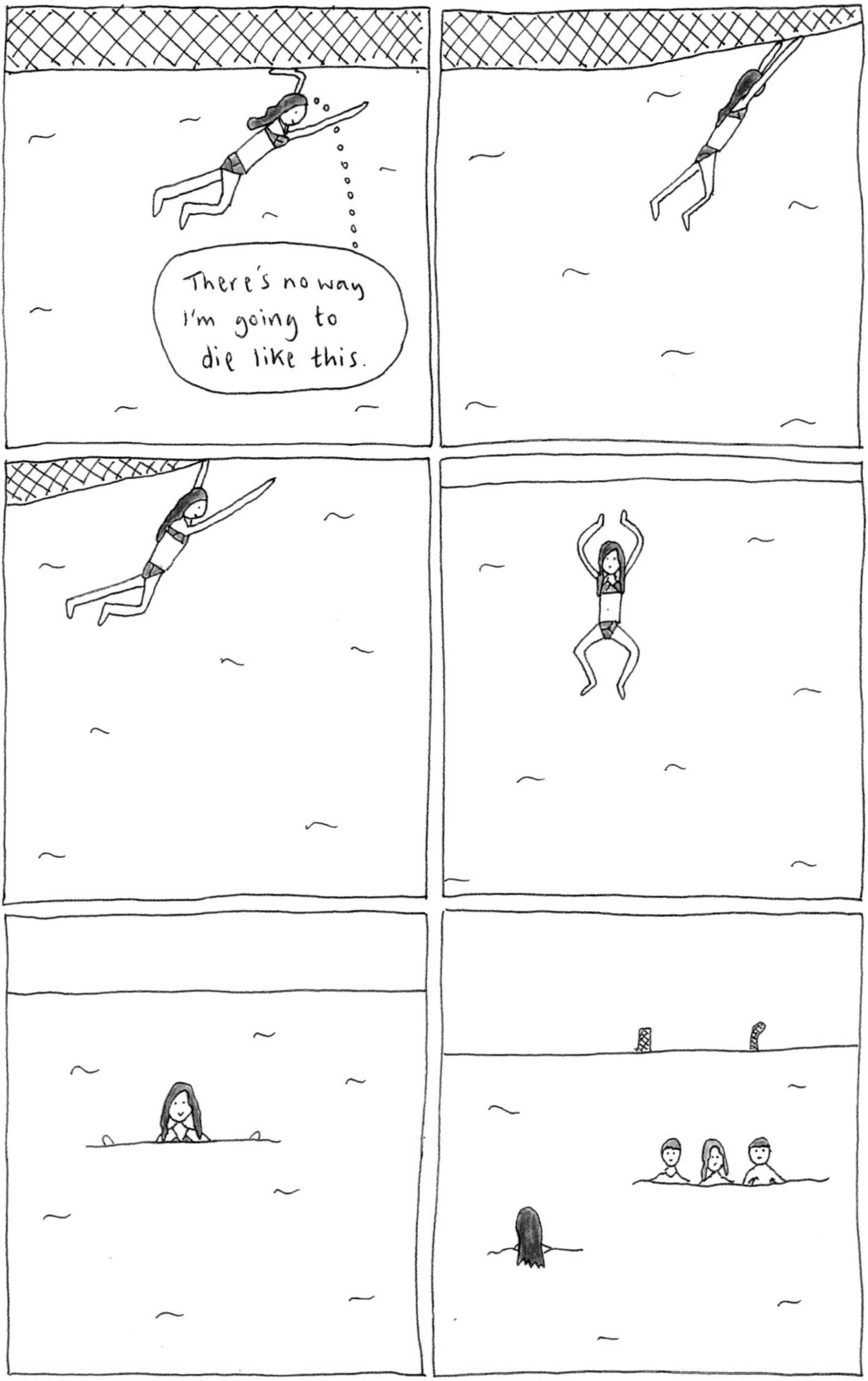
There's no way
I'm going to
die like this.

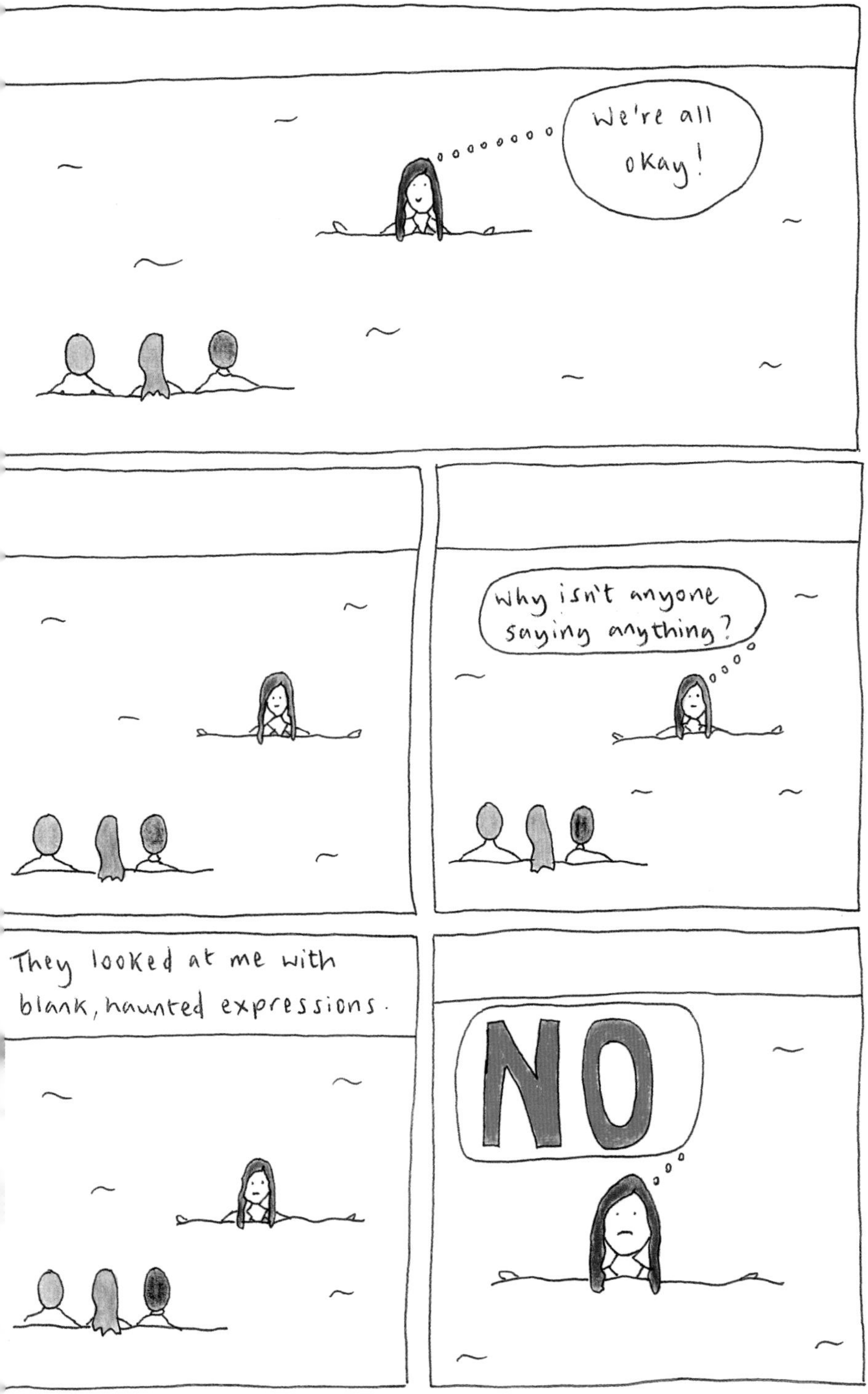
We're all okay!
Why isn't anyone saying anything?
They looked at me with blank, haunted expressions.
NO

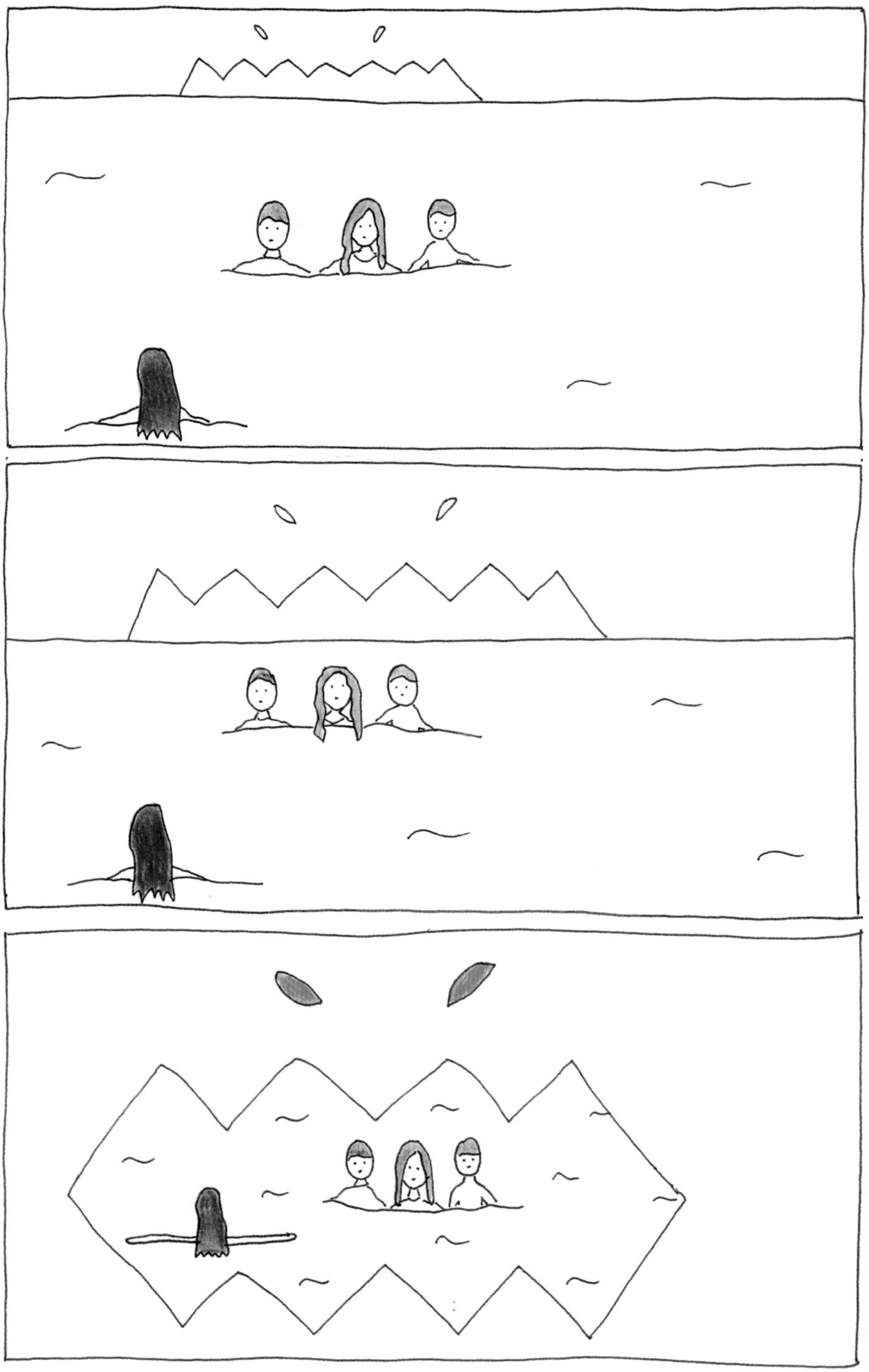

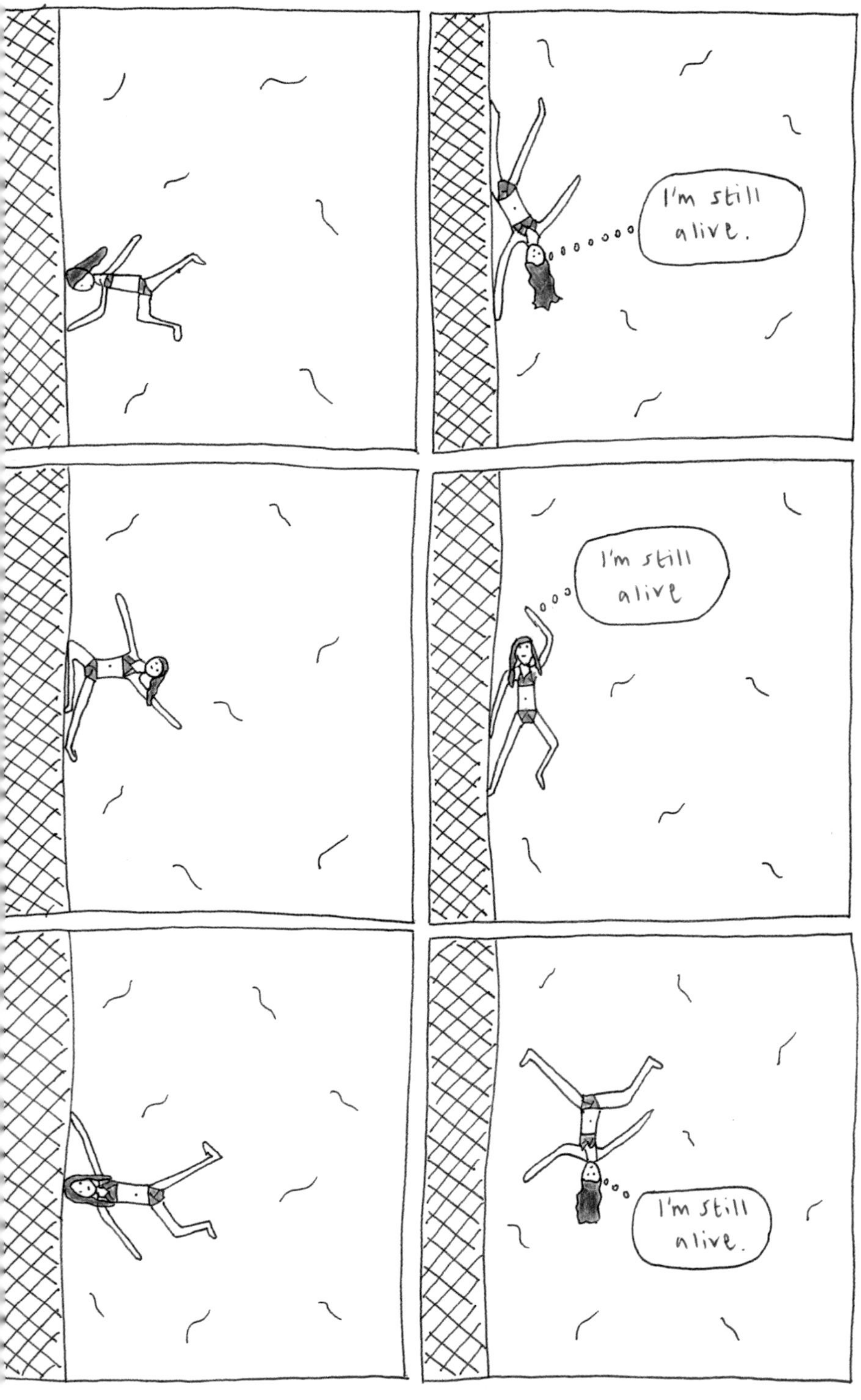
I'm still alive.
I'm still alive
I'm still alive.

Start
On
Off
Spin
G
90
75
Rinse
60
30
40
40
Wool
30
40
30
Delicates
Start
On
Off
Spin
G
90
75
Rinse
60
30
40
40
Wool
30
40
30
Delicates
Start
On
Off
Spin
G
90
75
Rinse
60
30
40
40
Wool
30
40
30
Delicates
Start
On
Off
Spin
G
90
75
Rinse
60
30
40
40
Wool
30
40
30
Delicates

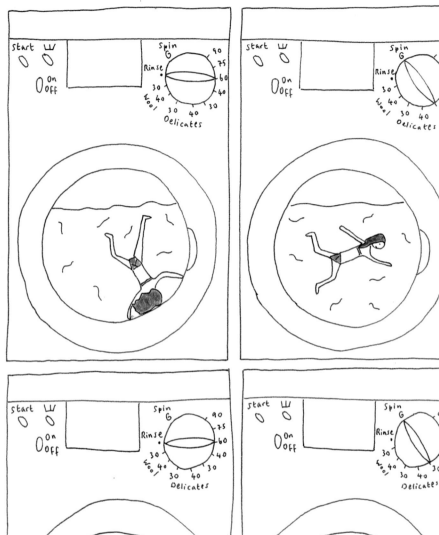

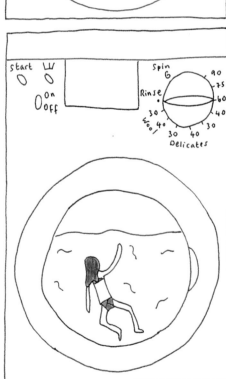

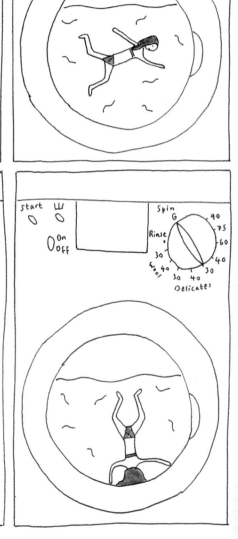

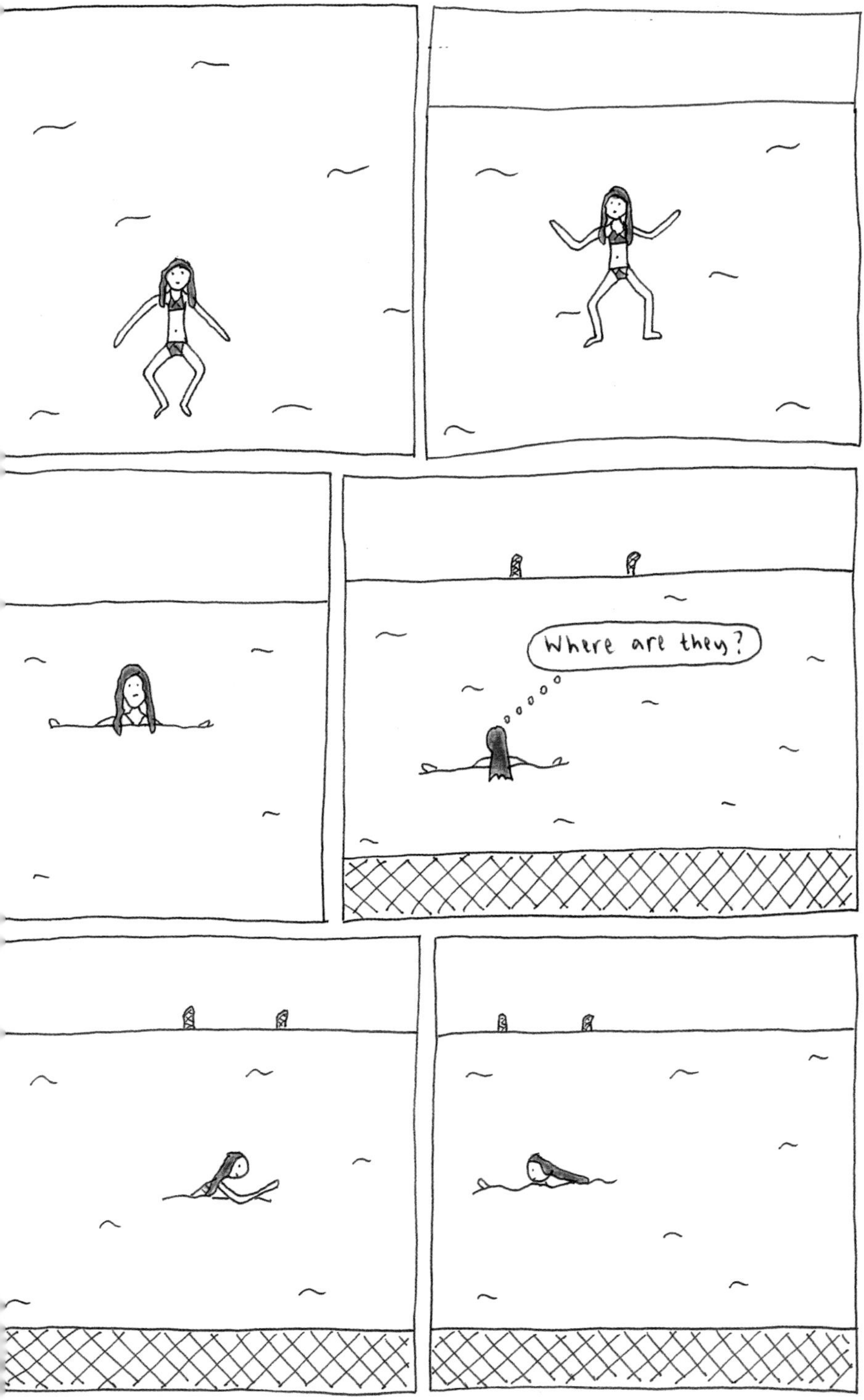
Where are they?

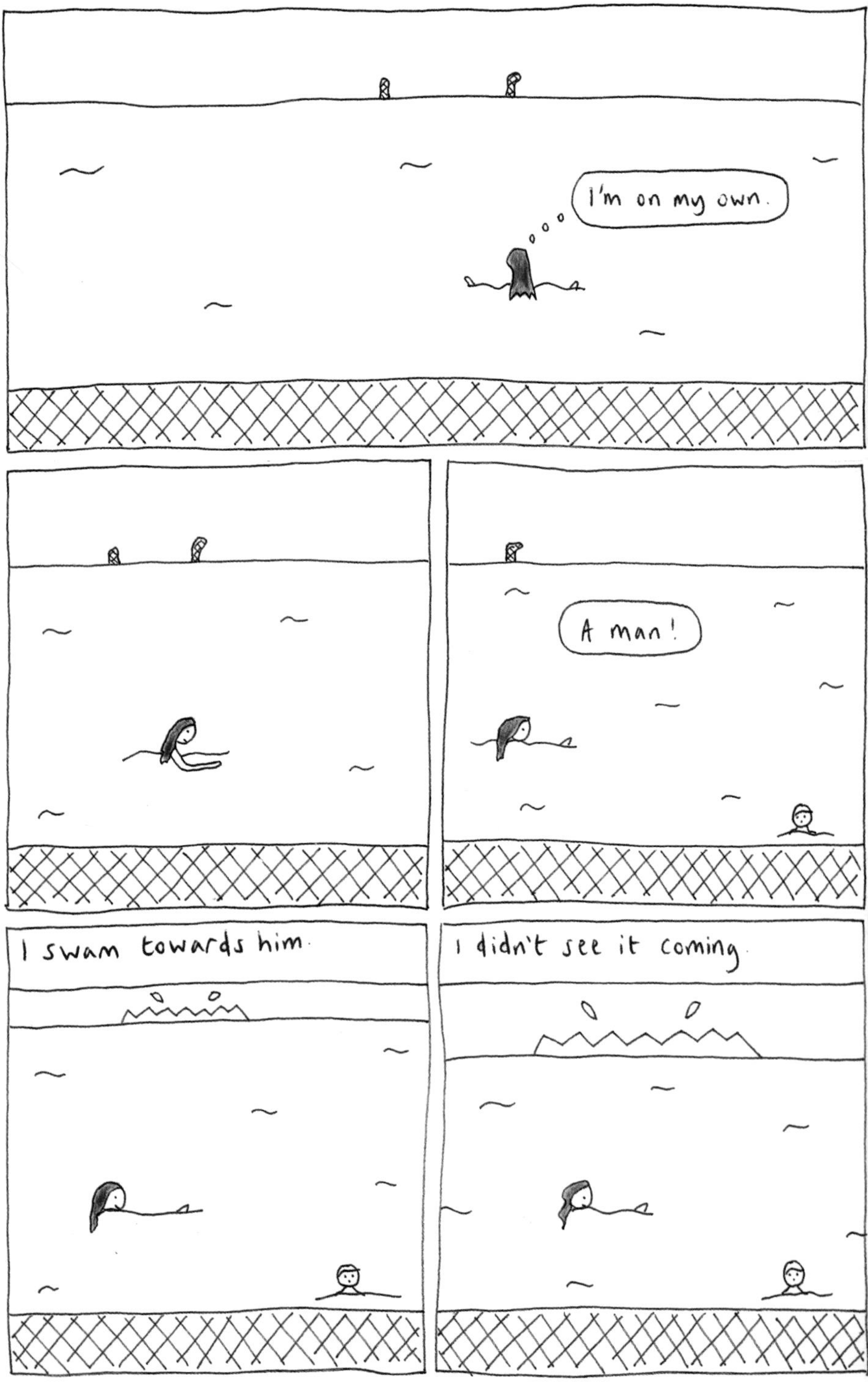
I'm on my own.
A man!
I swam towards him.
I didn't see it coming.

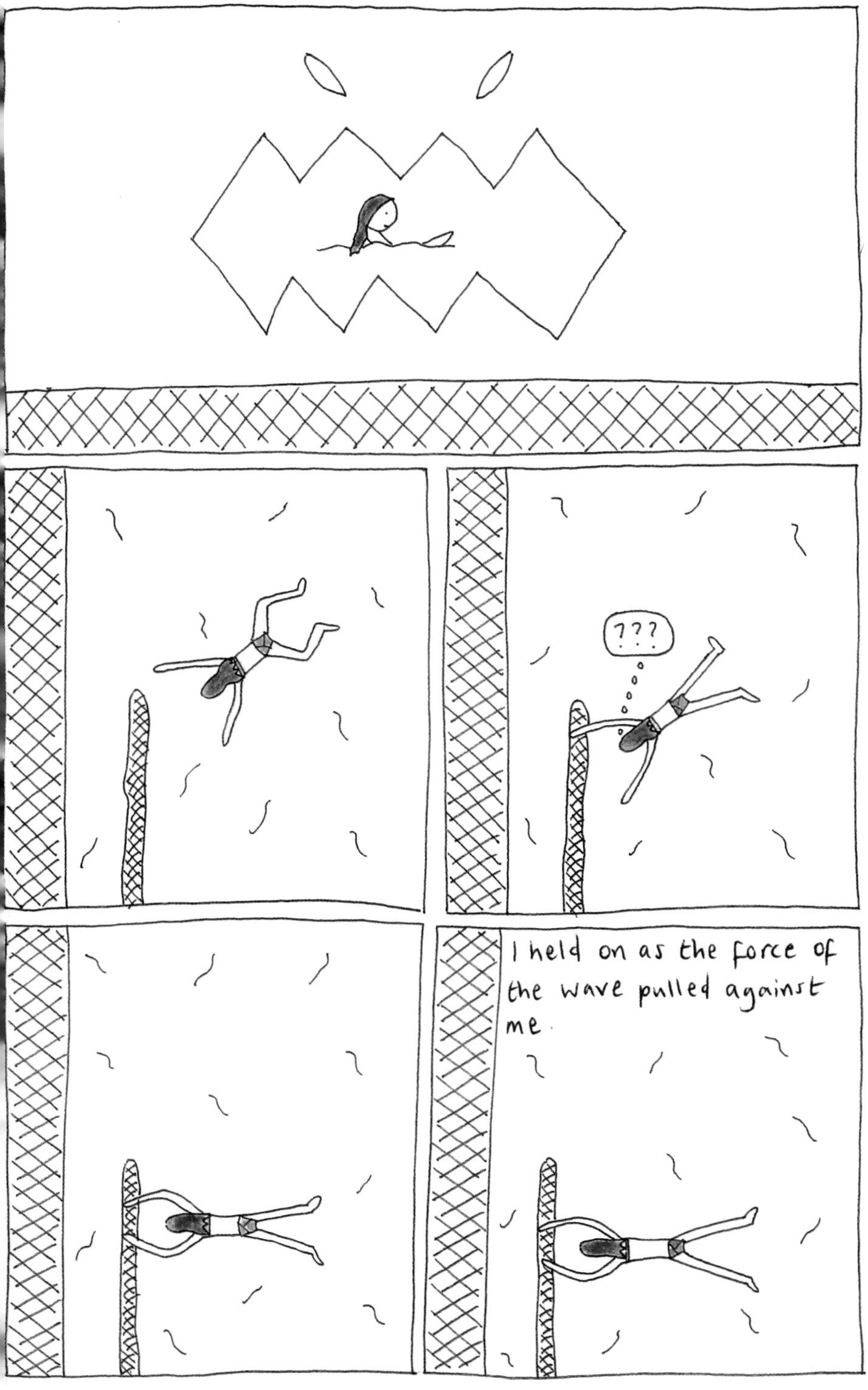
???
I held on as the force of the wave pulled against me.

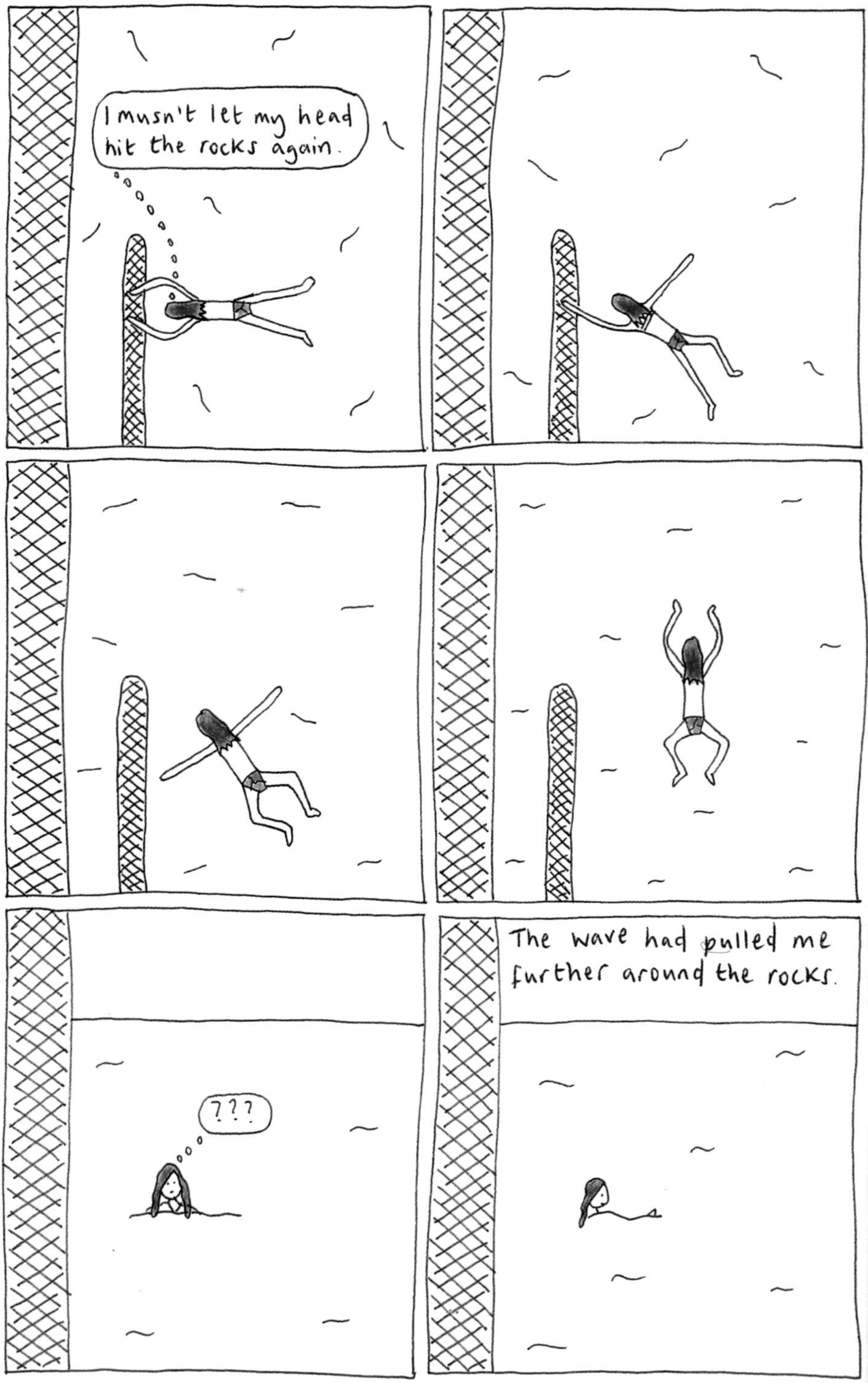
I musn't let my head hit the rocks again.
???
The wave had pulled me further around the rocks.

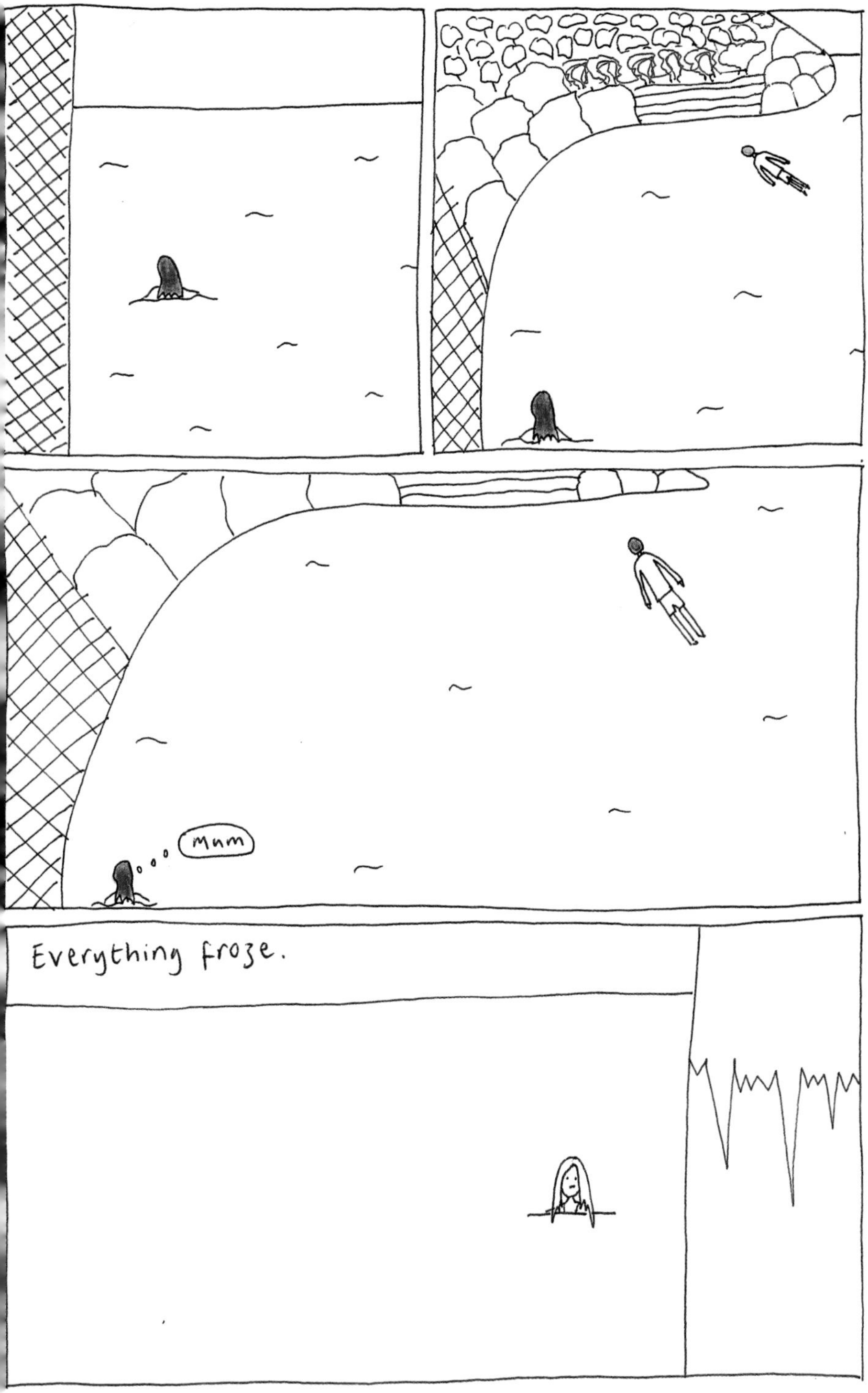
Mum
Everything froze.

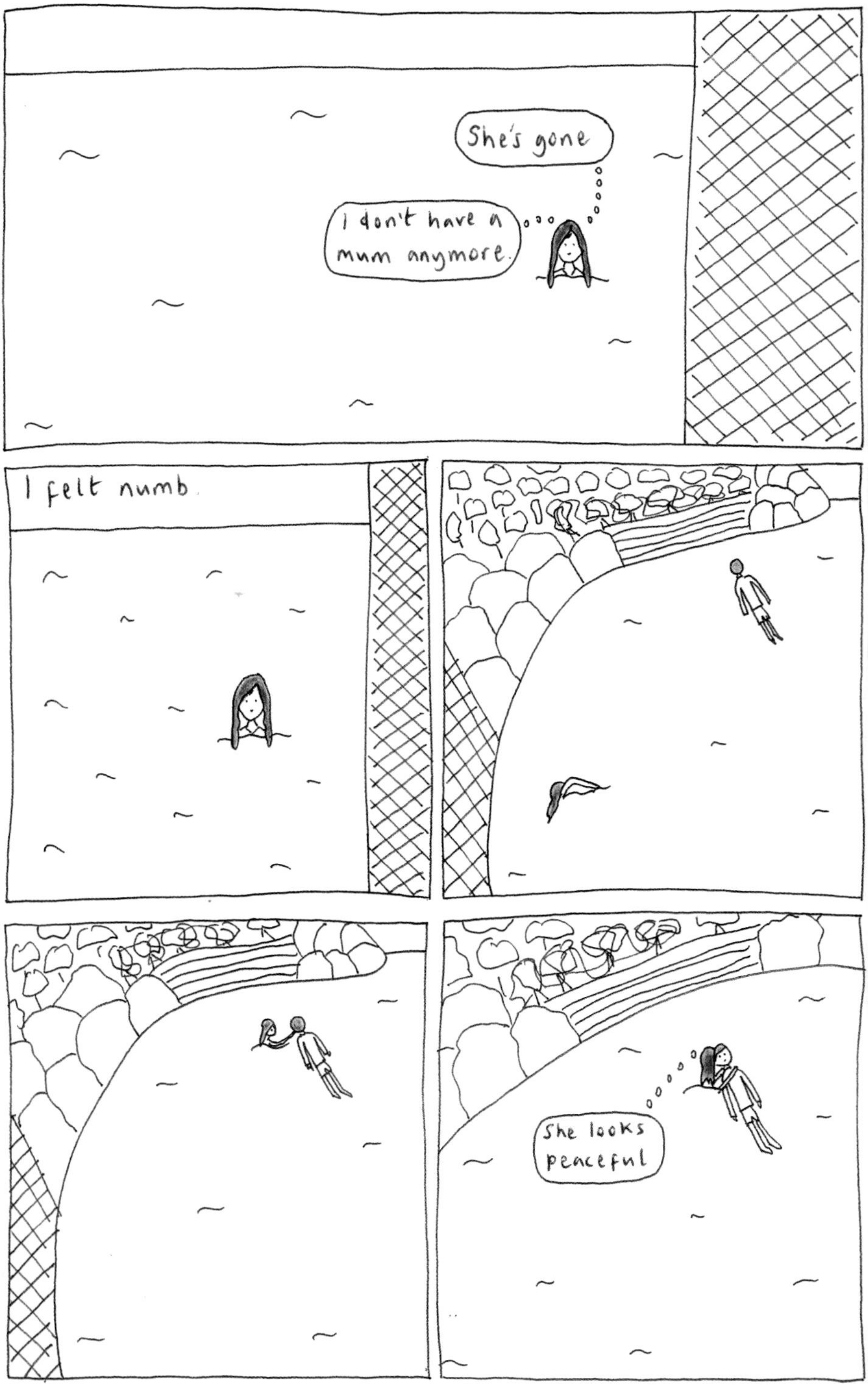

I don't have a mum anymore.
She's gone
I felt numb.
She looks peaceful

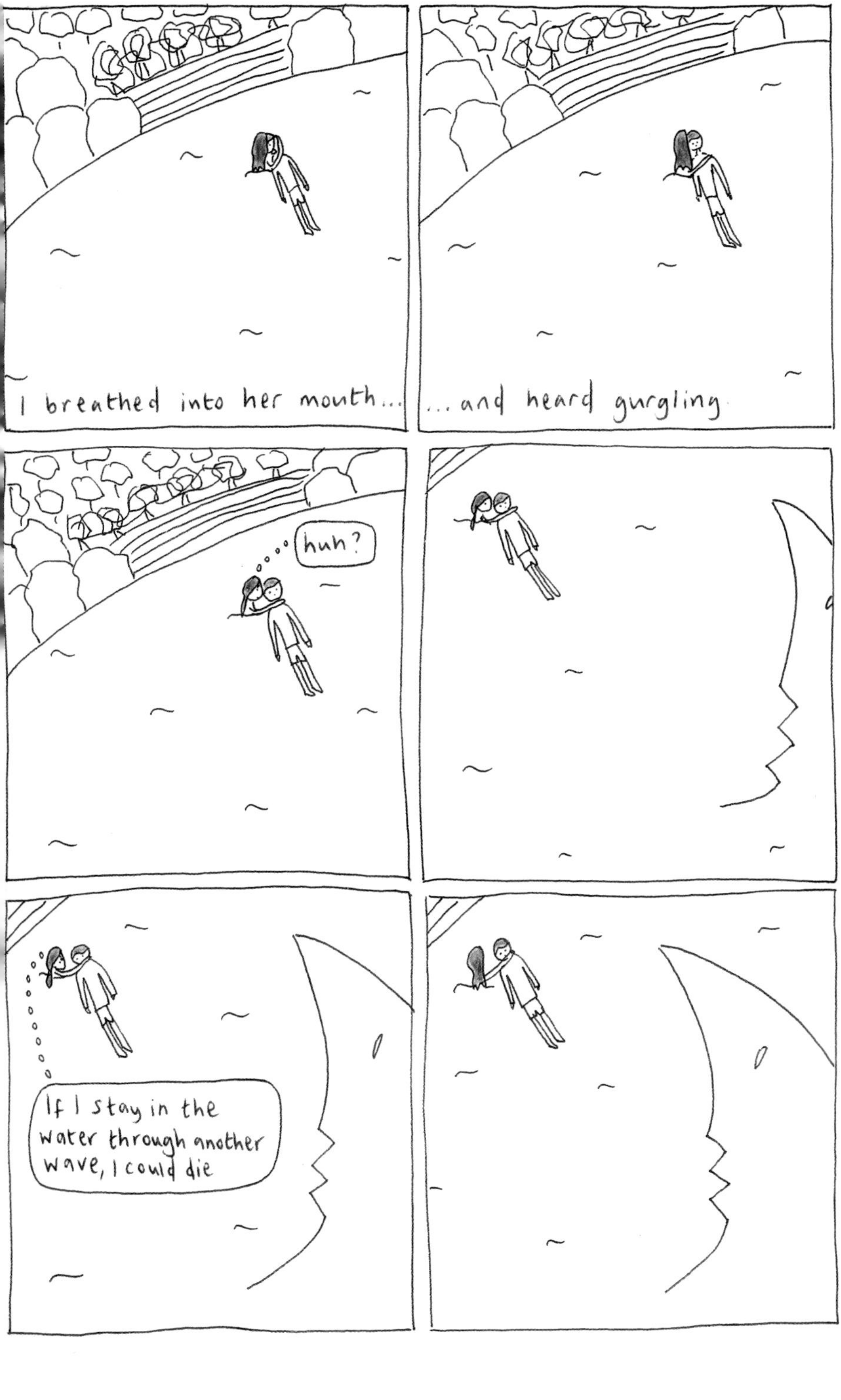
I breathed into her mouth...
...and heard gurgling.
huh?
If I stay in the water through another wave, I could die

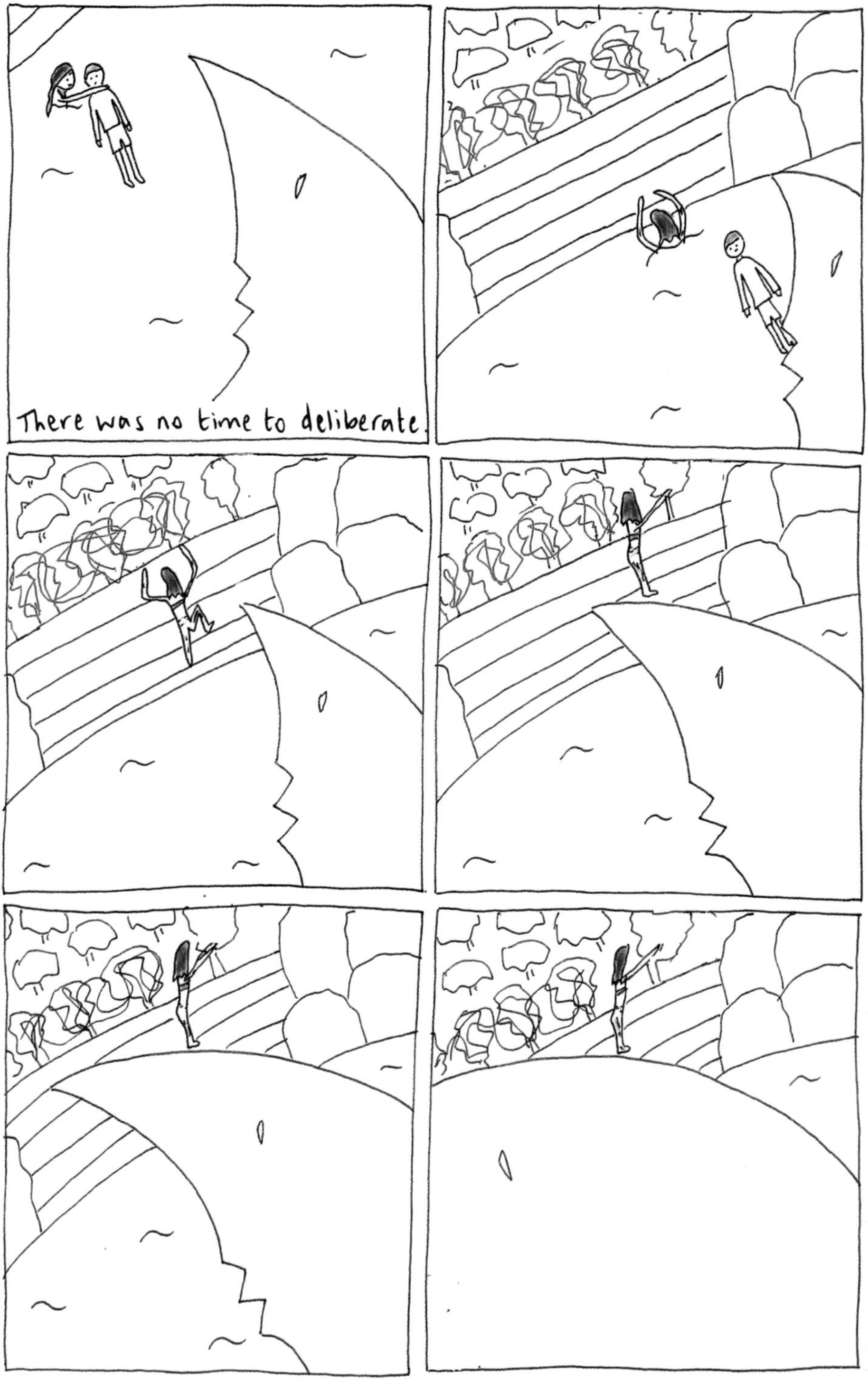
There was no time to deliberate.

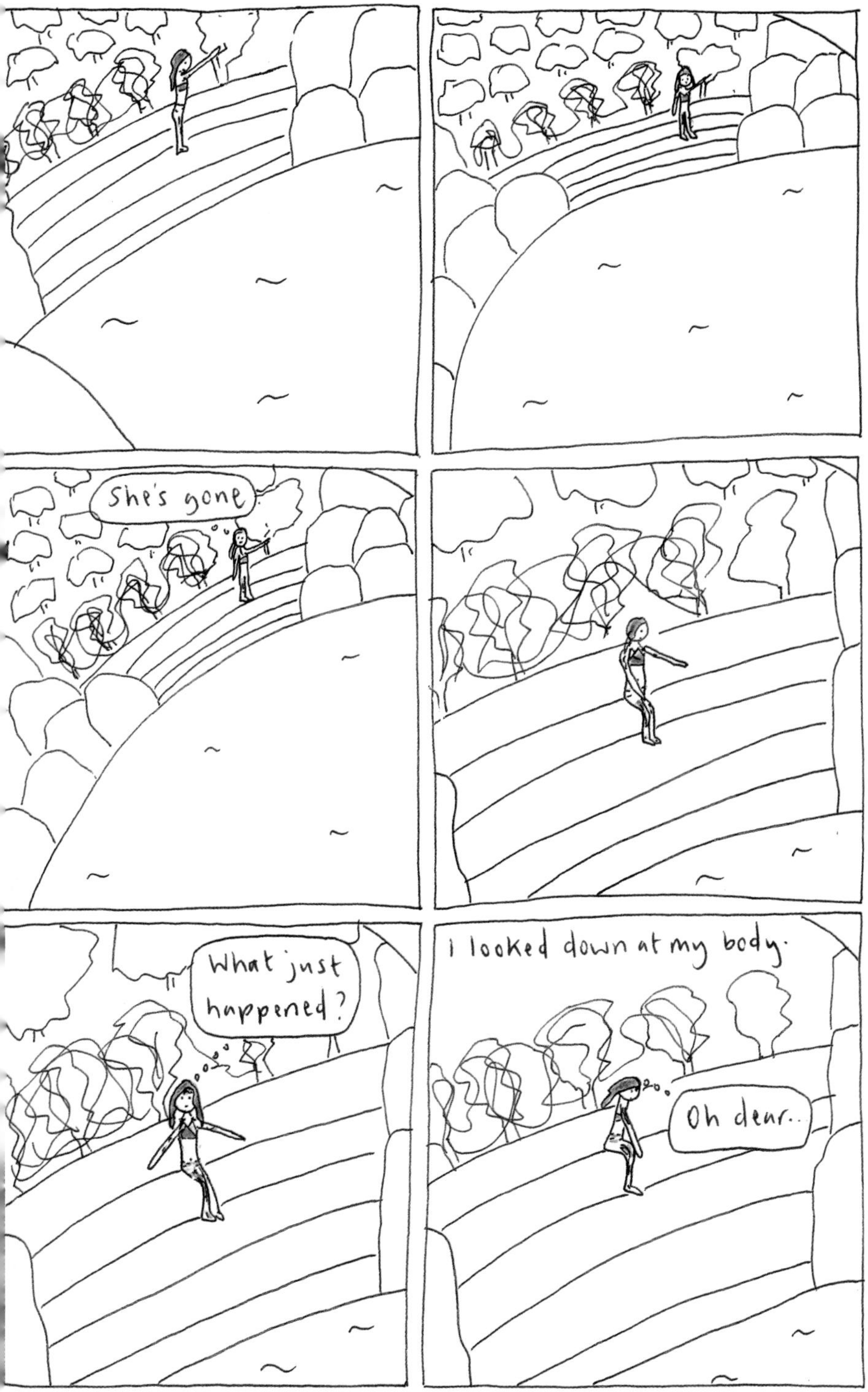
She's gone
What just happened?
I looked down at my body.
Oh dear..

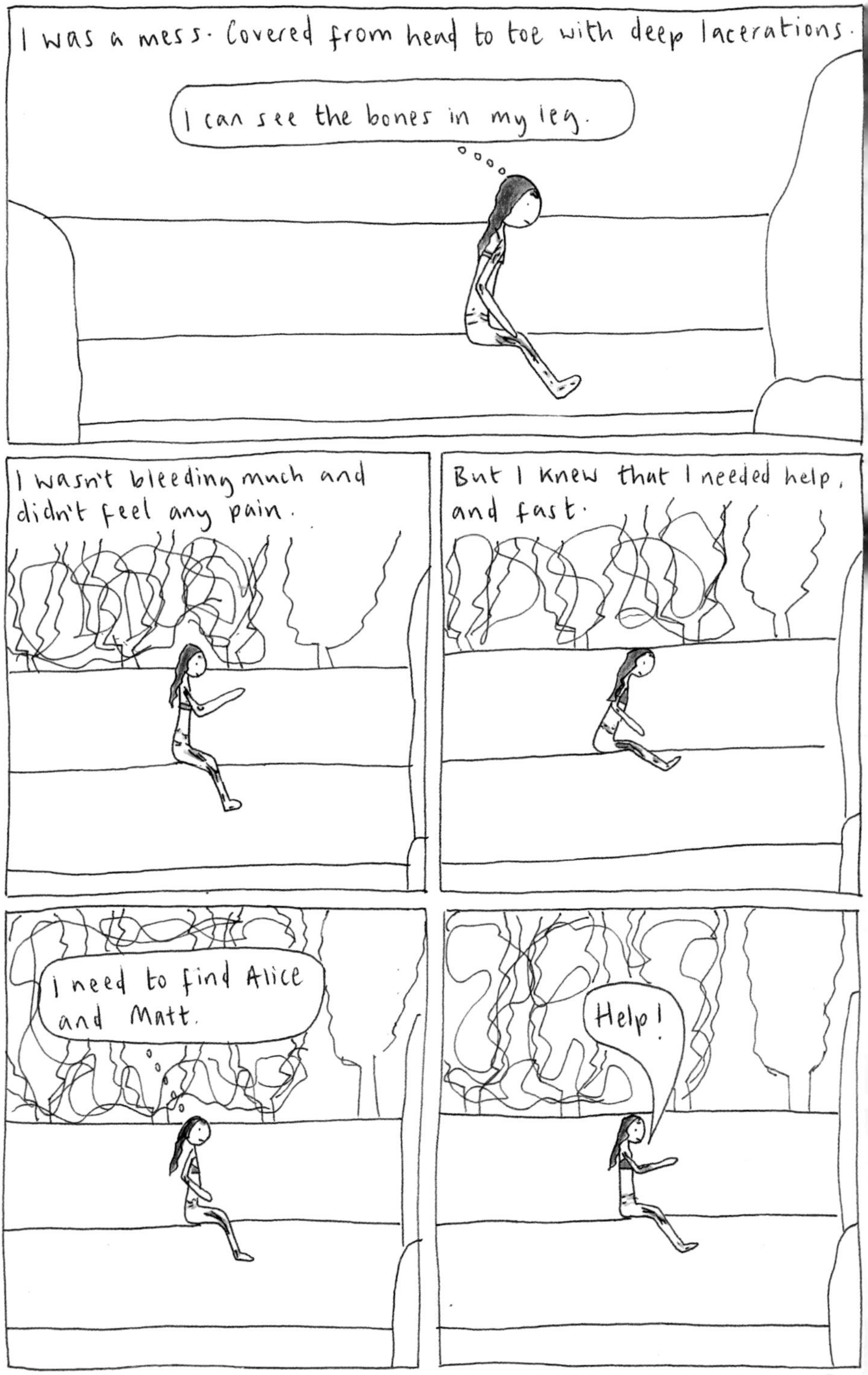
I was a mess. Covered from head to toe with deep lacerations.
I can see the bones in my leg.
I wasn't bleeding much and didn't feel any pain.
But I knew that I needed help, and fast.
I need to find Alice and Matt.
Help!

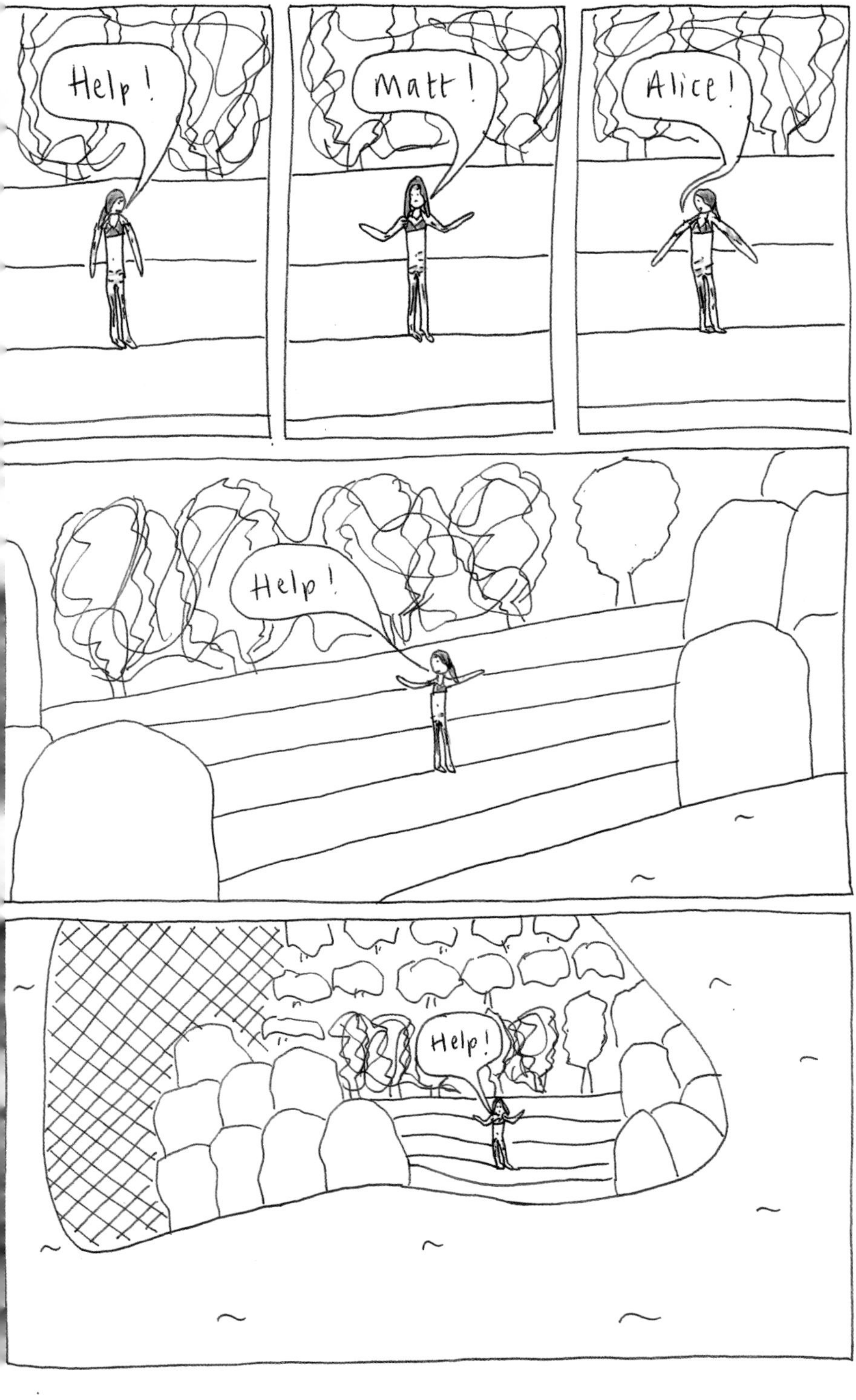
Help!
Matt!
Alice!
Help!
Help!

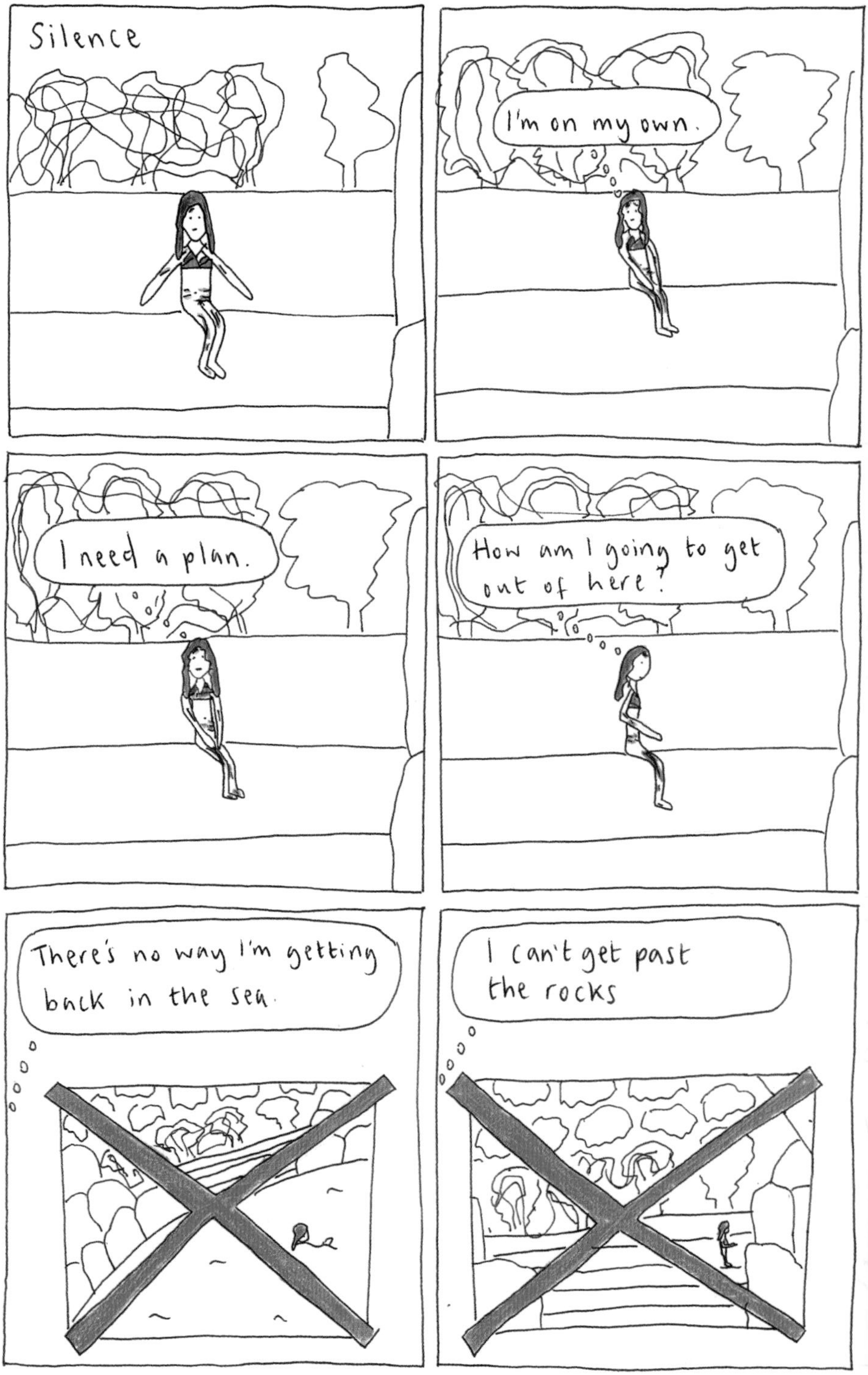
Silence
I'm on my own.
I need a plan.
How am I going to get out of here?
There's no way I'm getting back in the sea.
I can't get past the rocks

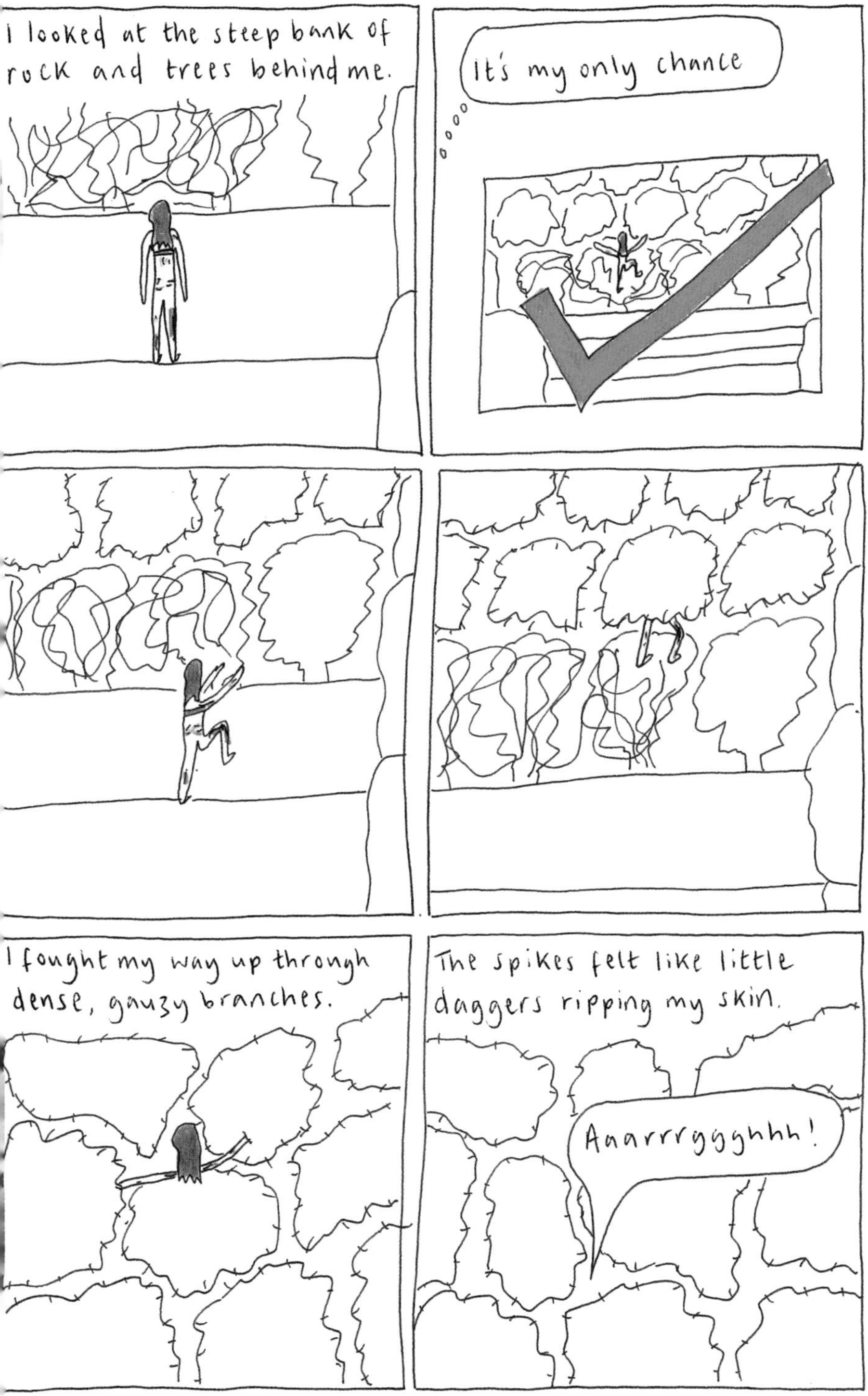

I looked at the steep bank of rock and trees behind me.
It's my only chance
I fought my way up through dense, gauzy branches.
The spikes felt like little daggers ripping my skin.
Aaarrrggghhh!

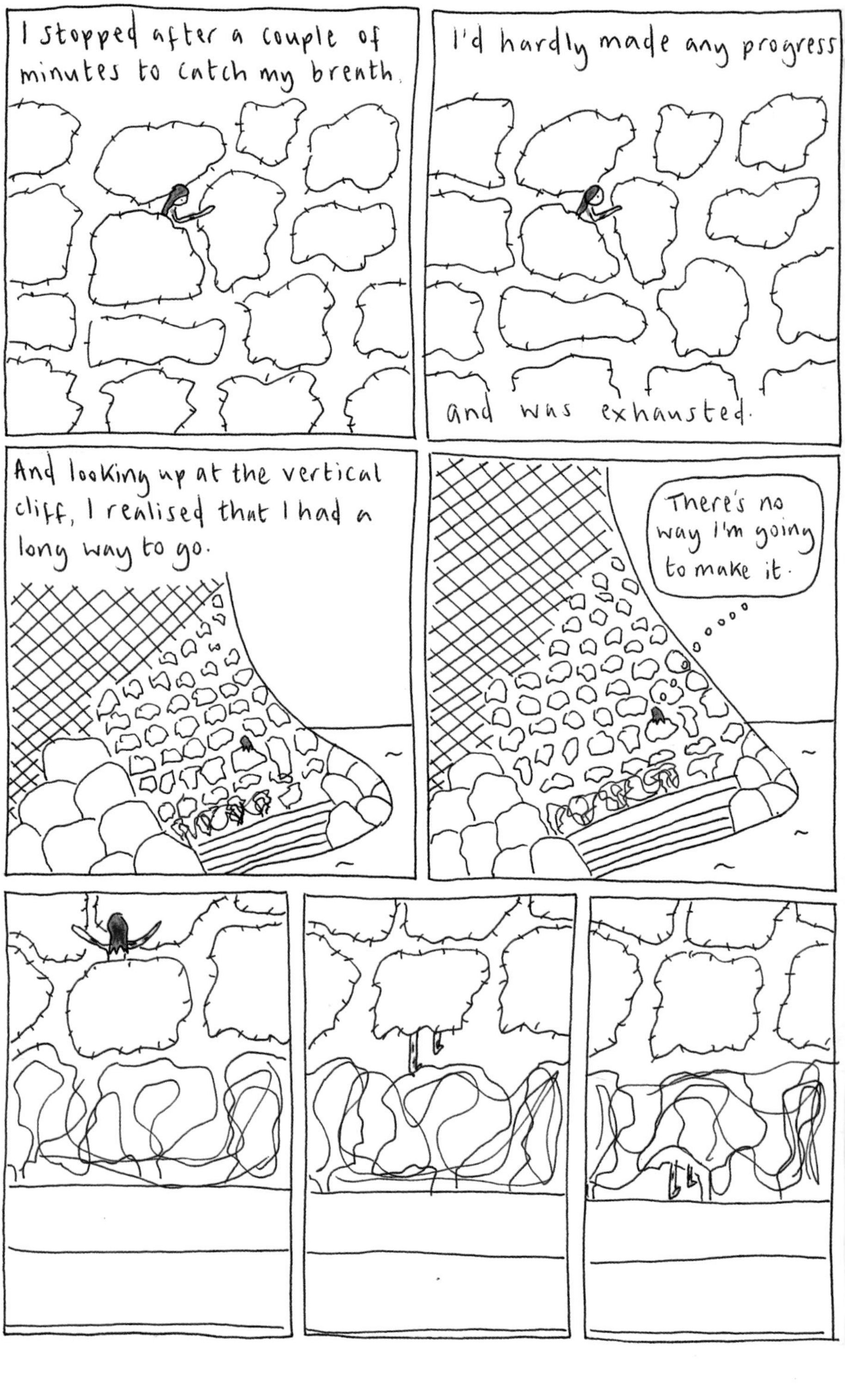
I stopped after a couple of minutes to catch my breath.
I'd hardly made any progress
and was exhausted.
And looking up at the vertical cliff, I realised that I had a long way to go.
There's no way I'm going to make it.

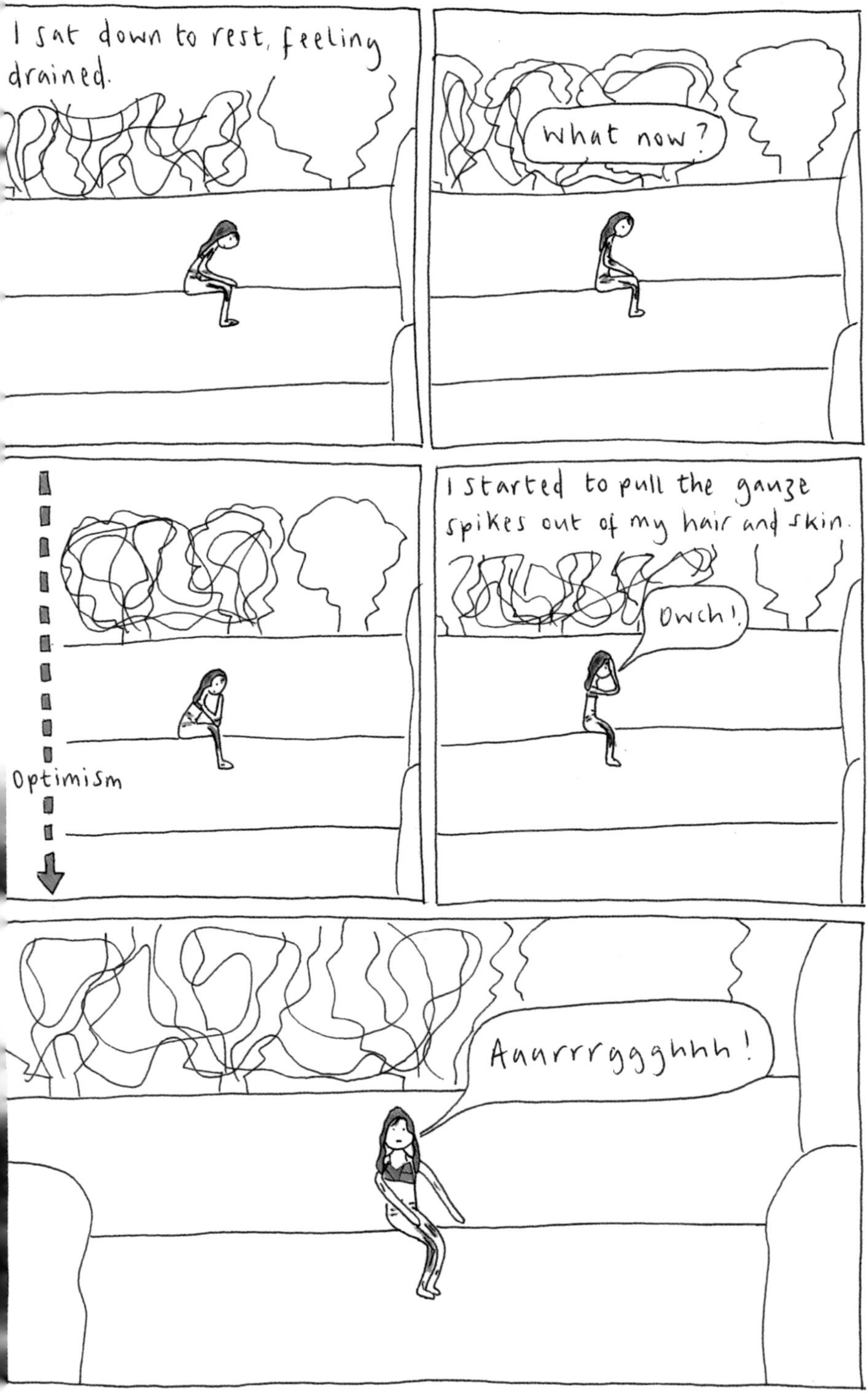
I sat down to rest, feeling drained.
What now?
Optimism
I started to pull the gauze spikes out of my hair and skin.
Owch!
Aaarrrggghhh!

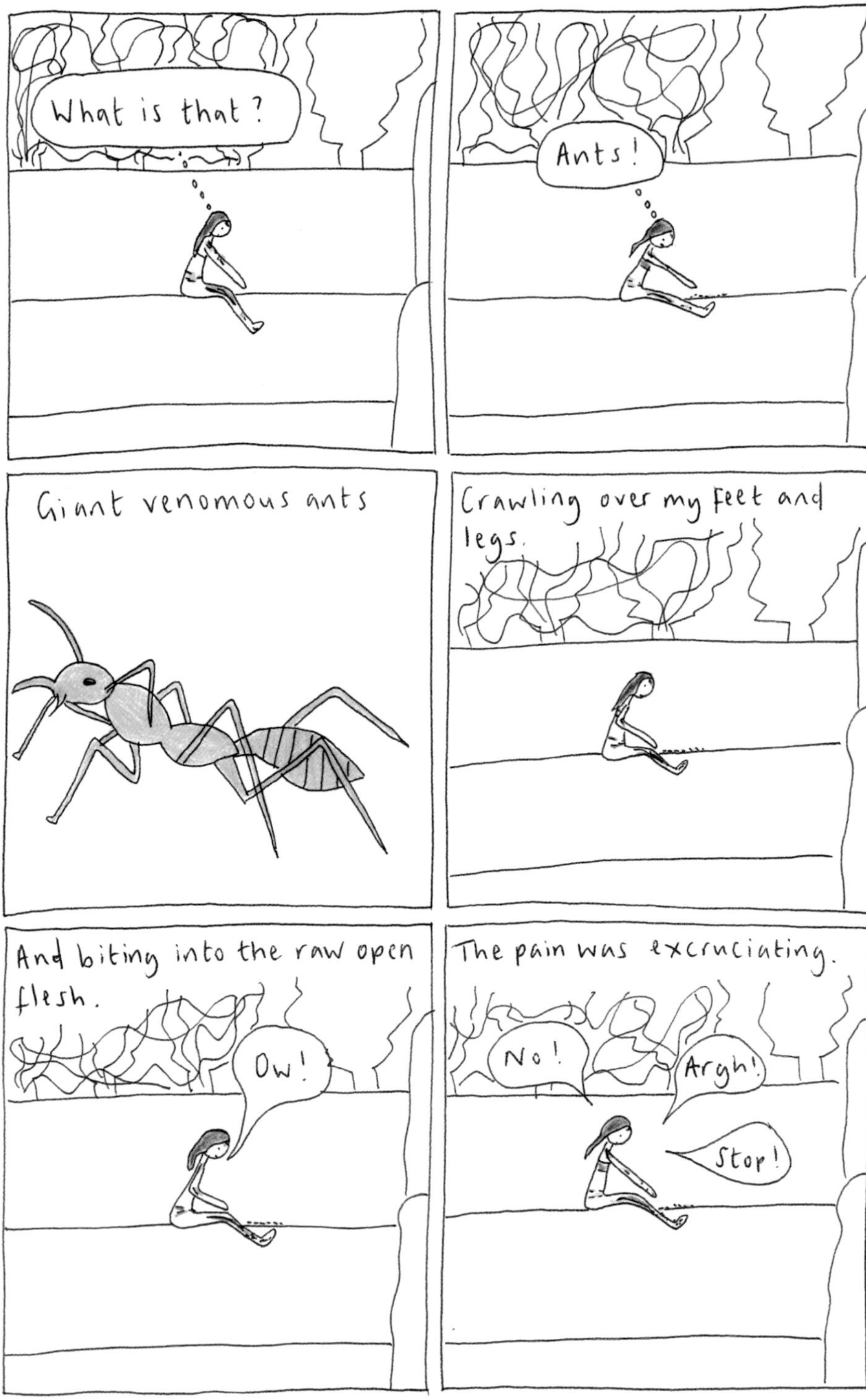
What is that?
Ants!
Giant venomous ants
Crawling over my feet and legs.
And biting into the raw open flesh.
Ow!
The pain was excruciating.
No!
Argh!
Stop!

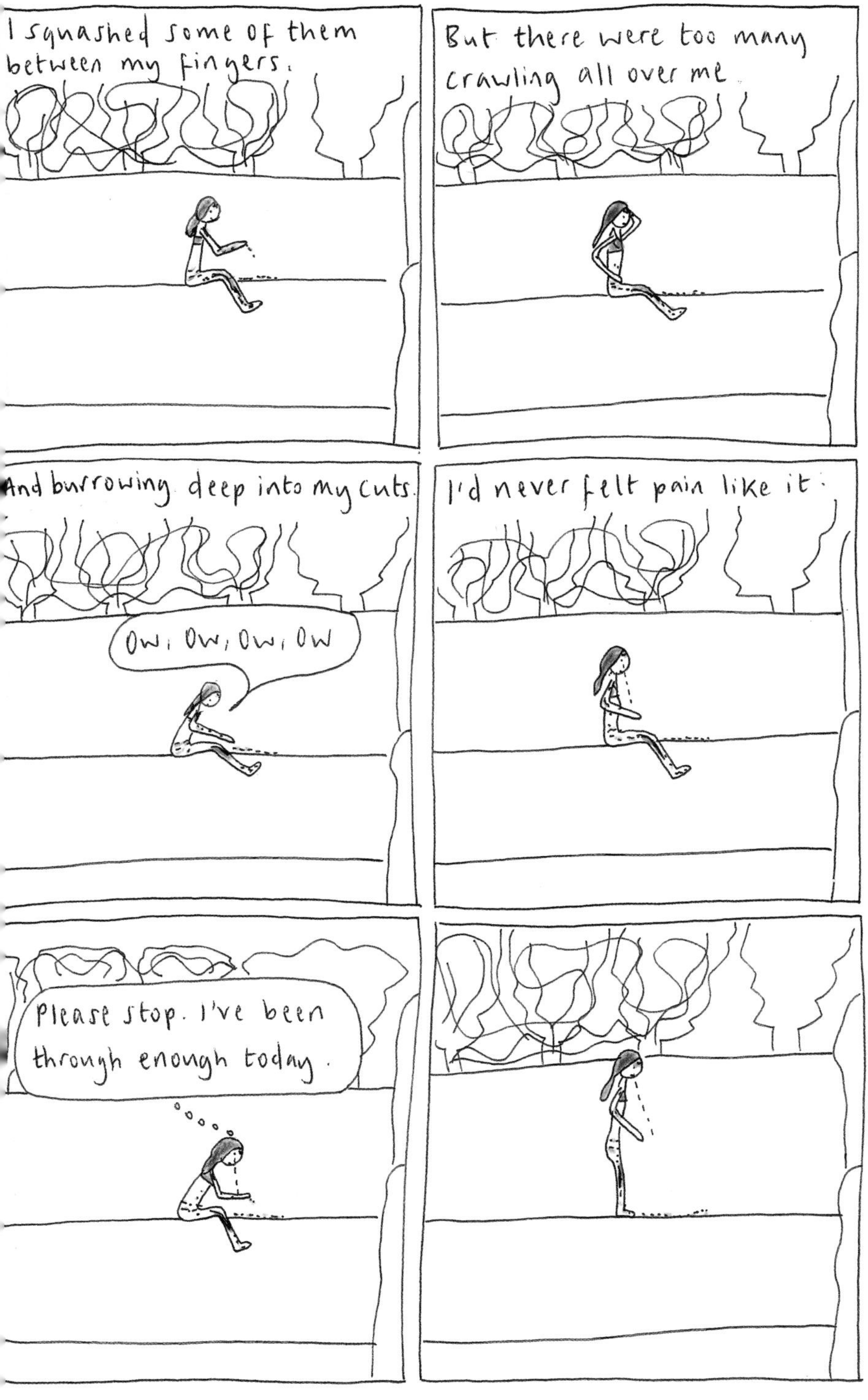
I squashed some of them between my fingers.
But there were too many crawling all over me.
And burrowing deep into my cuts.
Ow, Ow, Ow, Ow
I'd never felt pain like it.
Please stop. I've been through enough today.

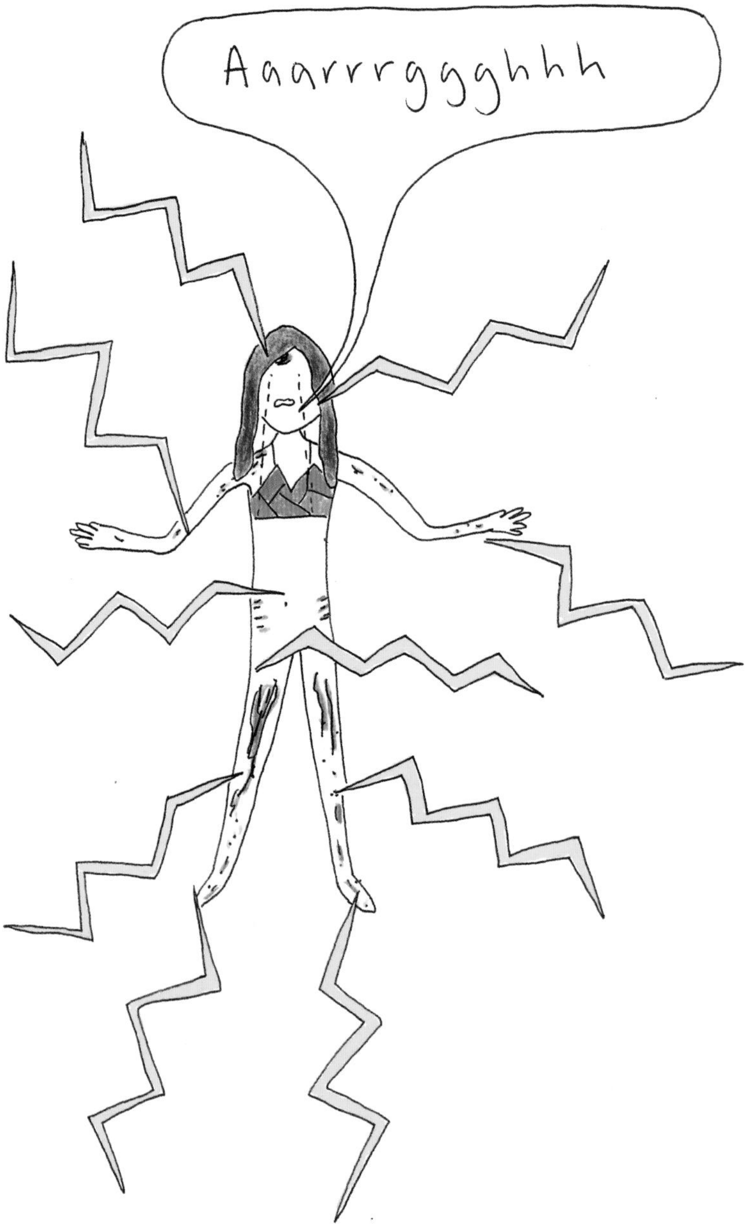
Aaarrrggghhh

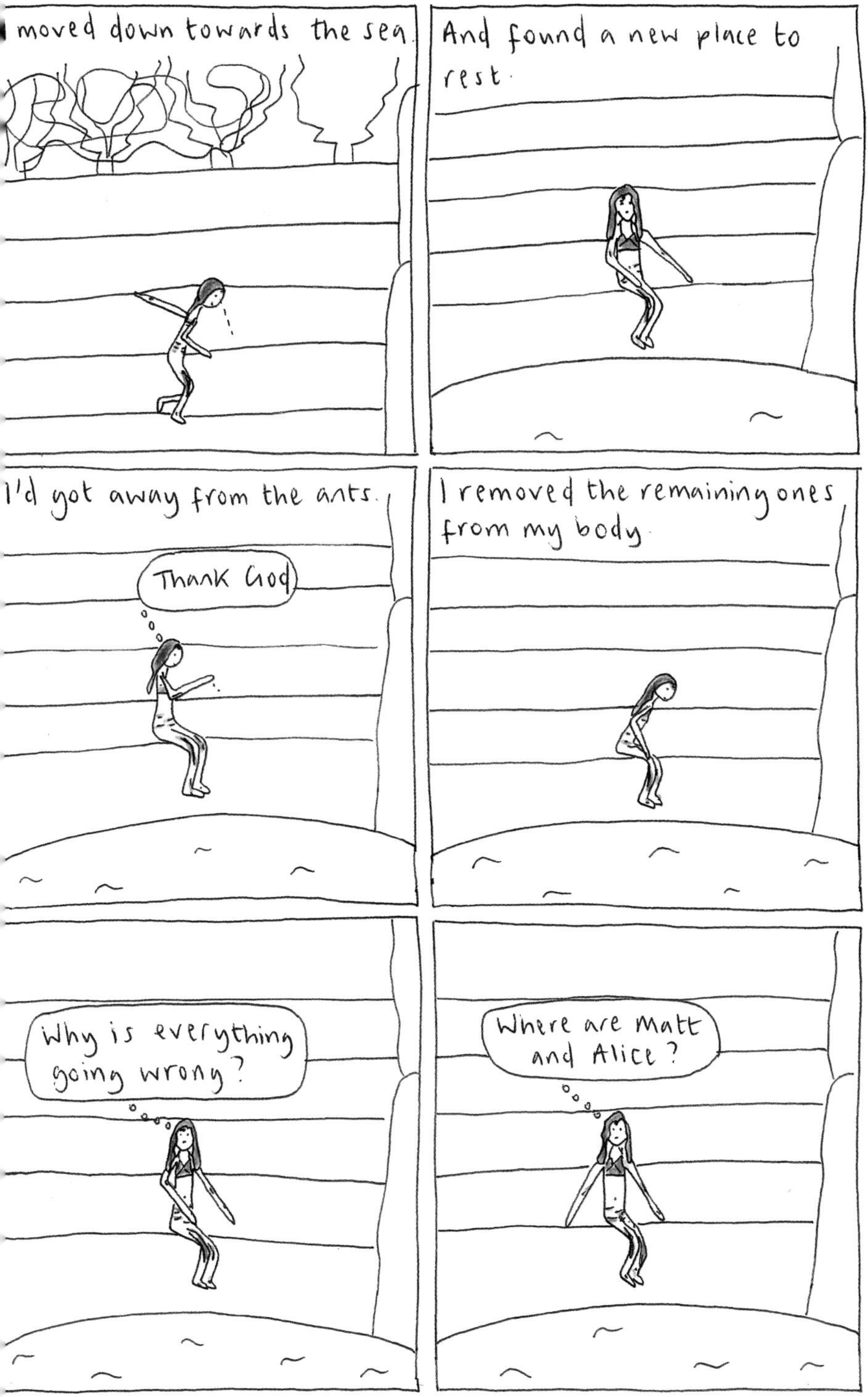
I moved down towards the sea.
And found a new place to rest.
I'd got away from the ants.
Thank God
I removed the remaining ones from my body.
Why is everything going wrong?
Where are Matt and Alice?

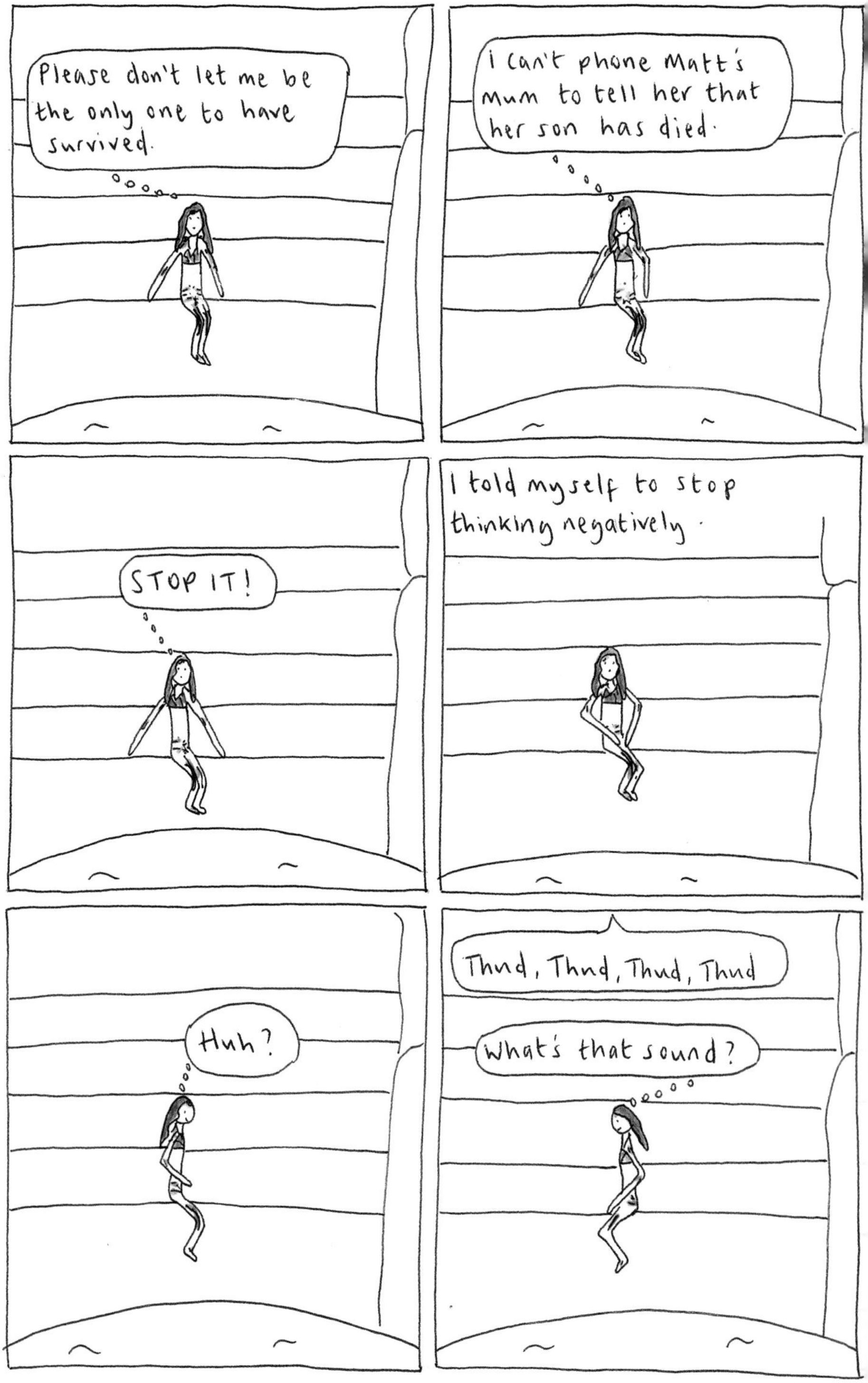
Please don't let me be the only one to have survived.
I can't phone Matt's Mum to tell her that her son has died.
STOP IT!
I told myself to stop thinking negatively.
Huh?
Thud, Thud, Thud, Thud
What's that sound?

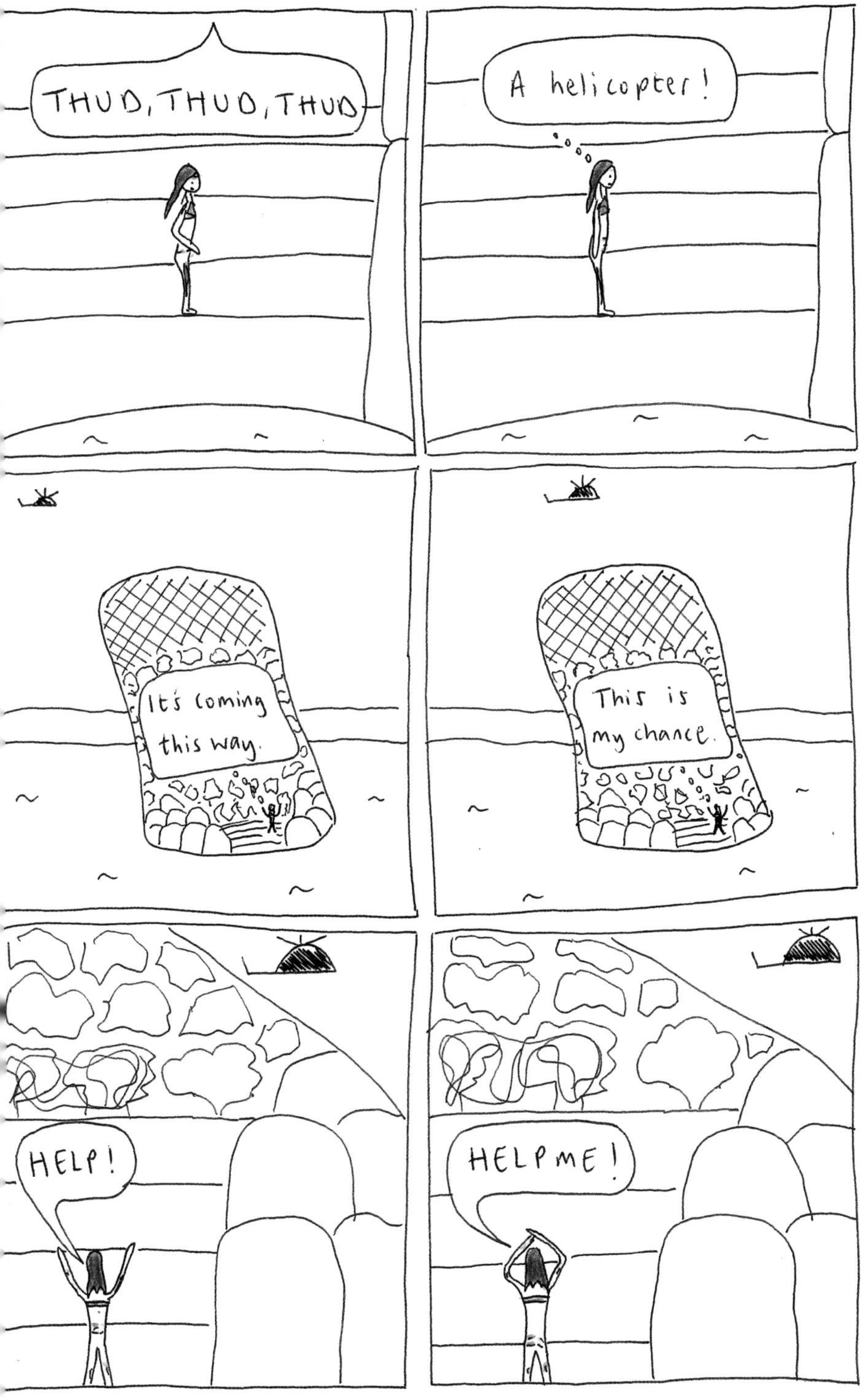
THUD, THUD, THUD
A helicopter!
It's coming this way.
This is my chance.
HELP!
HELP ME!

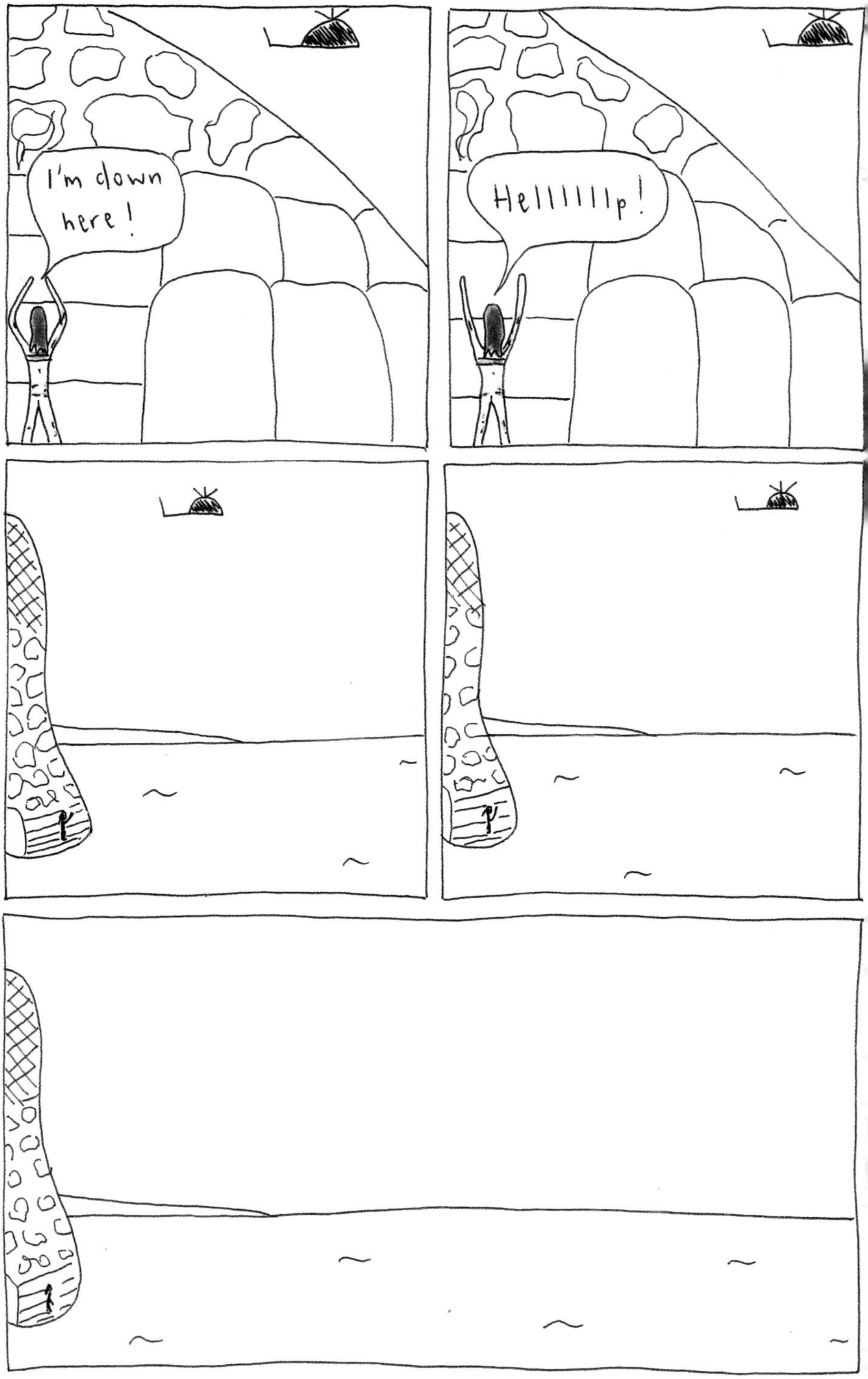
I'm down here!
Helllllllp!

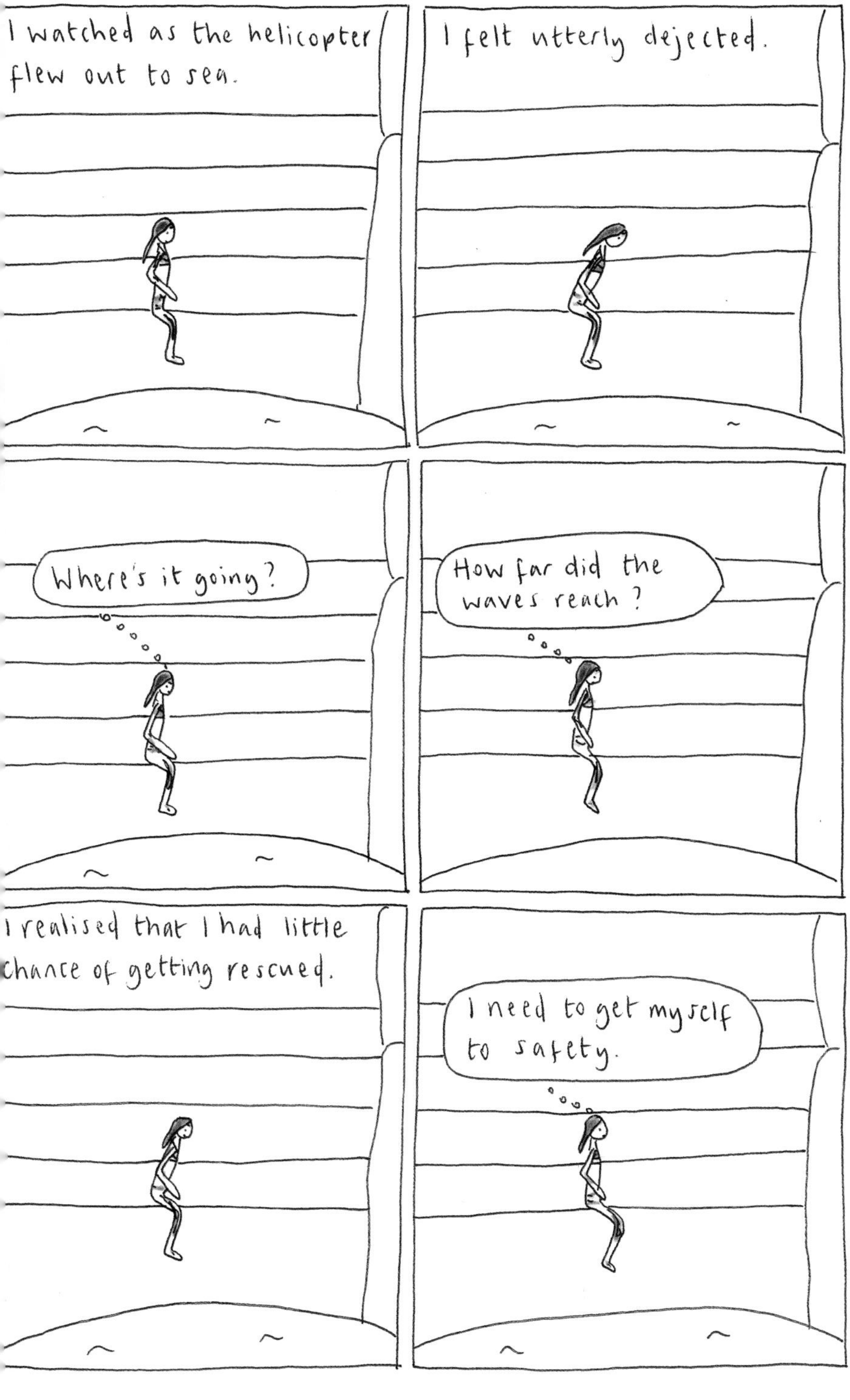
I watched as the helicopter flew out to sea.
I felt utterly dejected.
Where's it going?
How far did the waves reach?
I realised that I had little chance of getting rescued.
I need to get myself to safety.

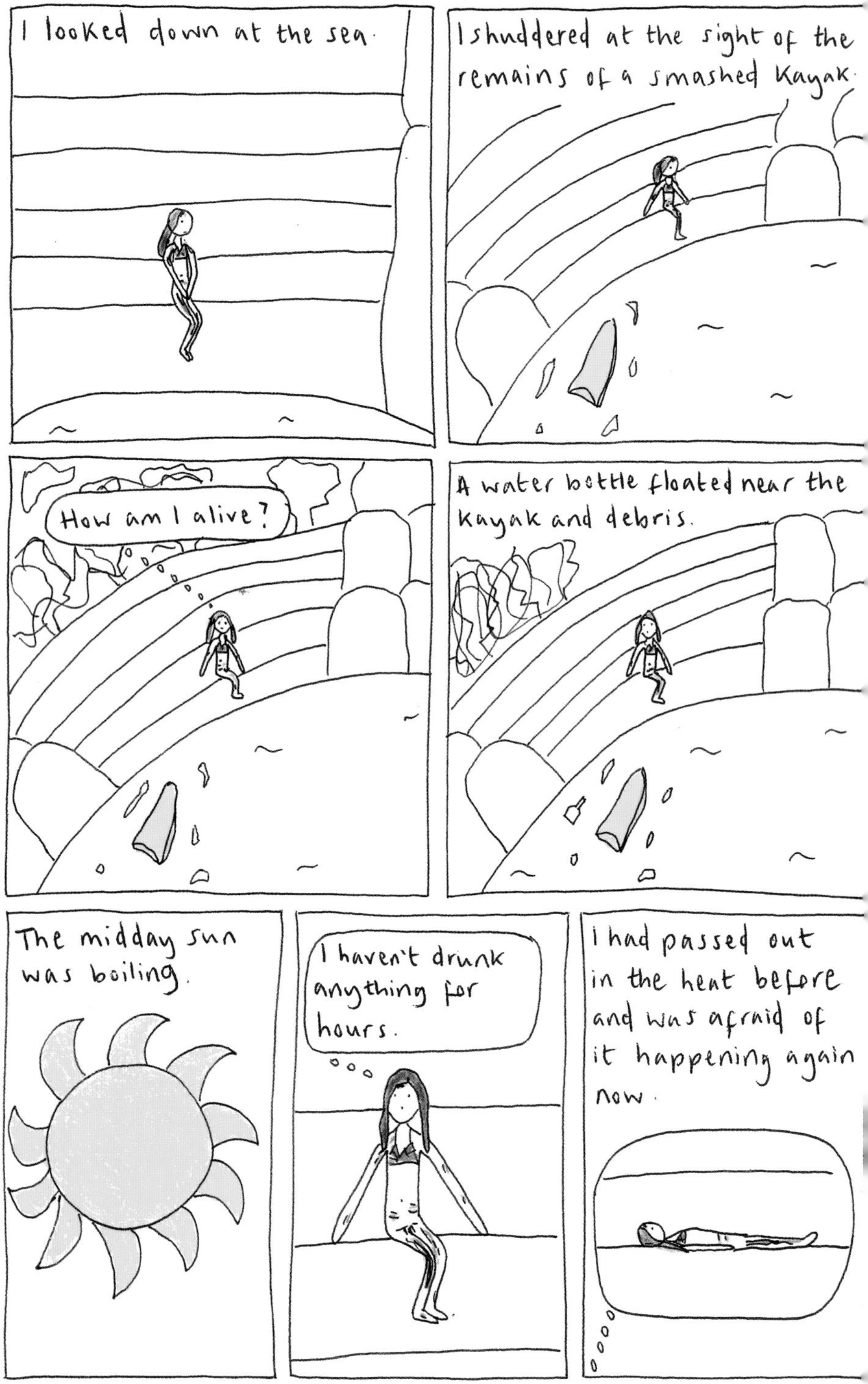
I looked down at the sea.
I shuddered at the sight of the remains of a smashed kayak.
How am I alive?
A water bottle floated near the kayak and debris.
The midday sun was boiling.
I haven't drunk anything for hours.
I had passed out in the heat before and was afraid of it happening again now.

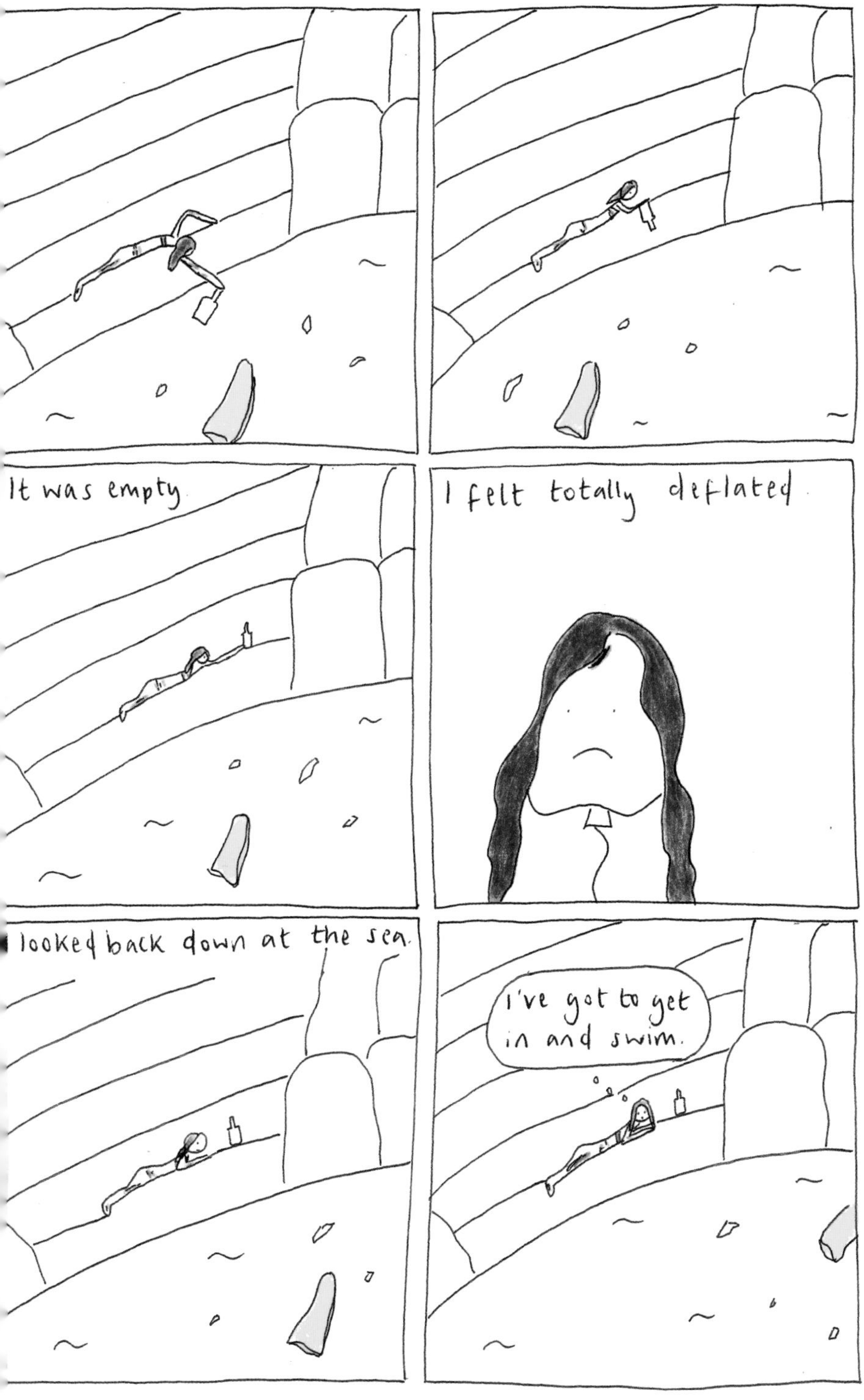
It was empty.
I felt totally deflated.
I looked back down at the sea.
I've got to get in and swim.

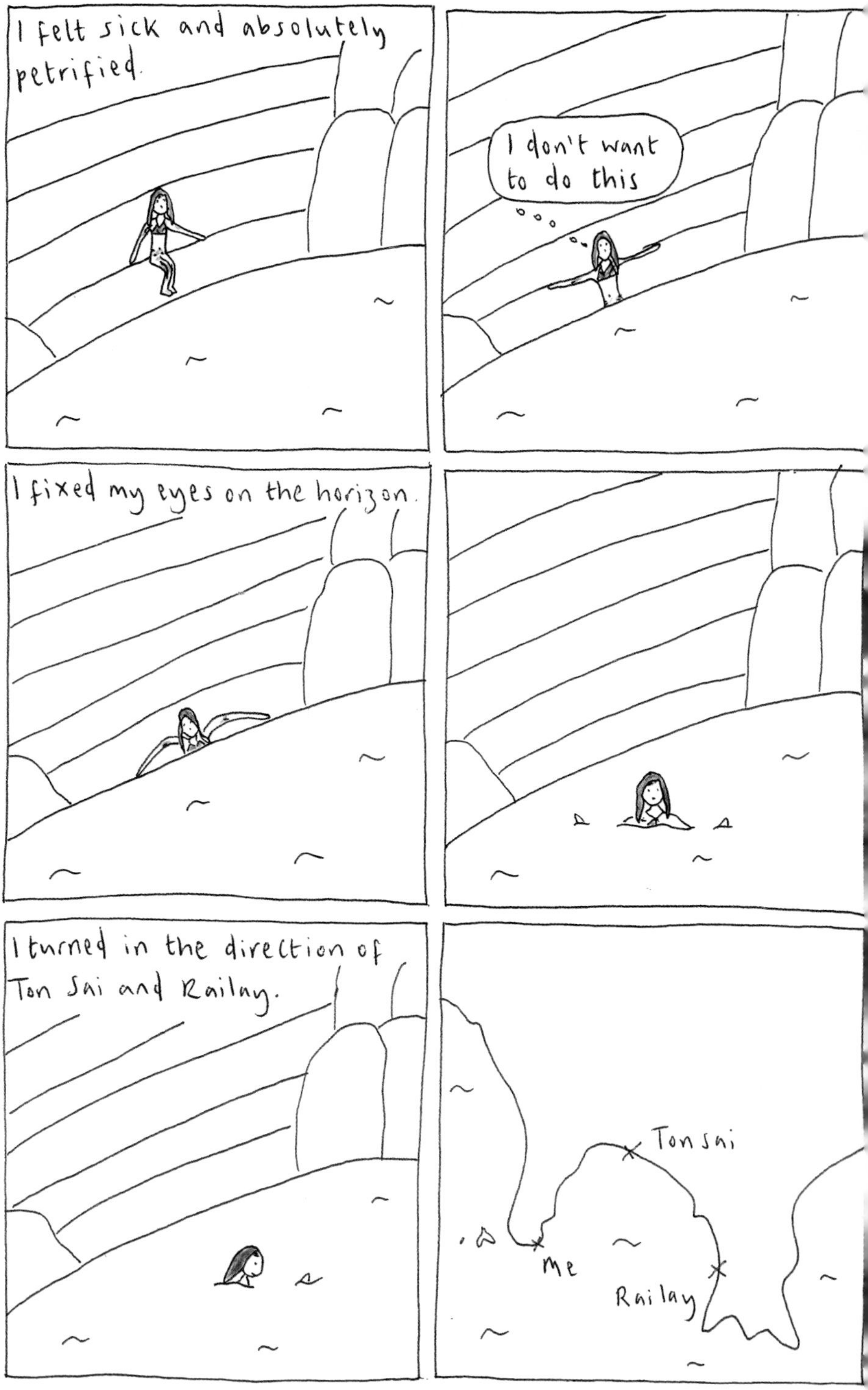
I felt sick and absolutely petrified.
I don't want to do this
I fixed my eyes on the horizon.
I turned in the direction of Ton Sai and Railay.
Ton sai
me
Railay

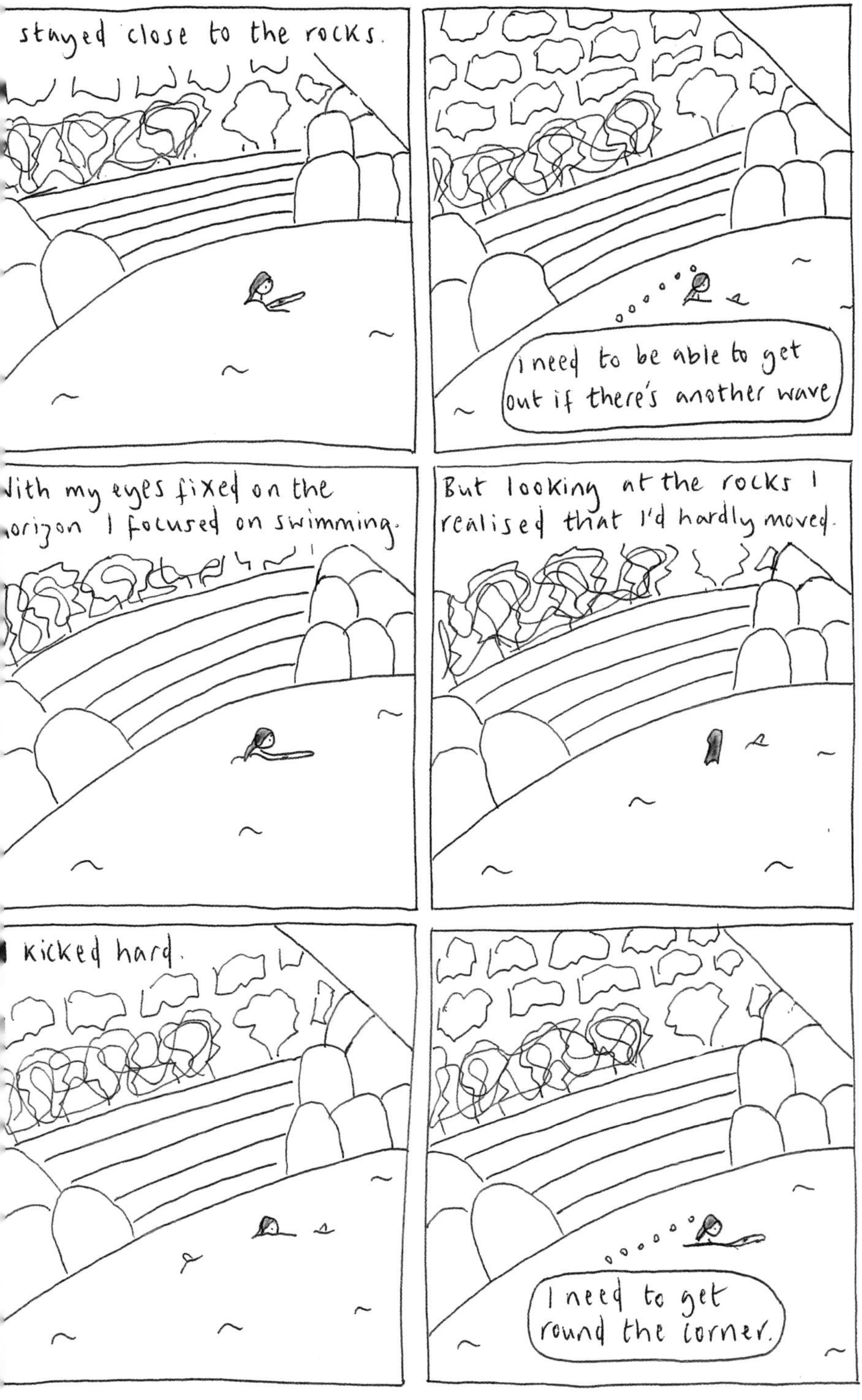
stayed close to the rocks.
I need to be able to get out if there's another wave
With my eyes fixed on the horizon I focused on swimming.
But looking at the rocks I realised that I'd hardly moved.
kicked hard.
I need to get round the corner.

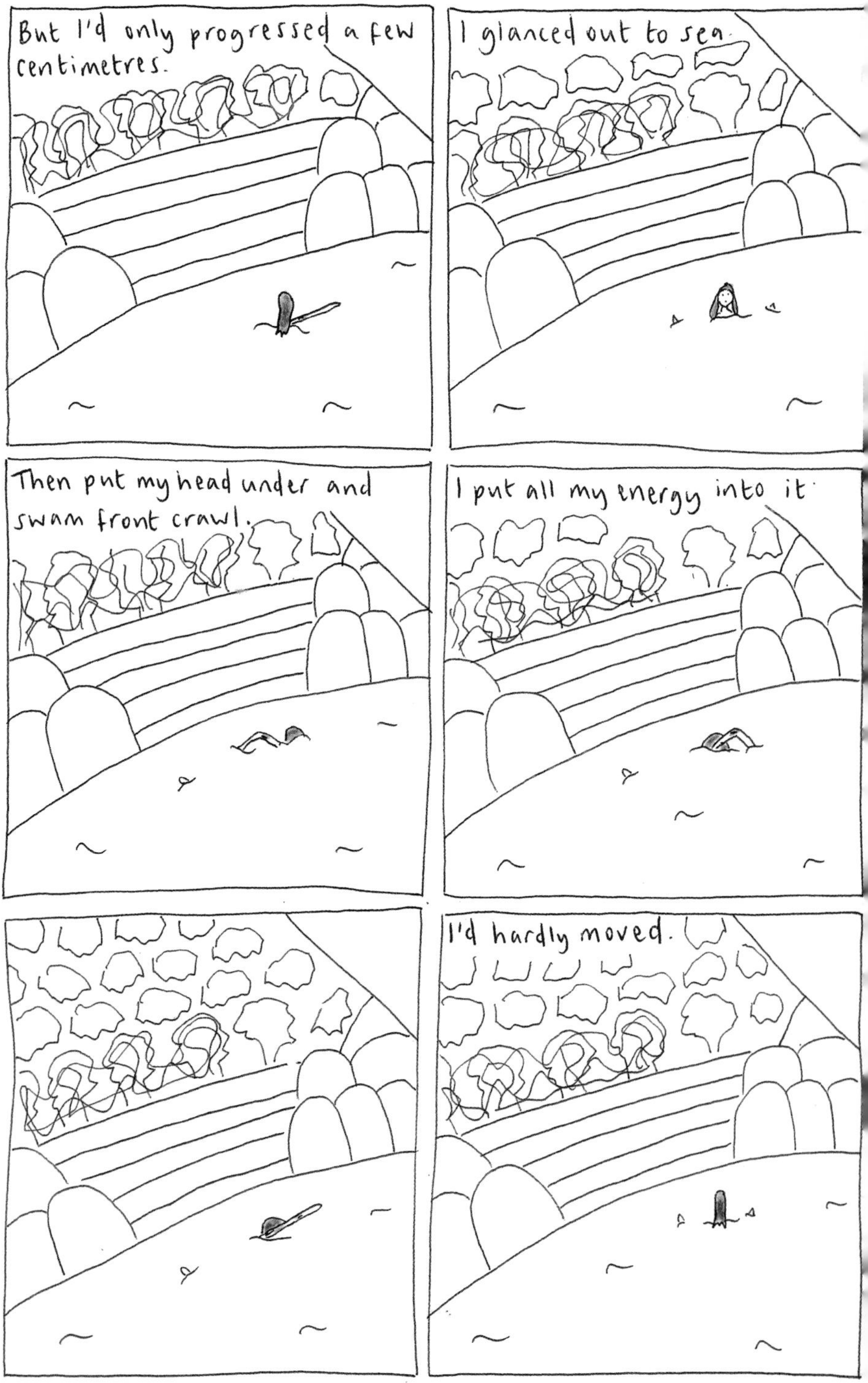
But I'd only progressed a few centimetres.
I glanced out to sea.
Then put my head under and swam front crawl.
I put all my energy into it.
I'd hardly moved.

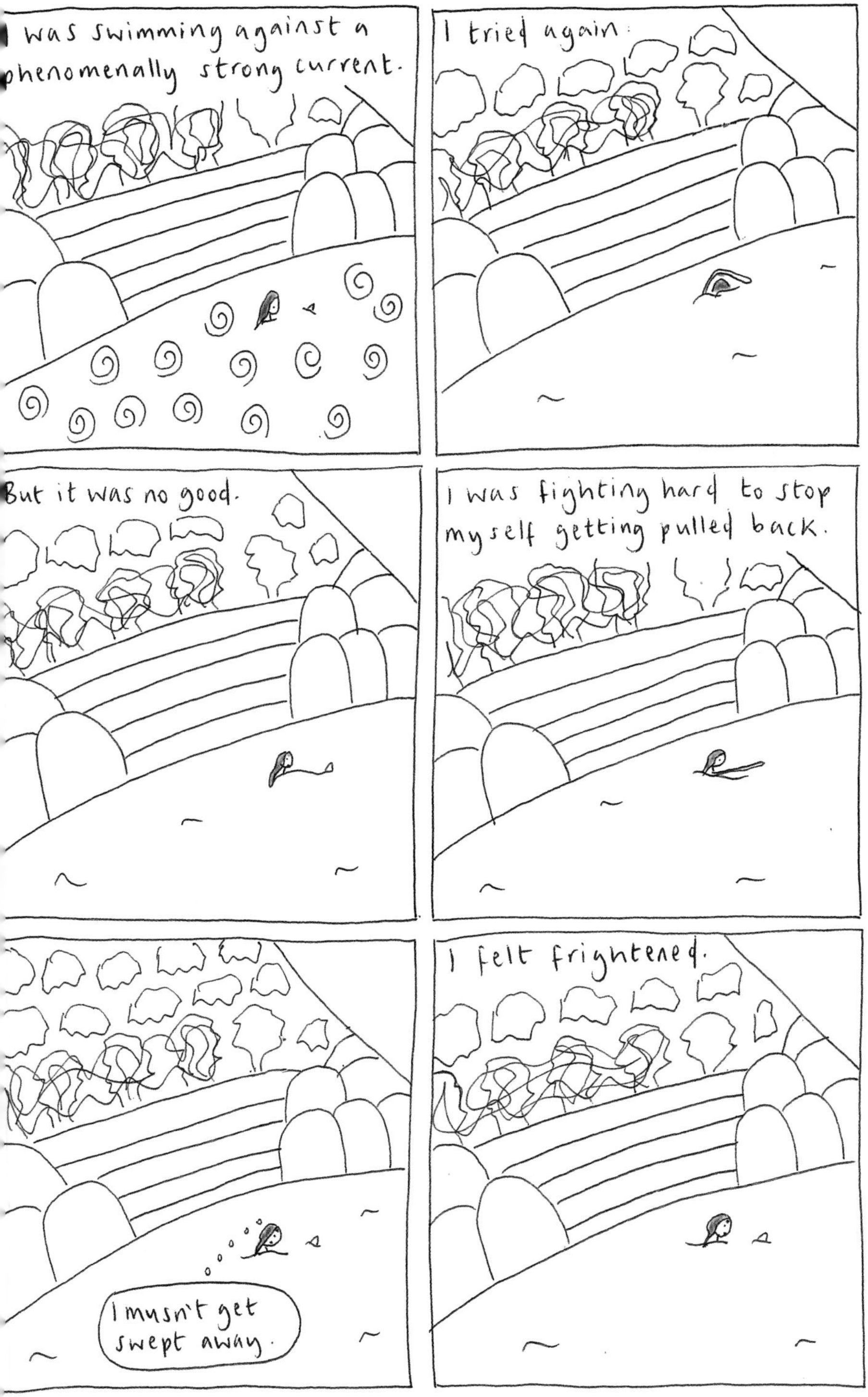
I was swimming against a phenomenally strong current.
I tried again.
But it was no good.
I was fighting hard to stop myself getting pulled back.
I musn't get swept away.
I felt frightened.

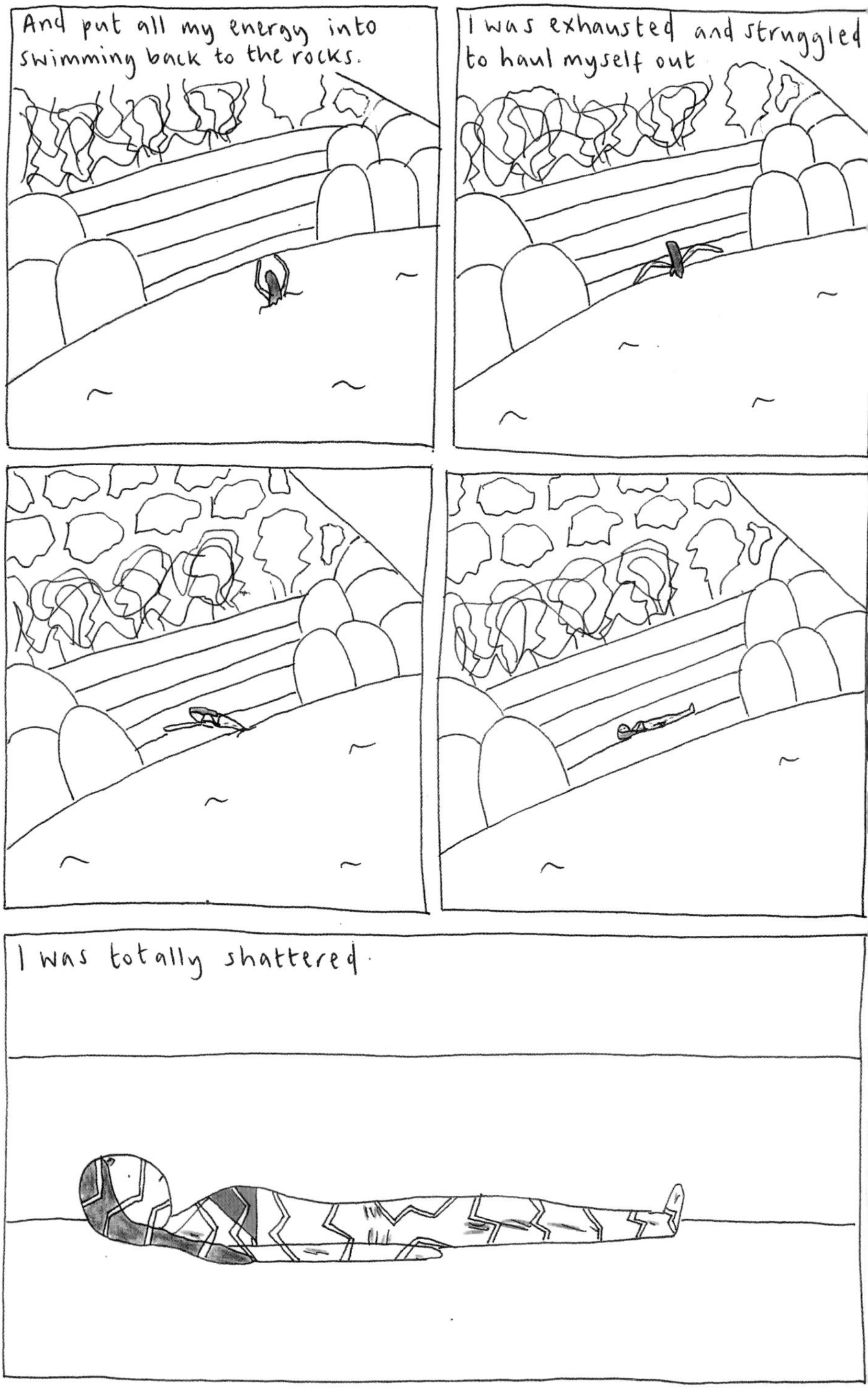
And put all my energy into swimming back to the rocks.
I was exhausted and struggled to haul myself out
I was totally shattered.

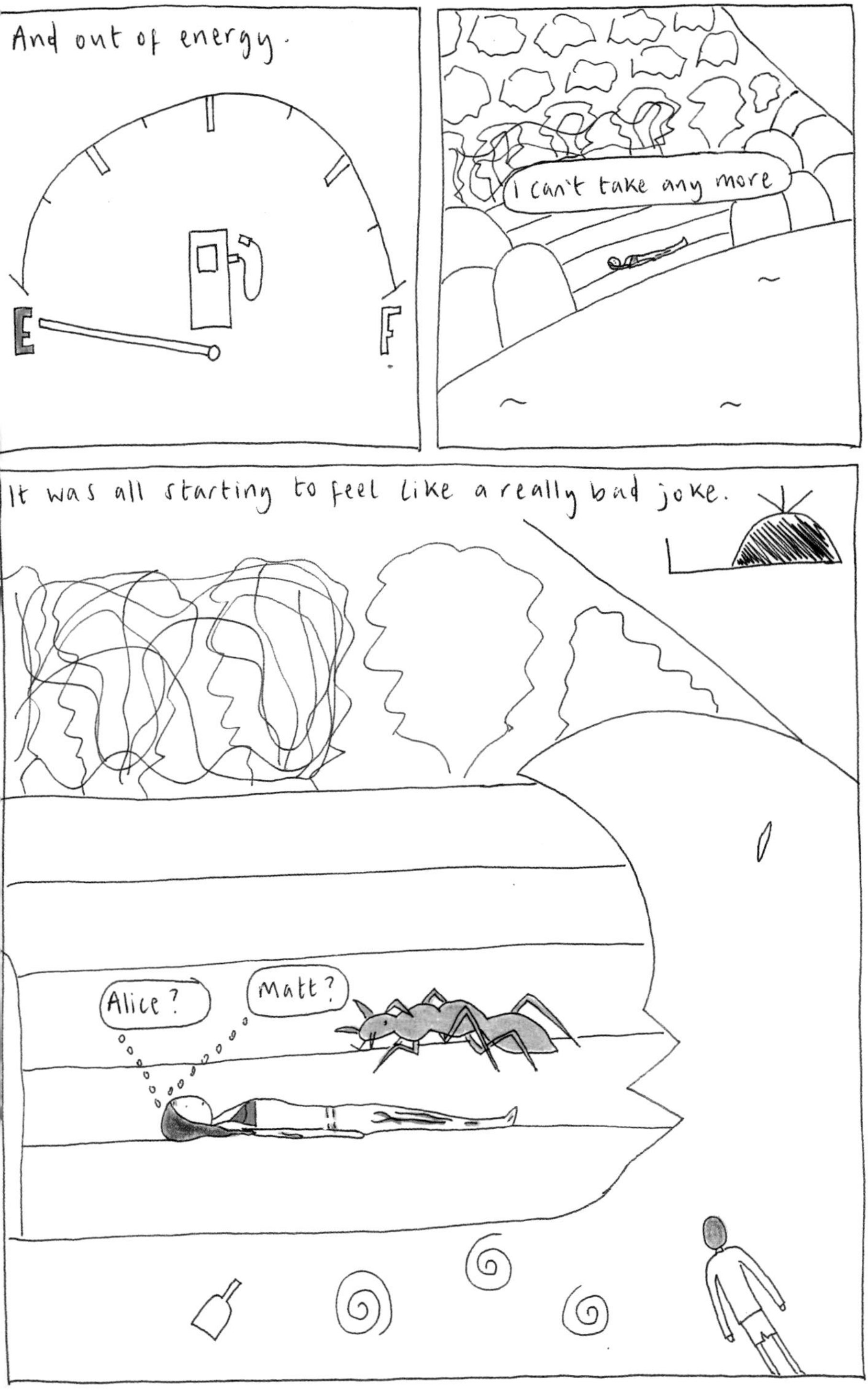
And out of energy.
E
F
I can't take any more
It was all starting to feel like a really bad joke.
Alice ?
Matt ?

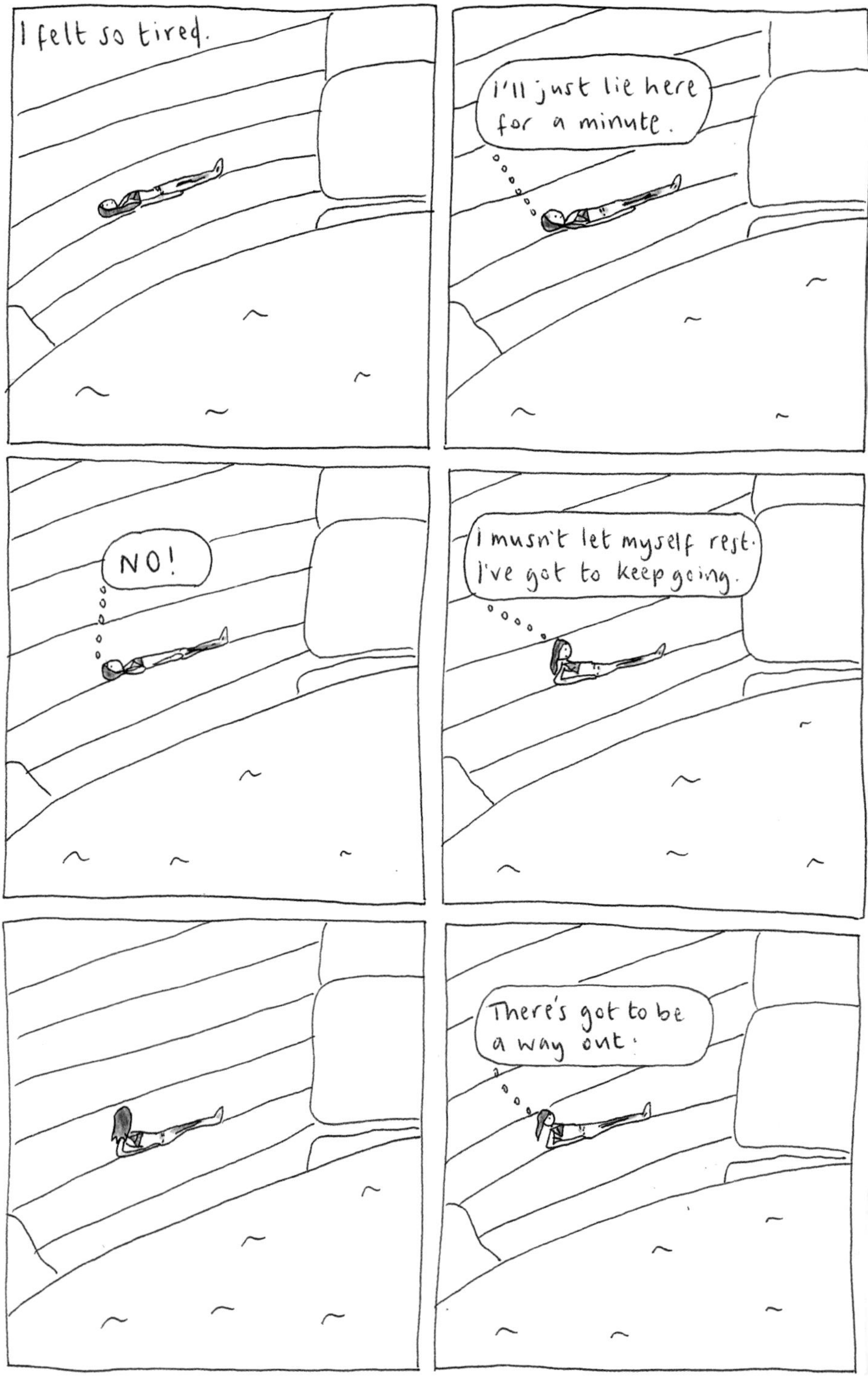
I felt so tired.
I'll just lie here for a minute.
NO!
I musn't let myself rest. I've got to keep going.
There's got to be a way out.

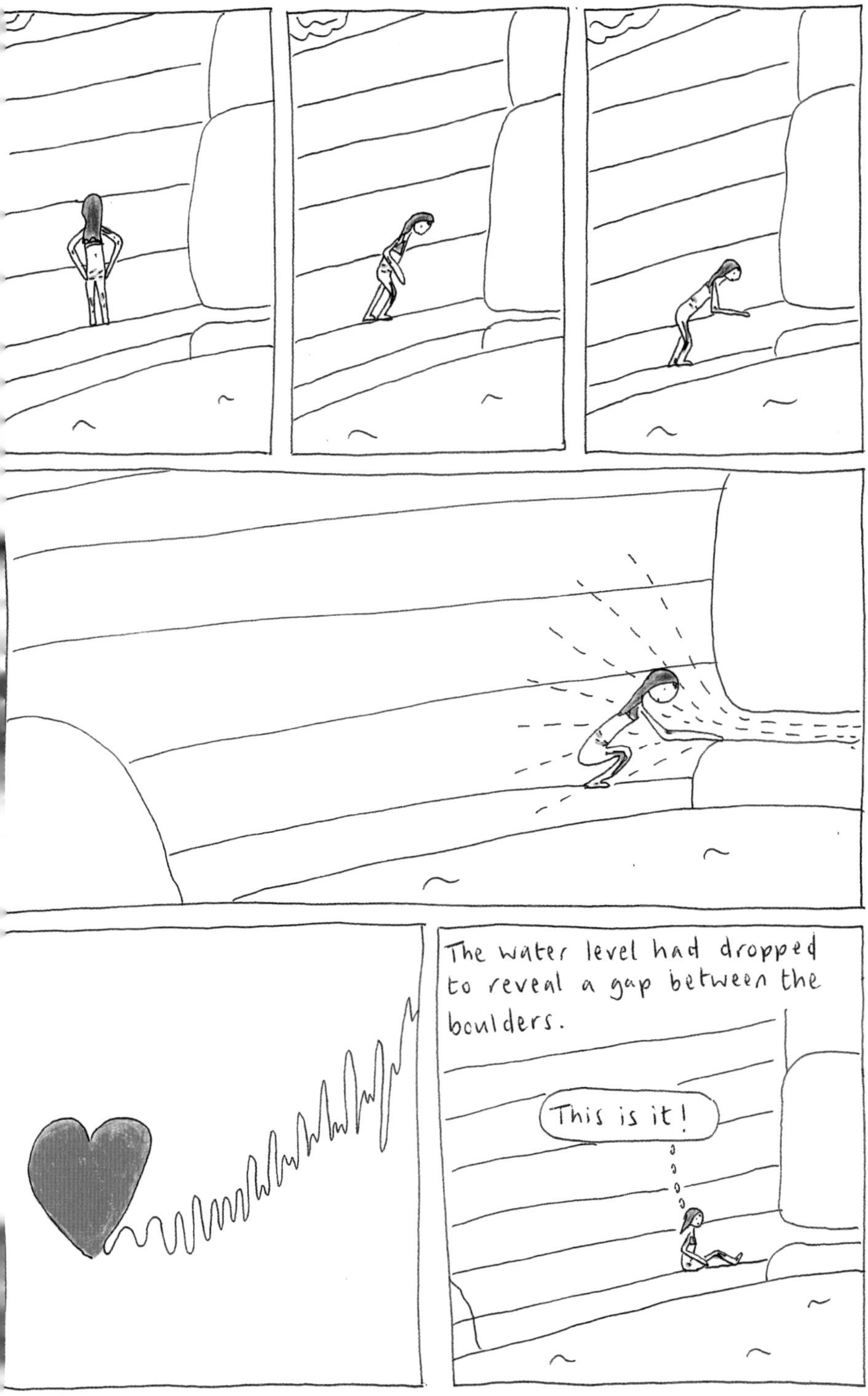
The water level had dropped to reveal a gap between the boulders.
This is it!

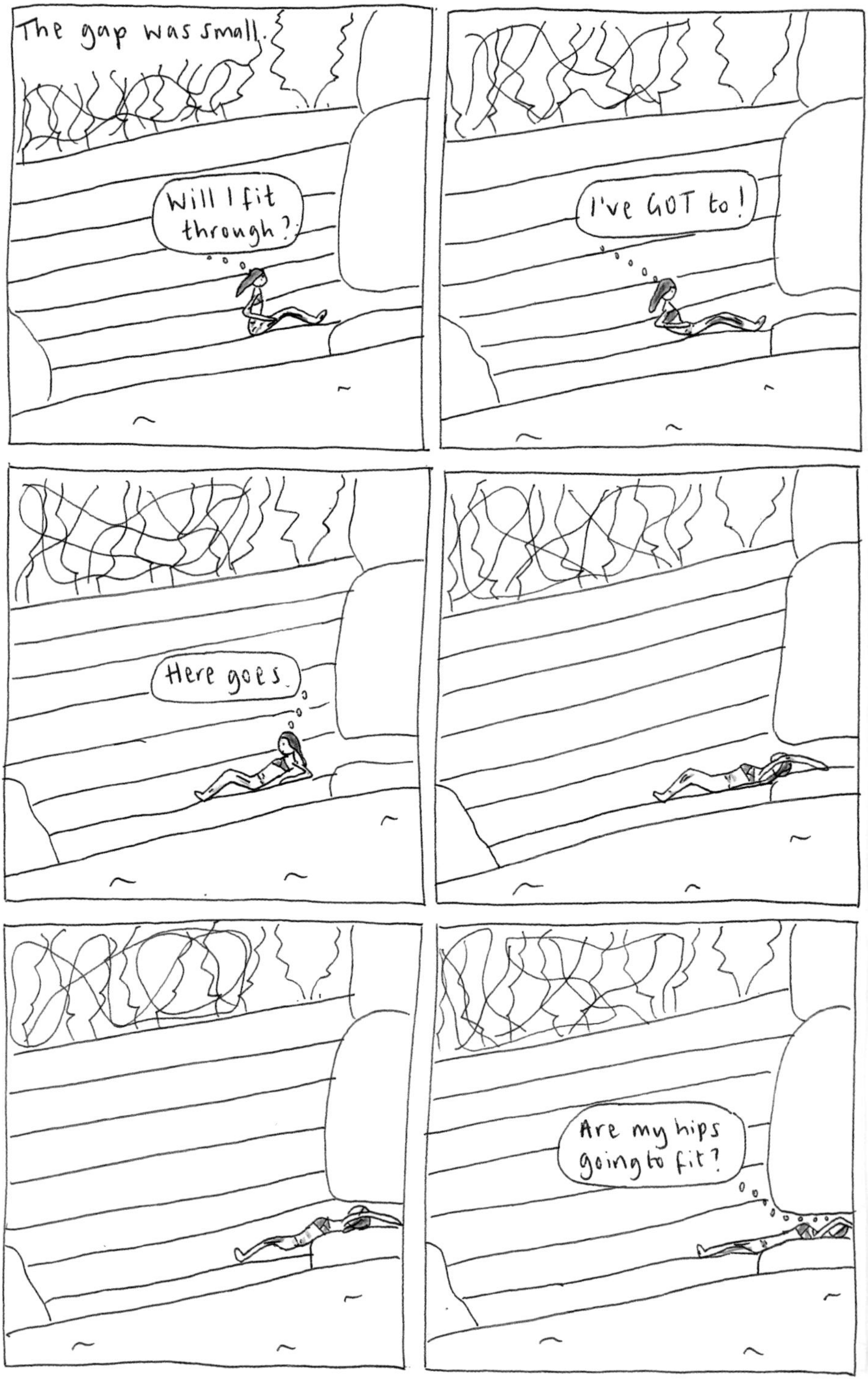
The gap was small.
Will I fit through?
I've GOT to!
Here goes.
Are my hips going to fit?

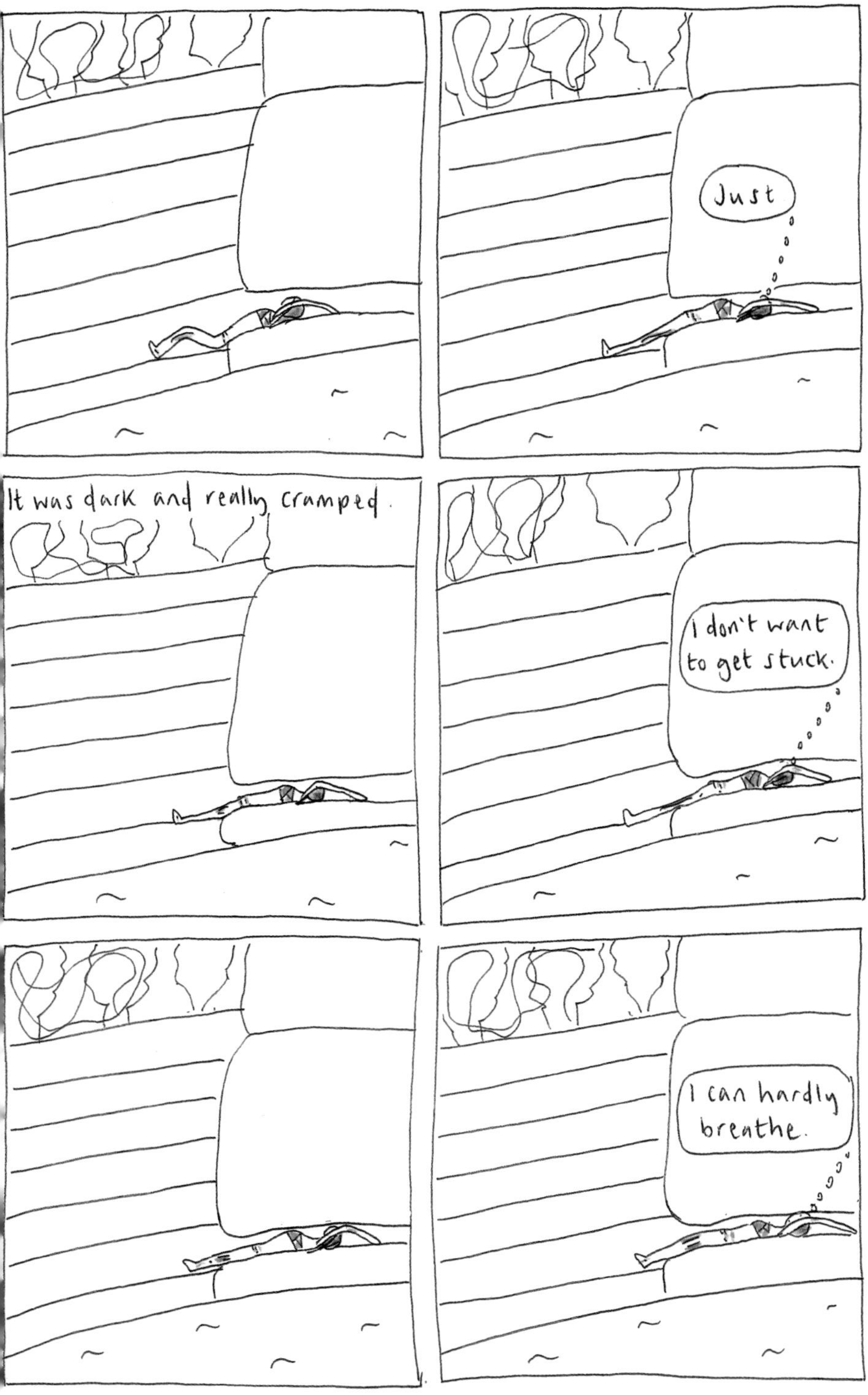
Just
It was dark and really cramped.
I don't want to get stuck.
I can hardly breathe.

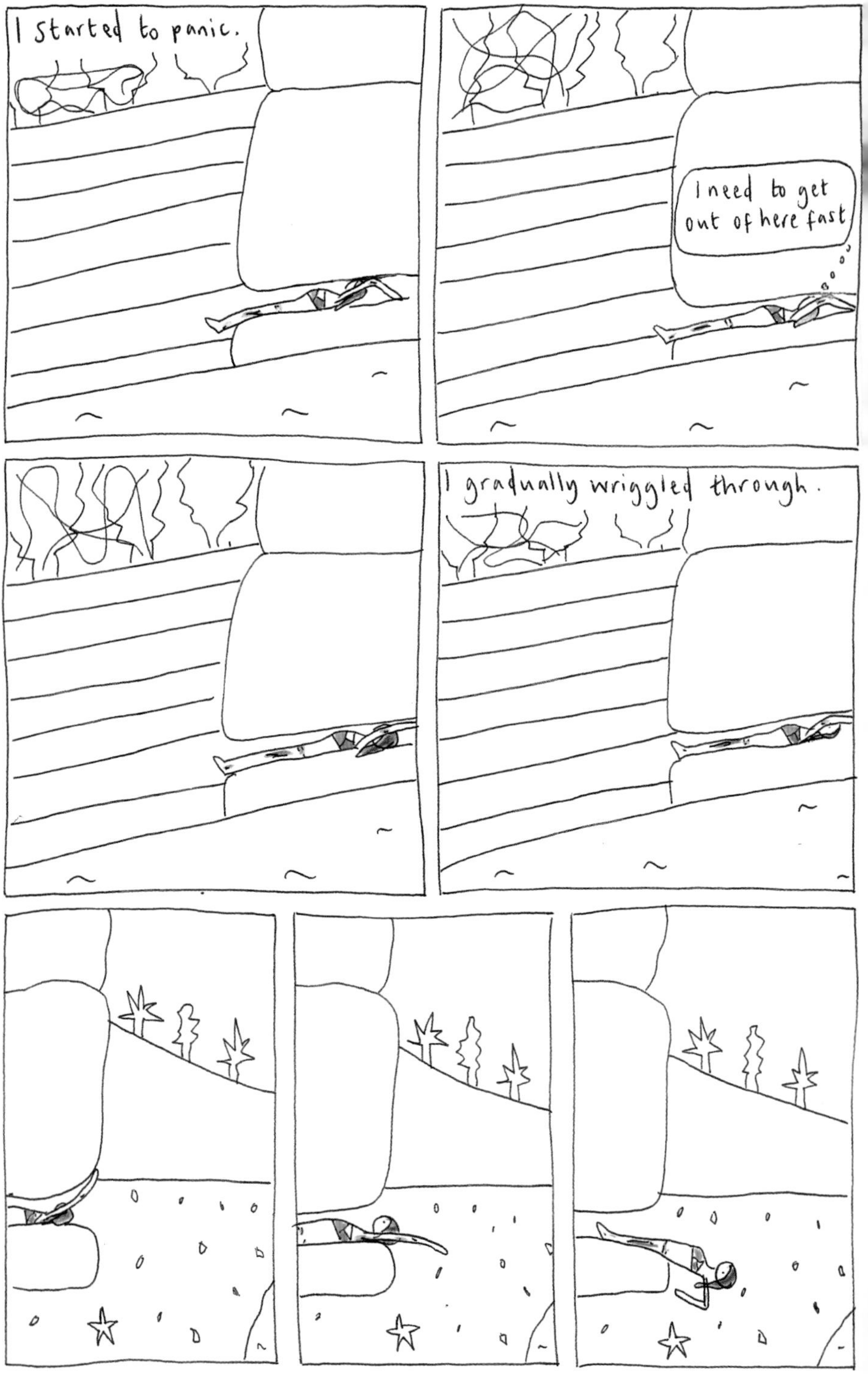
I started to panic.
I need to get out of here fast
I gradually wriggled through.

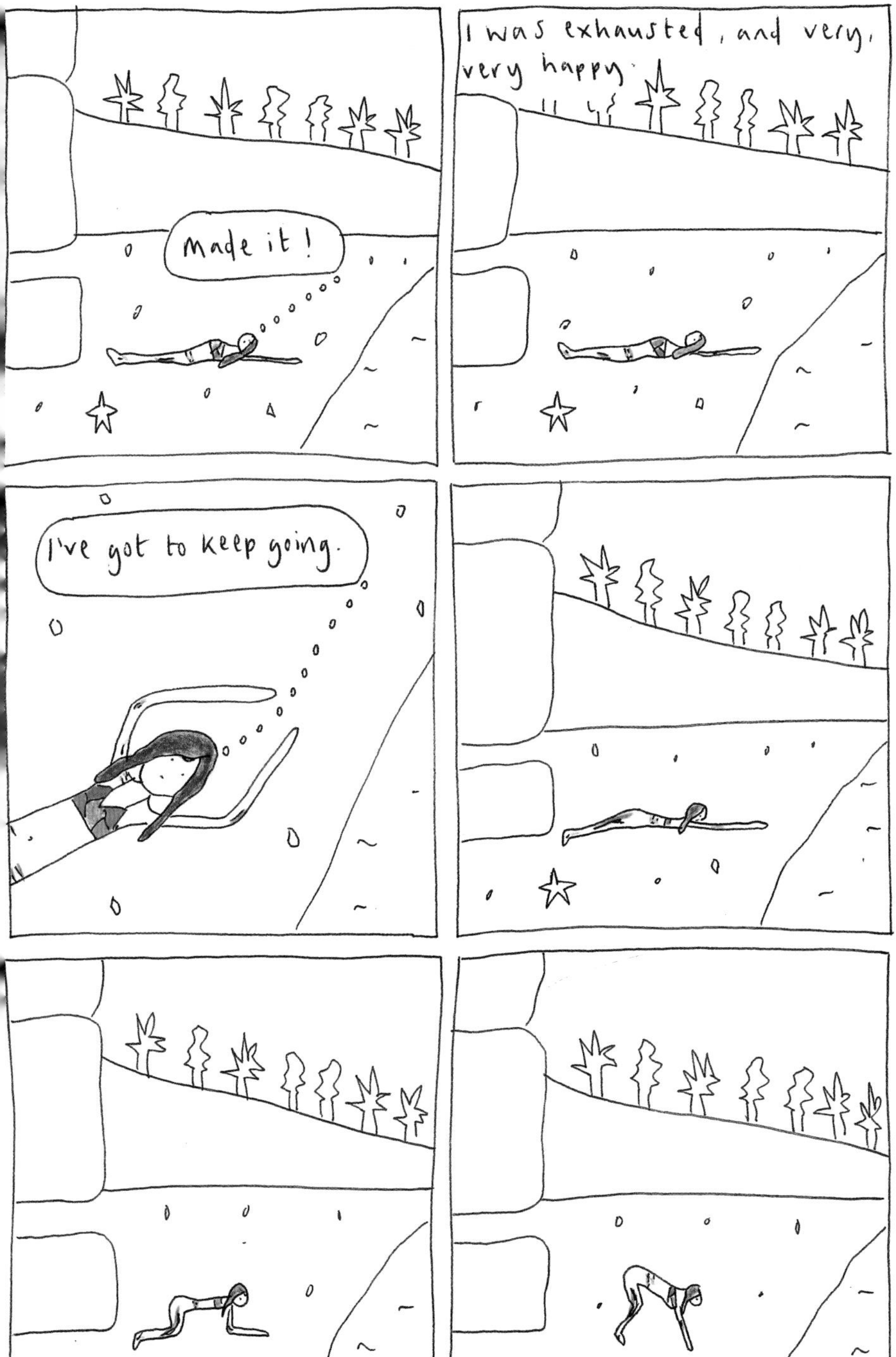
Made it!
I was exhausted, and very, very happy.
I've got to keep going.

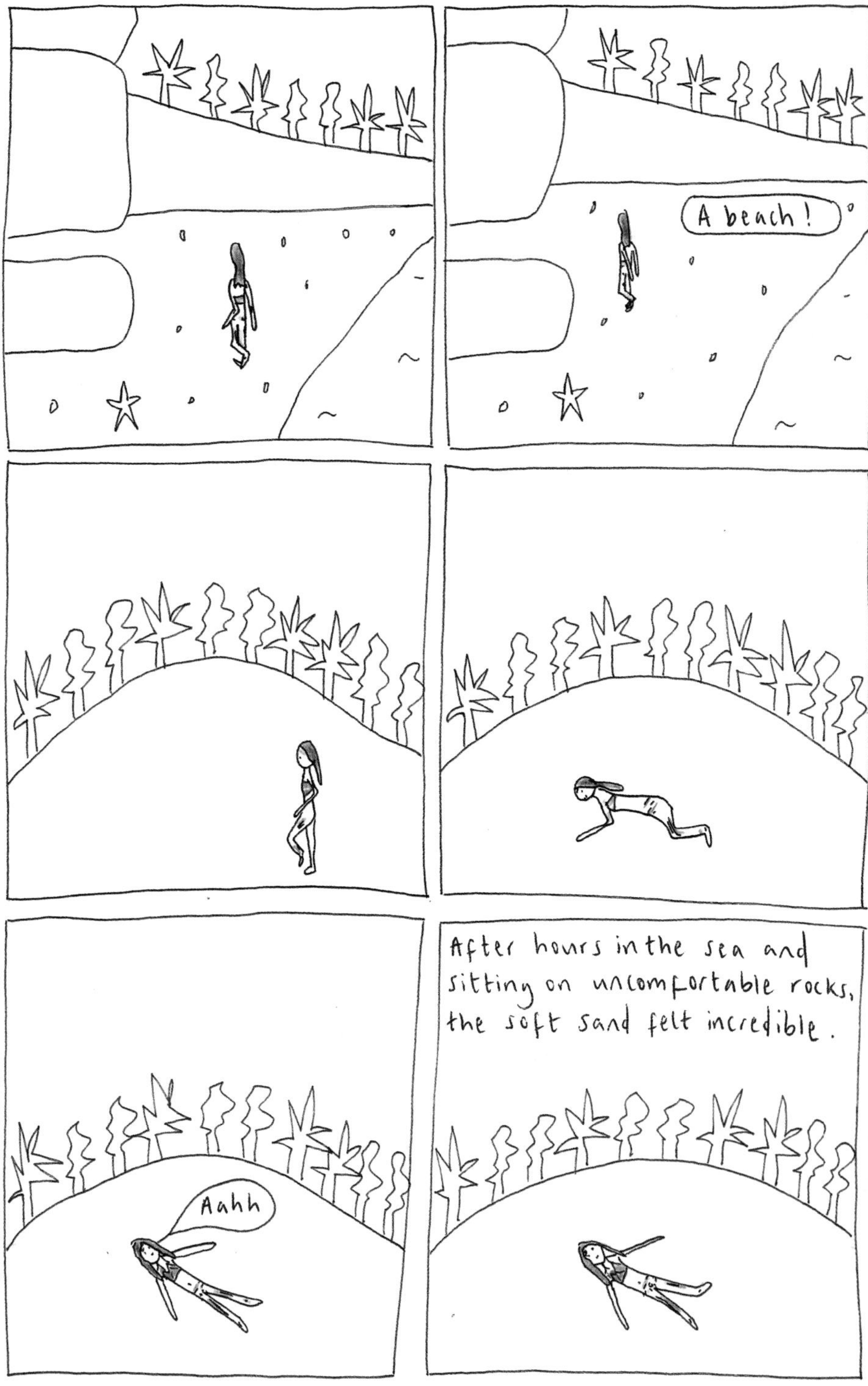
A beach!
Aahh
After hours in the sea and sitting on uncomfortable rocks, the soft sand felt incredible.

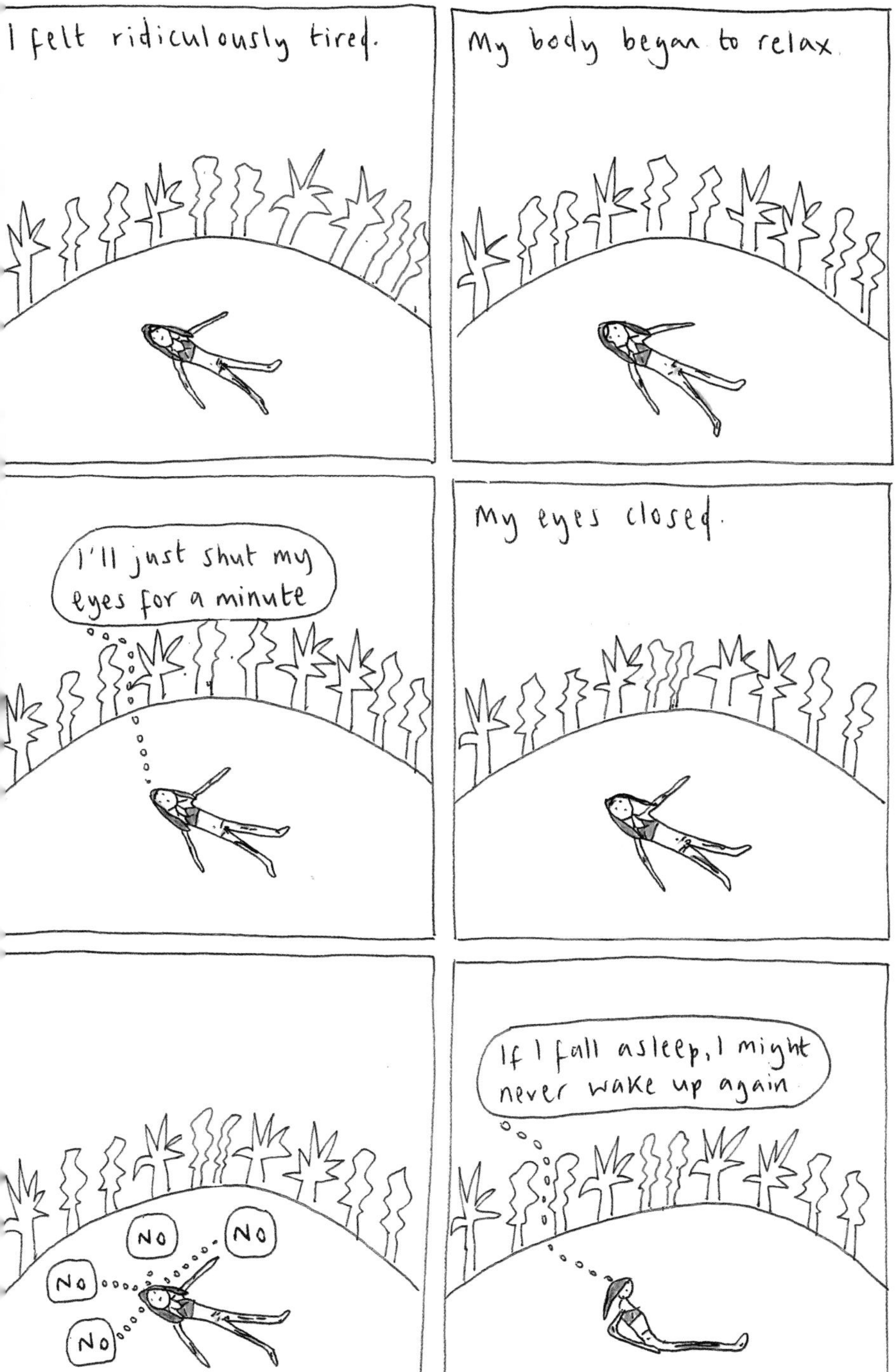
I felt ridiculously tired.
My body began to relax.
I'll just shut my eyes for a minute
My eyes closed.
NO
NO
No
No
If I fall asleep, I might never wake up again

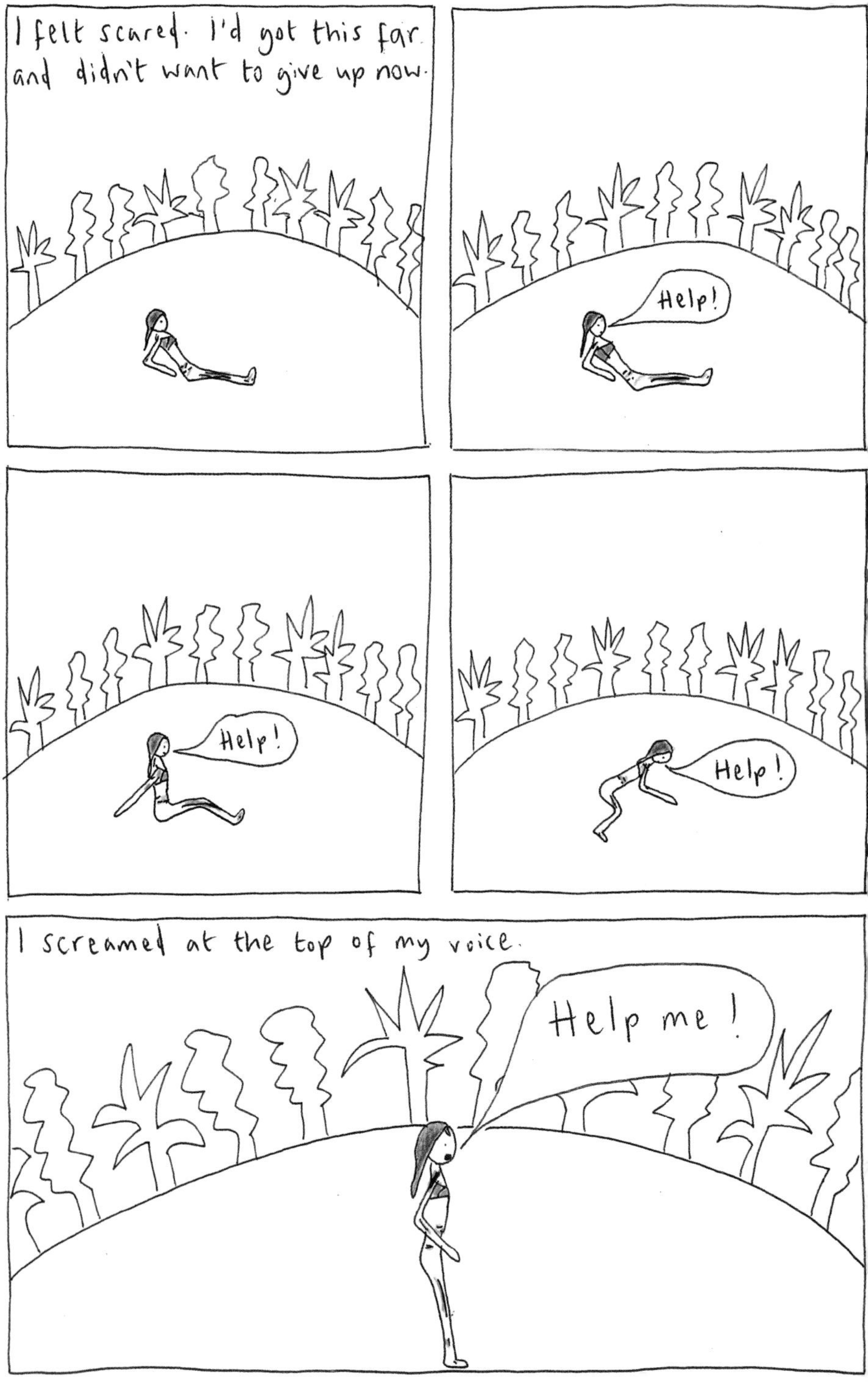
I felt scared. I'd got this far and didn't want to give up now.
Help!
Help!
Help!
I screamed at the top of my voice.
Help me!

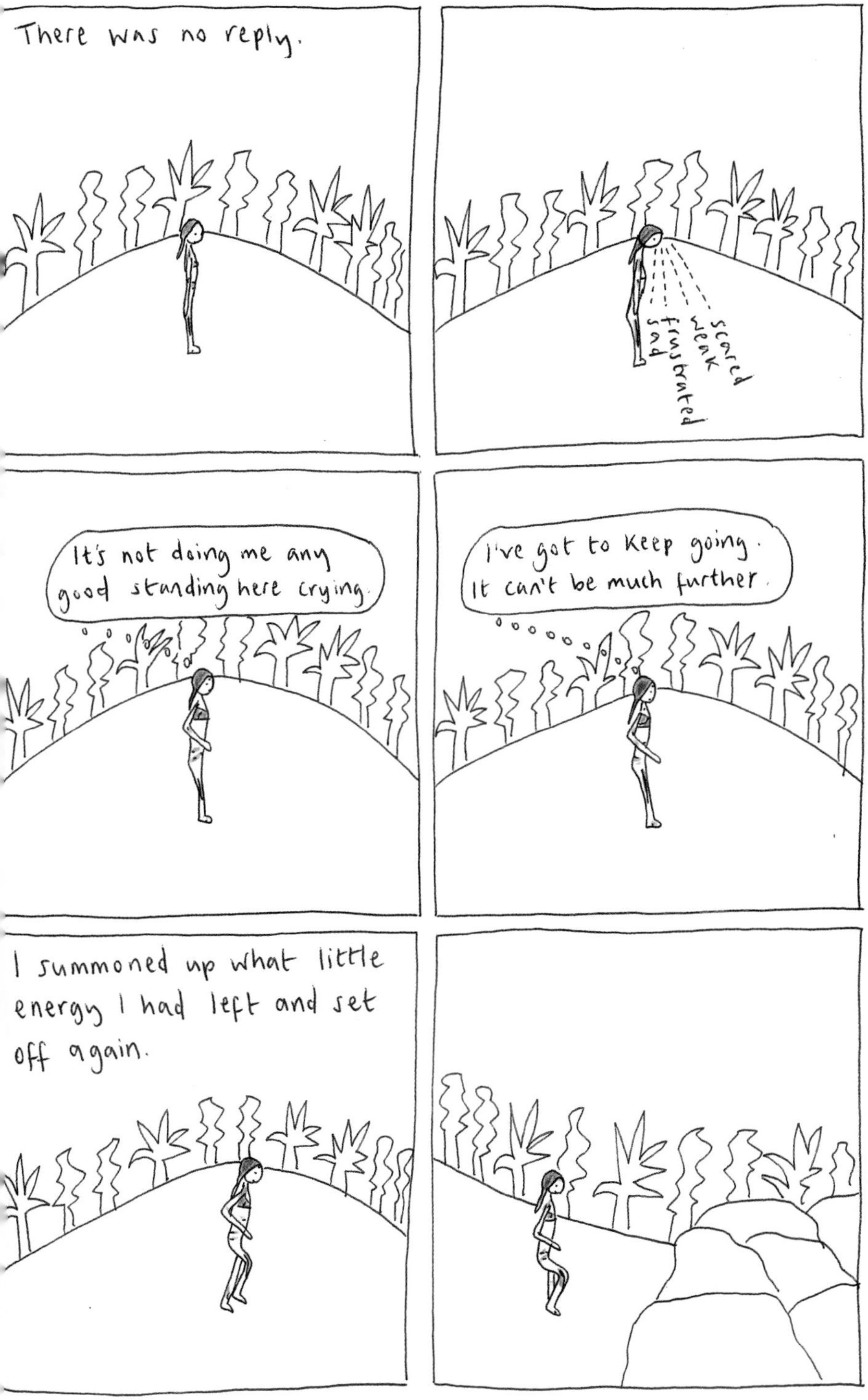
There was no reply.
scared
weak
frustrated
sad
It's not doing me any good standing here crying.
I've got to keep going. It can't be much further.
I summoned up what little energy I had left and set off again.

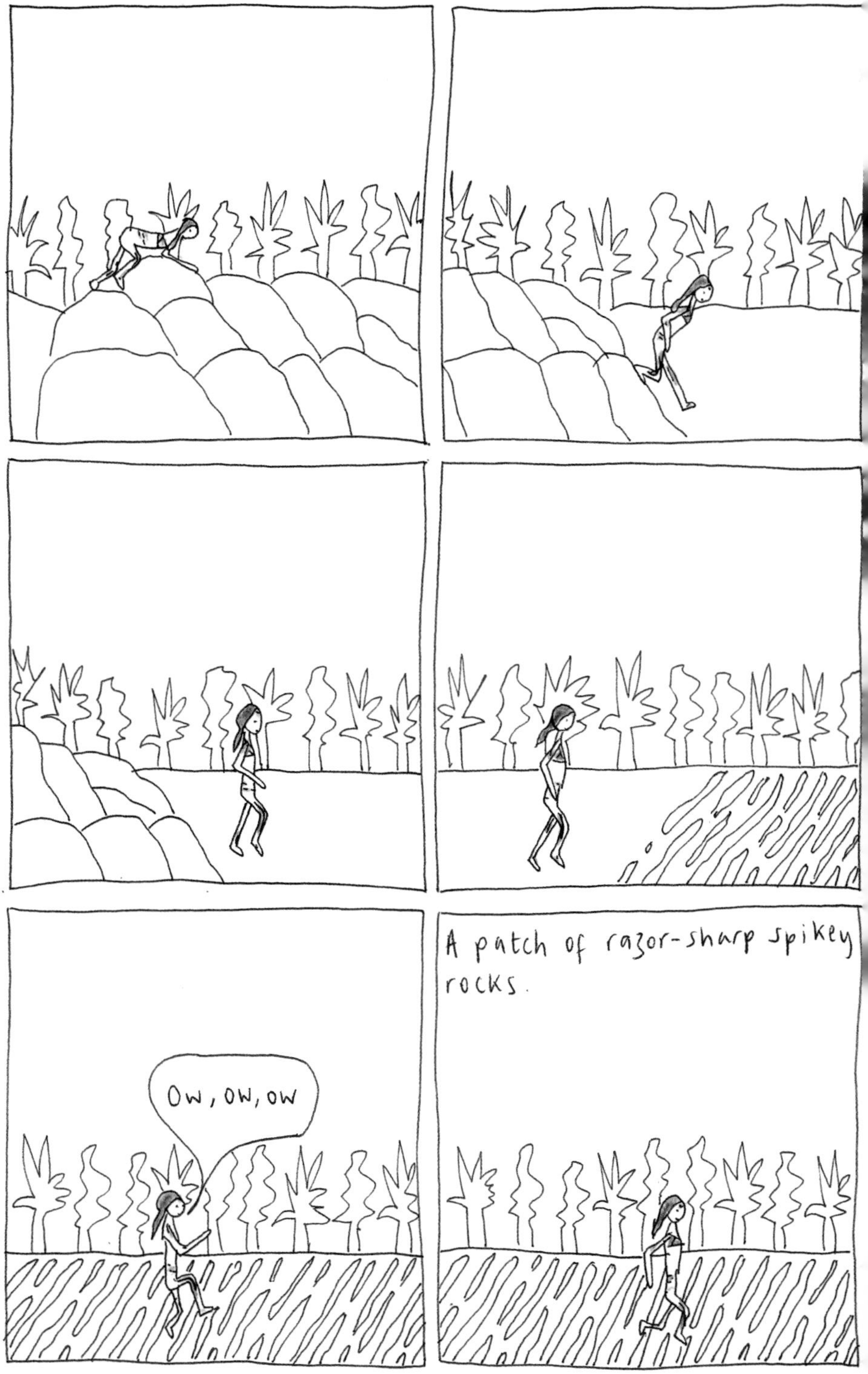
Ow, ow, ow
A patch of razor-sharp spikey rocks.

The rocks dug into the deep
cuts on the soles of my feet.
aarrgghh!
Thank goodness.
Soft sand again.
Huh?

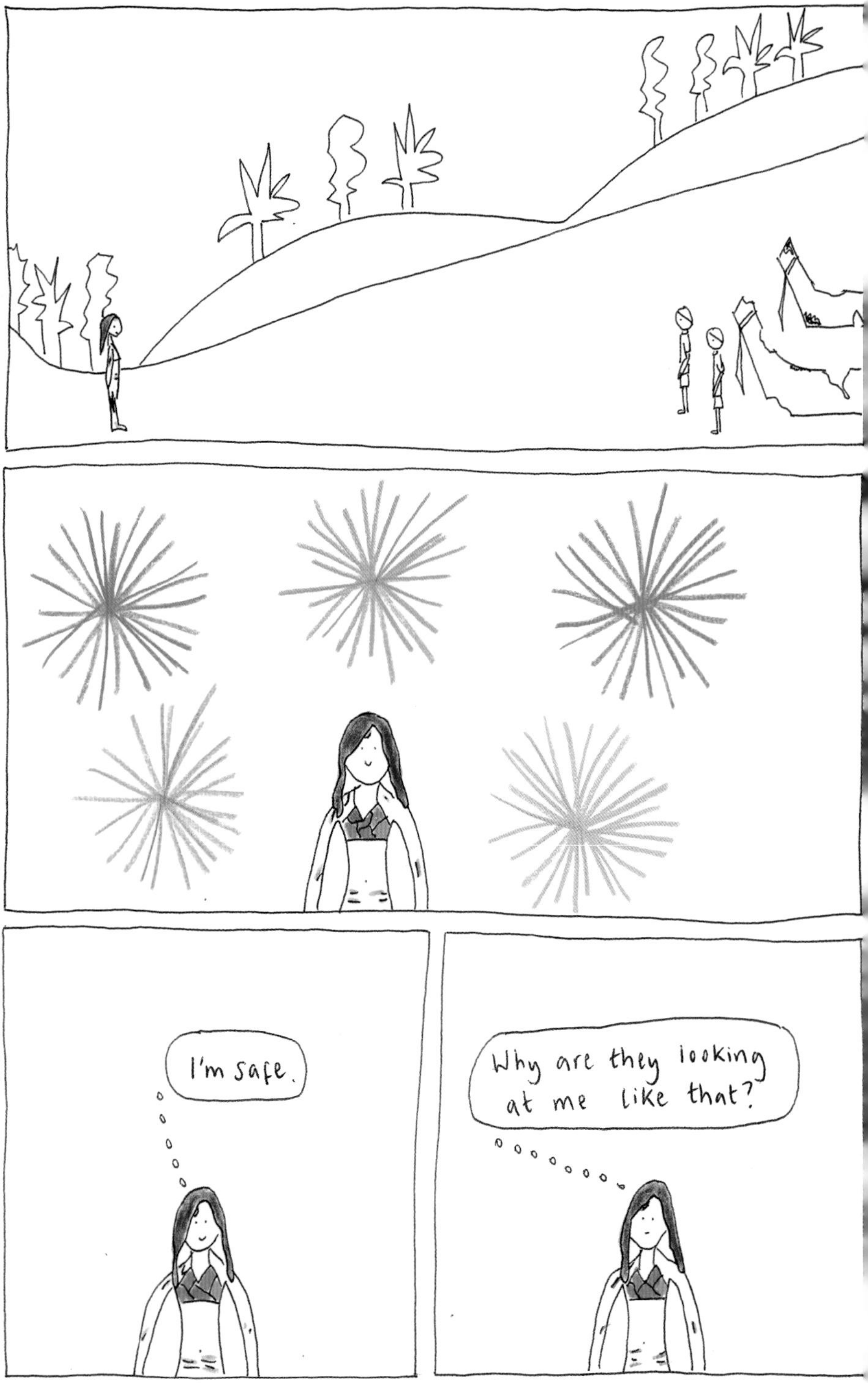
I'm safe.
Why are they looking at me like that?

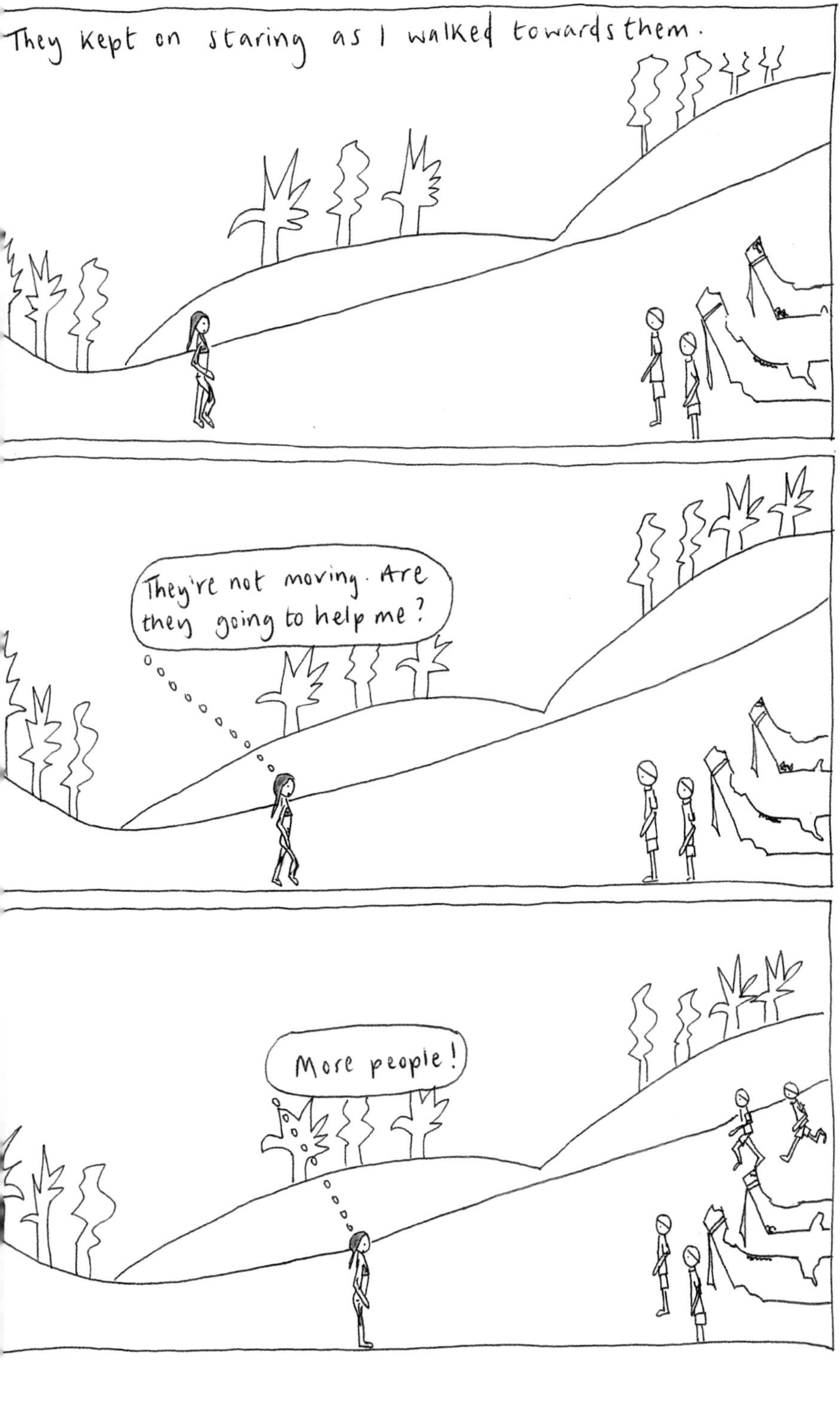
They kept on staring as I walked towards them.
They're not moving. Are they going to help me?
More people!

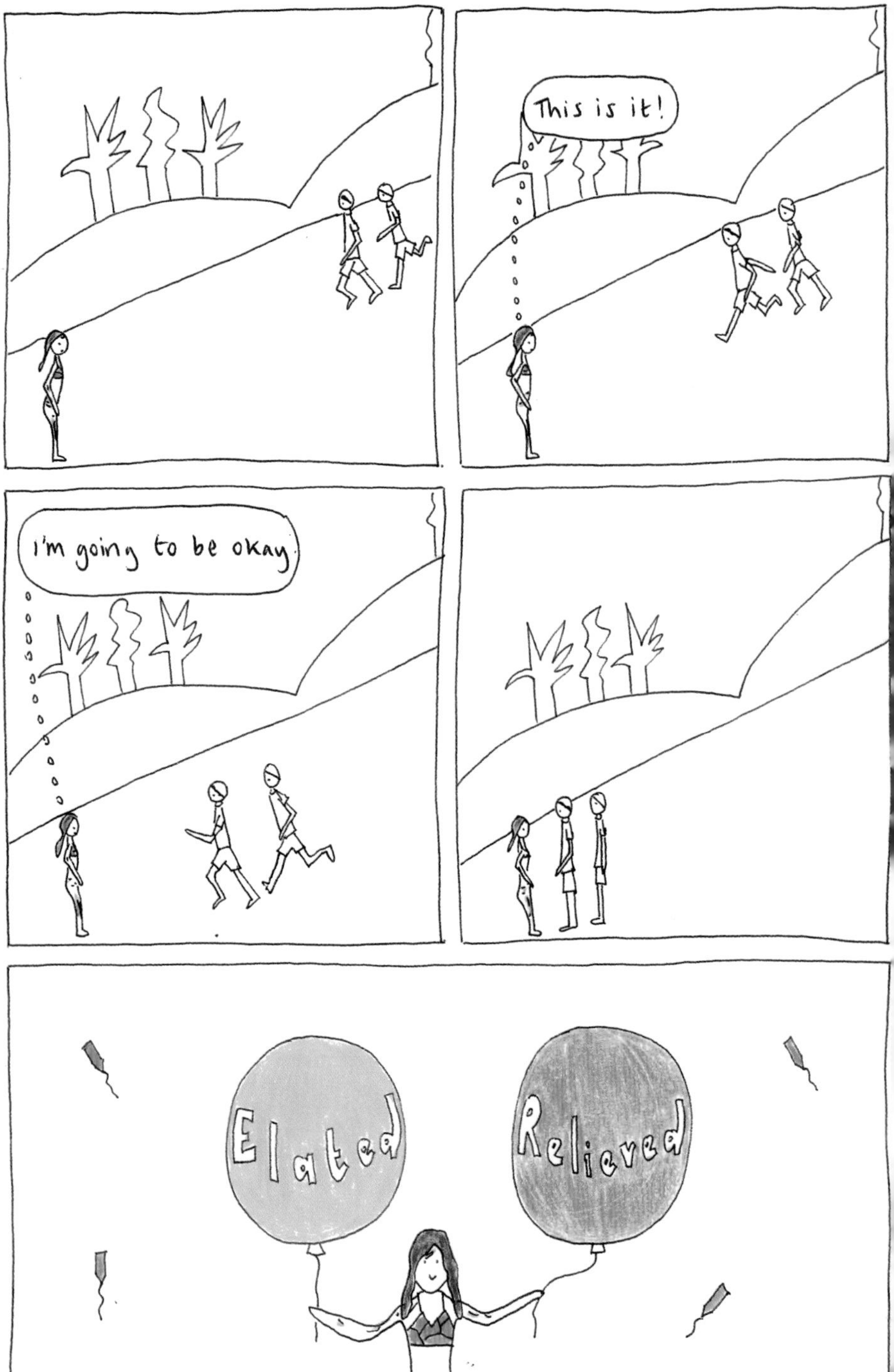
This is it!
I'm going to be okay
Elated
Relieved

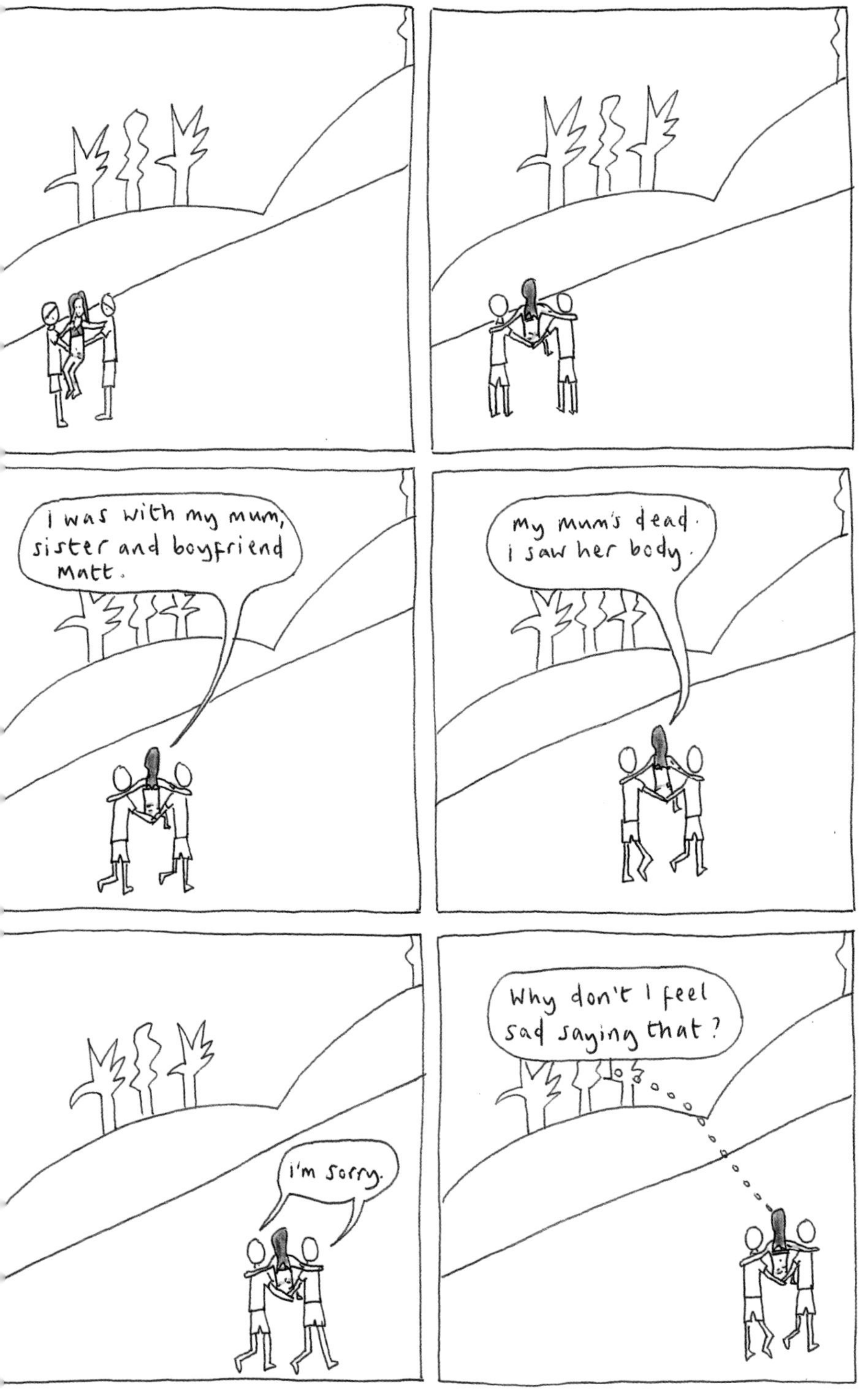
i was with my mum, sister and boyfriend Matt.
my mum's dead. i saw her body.
i'm sorry.
Why don't I feel sad saying that?

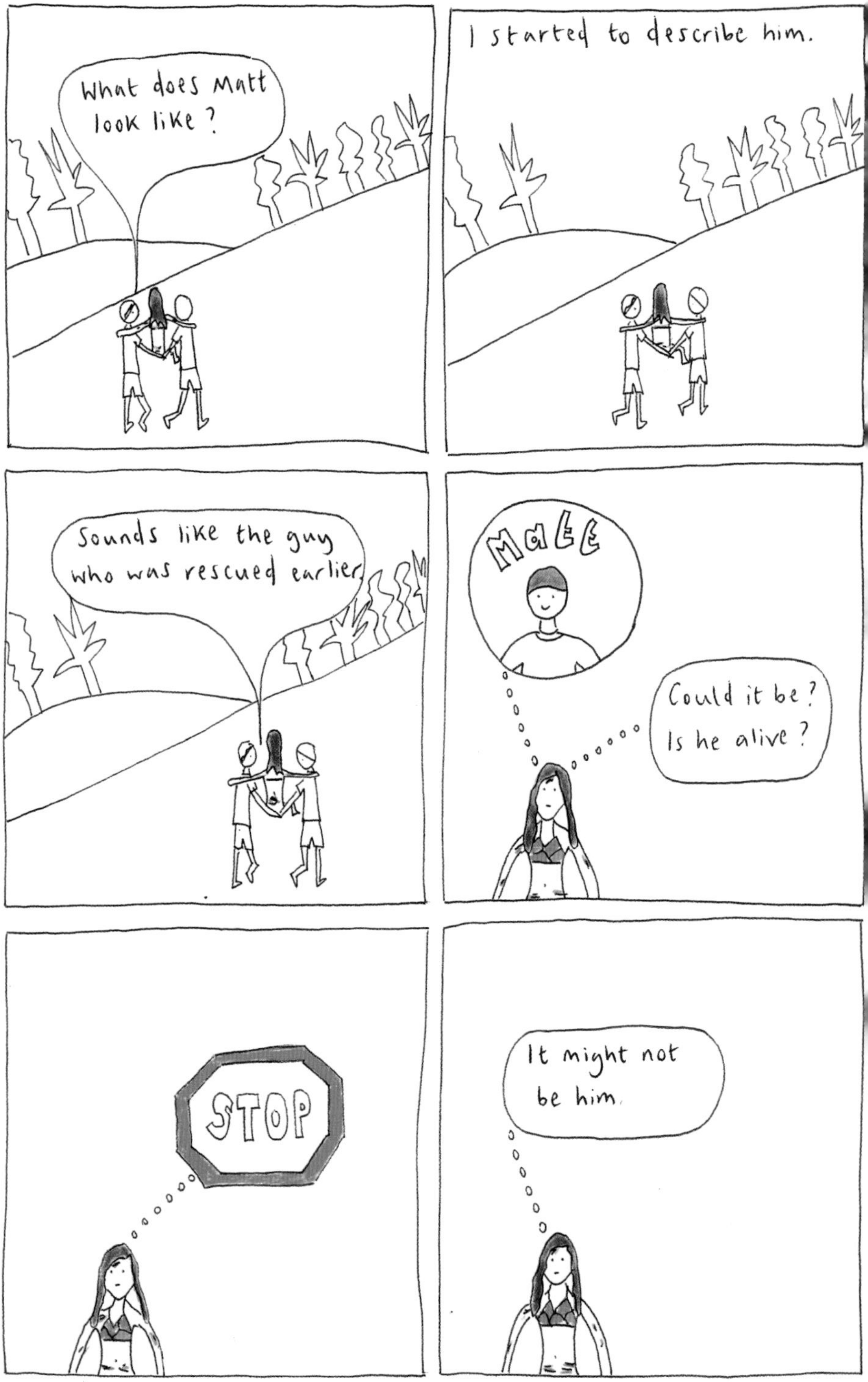
What does Matt look like?
I started to describe him.
Sounds like the guy who was rescued earlier.
Matt
Could it be? Is he alive?
STOP
It might not be him.

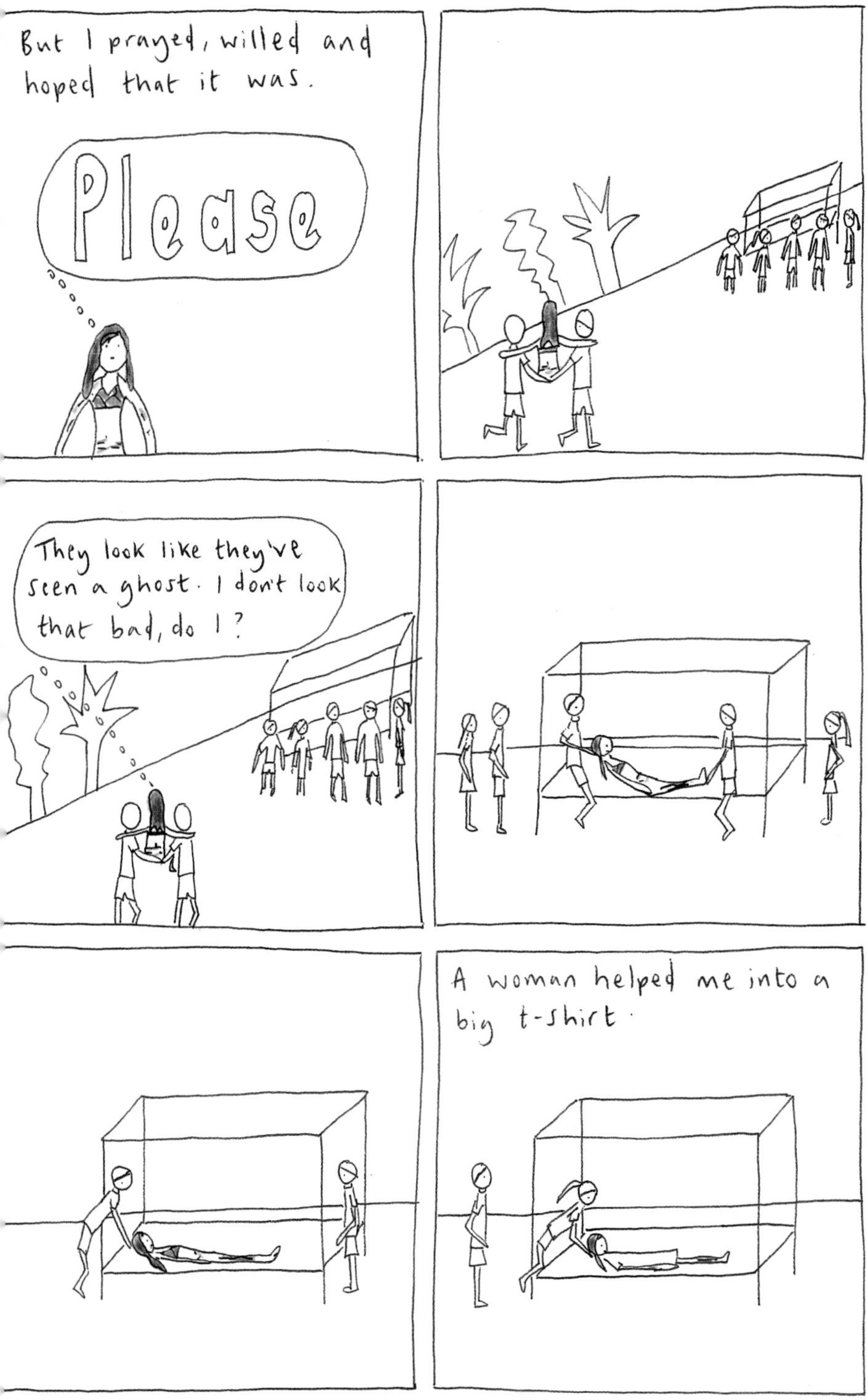
But I prayed, willed and hoped that it was.
Please
They look like they've seen a ghost. I don't look that bad, do I?
A woman helped me into a big t-shirt.

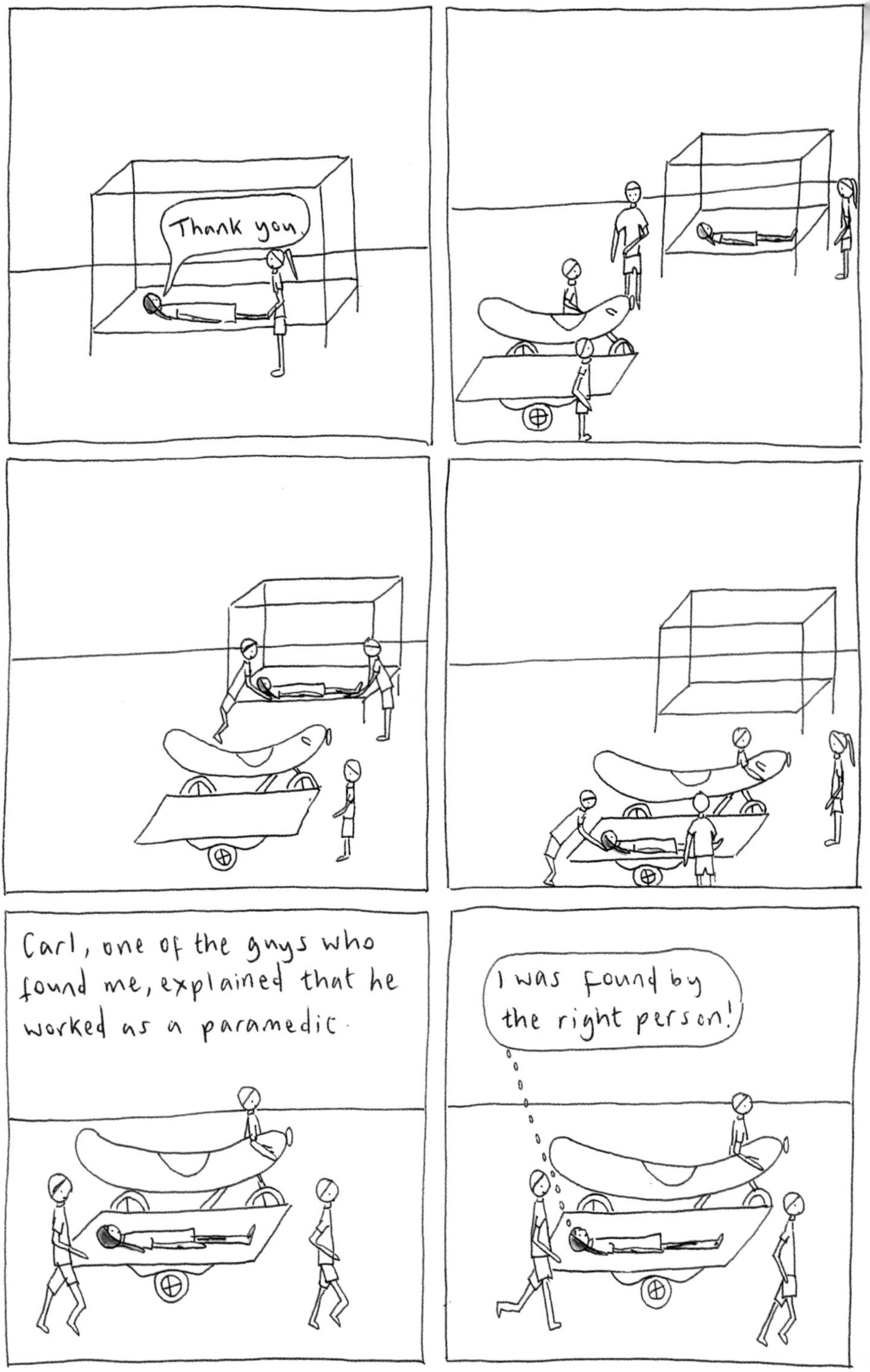

Thank you.
Carl, one of the guys who found me, explained that he worked as a paramedic.
I was found by the right person!

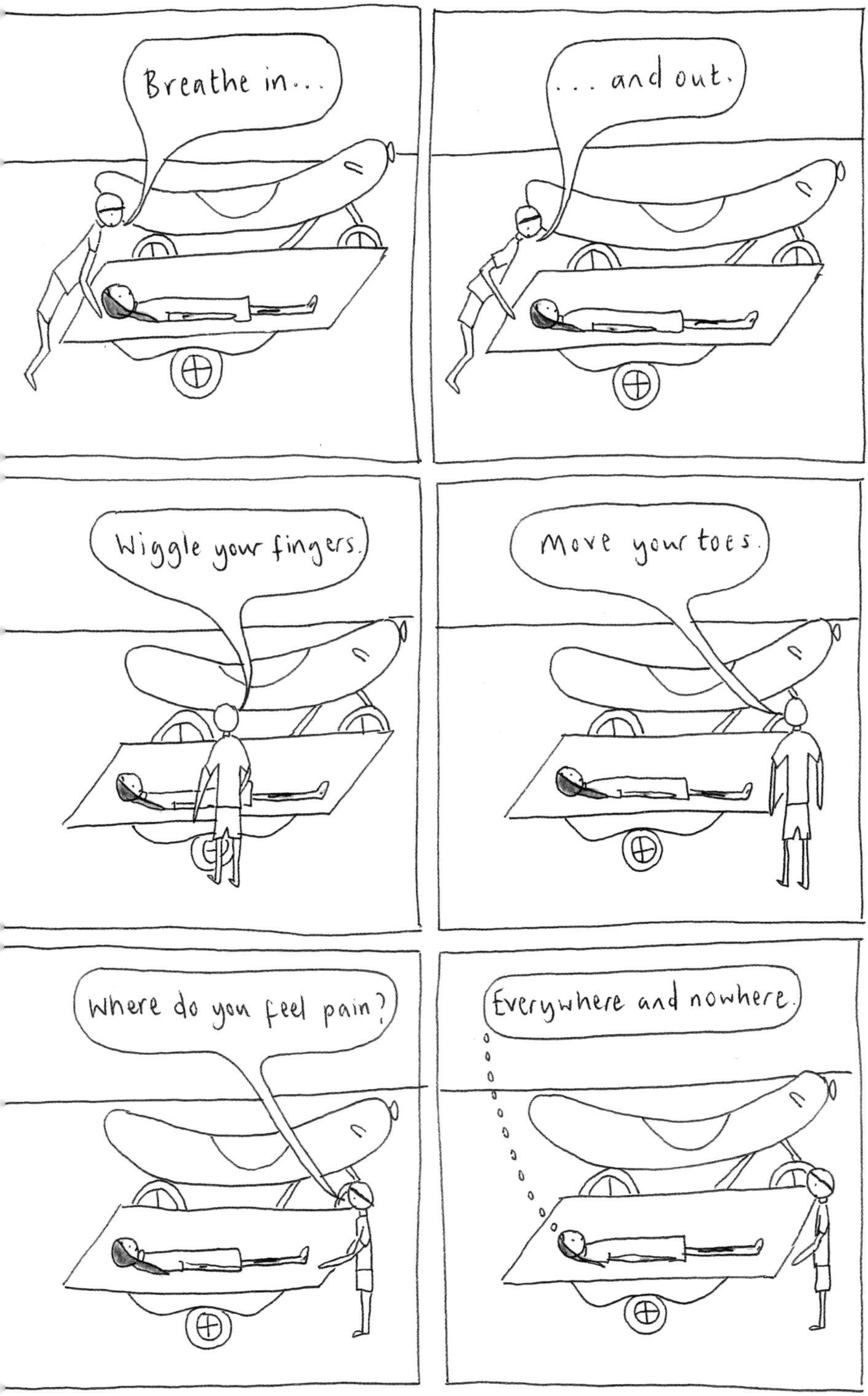
Breathe in...
... and out.
Wiggle your fingers.
Move your toes.
Where do you feel pain?
Everywhere and nowhere.

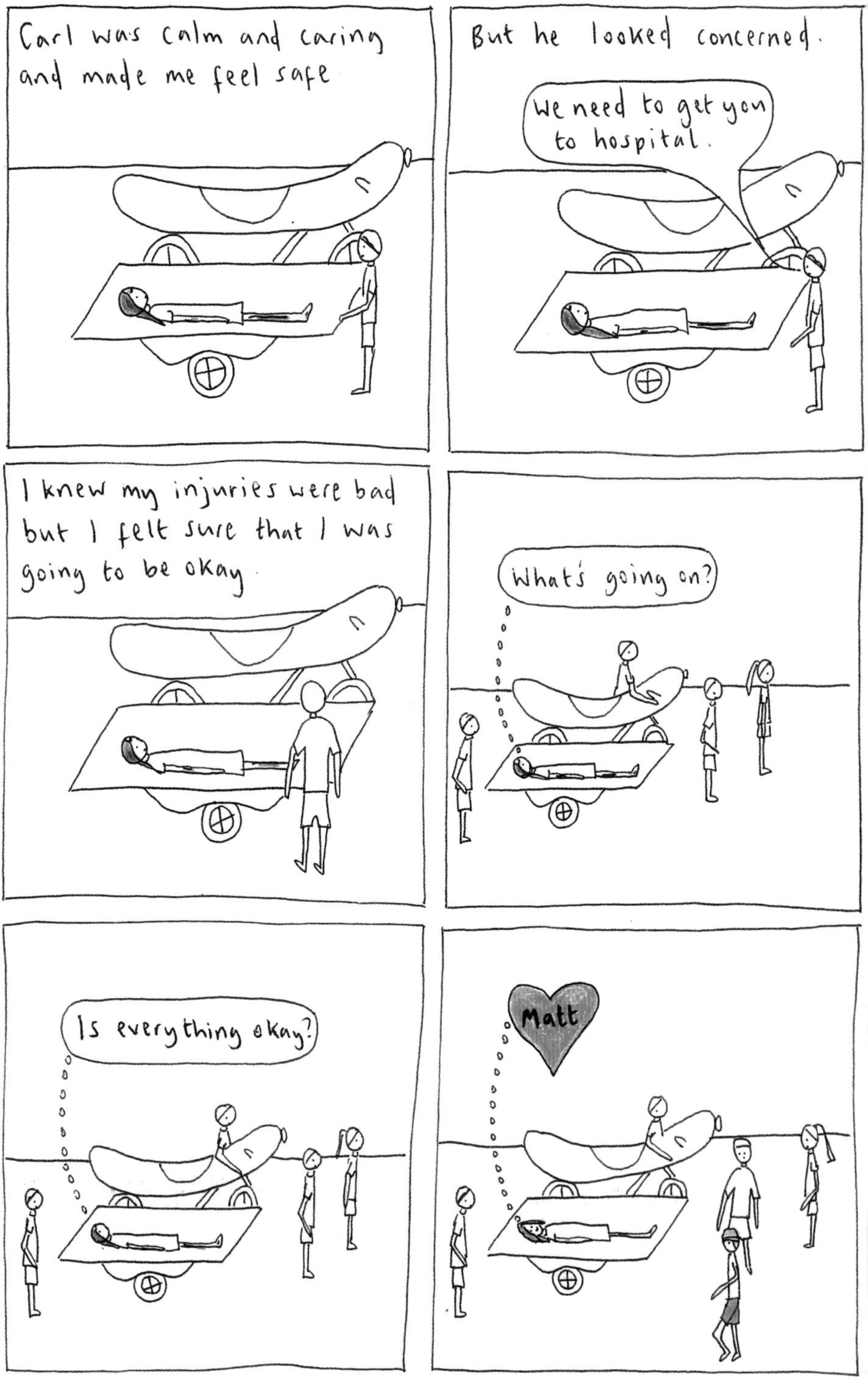
Carl was calm and caring and made me feel safe
But he looked concerned.
We need to get you to hospital.
I knew my injuries were bad but I felt sure that I was going to be okay.
What's going on?
Is everything okay?
Matt

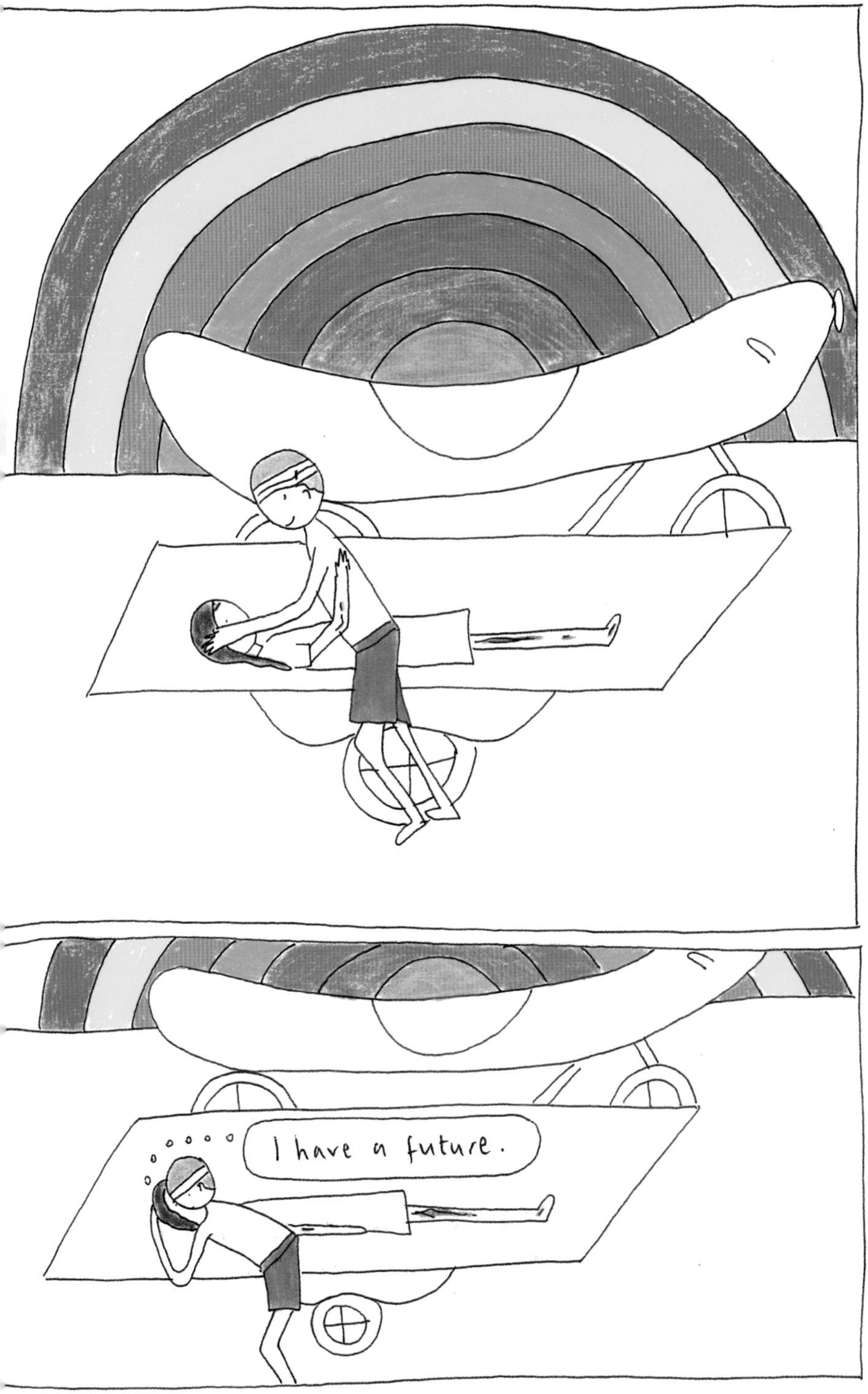
I have a future.

It was really him. Battered and bruised and with a hollow look of shock in his eyes. But alive.

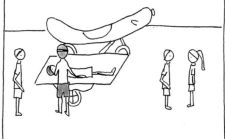

I knew that whatever lay ahead, we'd get through it together.

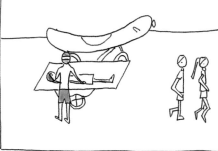

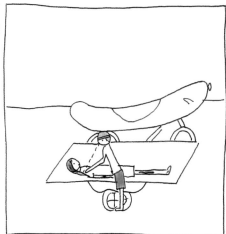

Mum died.

No.

Why don't I feel any emotion?

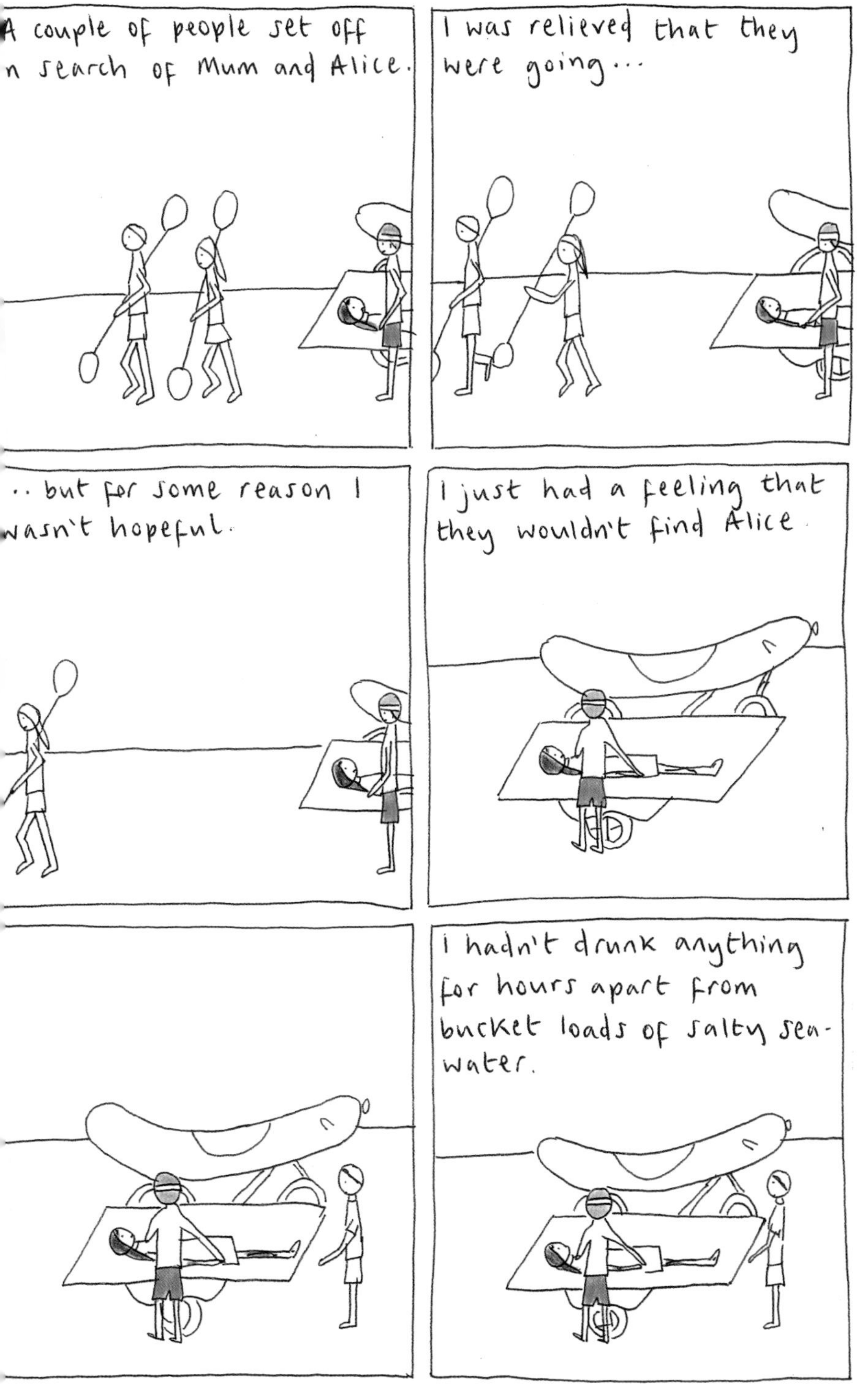
A couple of people set off
n search of Mum and Alice.
I was relieved that they
were going...
.. but for some reason I
wasn't hopeful.
I just had a feeling that
they wouldn't find Alice.
I hadn't drunk anything
for hours apart from
bucket loads of salty sea-
water.

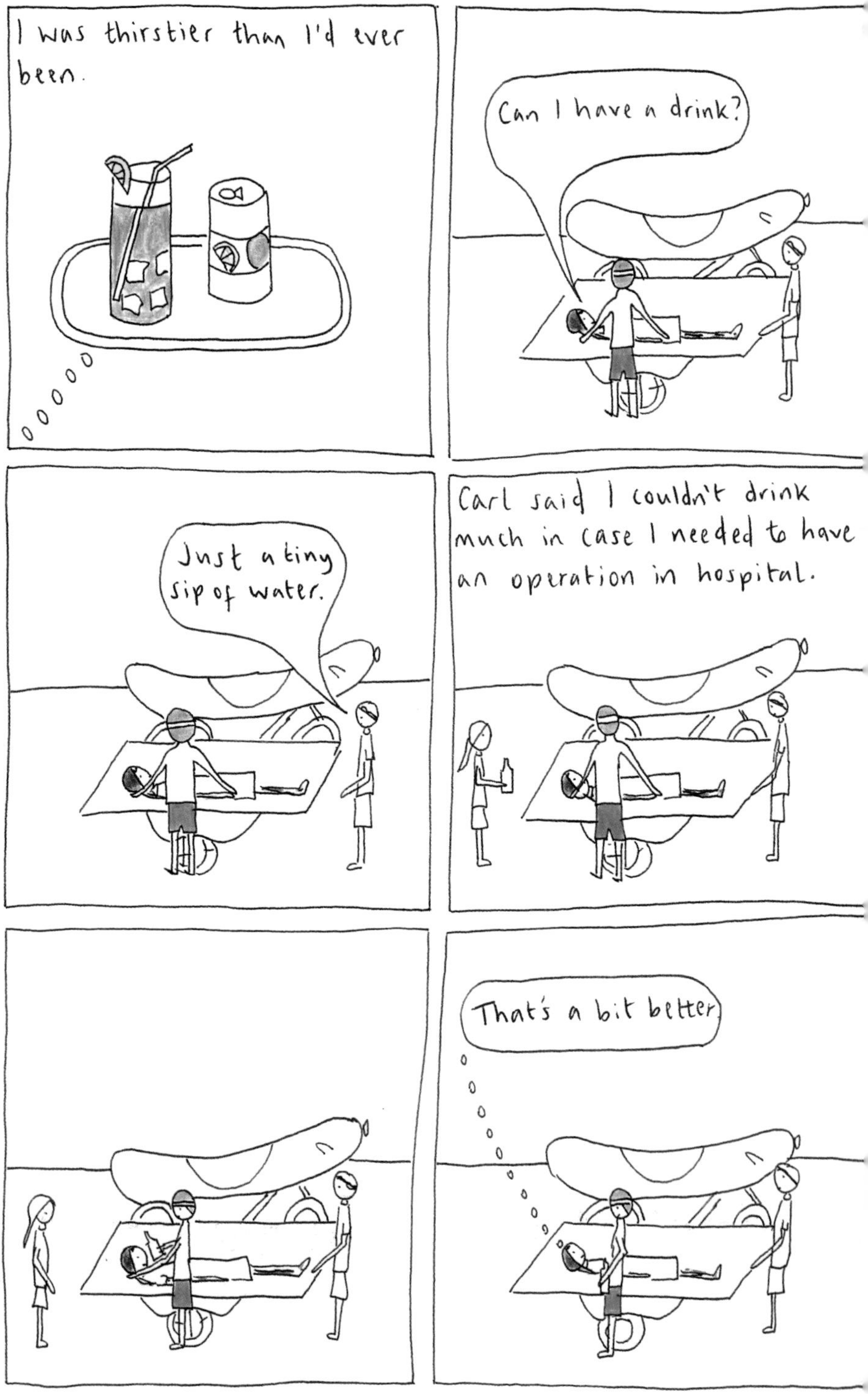
I was thirstier than I'd ever been.
Can I have a drink?
Just a tiny sip of water.
Carl said I couldn't drink much in case I needed to have an operation in hospital.
That's a bit better

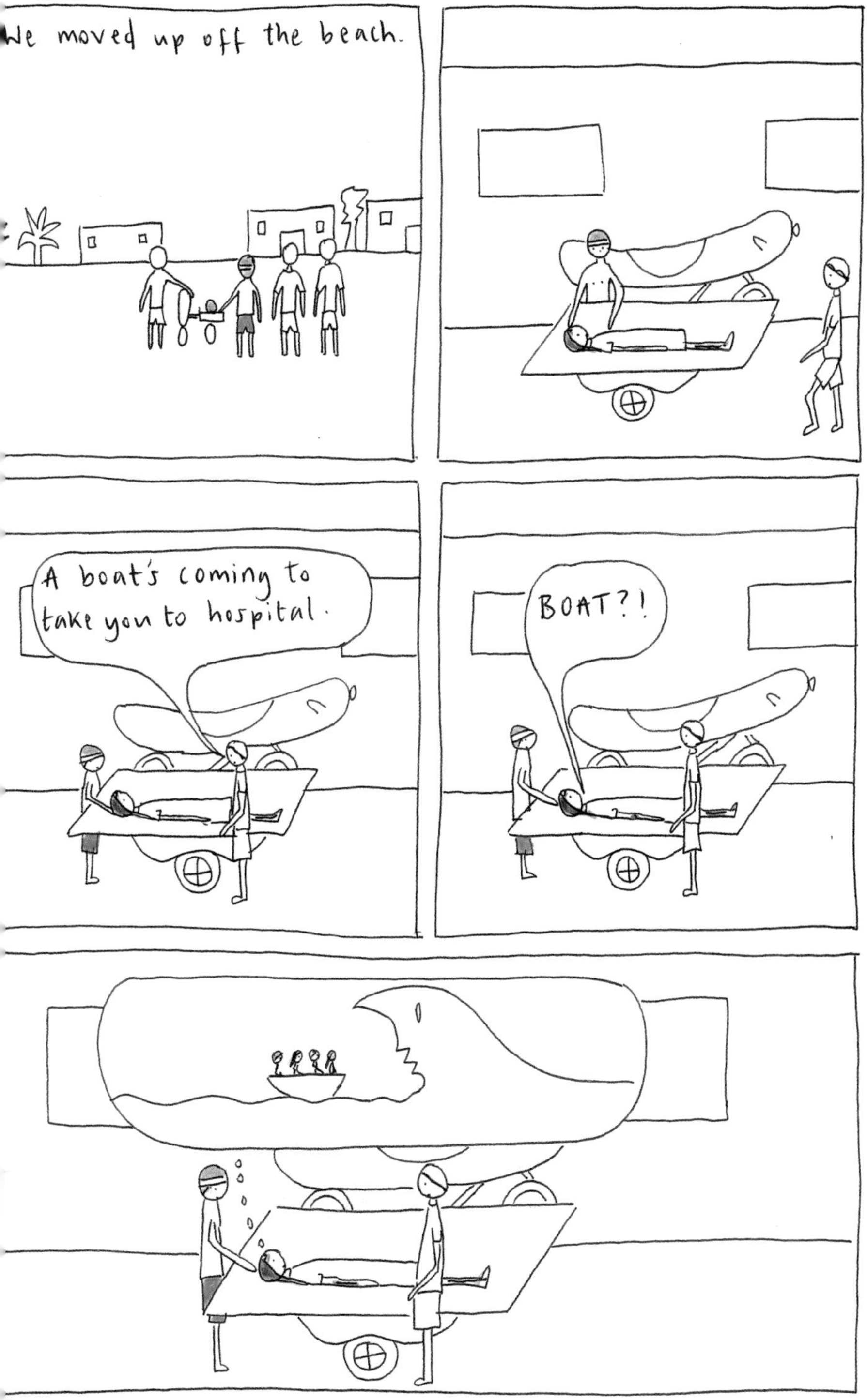
We moved up off the beach.
A boat's coming to take you to hospital.
BOAT?!

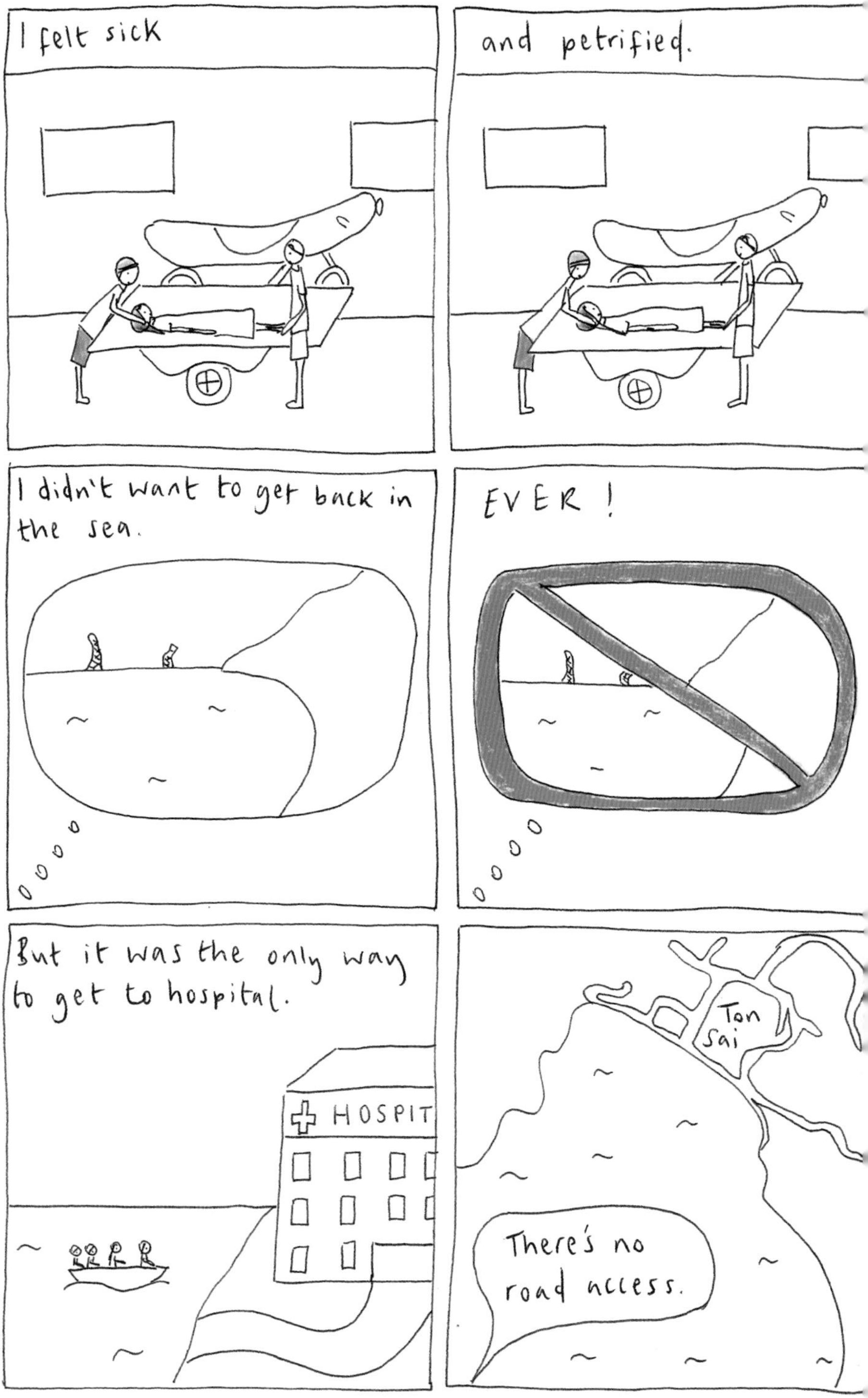
I felt sick
and petrified.
I didn't want to get back in the sea.
EVER!
But it was the only way to get to hospital.
HOSPIT
Ton Sai
There's no road access.

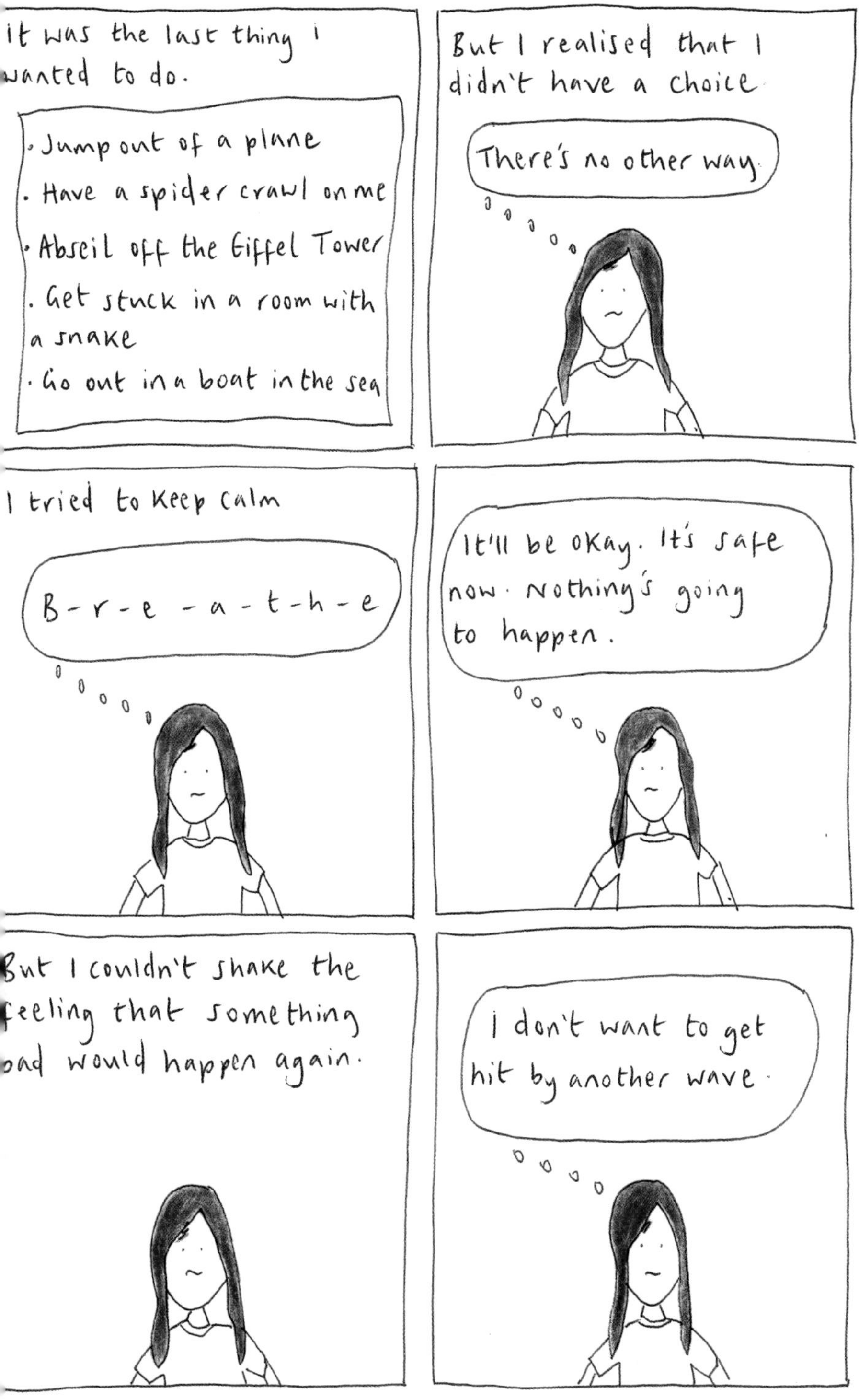
it was the last thing i wanted to do.
• Jump out of a plane
• Have a spider crawl on me
• Abseil off the Eiffel Tower
• Get stuck in a room with a snake
• Go out in a boat in the sea
But I realised that I didn't have a choice.
There's no other way.
I tried to keep calm
B-r-e-a-t-h-e
It'll be okay. It's safe now. Nothing's going to happen.
But I couldn't shake the feeling that something bad would happen again.
I don't want to get hit by another wave.

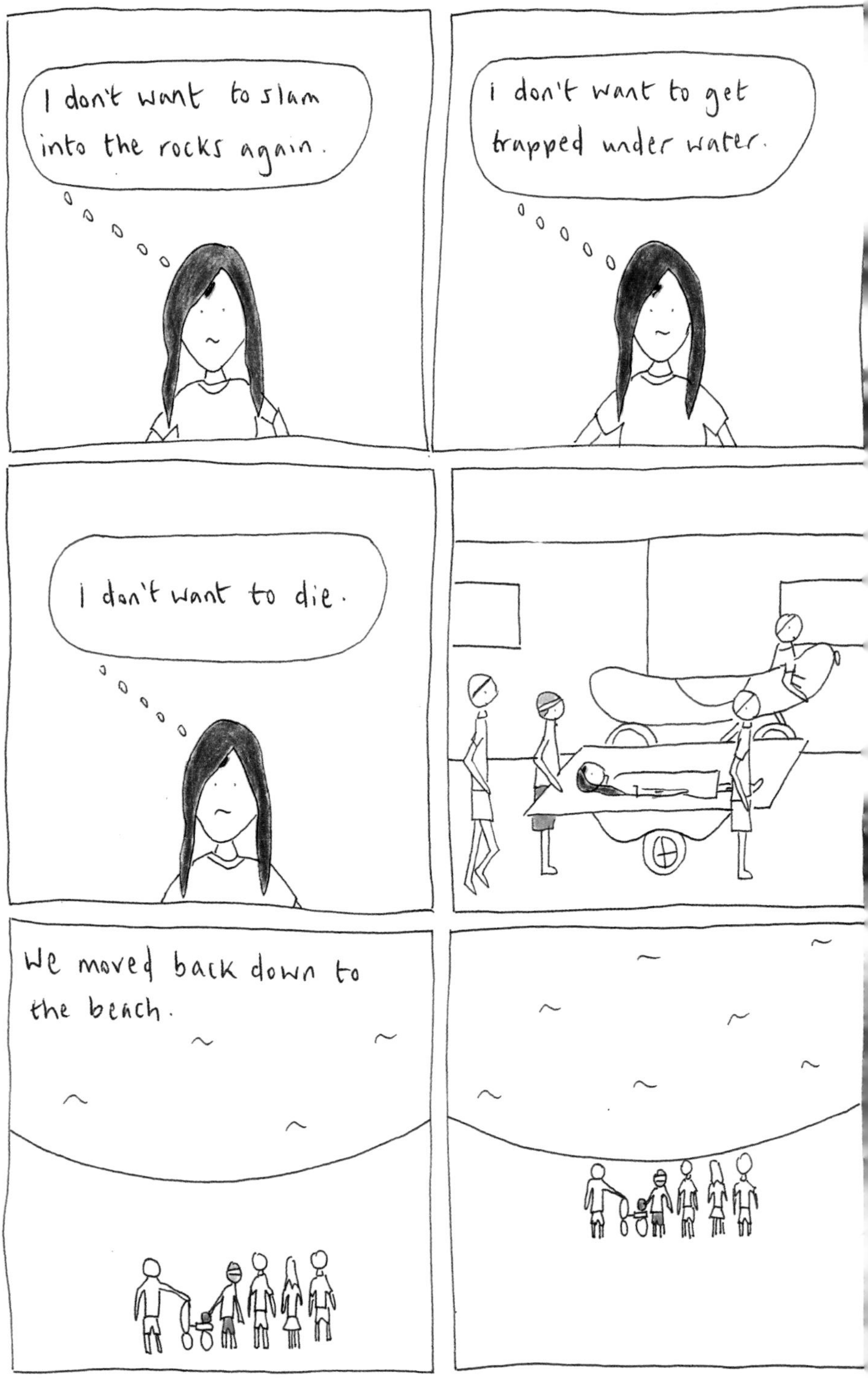
I don't want to slam into the rocks again.
i don't want to get trapped under water.
I don't want to die.
We moved back down to the beach.

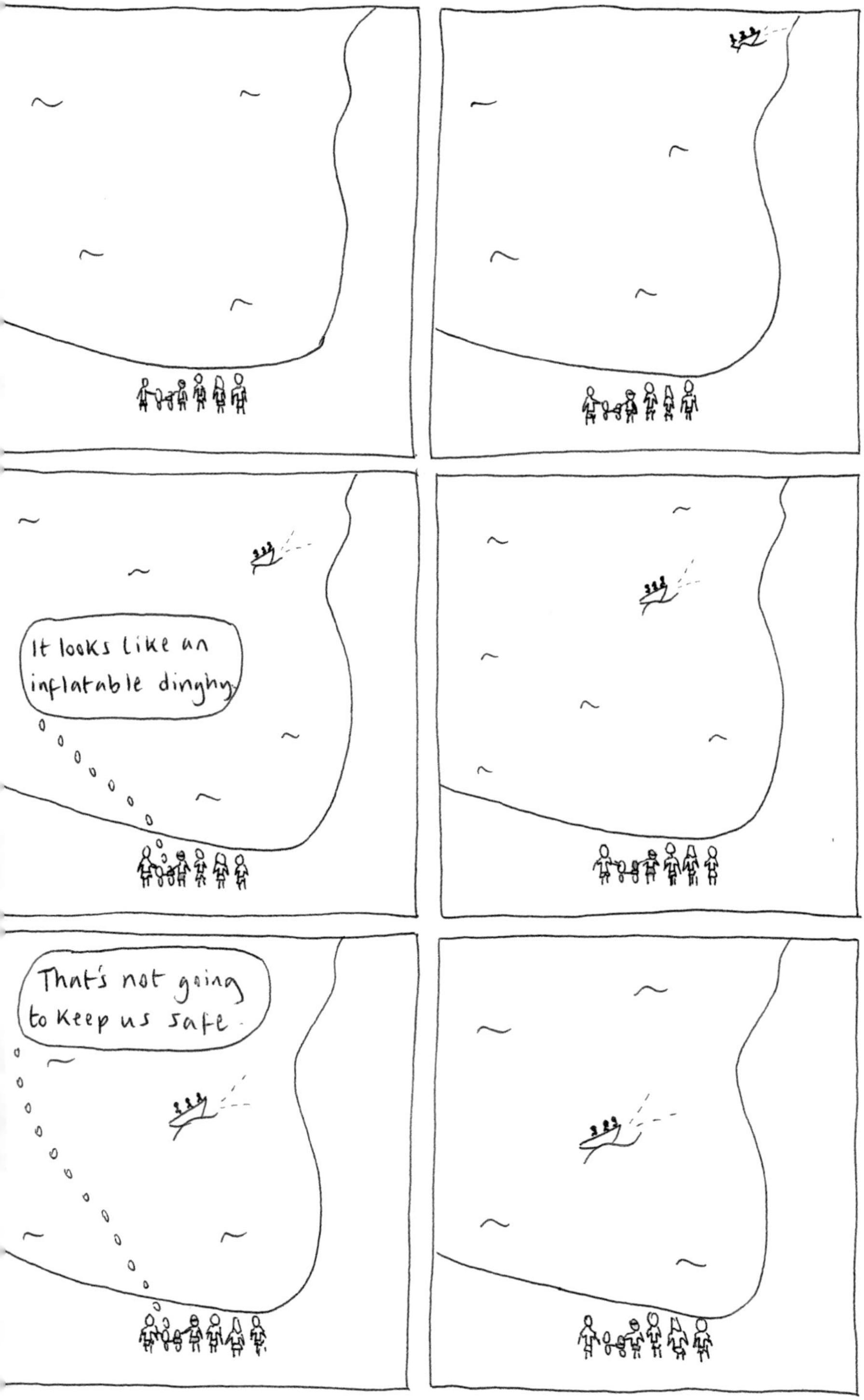
It looks like an inflatable dinghy
That's not going to keep us safe

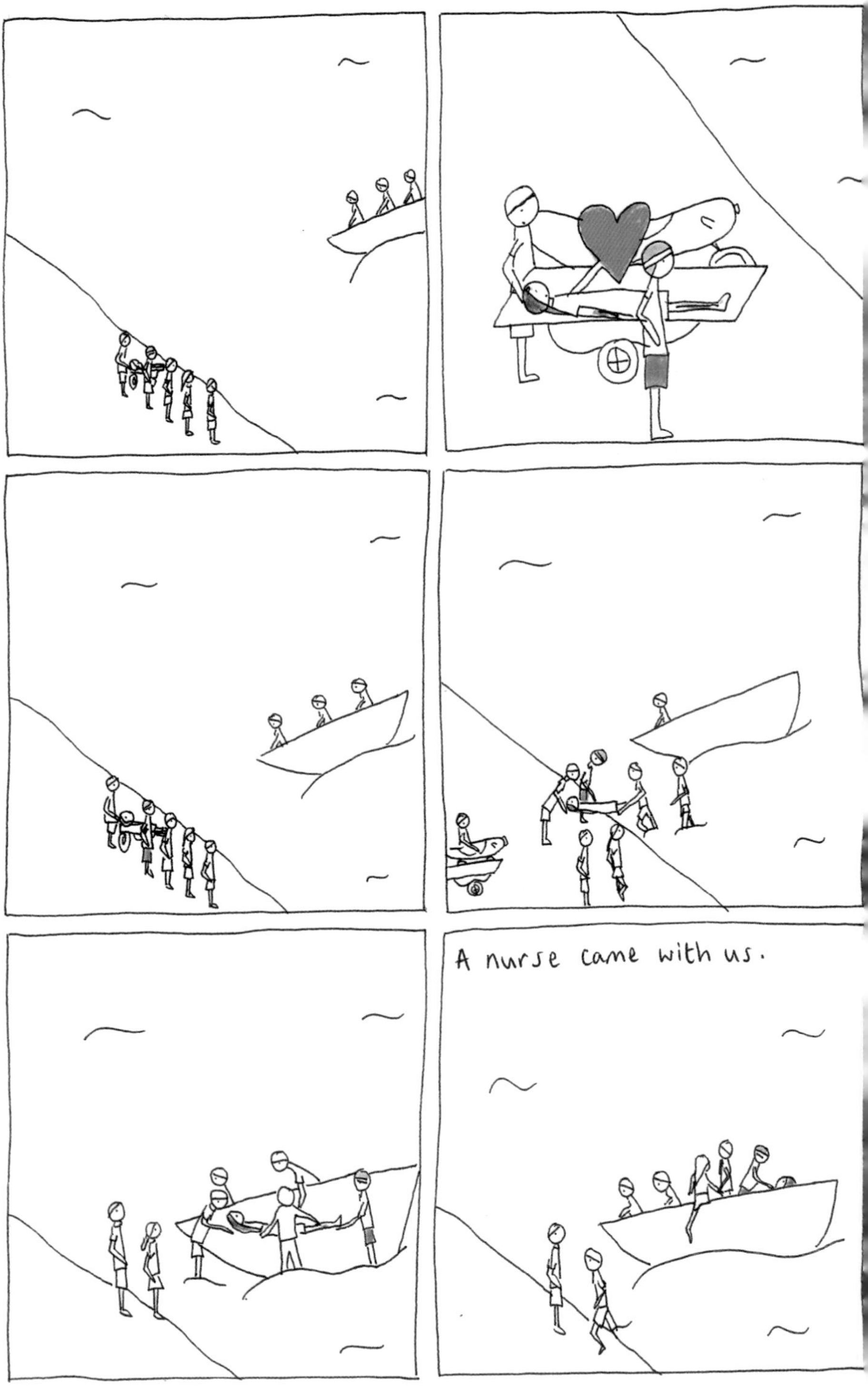
A nurse came with us.

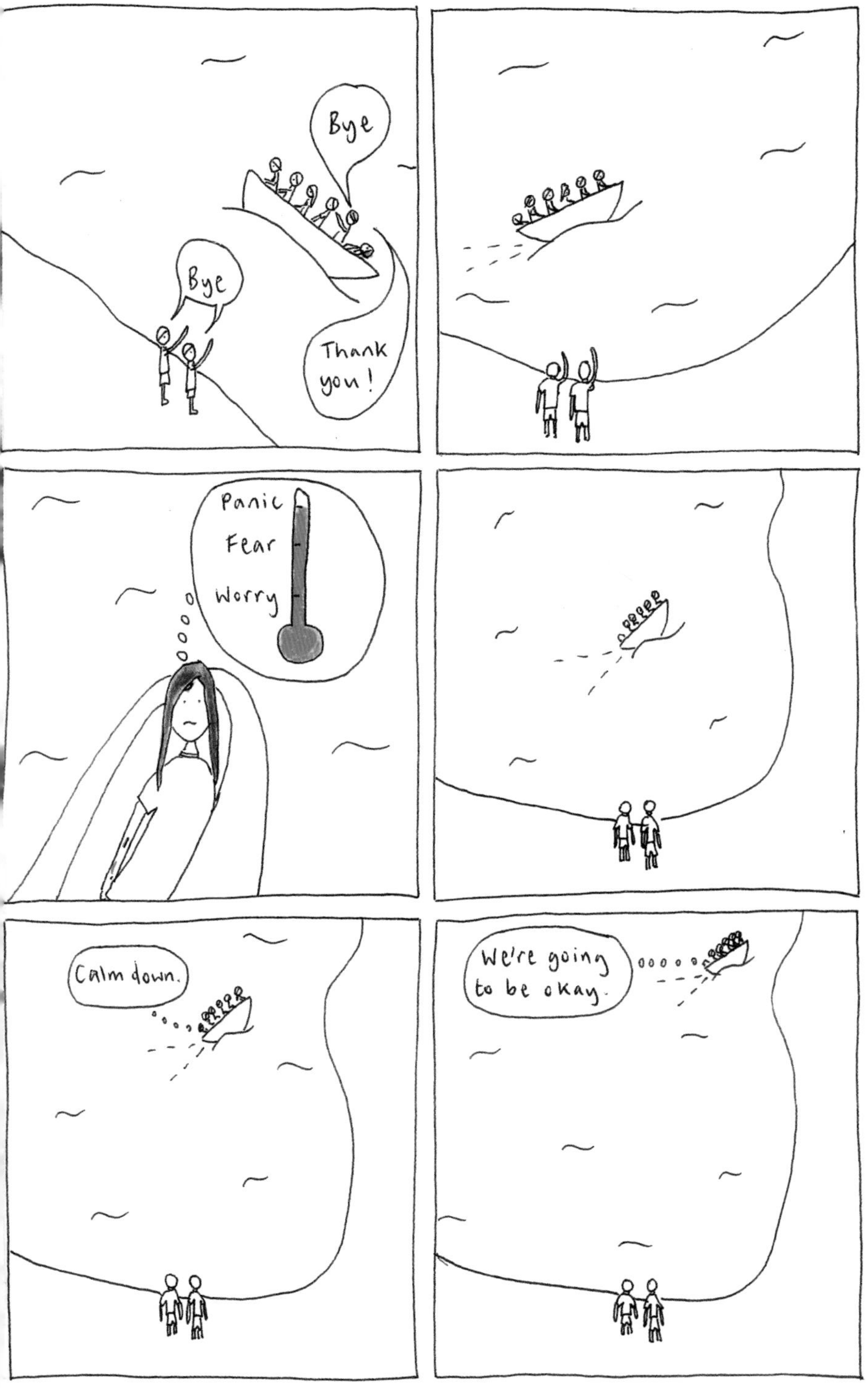
Bye
Bye
Thank you!
Panic
Fear
Worry
Calm down.
We're going to be okay.

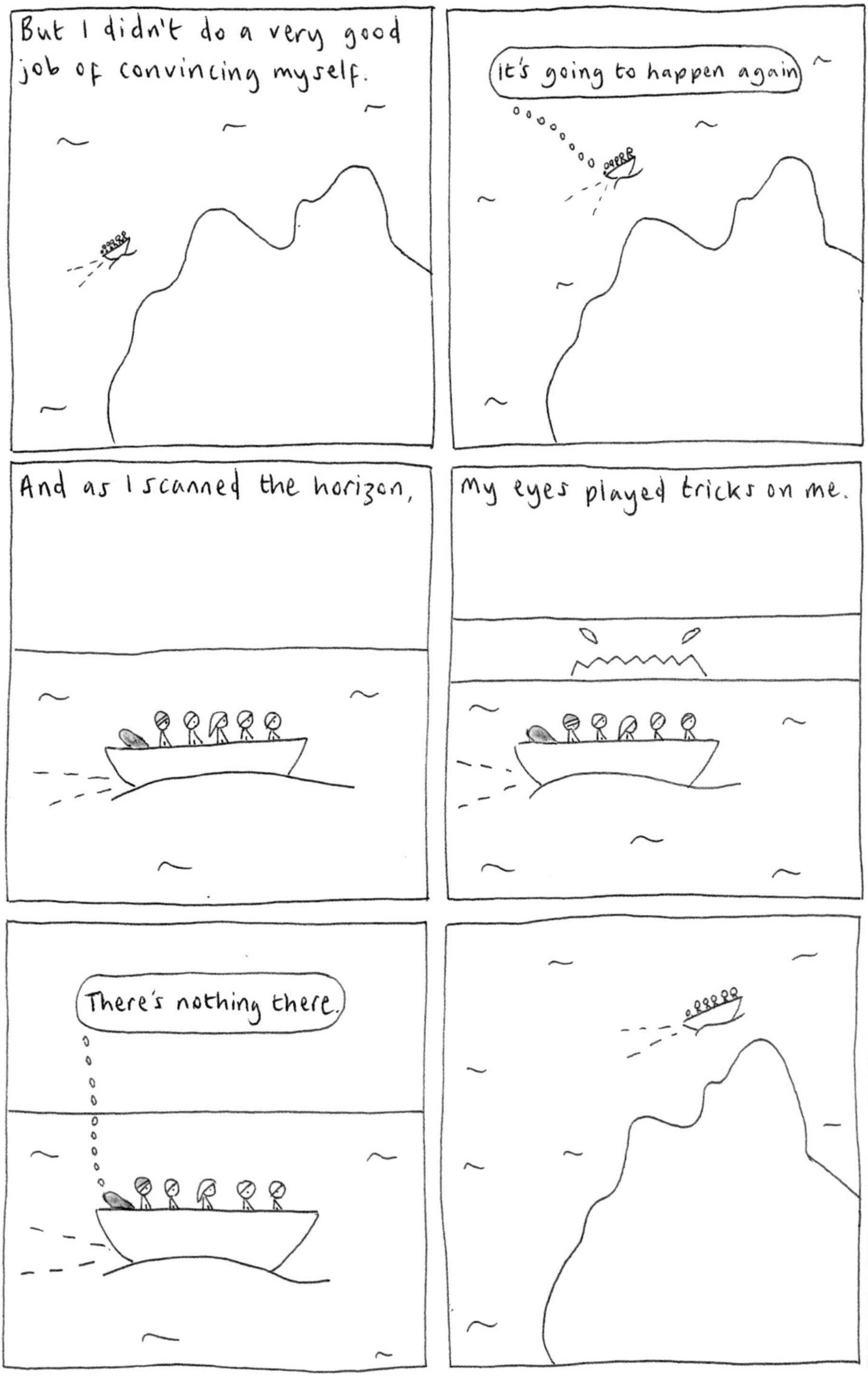
But I didn't do a very good job of convincing myself.
It's going to happen again
And as I scanned the horizon,
My eyes played tricks on me.
There's nothing there.

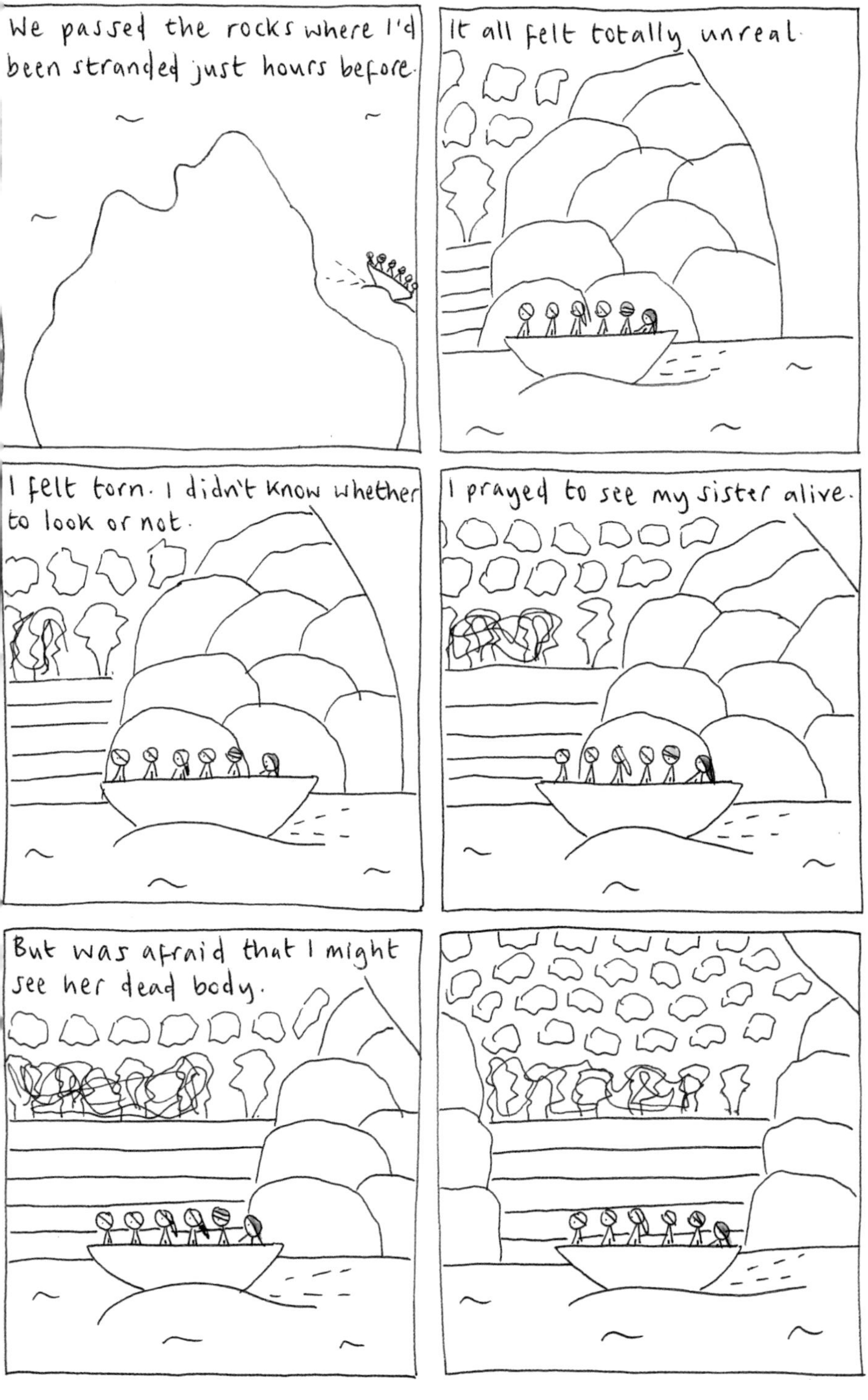
We passed the rocks where I'd been stranded just hours before.
It all felt totally unreal.
I felt torn. I didn't know whether to look or not.
I prayed to see my sister alive.
But was afraid that I might see her dead body.

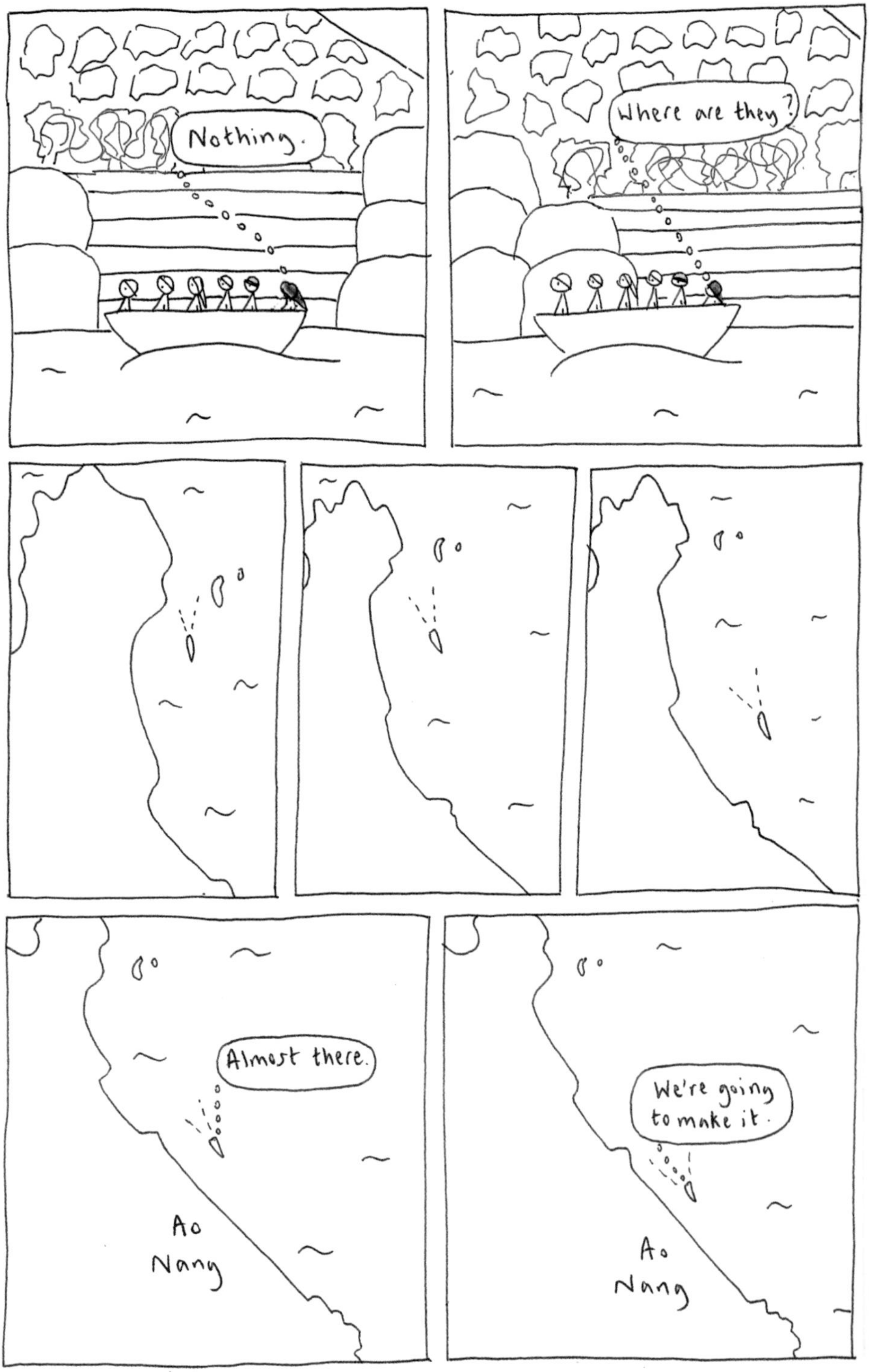
Nothing.
Where are they?
Almost there.
Ao Nang
We're going to make it.
Ao Nang

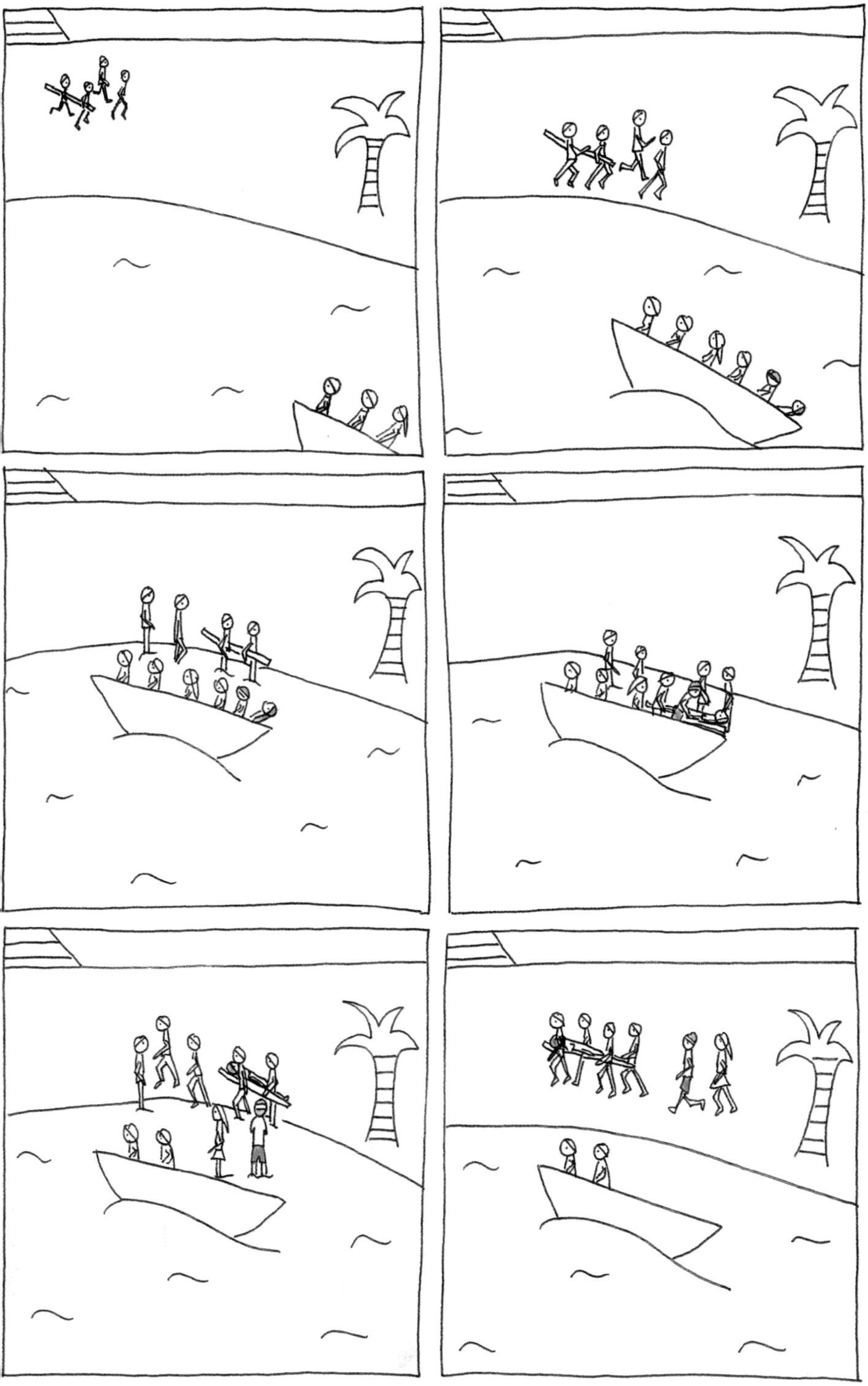

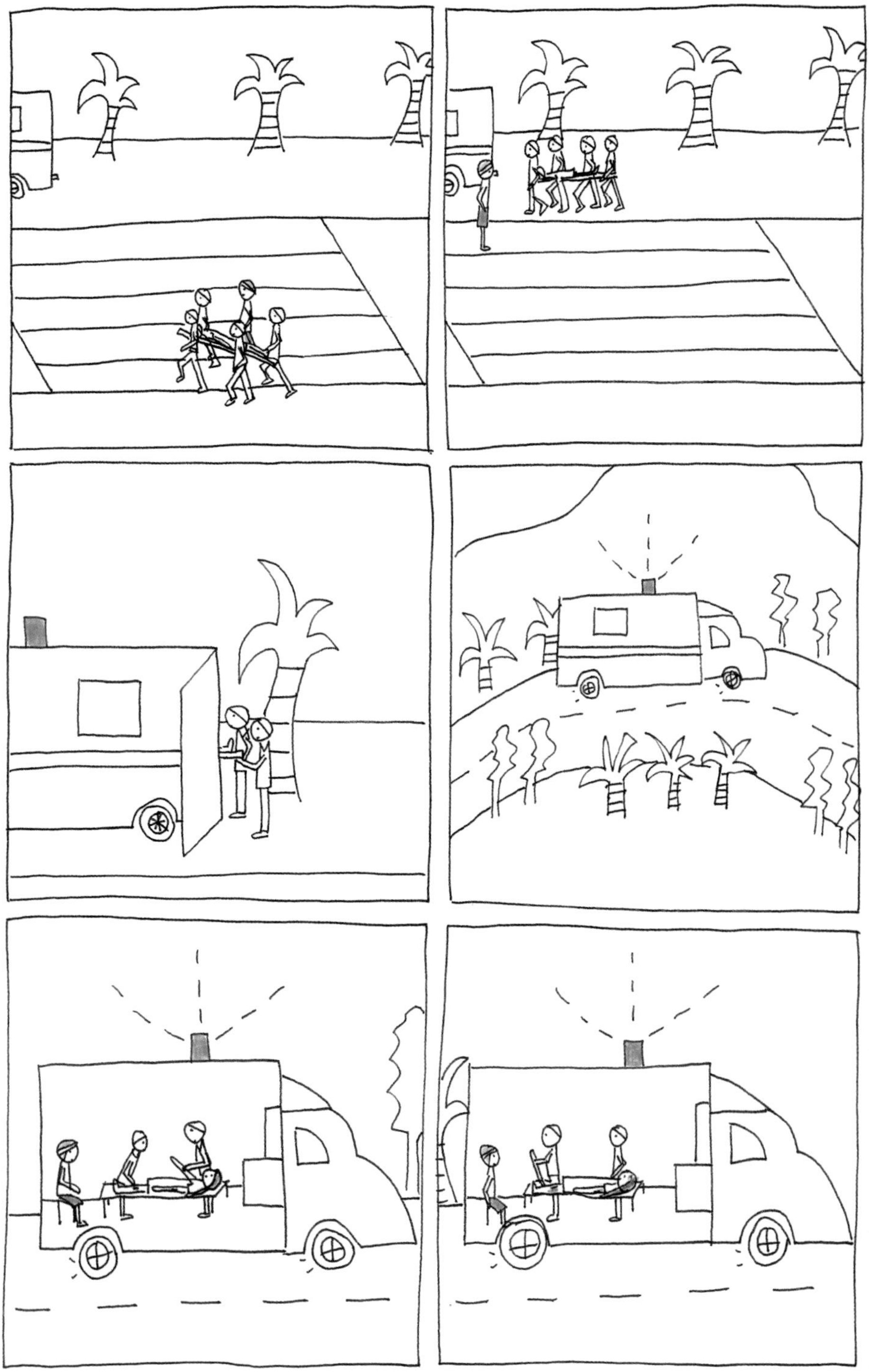

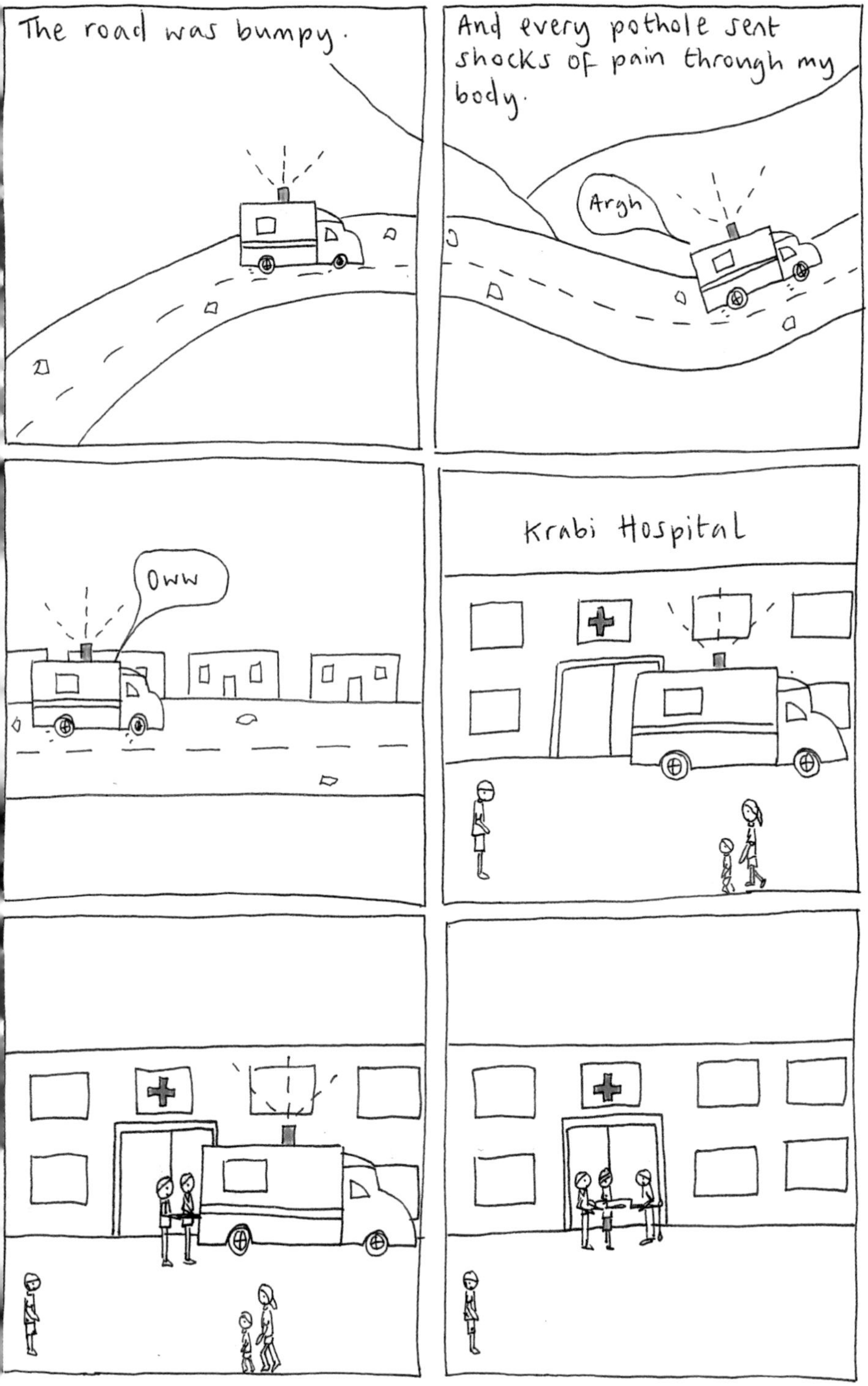
The road was bumpy.
And every pothole sent shocks of pain through my body.
Argh
Oww
Krabi Hospital

I'd never seen anything like it.

Injured, bloody people everywhere.

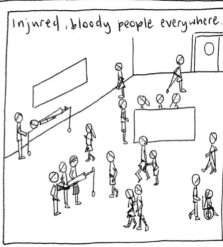

There was a confused hum of noise.

And an uneasy feeling hung in the air.

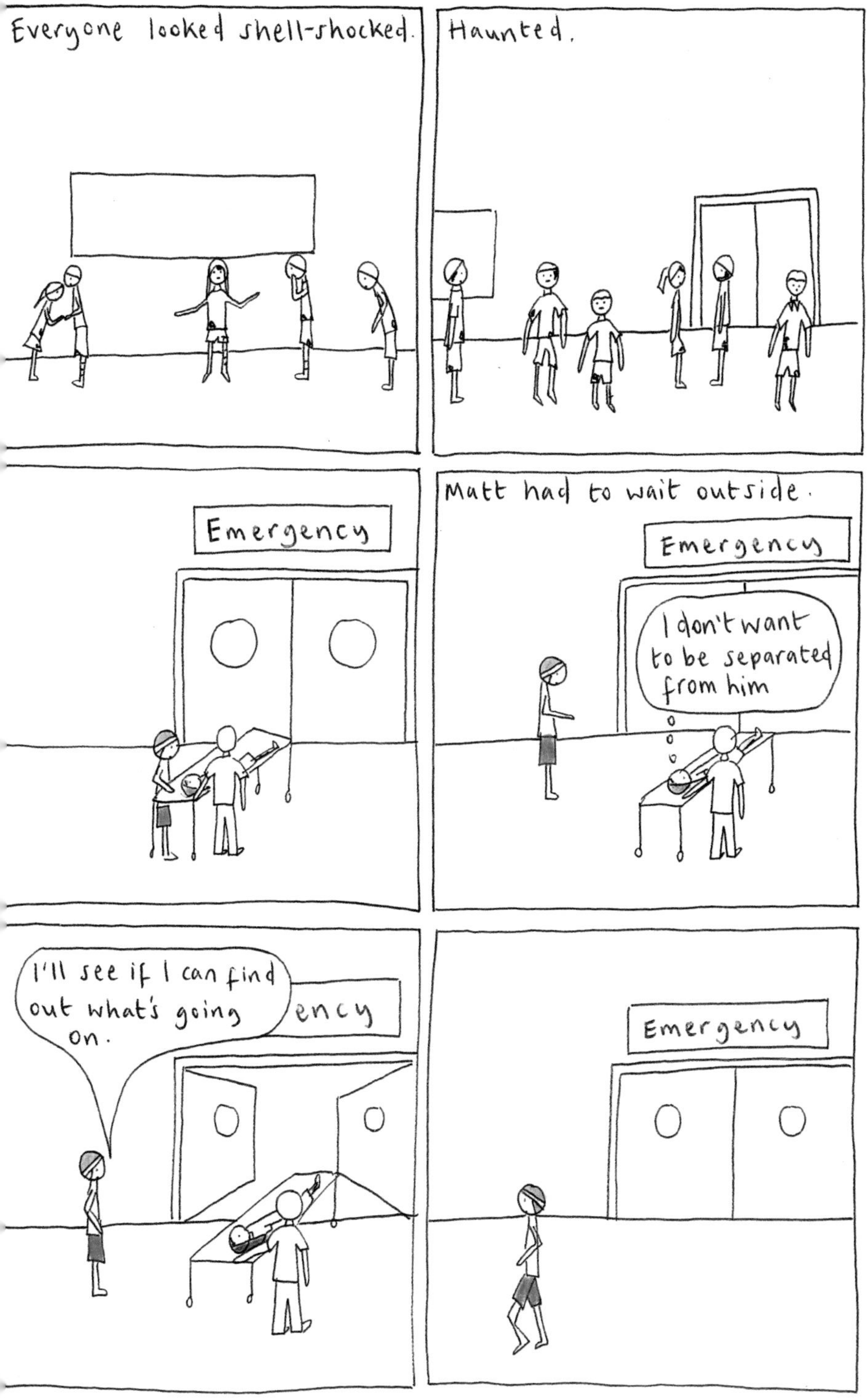
Everyone looked shell-shocked.
Haunted.
Emergency
Matt had to wait outside.
Emergency
I don't want to be separated from him
I'll see if I can find out what's going on.
ency
Emergency

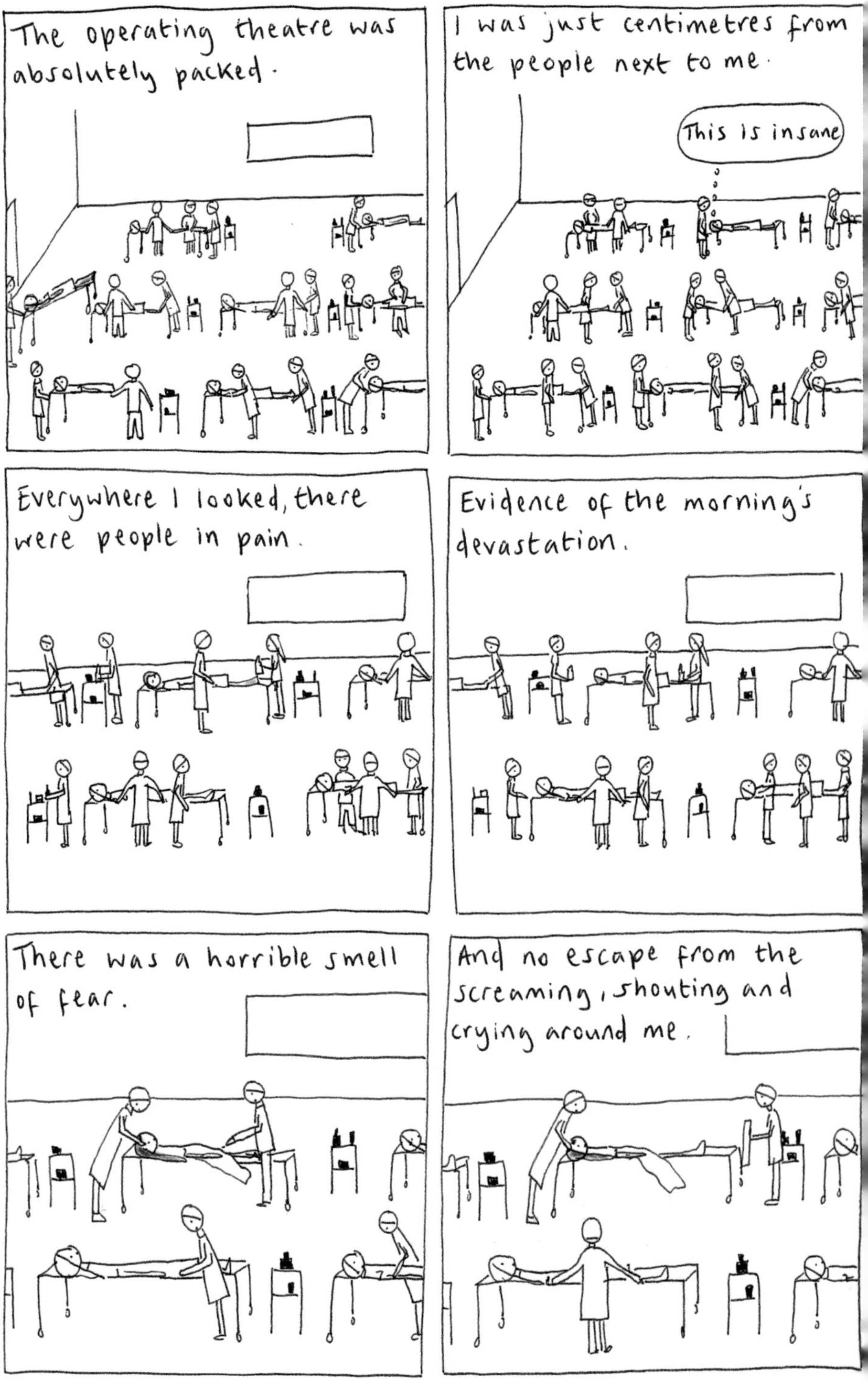

The operating theatre was absolutely packed.
I was just centimetres from the people next to me.
This is insane
Everywhere I looked, there were people in pain.
Evidence of the morning's devastation.
There was a horrible smell of fear.
And no escape from the screaming, shouting and crying around me.

The gravity of what had happened really started to hit me.
They cleaned my wounds from head to toe.
I felt sharp, painful stings all over.
And when they got to the big hole in my right leg, it was agony.
They all looked very serious.
This is very badly infected.
That doesn't sound good.

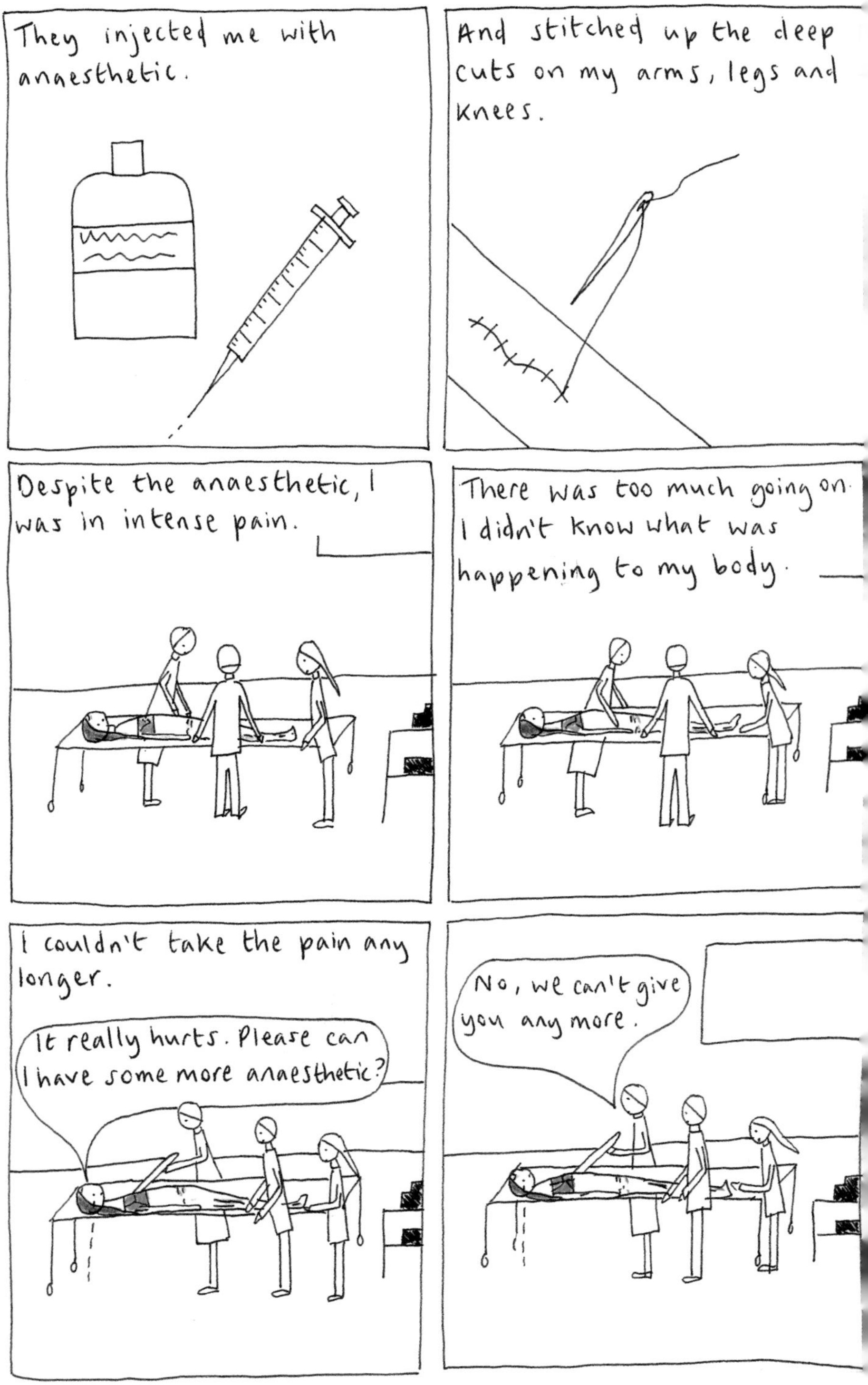
They injected me with anaesthetic.
And stitched up the deep cuts on my arms, legs and knees.
Despite the anaesthetic, I was in intense pain.
There was too much going on. I didn't know what was happening to my body.
I couldn't take the pain any longer.
It really hurts. Please can I have some more anaesthetic?
No, we can't give you any more.

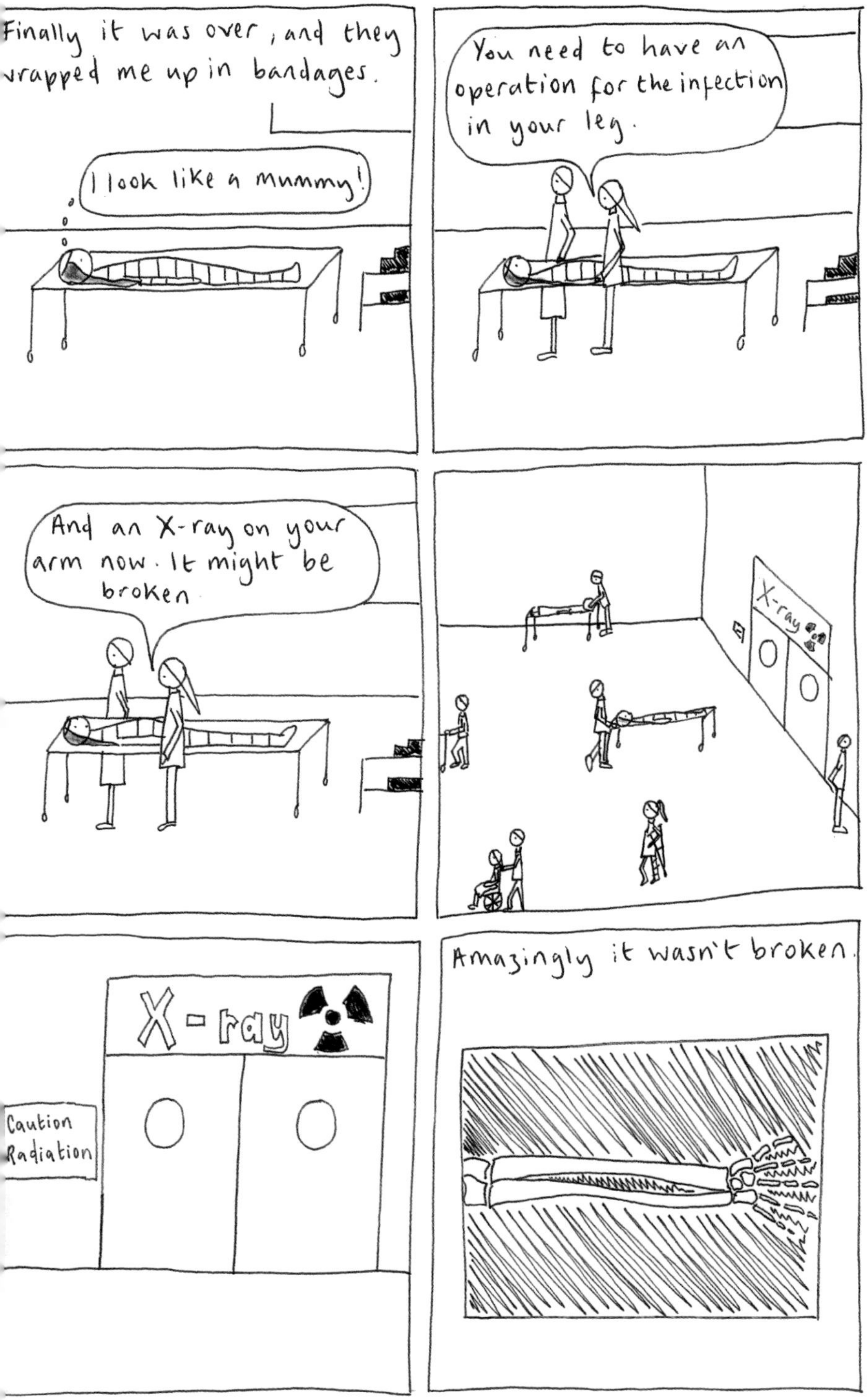
Finally it was over, and they wrapped me up in bandages.
I look like a mummy!
You need to have an operation for the infection in your leg.
And an X-ray on your arm now. It might be broken
X-ray
X-ray
Caution Radiation
Amazingly it wasn't broken.

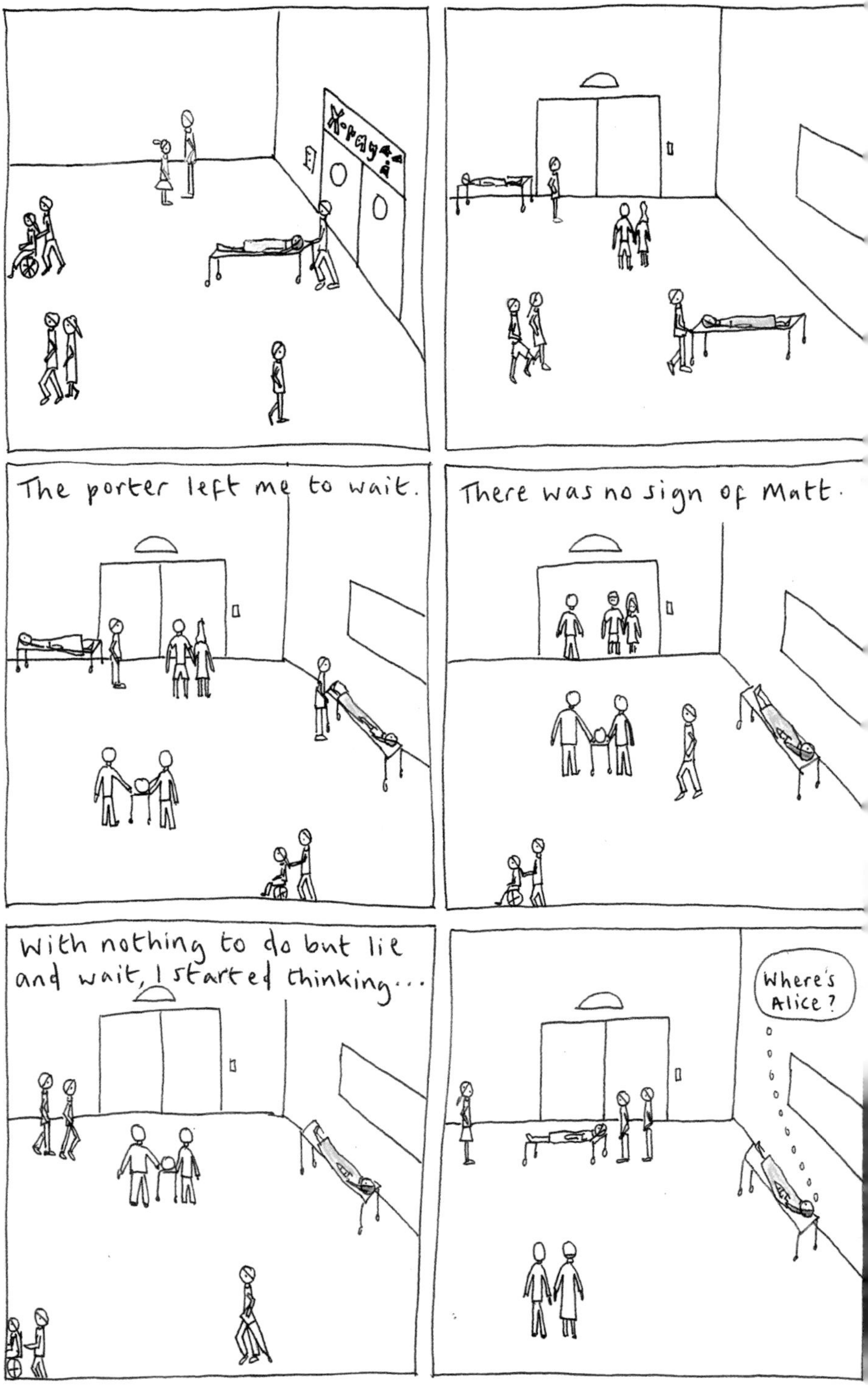
The porter left me to wait.
There was no sign of Matt.
With nothing to do but lie and wait, I started thinking...
Where's Alice?

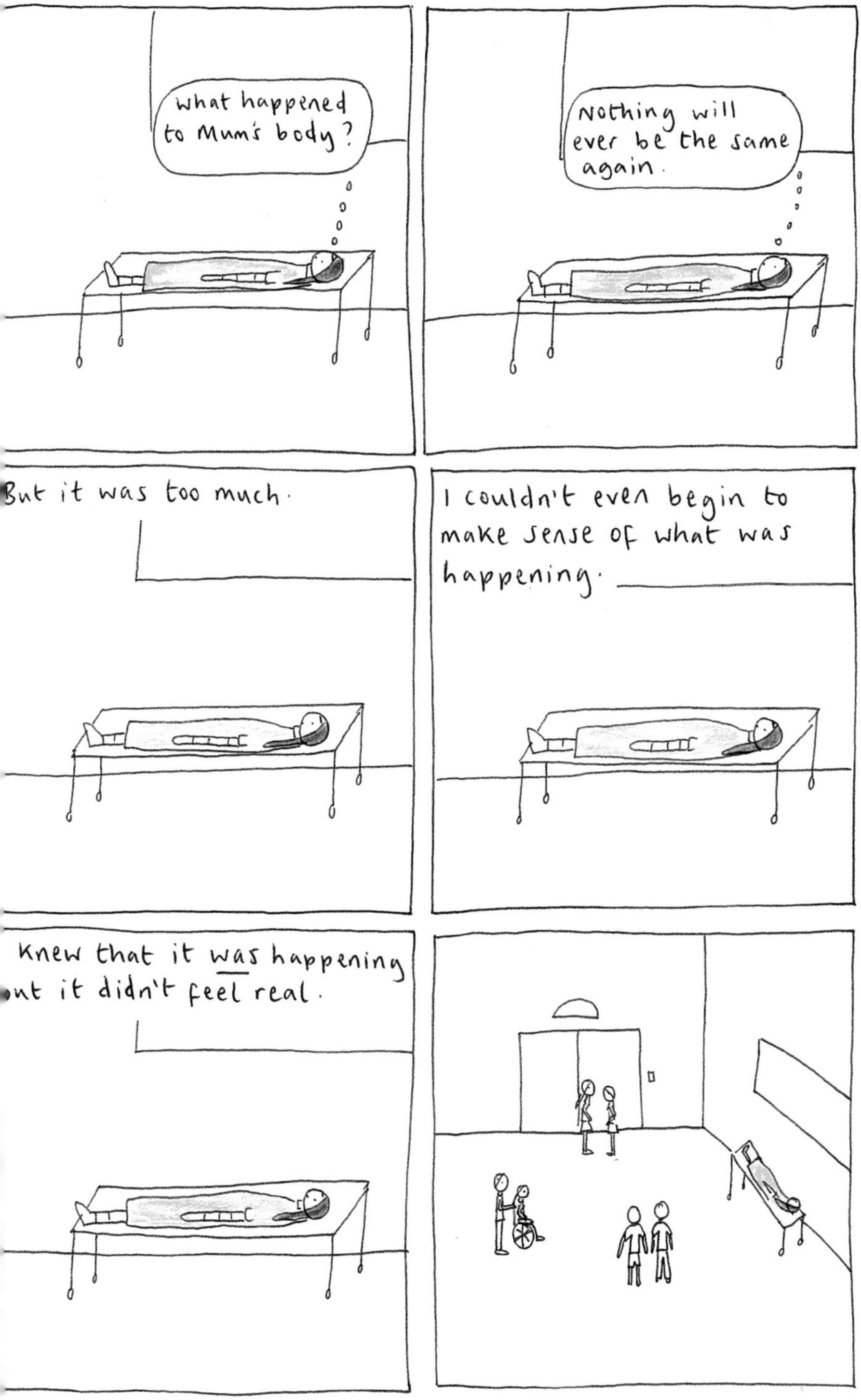
what happened to Mum's body?
Nothing will ever be the same again.
But it was too much.
I couldn't even begin to make sense of what was happening.
knew that it was happening
ut it didn't feel real.

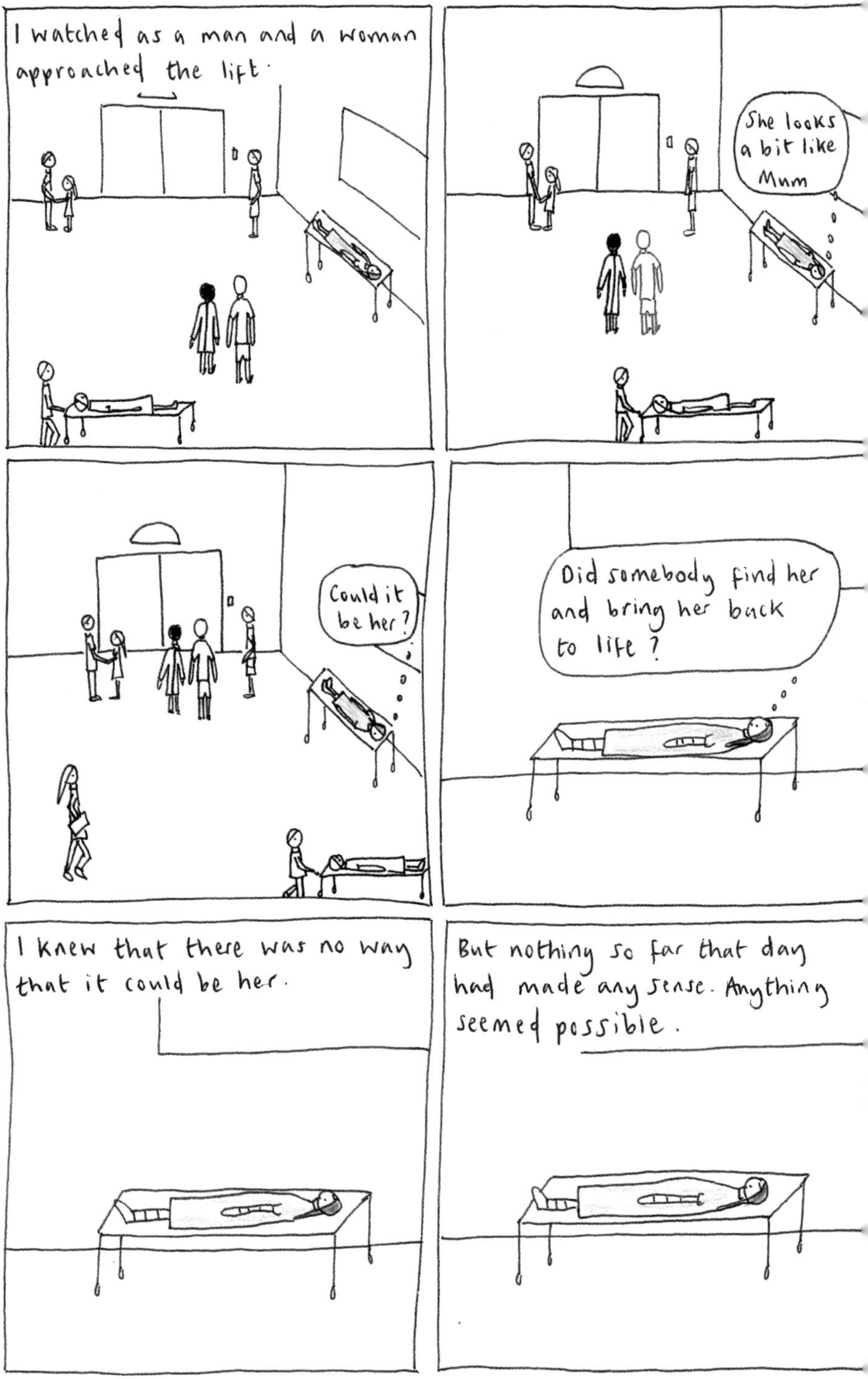
I watched as a man and a woman approached the lift.
She looks a bit like Mum
Could it be her?
Did somebody find her and bring her back to life?
I knew that there was no way that it could be her.
But nothing so far that day had made any sense. Anything seemed possible.

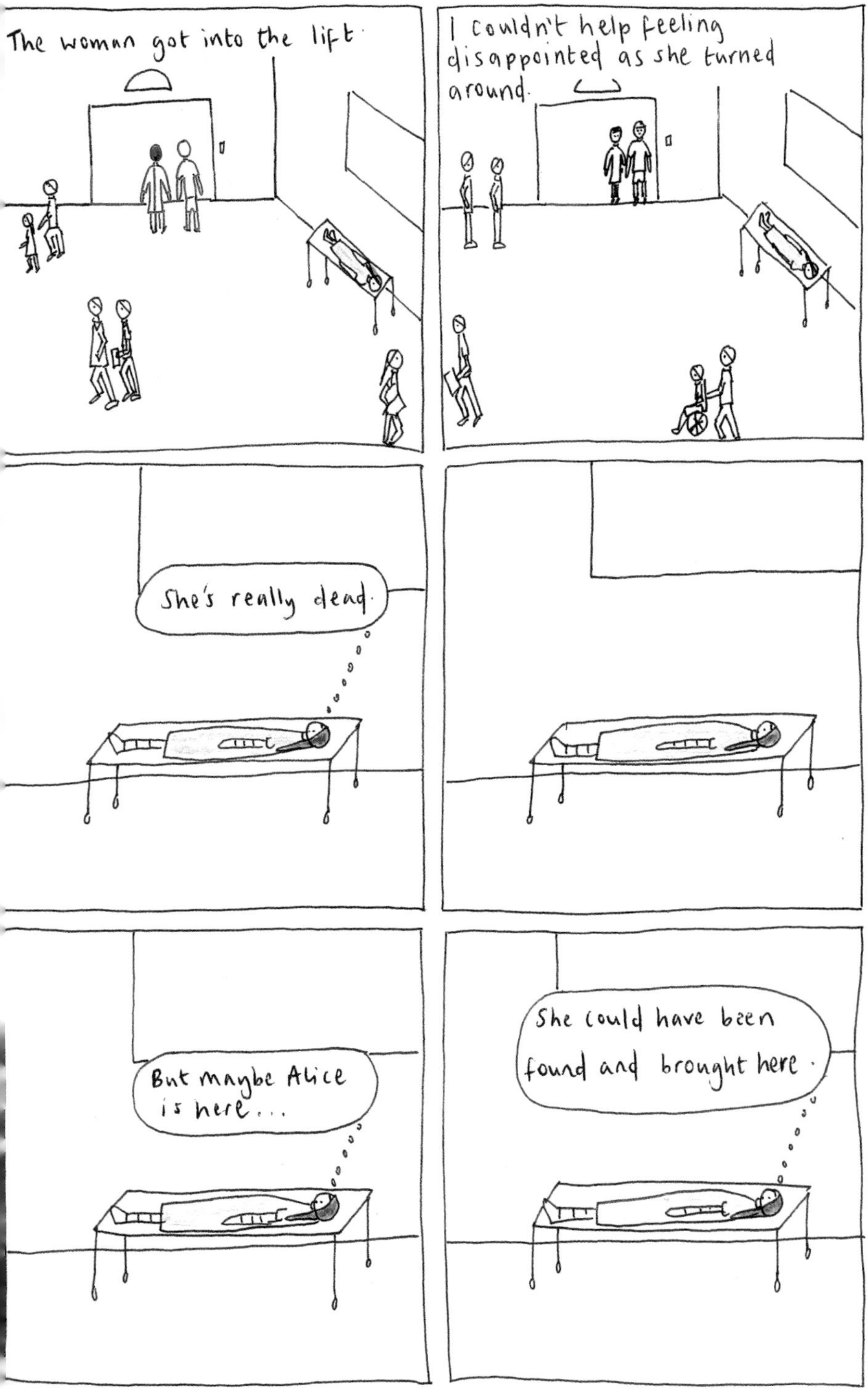
The woman got into the lift.
I couldn't help feeling disappointed as she turned around.
She's really dead.
But maybe Alice is here...
She could have been found and brought here.

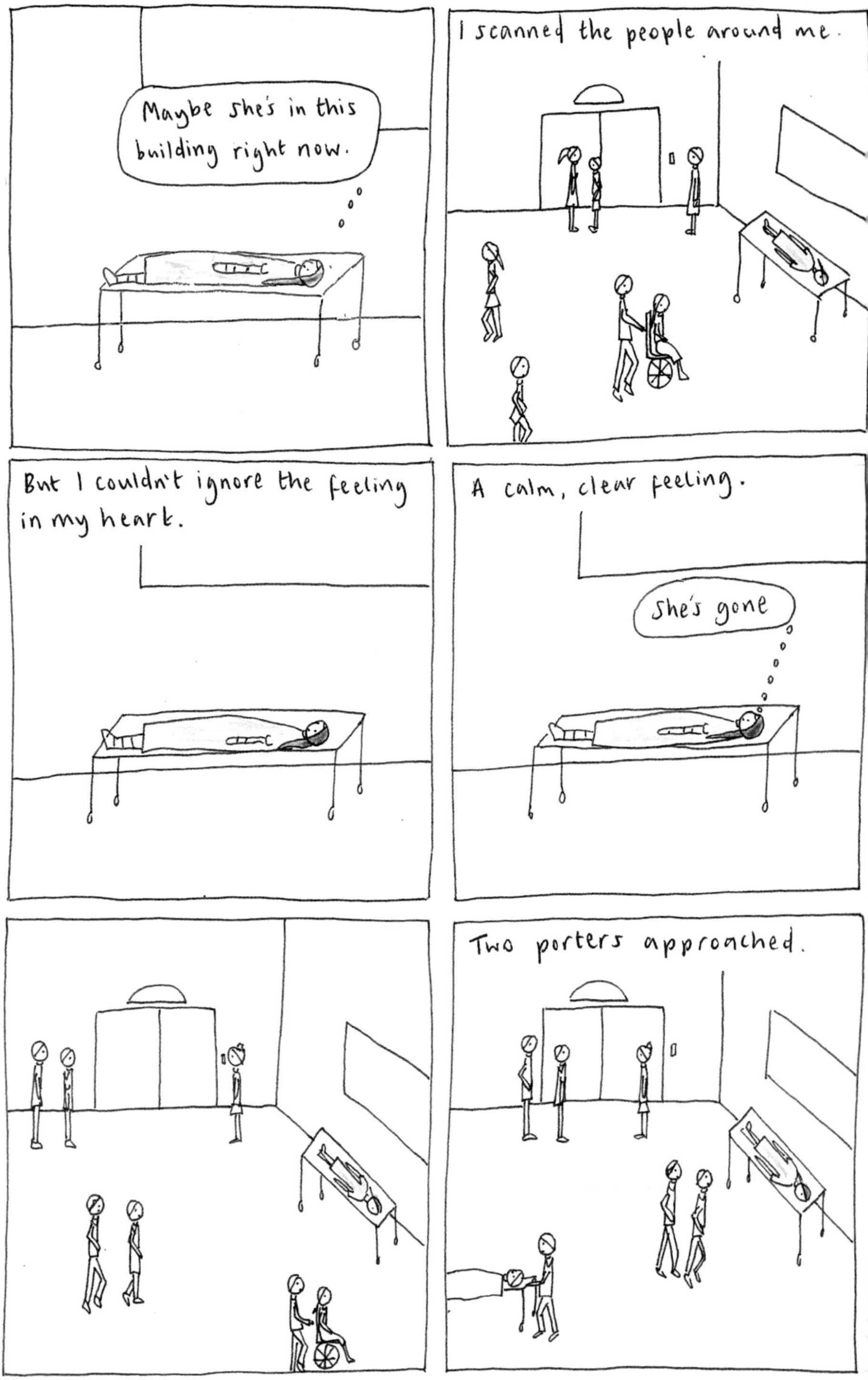

Maybe she's in this building right now.
I scanned the people around me.
But I couldn't ignore the feeling in my heart.
A calm, clear feeling.
She's gone
Two porters approached.

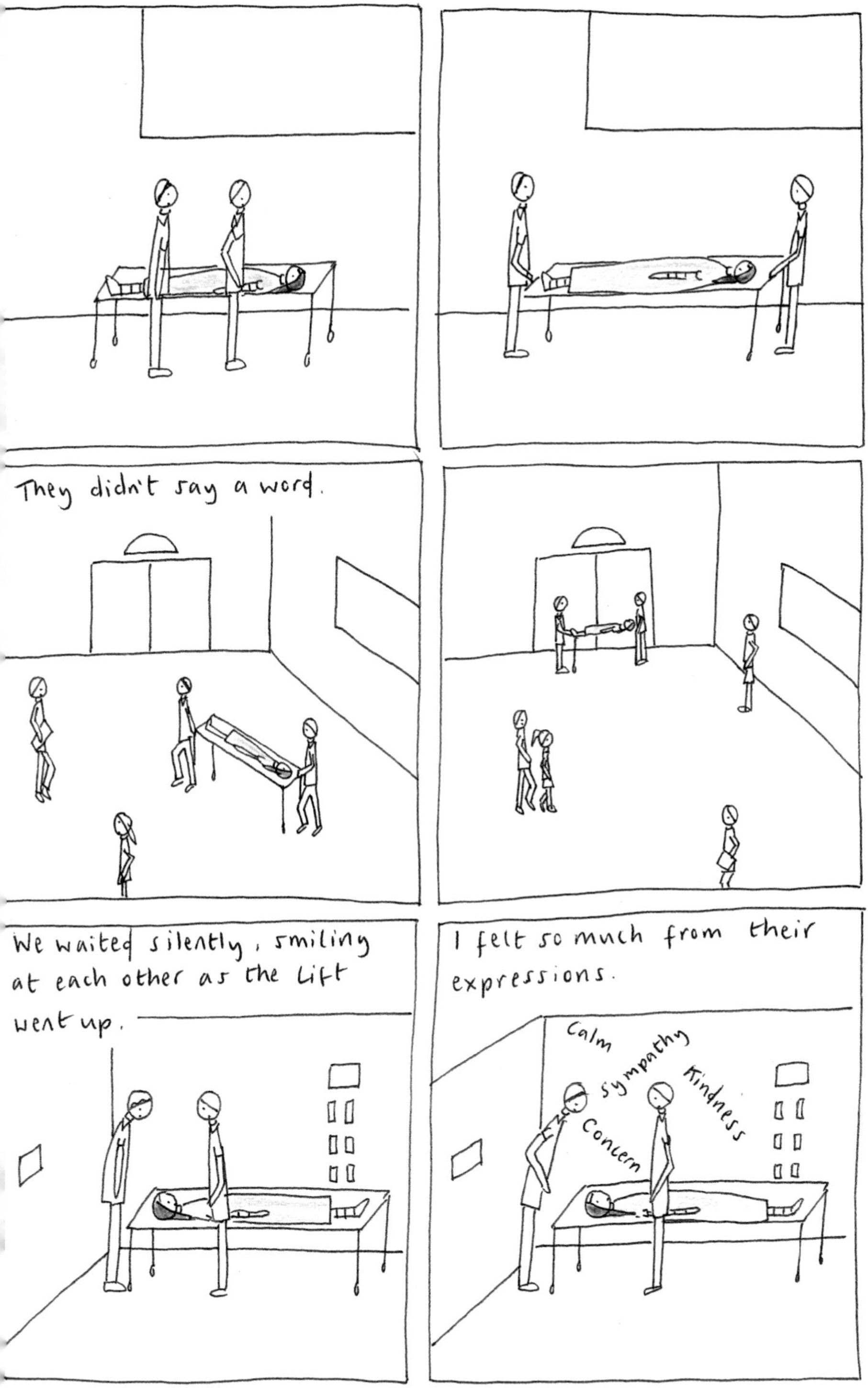
They didn't say a word.
We waited silently, smiling at each other as the lift went up.
I felt so much from their expressions.
Calm
Sympathy
Kindness
Concern

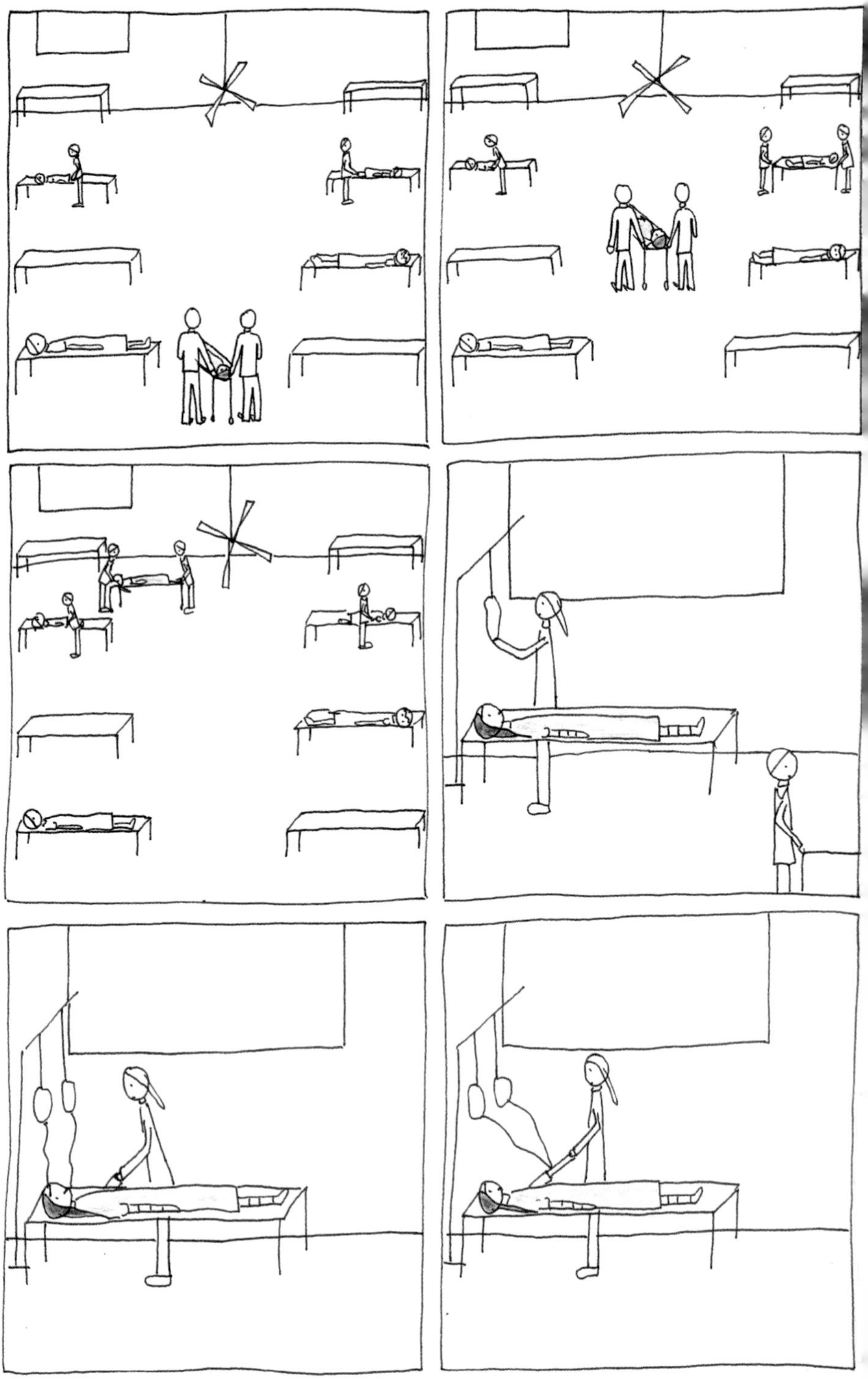

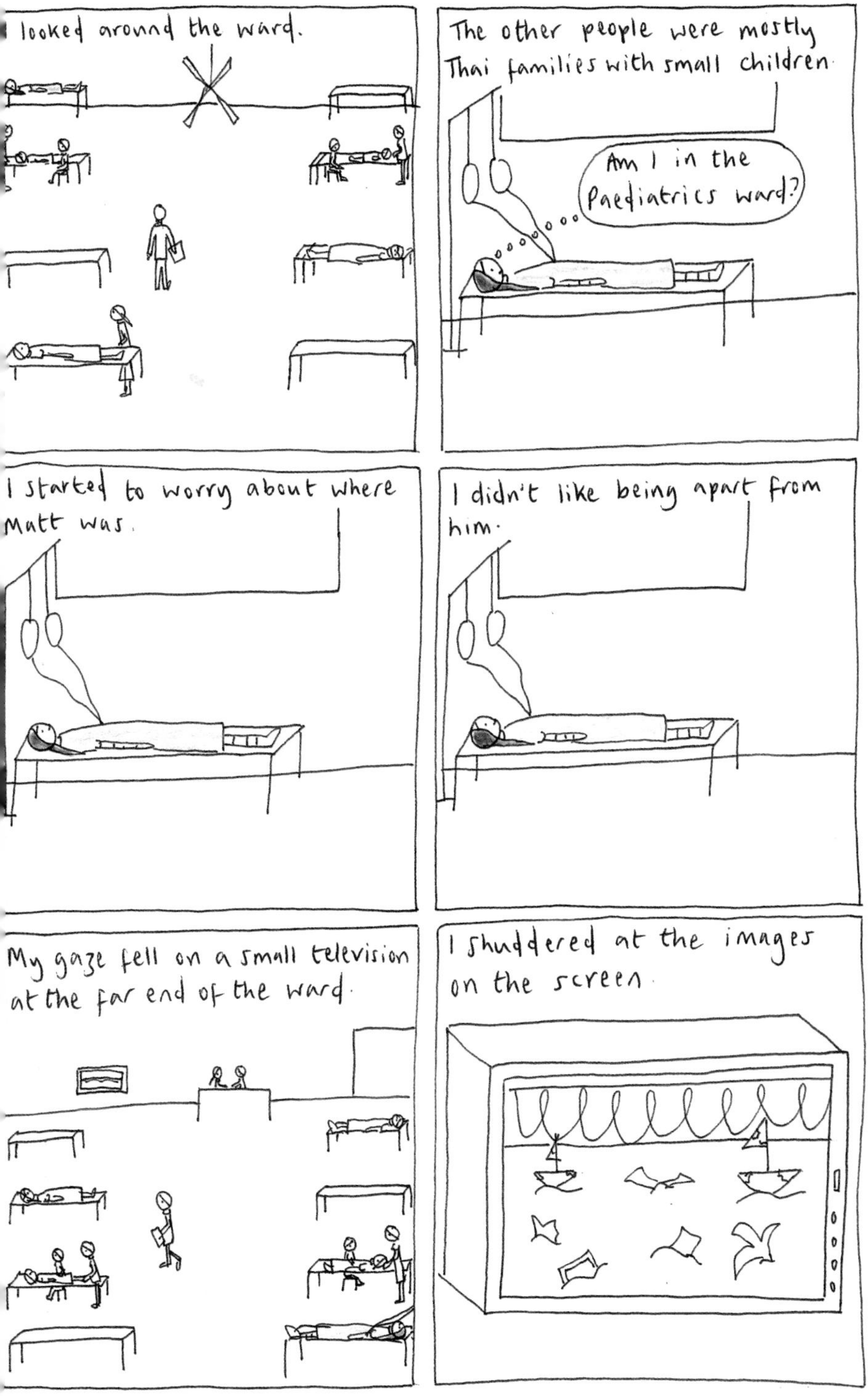
I looked around the ward.
The other people were mostly Thai families with small children.
Am I in the Paediatrics ward?
I started to worry about where Matt was.
I didn't like being apart from him.
My gaze fell on a small television at the far end of the ward.
I shuddered at the images on the screen.

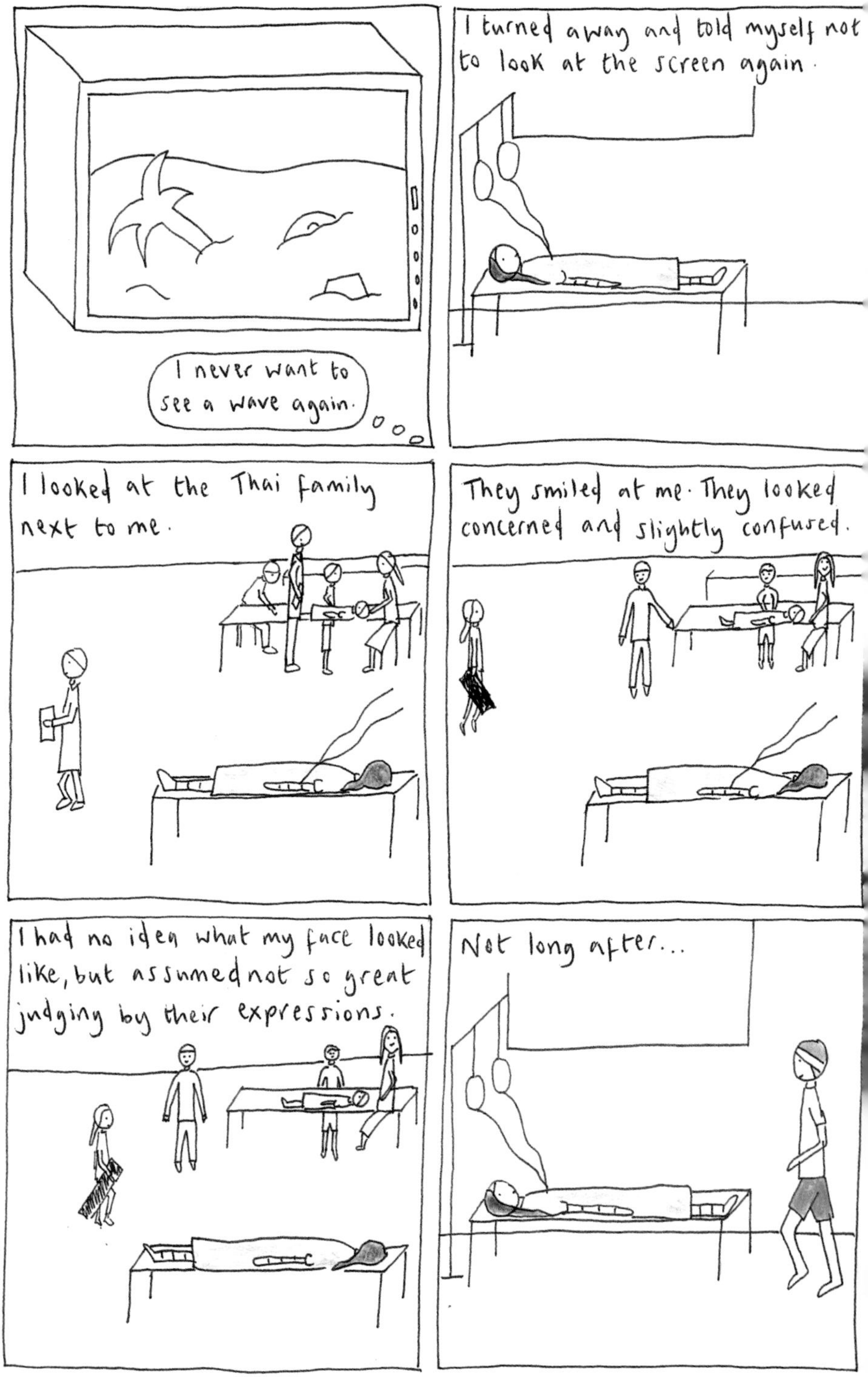
I never want to see a wave again.
I turned away and told myself not to look at the screen again.
I looked at the Thai family next to me.
They smiled at me. They looked concerned and slightly confused.
I had no idea what my face looked like, but assumed not so great judging by their expressions.
Not long after...

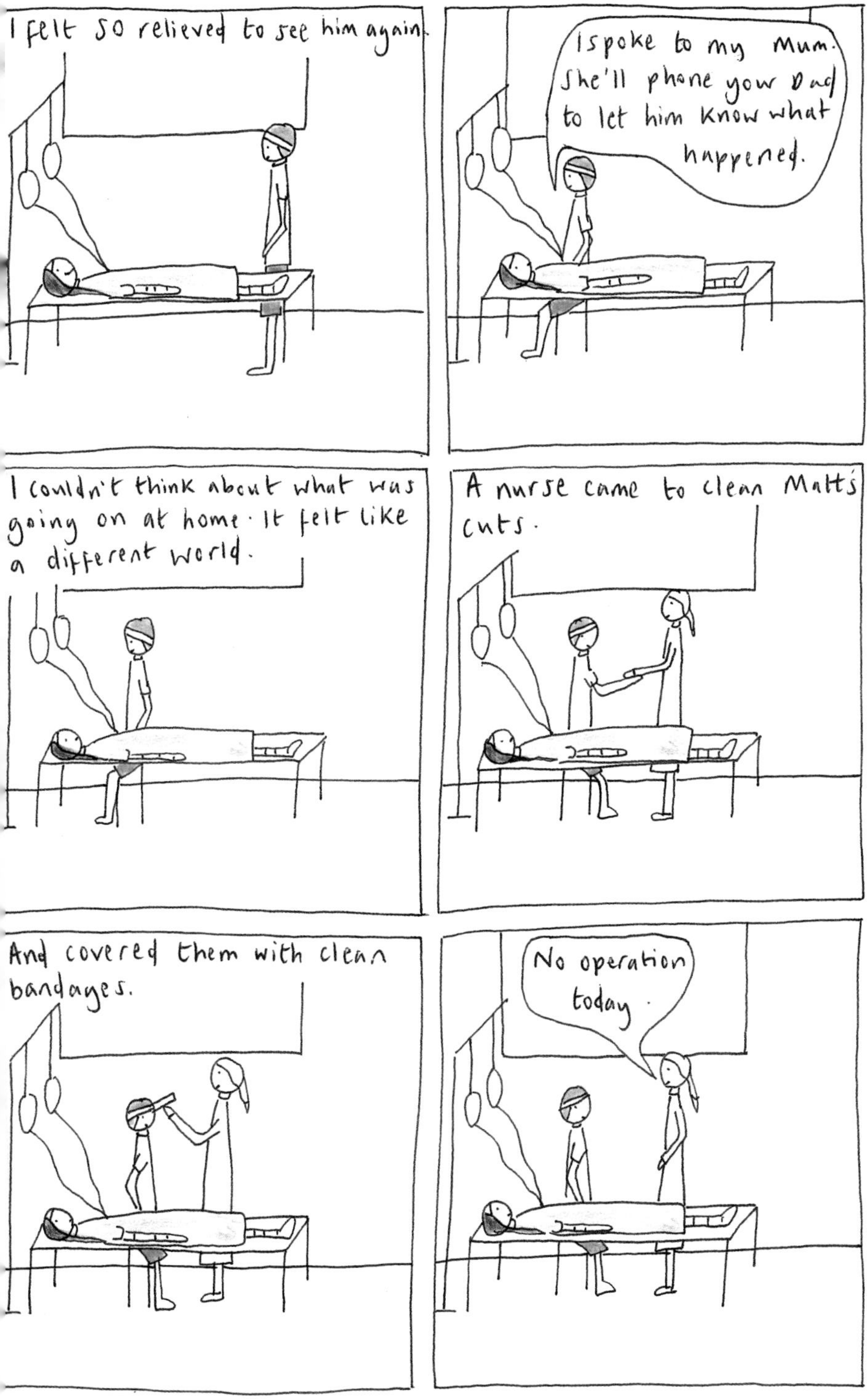
I felt so relieved to see him again.
I spoke to my Mum. She'll phone your Dad to let him know what happened.
I couldn't think about what was going on at home. It felt like a different world.
A nurse came to clean Matt's cuts.
And covered them with clean bandages.
No operation today.

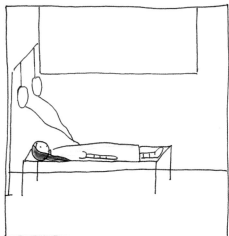

That means I can have a drink
I'll go to the shop
THUD
THUD
THUD
What's that?
My senses were still on high alert and I tensed up at the unidentified sound.

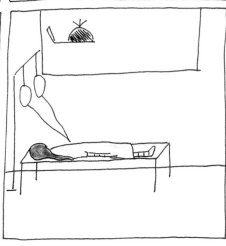

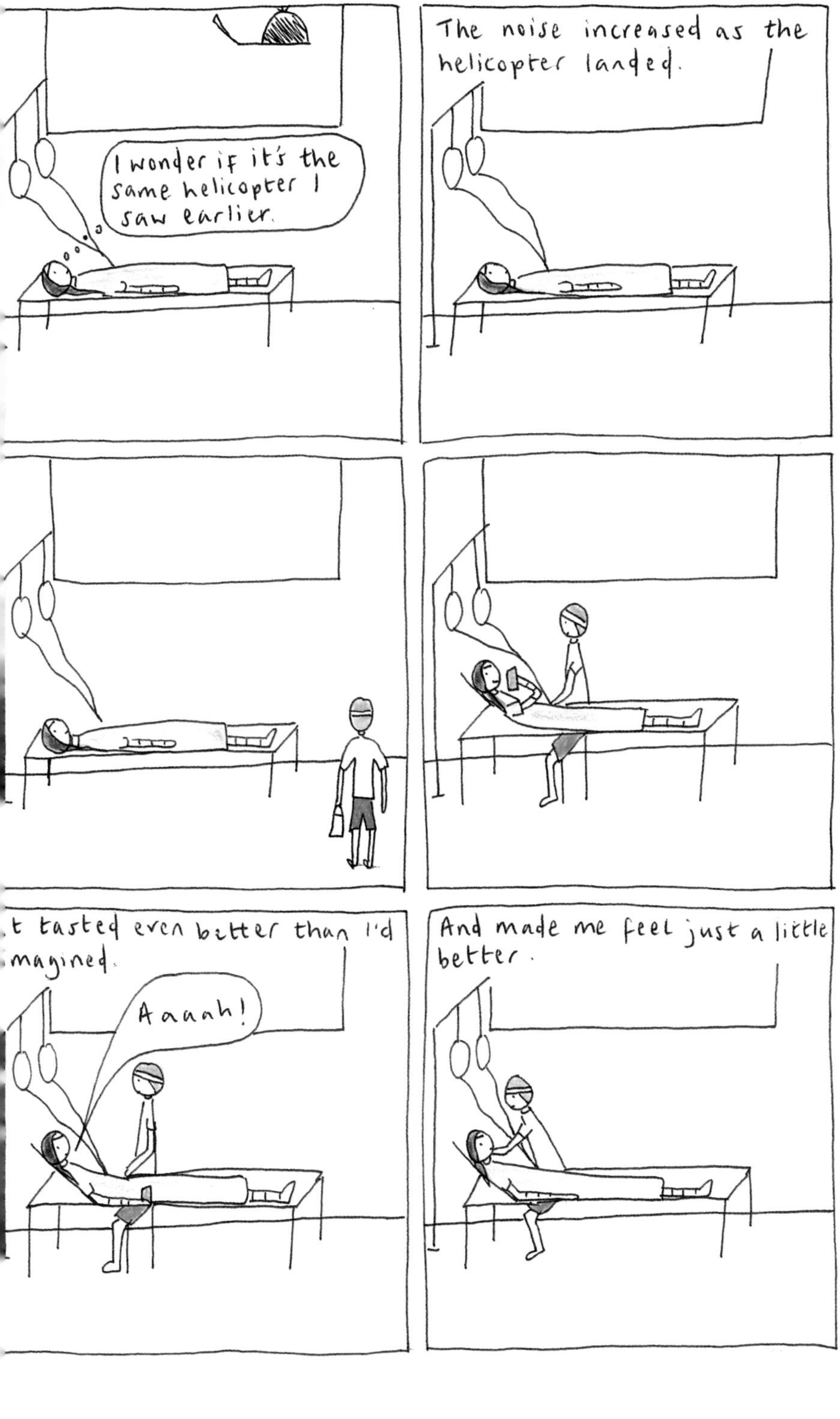
I wonder if it's the same helicopter I saw earlier.
The noise increased as the helicopter landed.
t tasted even better than I'd magined.
Aaaah!
And made me feel just a little better.

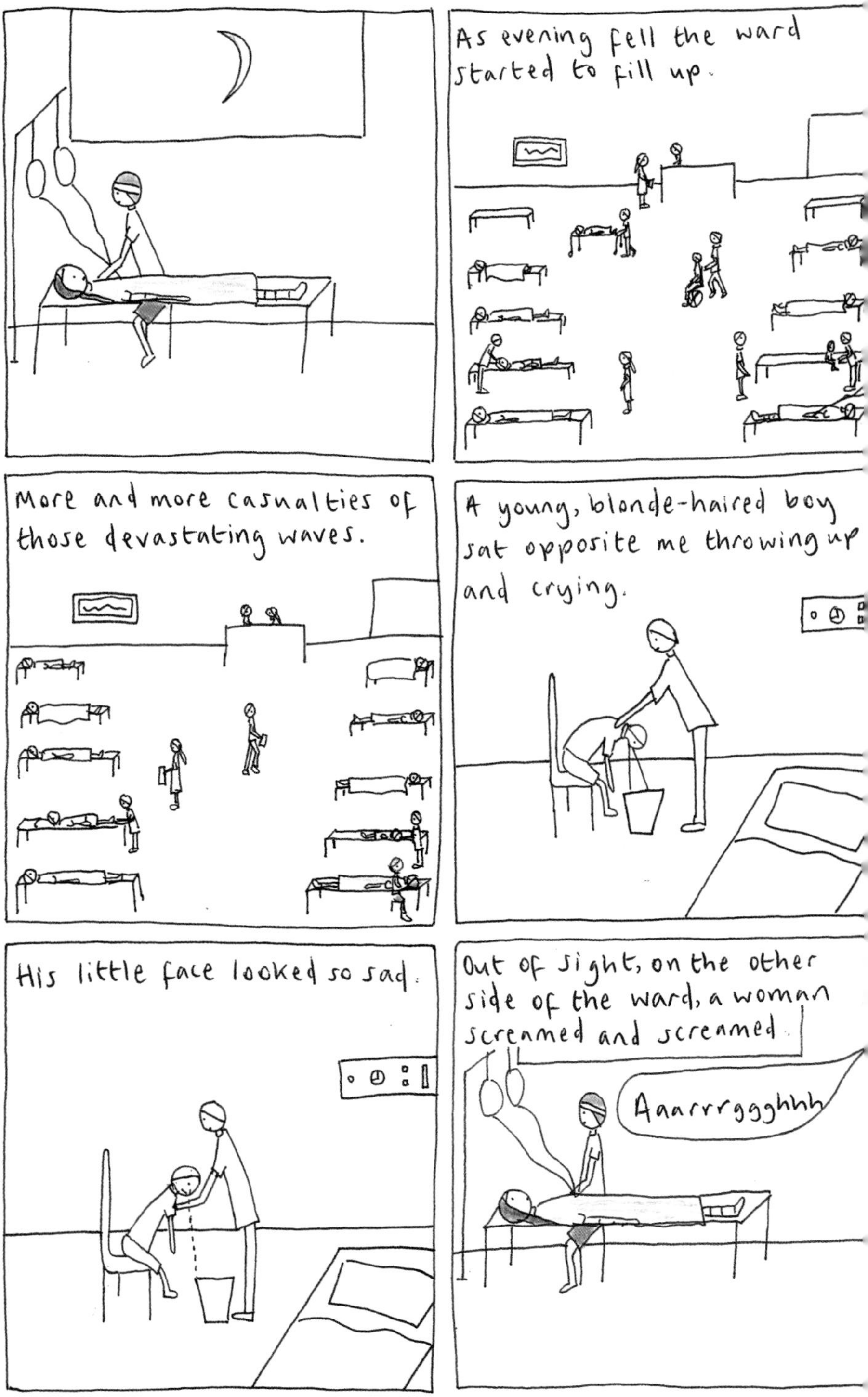
As evening fell the ward started to fill up.
More and more casualties of those devastating waves.
A young, blonde-haired boy sat opposite me throwing up and crying.
His little face looked so sad.
Out of sight, on the other side of the ward, a woman screamed and screamed.
Aaarrrggghhh

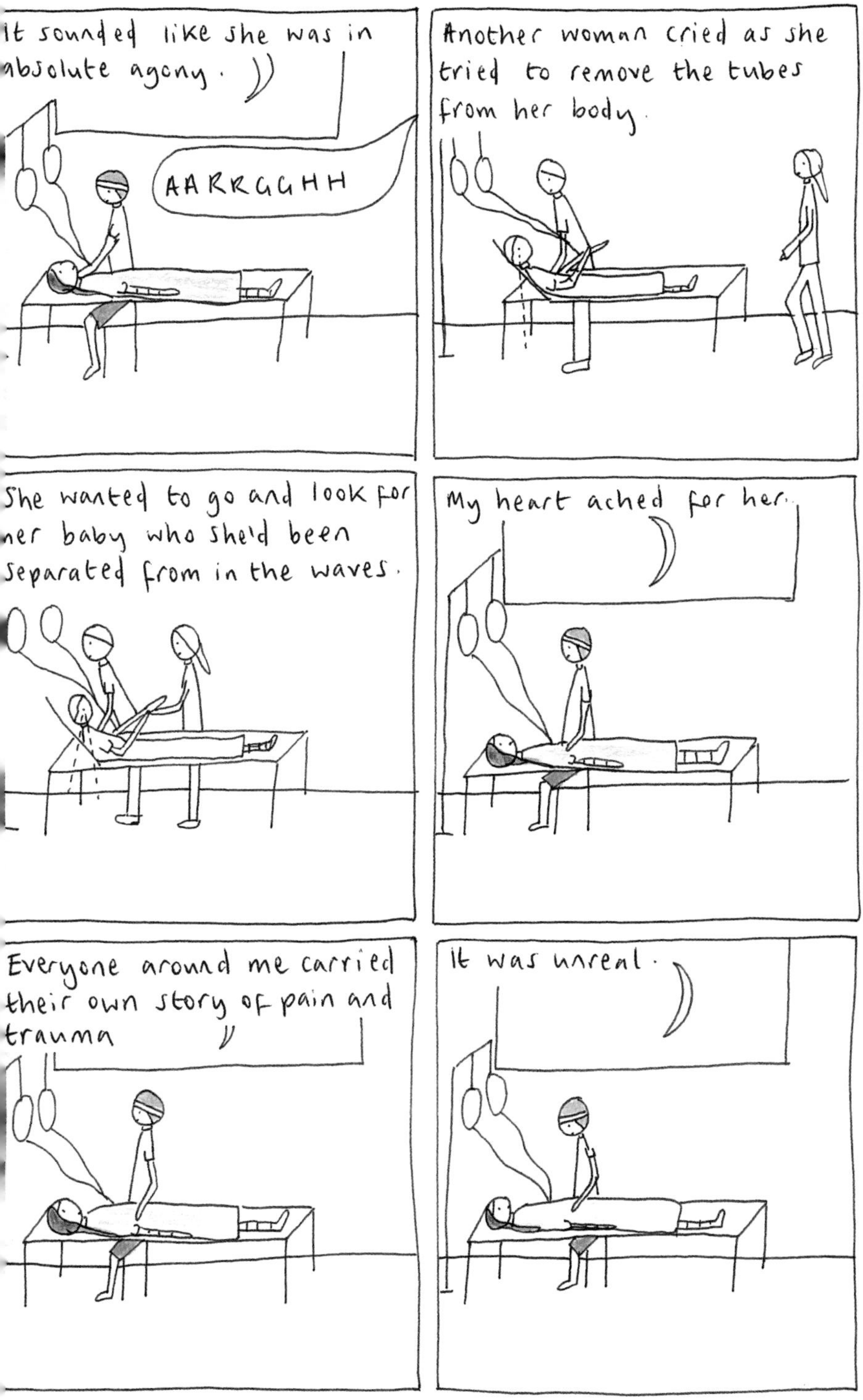

it sounded like she was in absolute agony.
AARRGGHH
Another woman cried as she tried to remove the tubes from her body.
She wanted to go and look for her baby who she'd been separated from in the waves.
My heart ached for her.
Everyone around me carried their own story of pain and trauma
It was unreal.

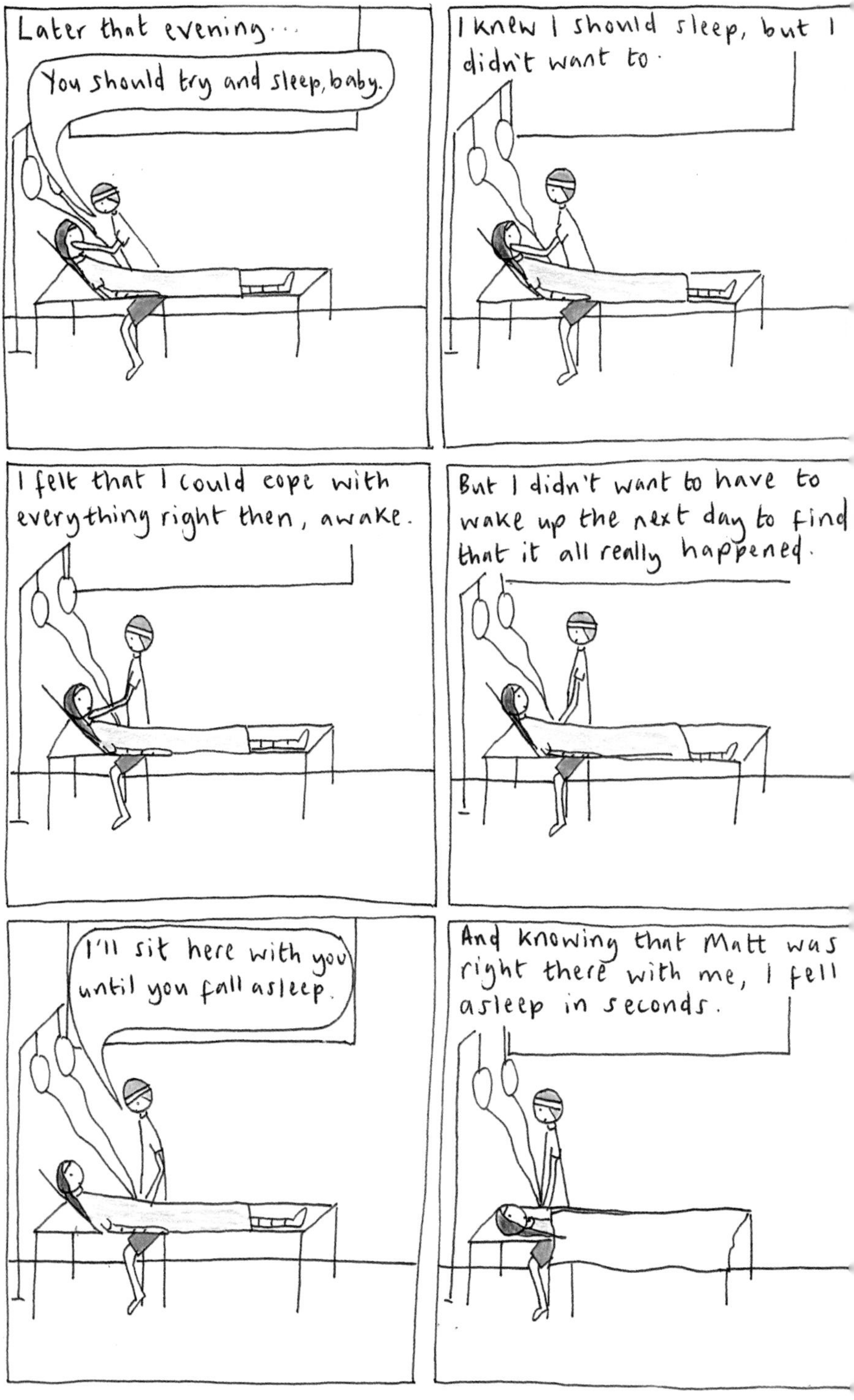

Later that evening...
You should try and sleep, baby.
I knew I should sleep, but I didn't want to.
I felt that I could cope with everything right then, awake.
But I didn't want to have to wake up the next day to find that it all really happened.
I'll sit here with you until you fall asleep.
And knowing that Matt was right there with me, I fell asleep in seconds.

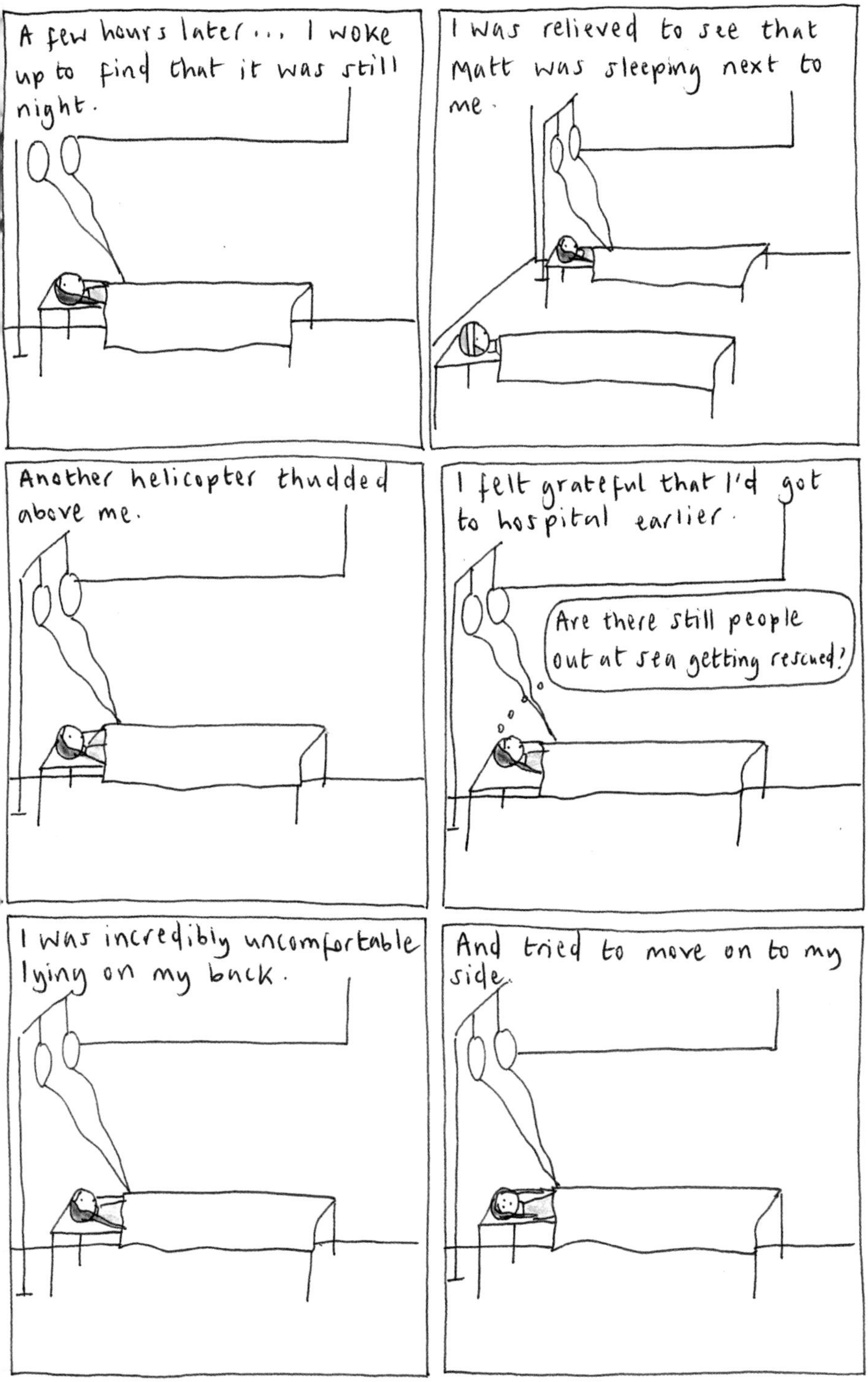
A few hours later... I woke up to find that it was still night.
I was relieved to see that Matt was sleeping next to me.
Another helicopter thudded above me.
I felt grateful that I'd got to hospital earlier.
Are there still people out at sea getting rescued?
I was incredibly uncomfortable lying on my back.
And tried to move on to my side.

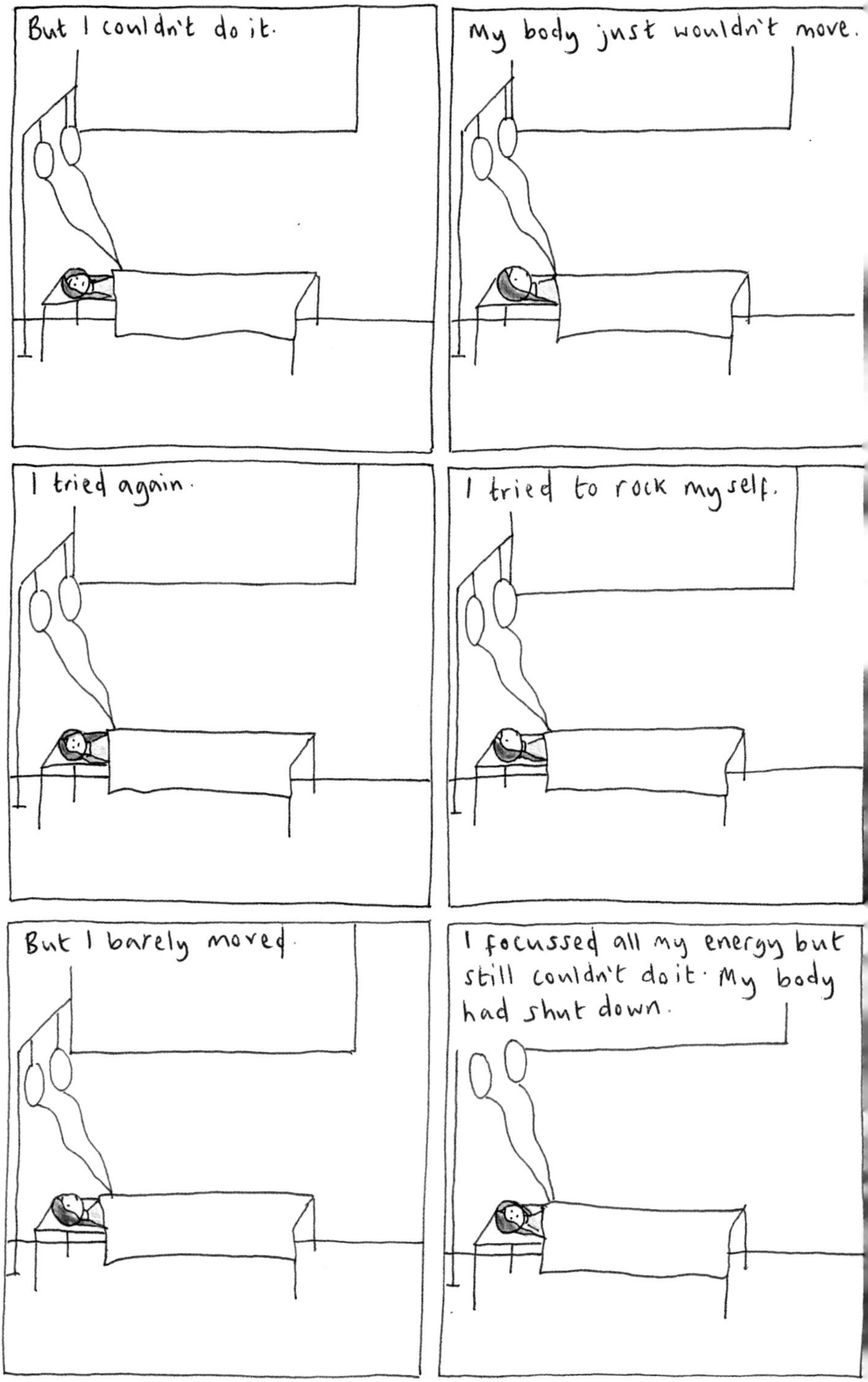

But I couldn't do it.
My body just wouldn't move.
I tried again.
I tried to rock myself.
But I barely moved.
I focussed all my energy but still couldn't do it. My body had shut down.

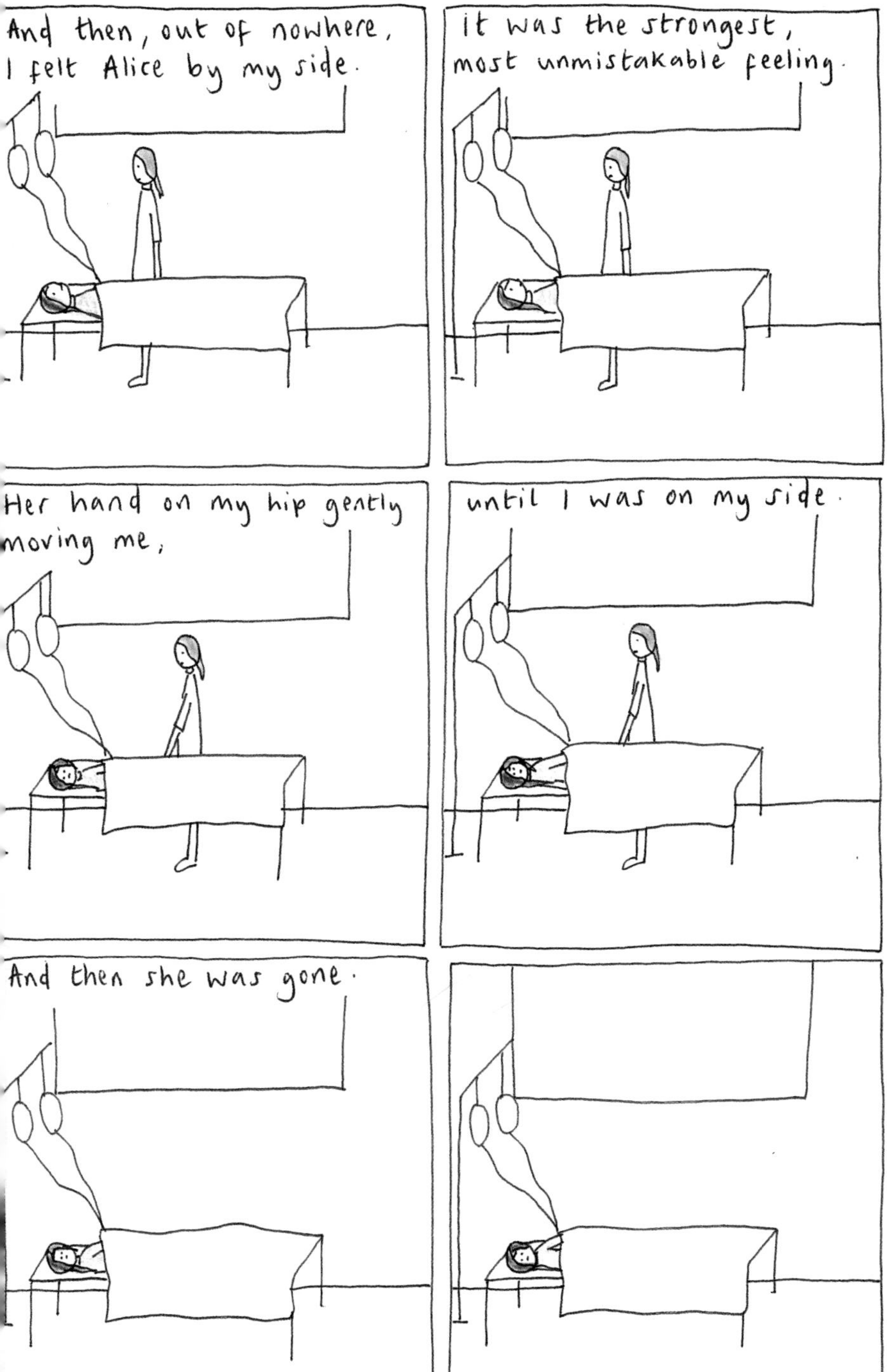
And then, out of nowhere, I felt Alice by my side.
It was the strongest, most unmistakable feeling.
Her hand on my hip gently moving me,
until I was on my side.
And then she was gone.

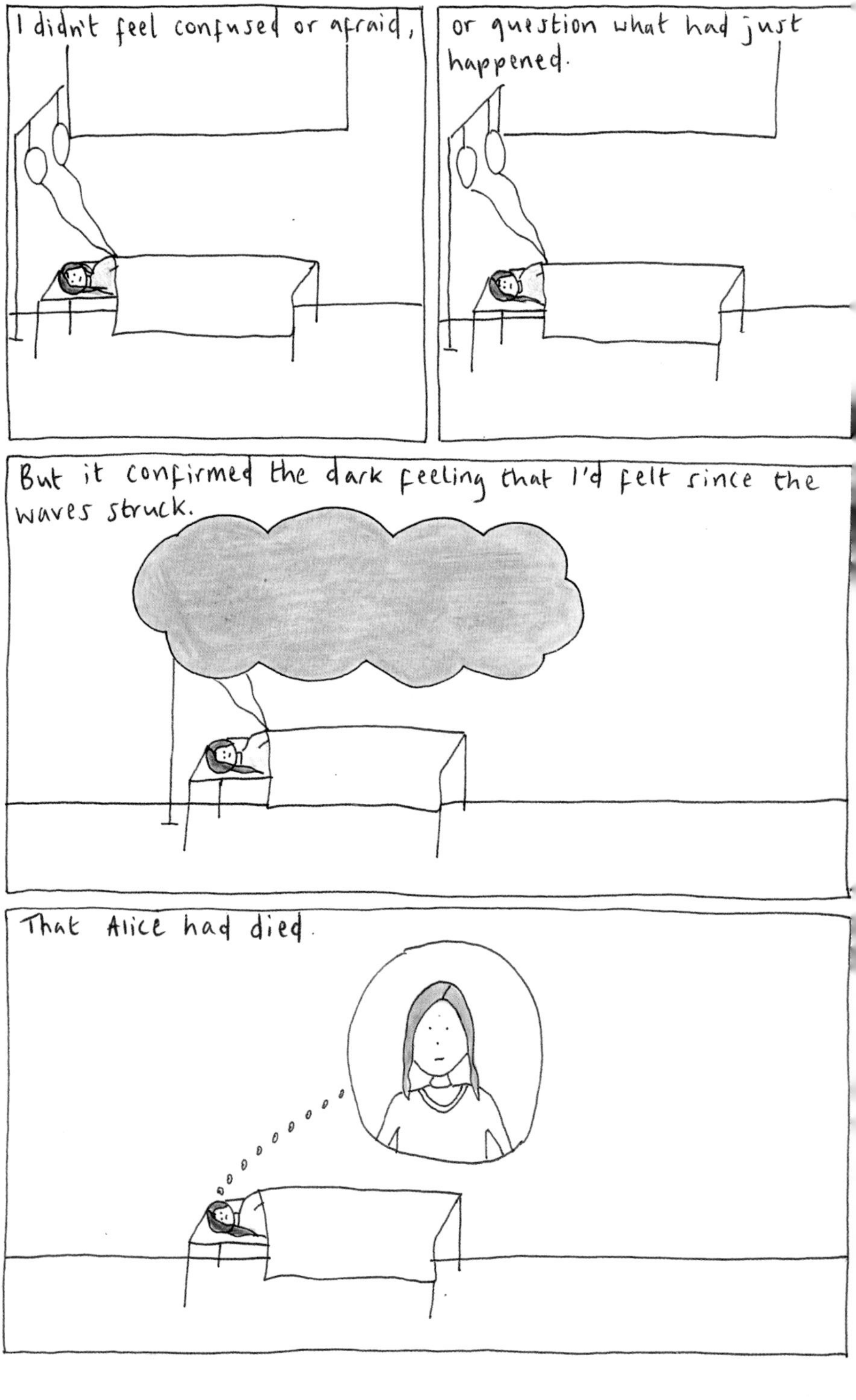
I didn't feel confused or afraid,
or question what had just happened.
But it confirmed the dark feeling that I'd felt since the waves struck.
That Alice had died.

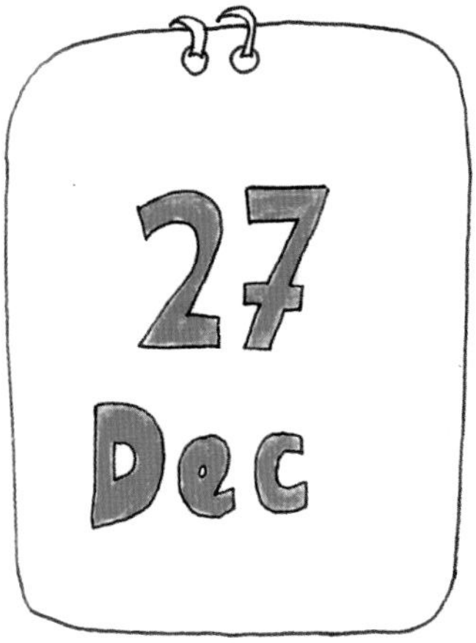
27
Dec

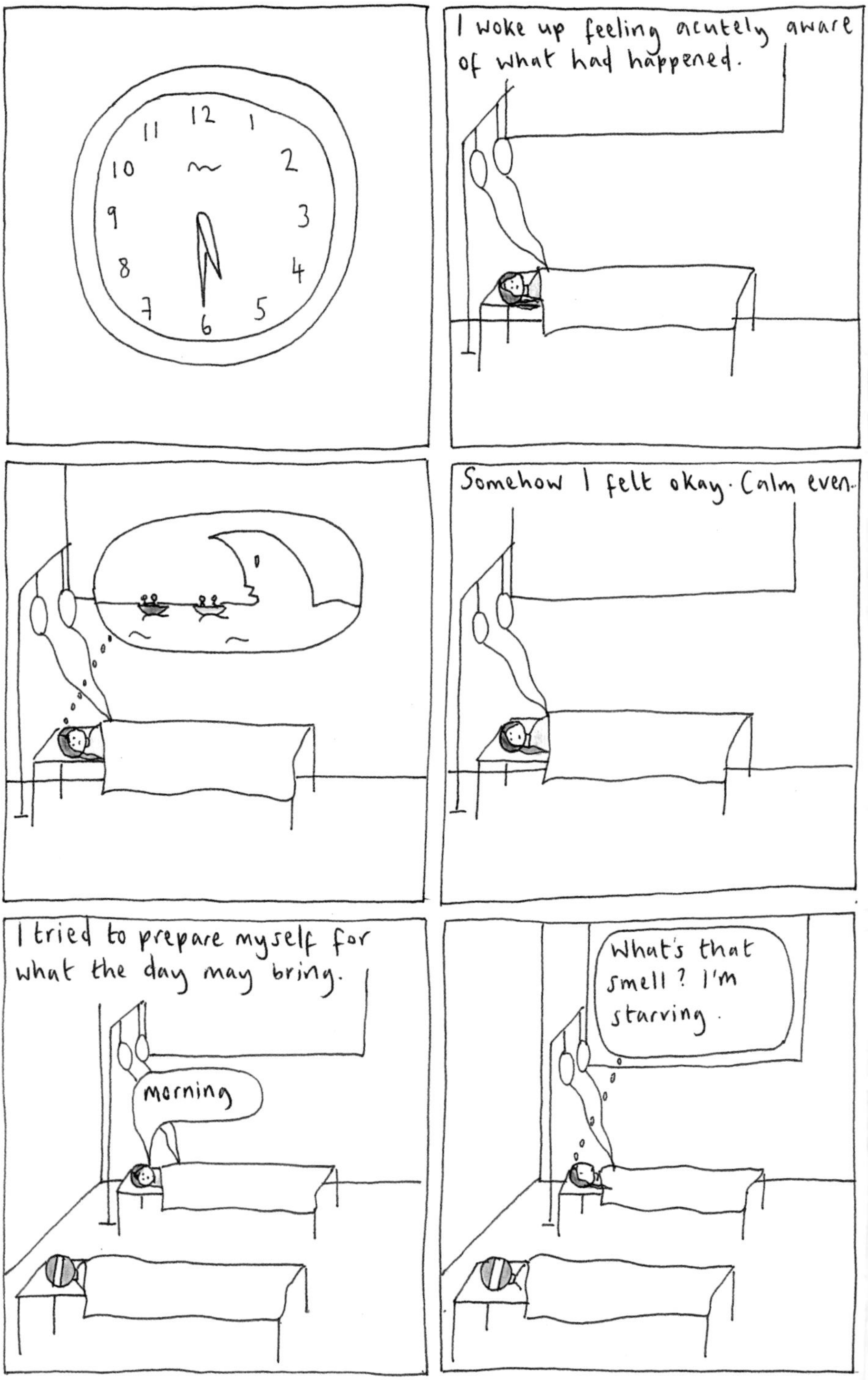
12
1
2
3
4
5
6
7
8
9
10
11
I woke up feeling acutely aware of what had happened.
Somehow I felt okay. Calm even.
I tried to prepare myself for what the day may bring.
morning
What's that smell? I'm starving.

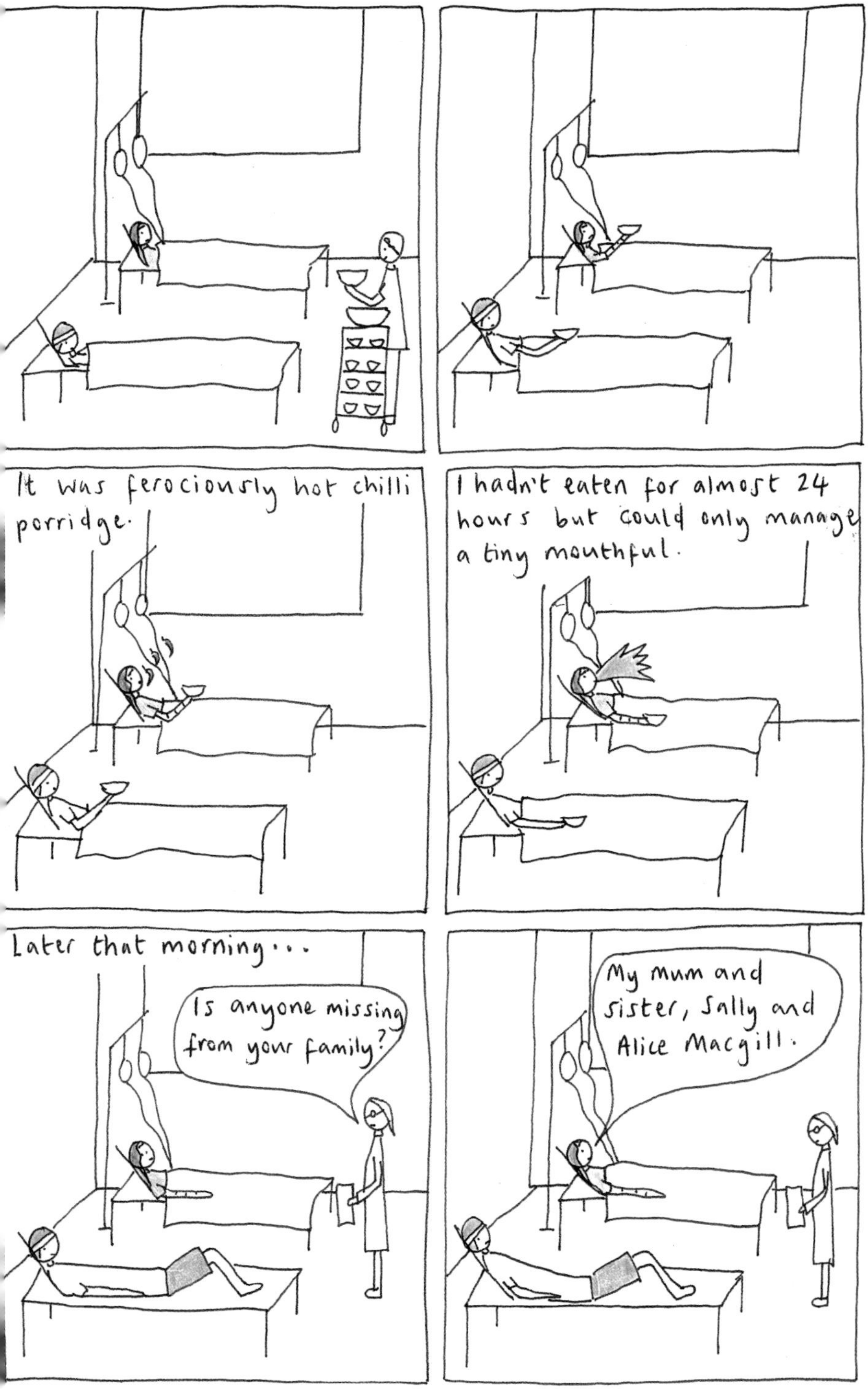

It was ferociously hot chilli porridge.
I hadn't eaten for almost 24 hours but could only manage a tiny mouthful.
Later that morning...
Is anyone missing from your family?
My mum and sister, Sally and Alice Macgill.

Your mother is down here as deceased and your sister is missing

It wasn't exactly news, but still it felt surreal hearing someone else saying it.

I knew that mum had died, but was too numb for it to sink in.

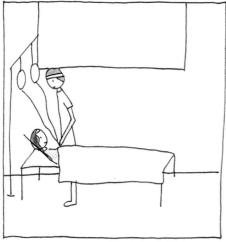

I tried to be open-minded and positive about Alice.

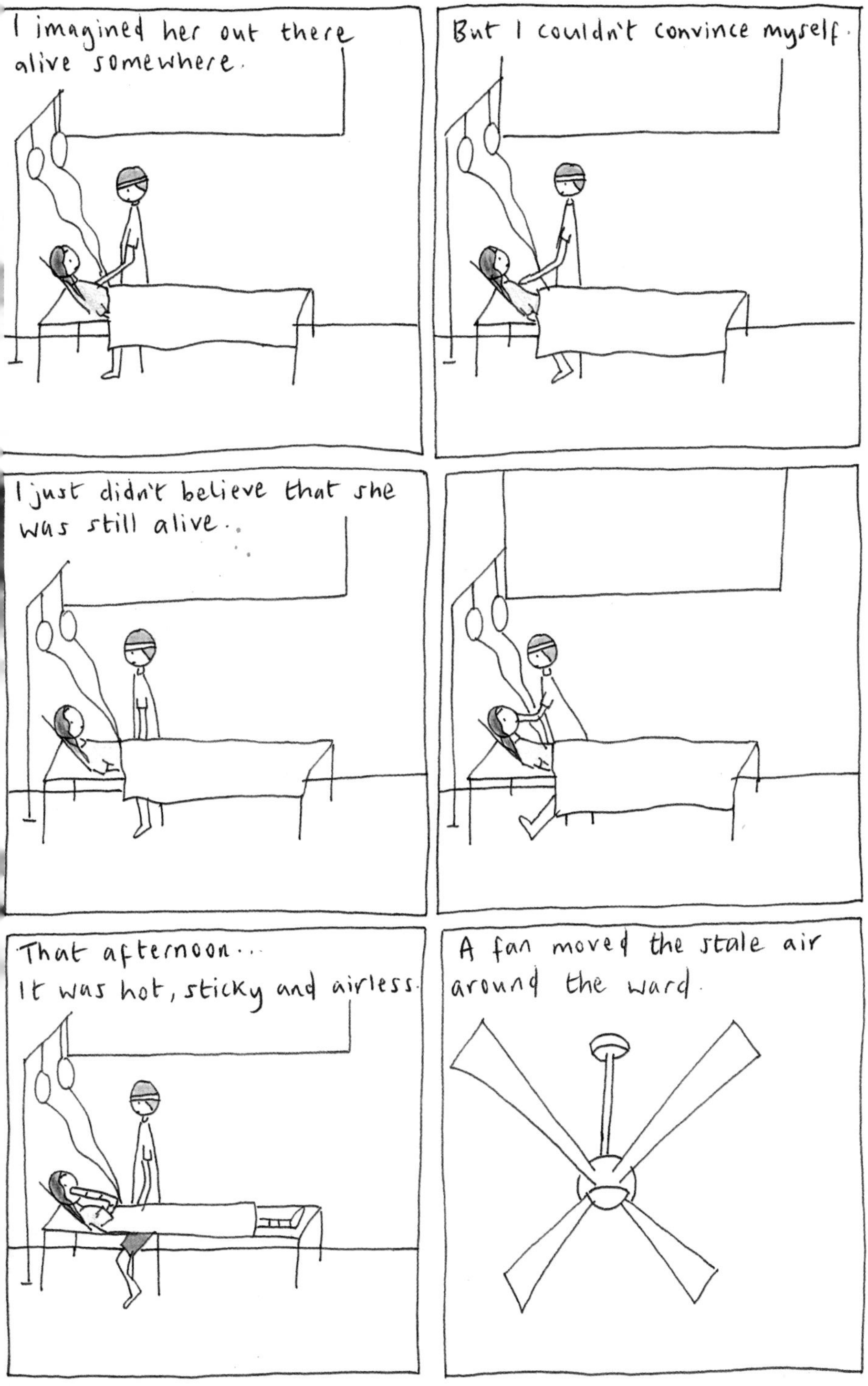
I imagined her out there alive somewhere.
But I couldn't convince myself.
I just didn't believe that she was still alive...
That afternoon...
It was hot, sticky and airless.
A fan moved the stale air around the ward.

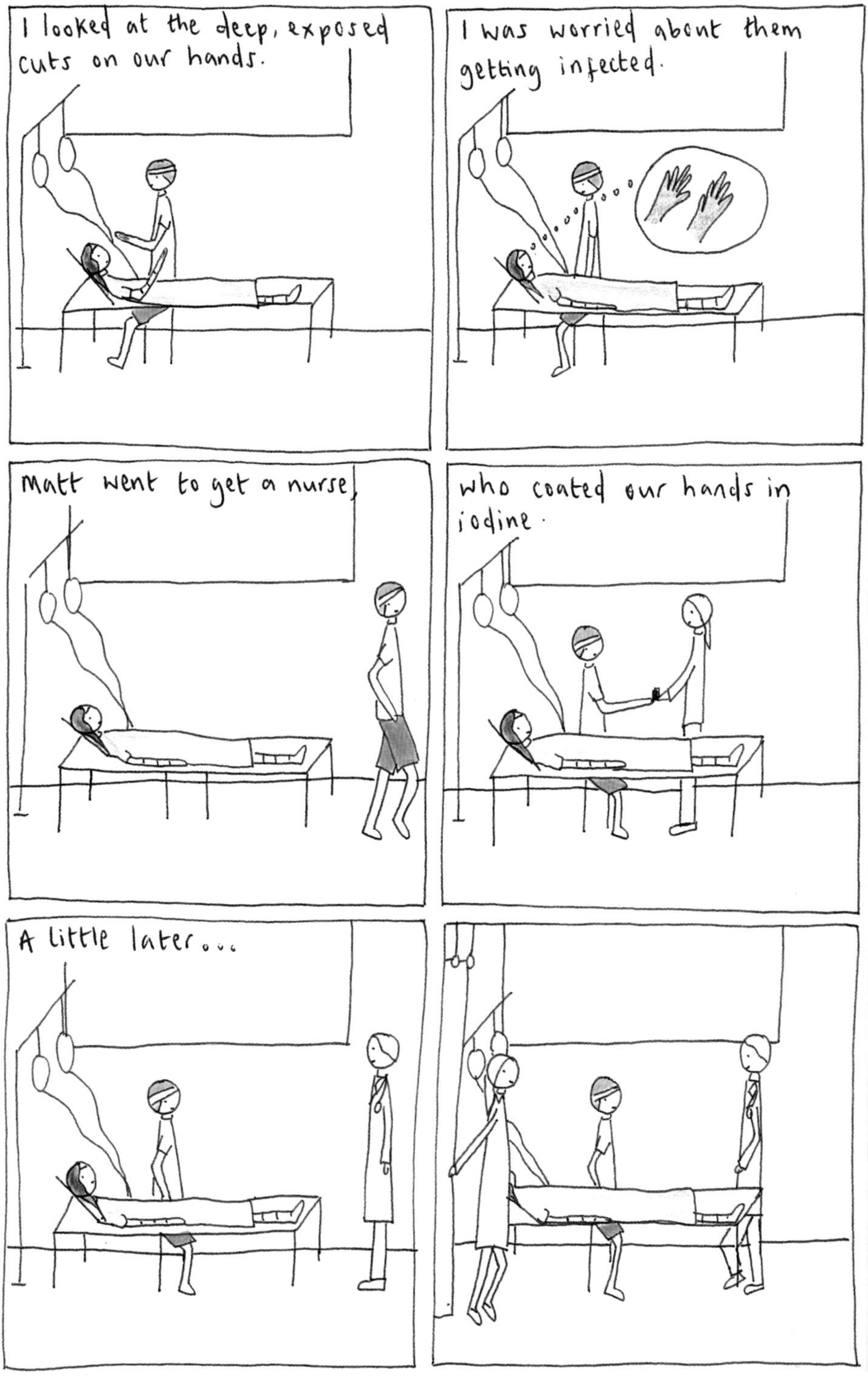

I looked at the deep, exposed cuts on our hands.
I was worried about them getting infected.
Matt went to get a nurse,
who coated our hands in iodine.
A little later...

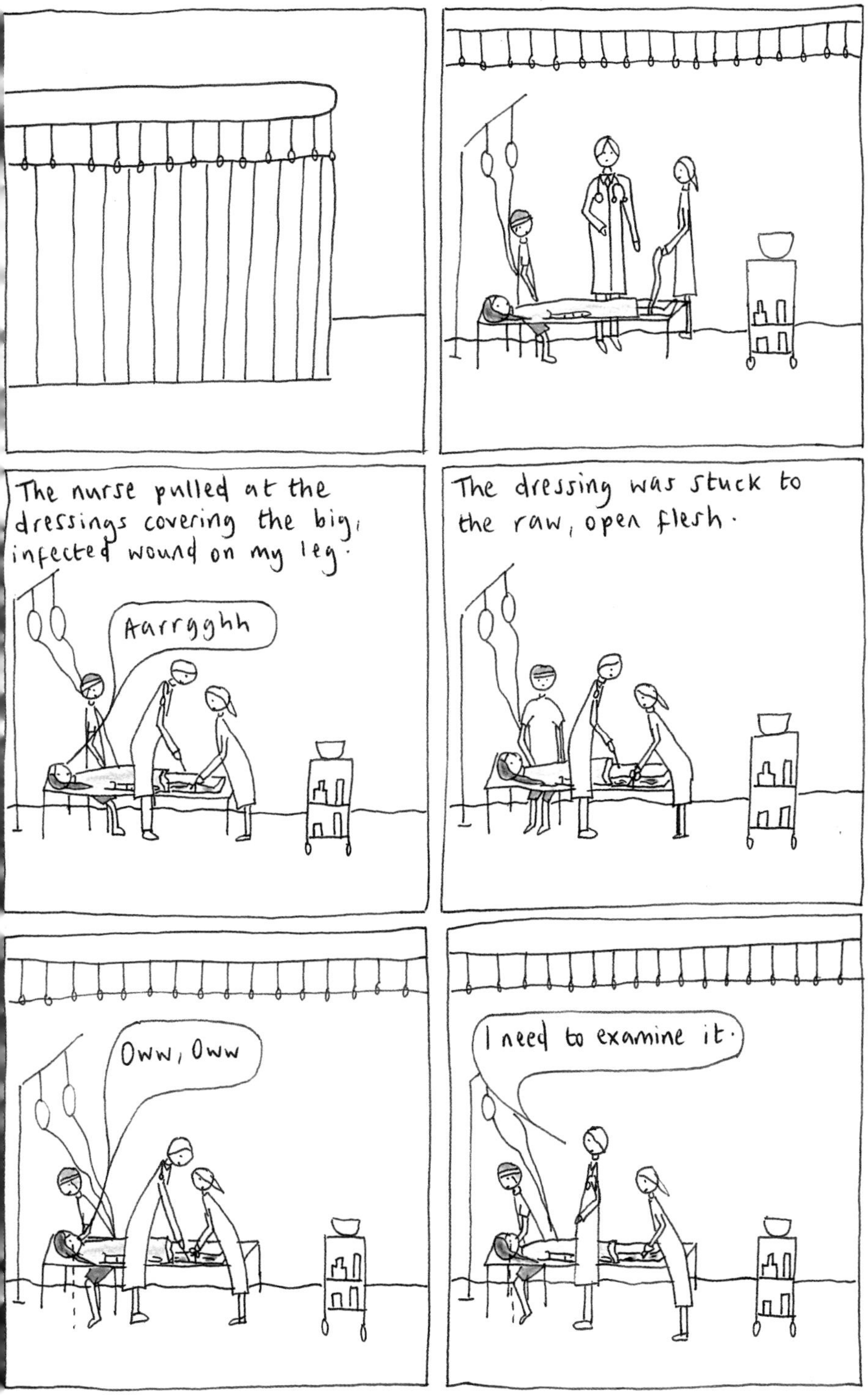

The nurse pulled at the dressings covering the big, infected wound on my leg.
Aarrgghh
The dressing was stuck to the raw, open flesh.
Oww, Oww
I need to examine it.

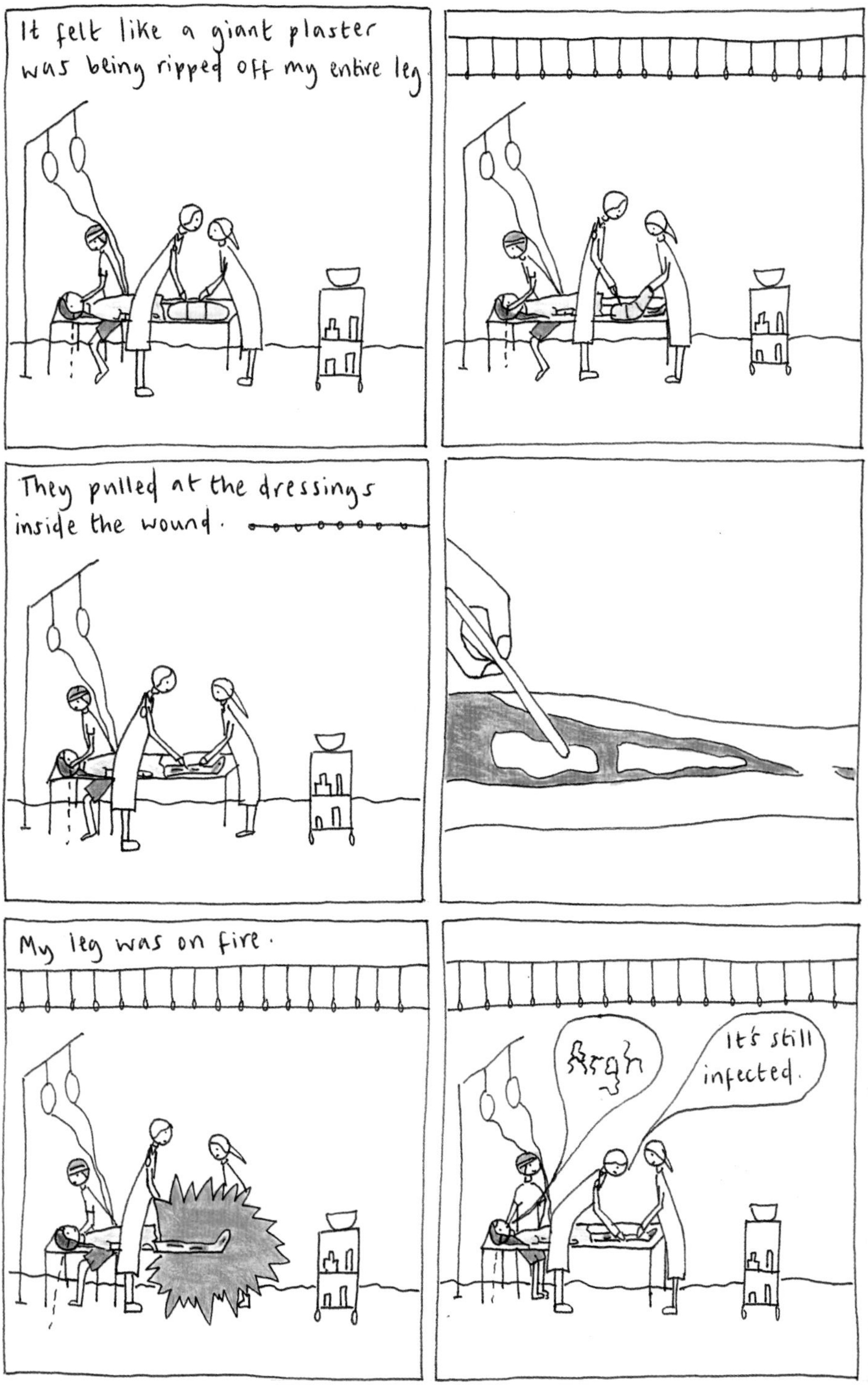
It felt like a giant plaster was being ripped off my entire leg.
They pulled at the dressings inside the wound.
My leg was on fire.
Argh
It's still infected.

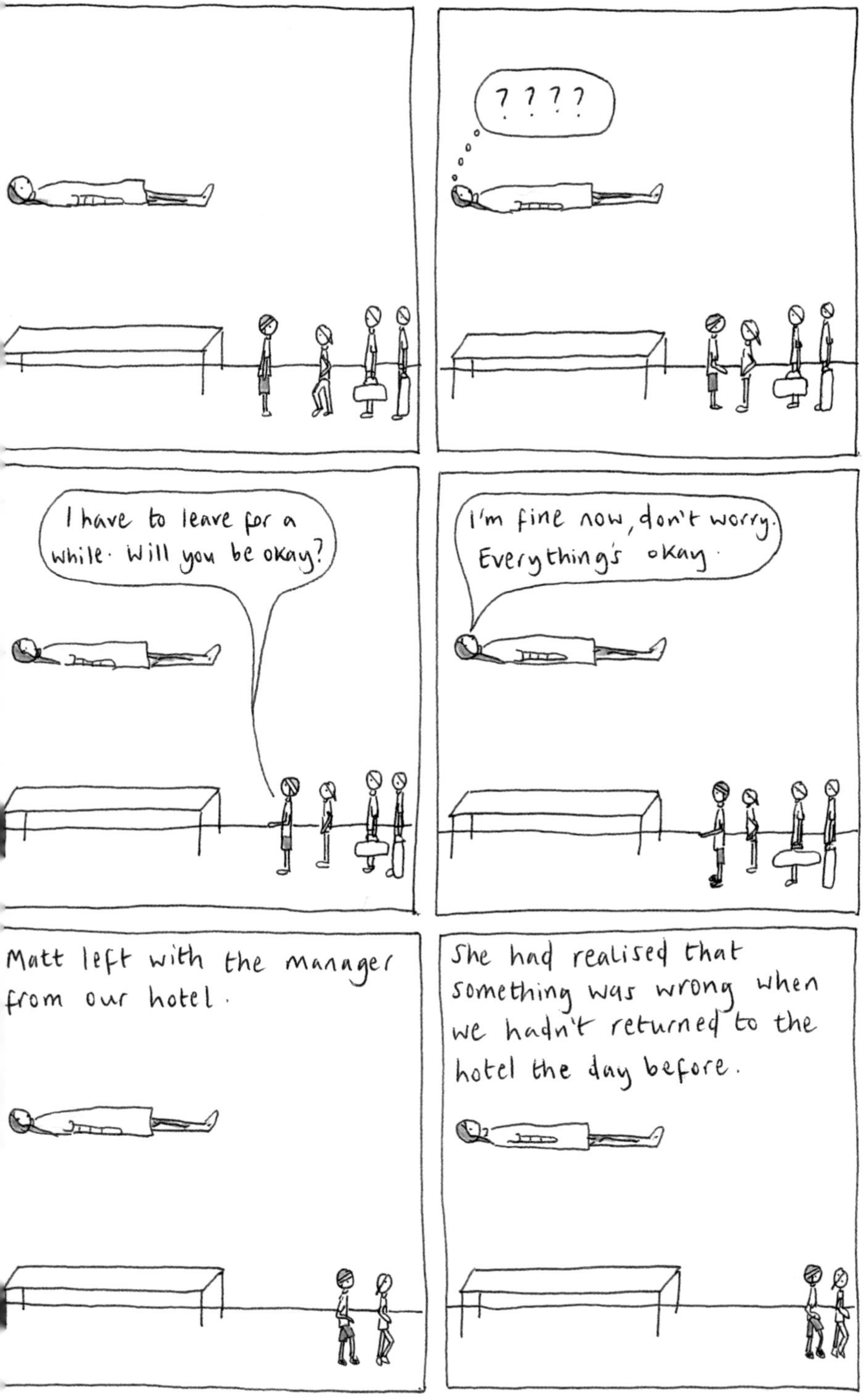
????
I have to leave for a while. Will you be okay?
I'm fine now, don't worry. Everything's okay.
Matt left with the manager from our hotel.
She had realised that something was wrong when we hadn't returned to the hotel the day before.

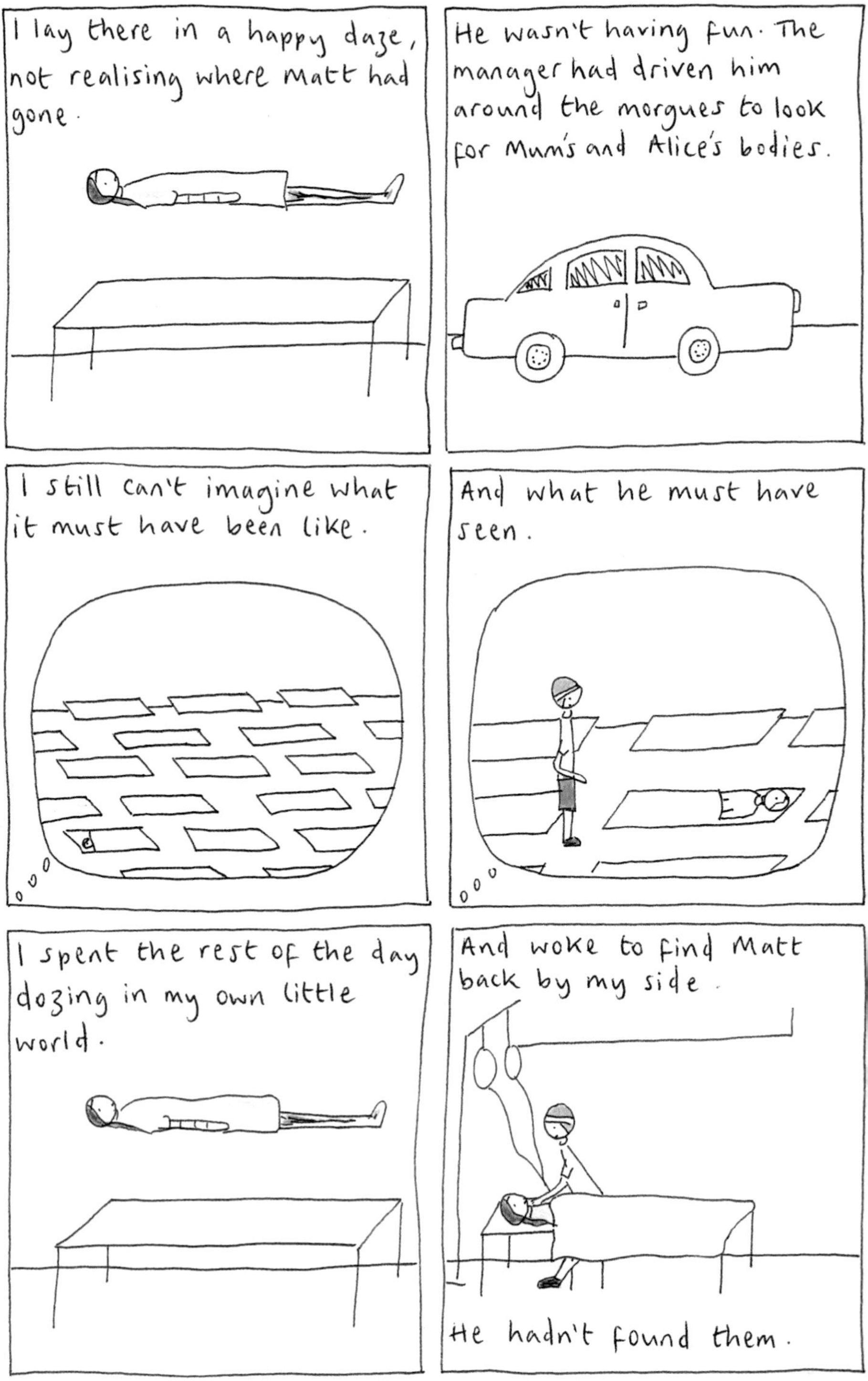
I lay there in a happy daze, not realising where Matt had gone.
He wasn't having fun. The manager had driven him around the morgues to look for Mum's and Alice's bodies.
I still can't imagine what it must have been like.
And what he must have seen.
I spent the rest of the day dozing in my own little world.
And woke to find Matt back by my side.
He hadn't found them.

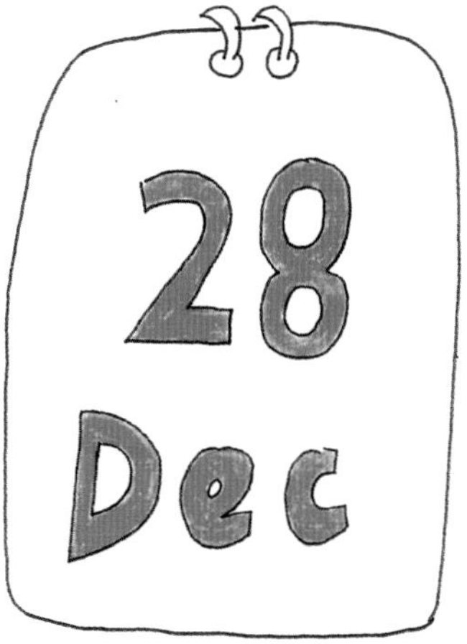
28
Dec

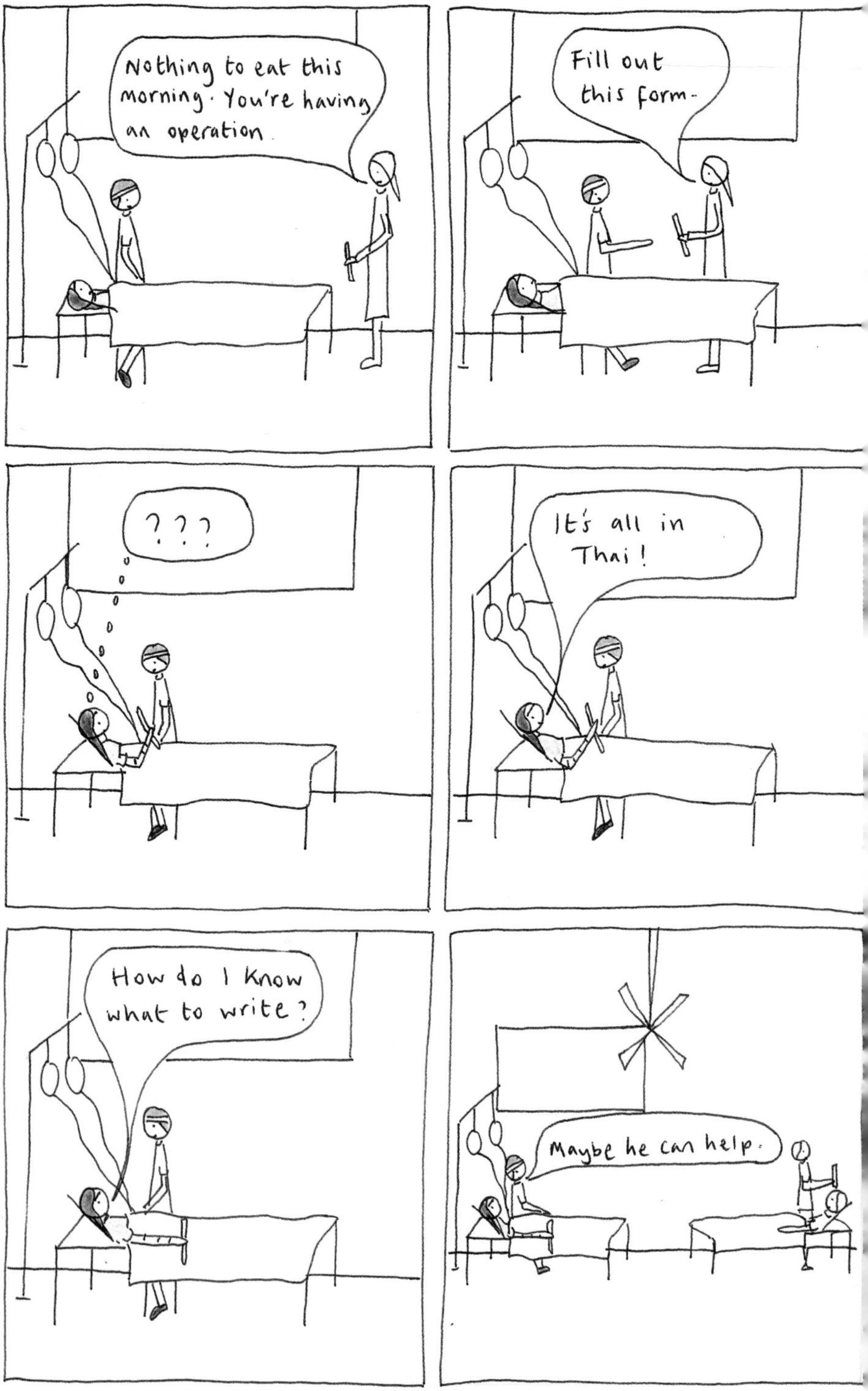
Nothing to eat this morning. You're having an operation.
Fill out this form.
???
It's all in Thai!
How do I know what to write?
Maybe he can help.

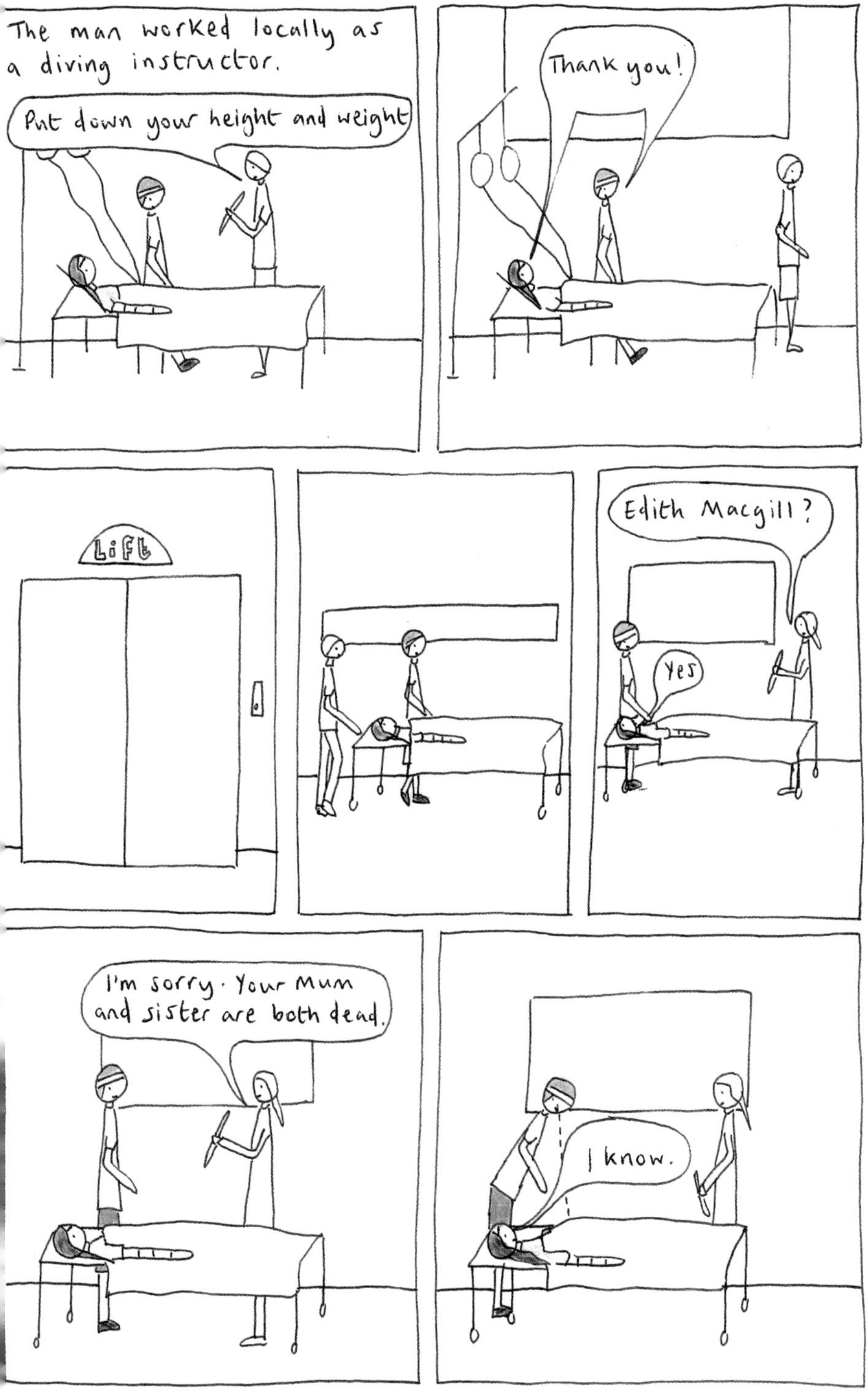
The man worked locally as a diving instructor.
Put down your height and weight
Thank you!
Lift
Edith Macgill?
Yes
I'm sorry. Your Mum and sister are both dead.
I know.

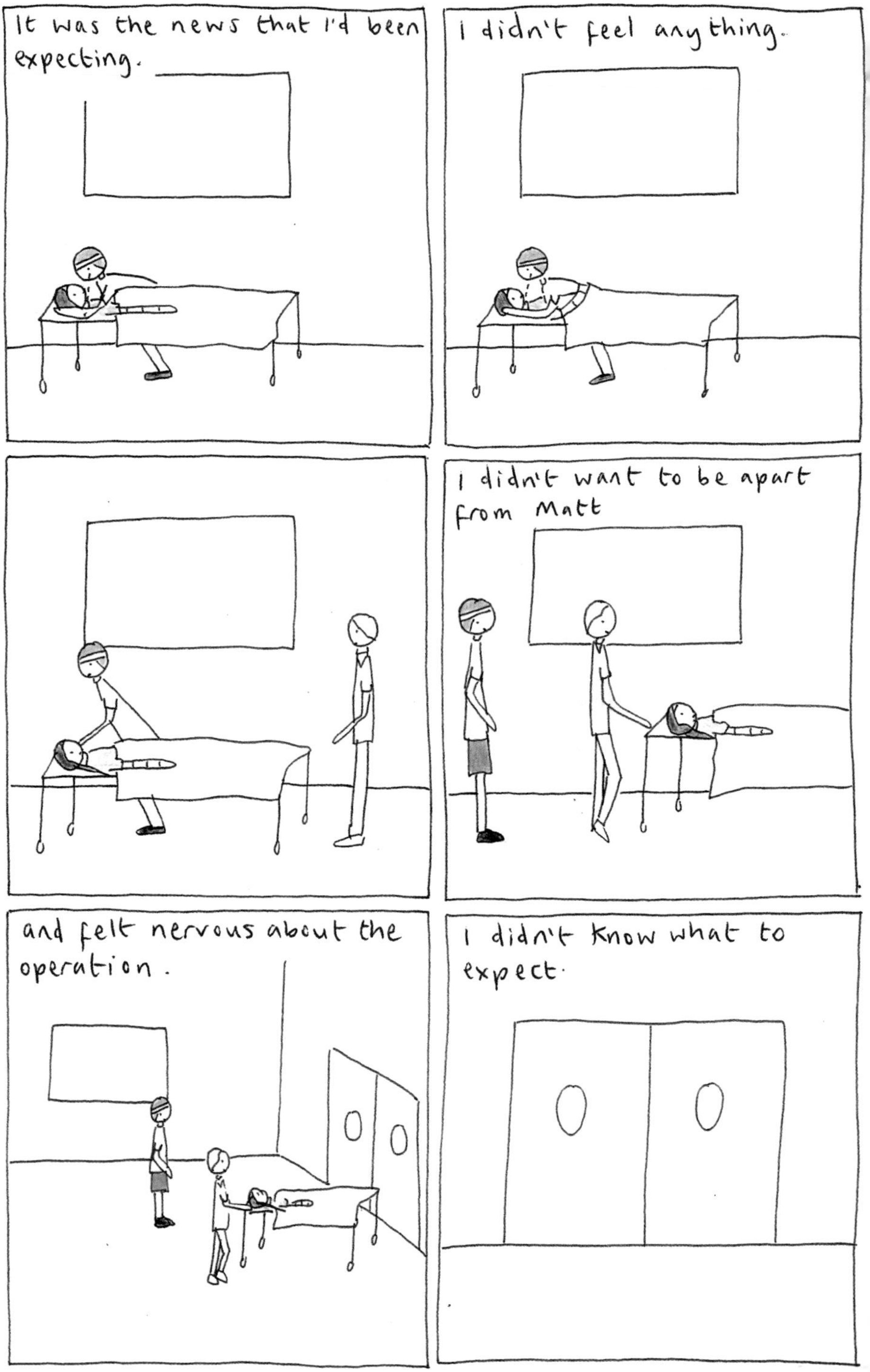
It was the news that I'd been expecting.
I didn't feel anything.
I didn't want to be apart from Matt
and felt nervous about the operation.
I didn't know what to expect.

They gave me a spinal anaesthetic to numb my lower body.

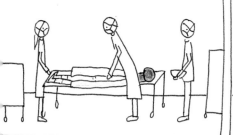

It felt really strange.

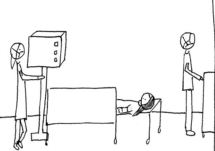

They hooked me up to a cardiac monitor

and began a debriding operation to remove the infected tissue.

I hated the feeling of being awake while they worked away.

I felt out of control and started to panic.

Panic

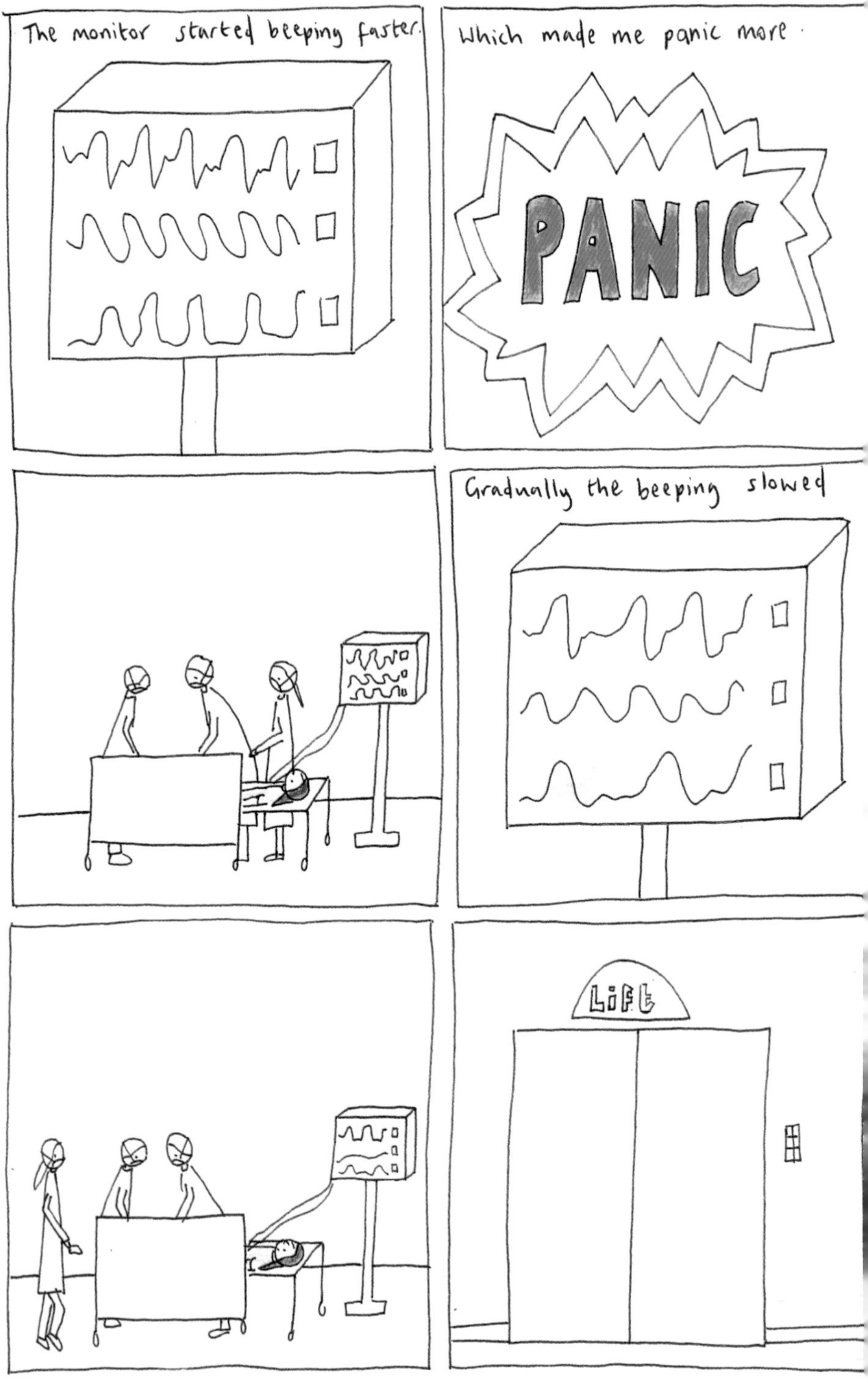
The monitor started beeping faster.
Which made me panic more.
PANIC
Gradually the beeping slowed
LiFt

Back on the ward....

Sandwiches!

Thank you

It was the first proper food that I'd eaten in days.

I hadn't realised how hungry I was.

Mmmmm

We found out that the couple owned a shop and had made piles of sandwiches to give out.

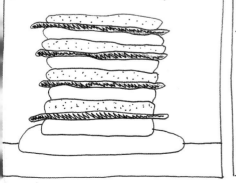

The hospital was usually used by local people and didn't have the capacity to cater for everyone.

In the afternoon Linny, a friend of Alice's came to visit with a friend.

I felt a confused mix of emotions.

Alice was the link between us, but Alice didn't exist any more.

I just didn't get it.

I felt like I was in a film, with no control of anything that was happening to me.

Production:

Scene	Take	Roll

Date: 28 · 12 · 04

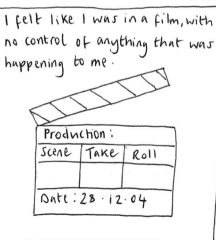

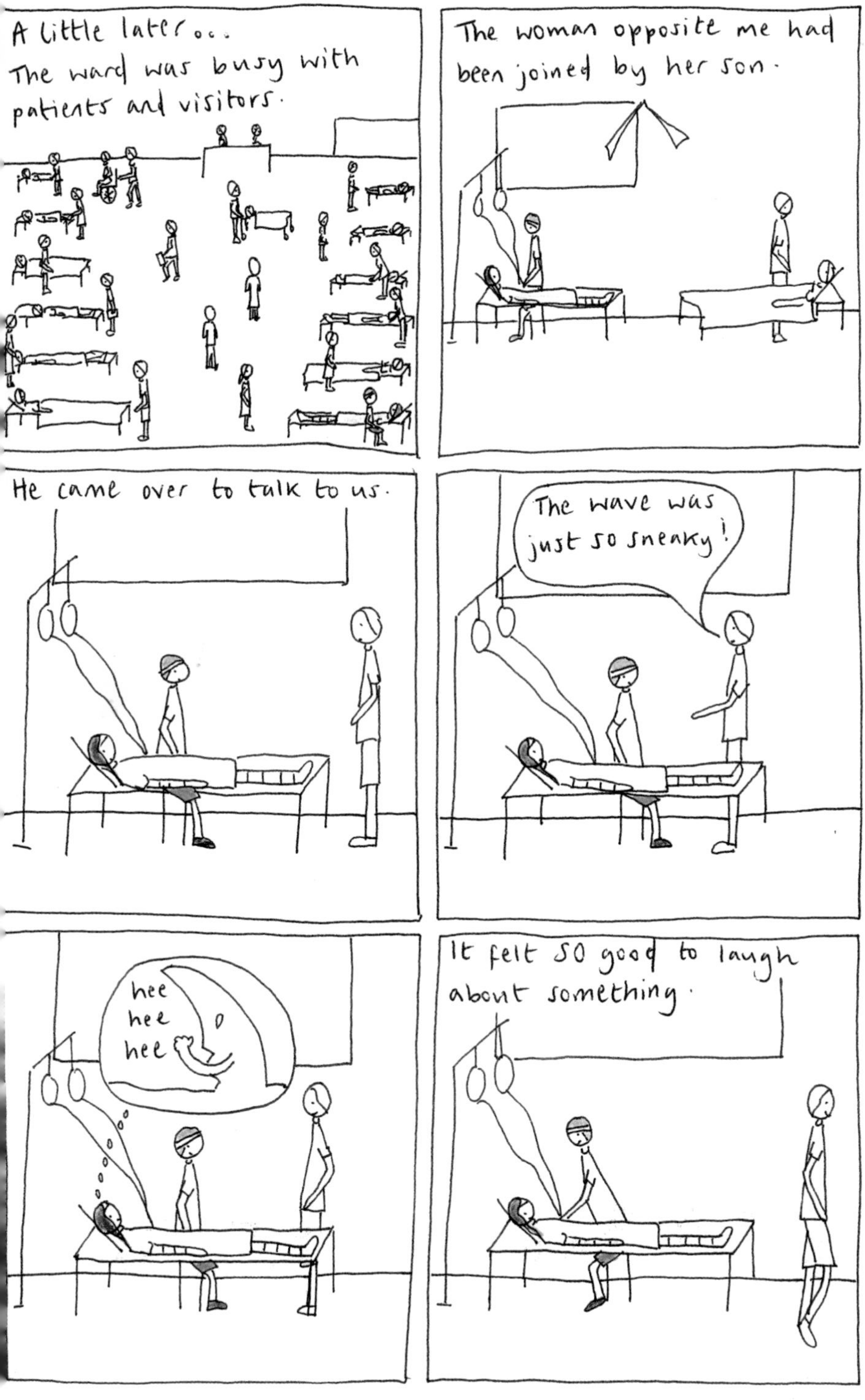
A little later...
The ward was busy with patients and visitors.
The woman opposite me had been joined by her son.
He came over to talk to us.
The wave was just so sneaky!
hee hee hee
It felt SO good to laugh about something.

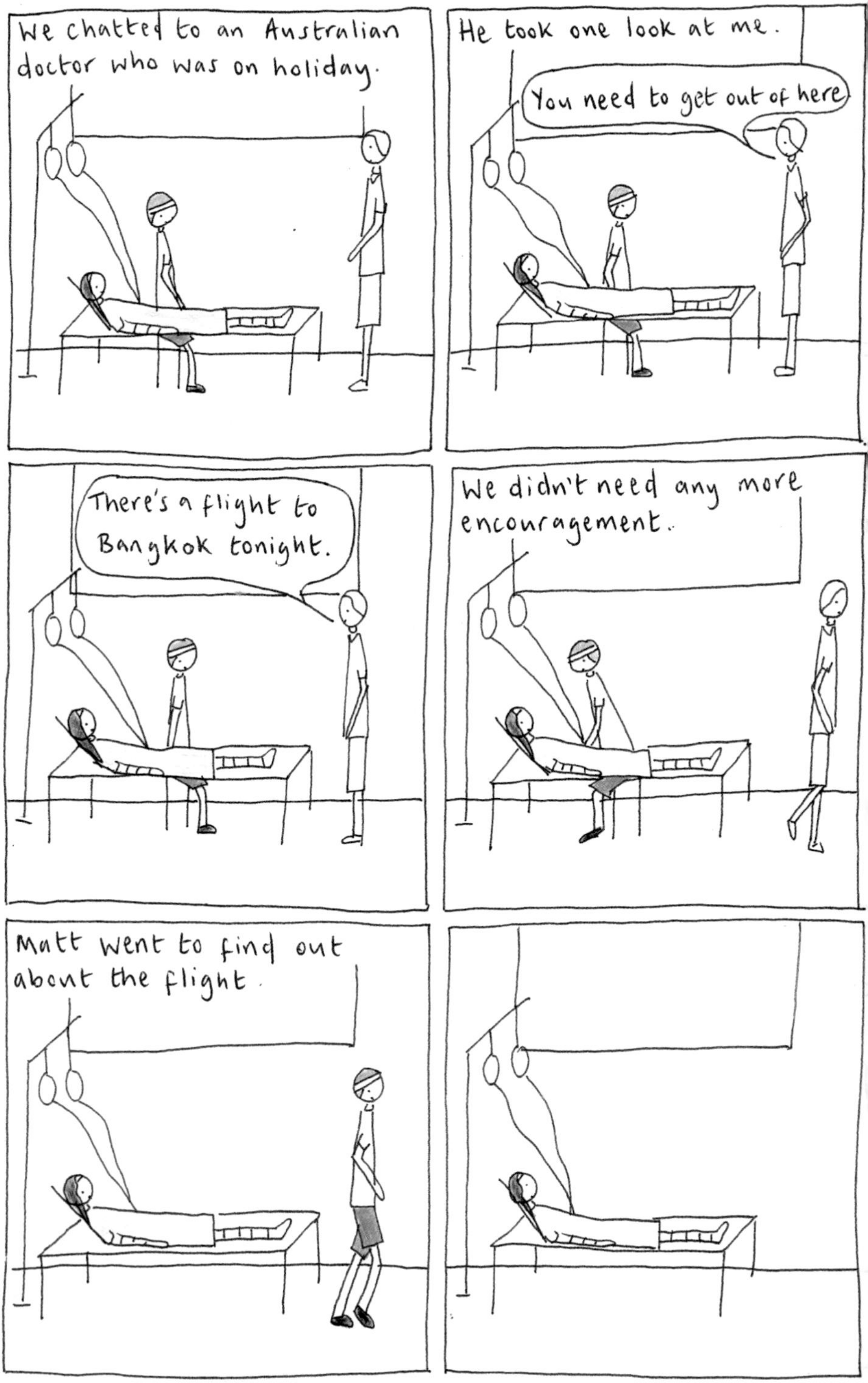
We chatted to an Australian doctor who was on holiday.
He took one look at me.
You need to get out of here
There's a flight to Bangkok tonight.
We didn't need any more encouragement.
Matt went to find out about the flight.

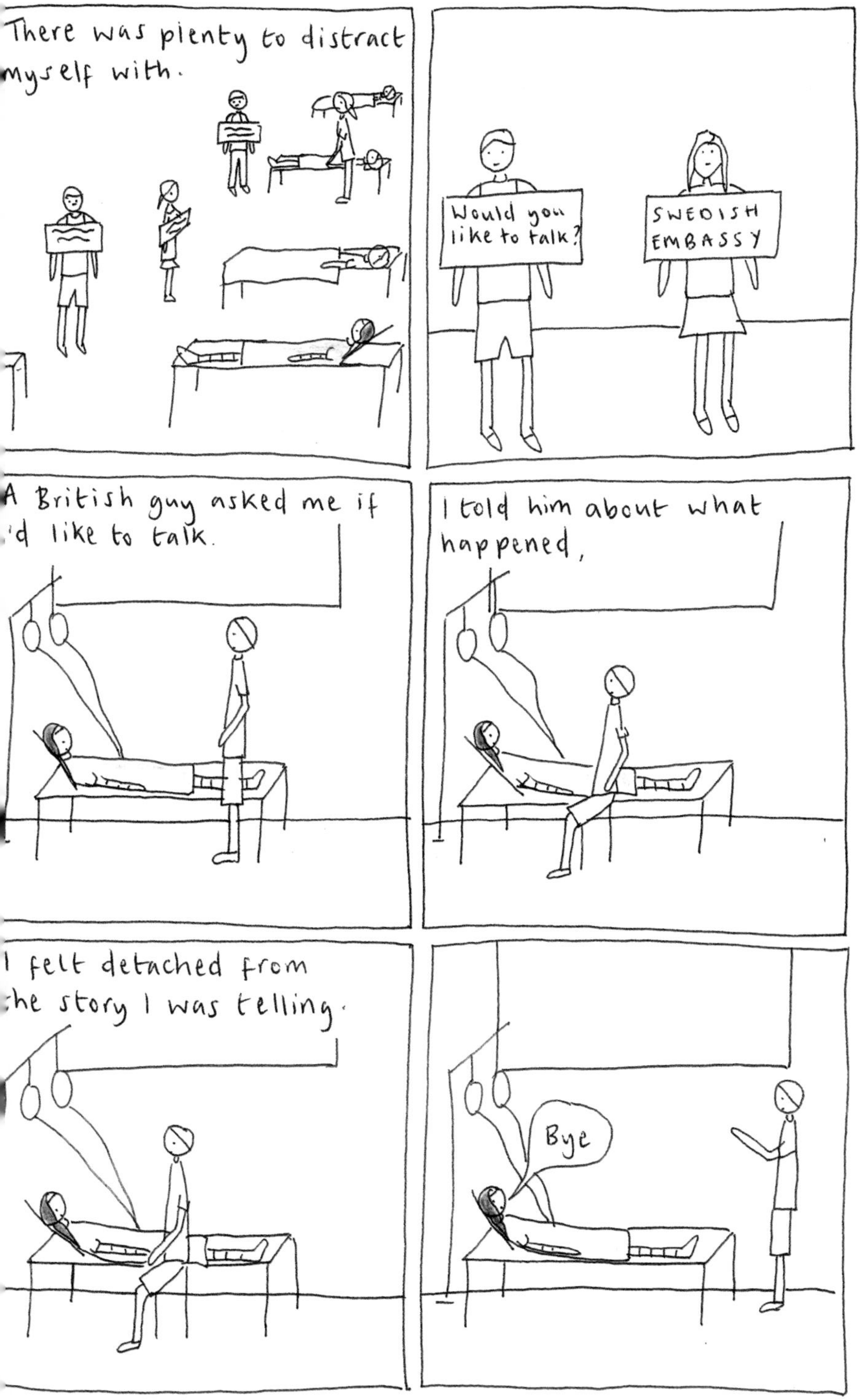
There was plenty to distract
myself with.
Would you like to talk?
SWEDISH EMBASSY
A British guy asked me if
'd like to talk.
I told him about what
happened,
I felt detached from
he story I was telling.
Bye

Matt had found someone from the British Consulate who sorted seats for us.

We're on the flight!

Confusingly he'd also been told that Alice was actually 'missing presumed dead'.

The news did nothing to raise my hopes.

You were down as dead...

Huh?

Matt spoke to the hospital staff and our insurance company.

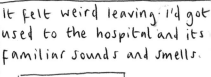

And then it was time to go.

It felt weird leaving. I'd got used to the hospital and its familiar sounds and smells.

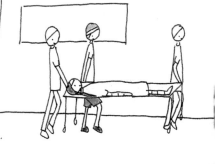

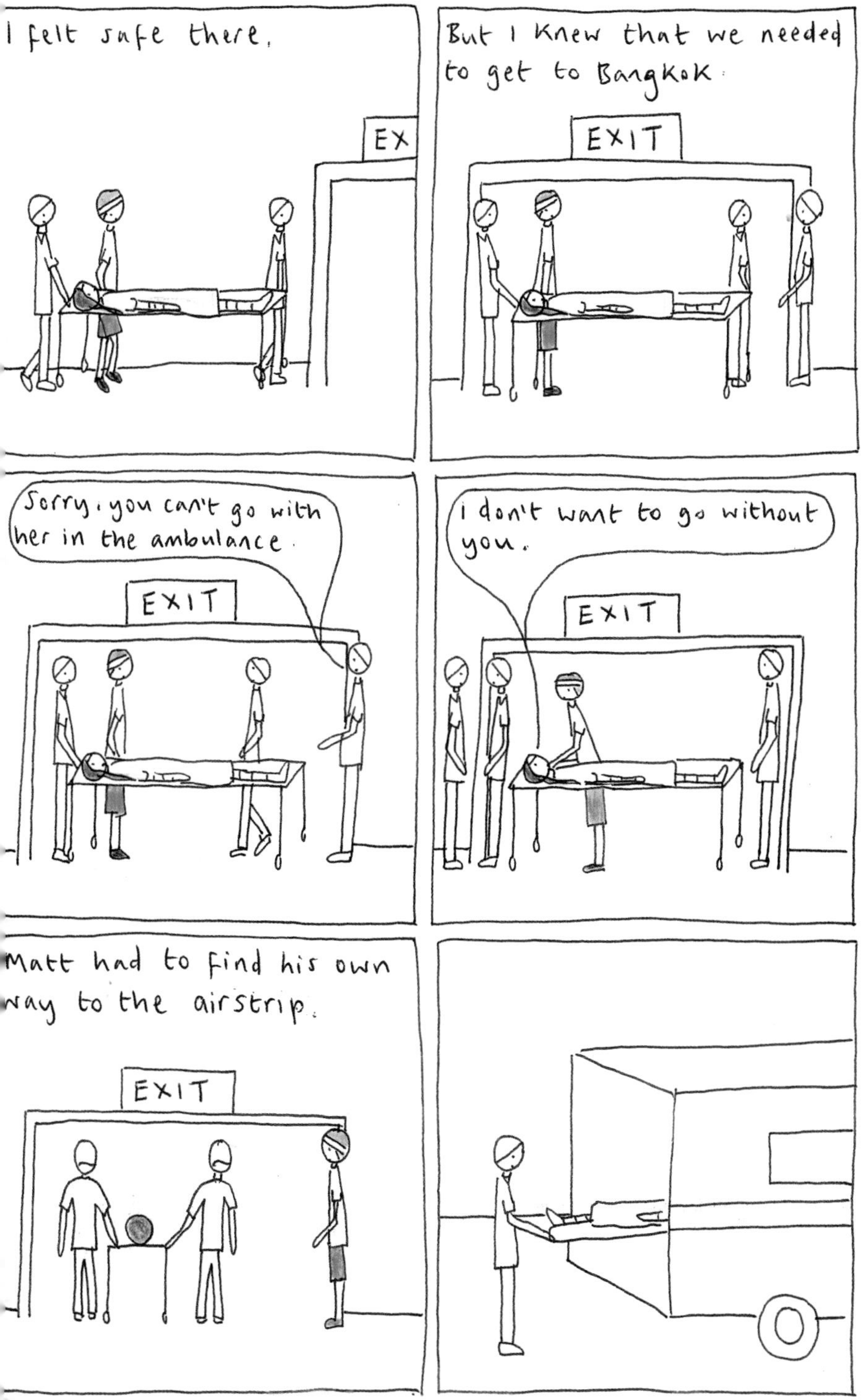
I felt safe there.
EX
But I knew that we needed to get to Bangkok.
EXIT
Sorry, you can't go with her in the ambulance.
EXIT
I don't want to go without you.
EXIT
Matt had to find his own way to the airstrip.
EXIT

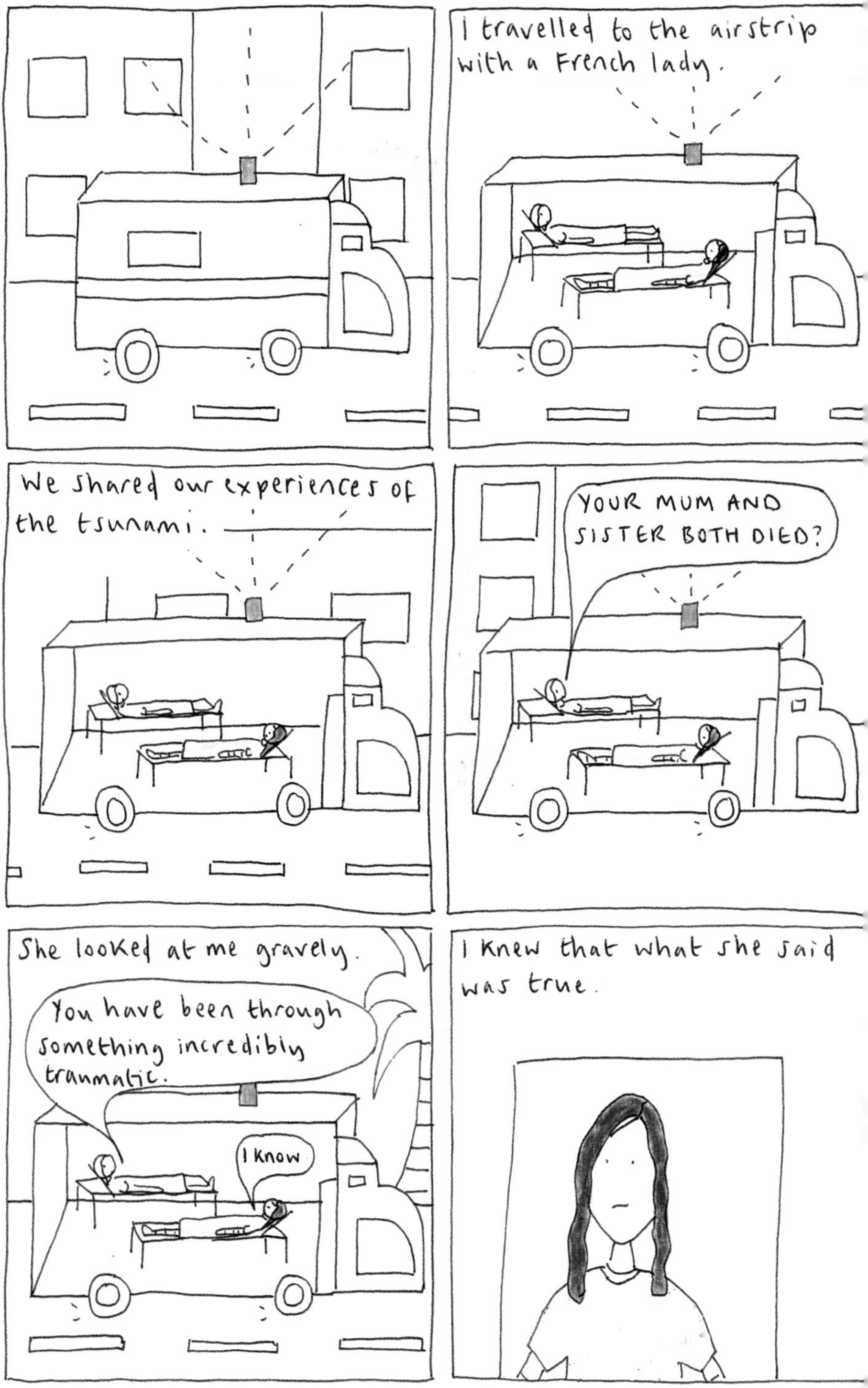

I travelled to the airstrip with a French lady.
We shared our experiences of the tsunami.
YOUR MUM AND SISTER BOTH DIED?
She looked at me gravely.
You have been through something incredibly traumatic.
I know
I knew that what she said was true.

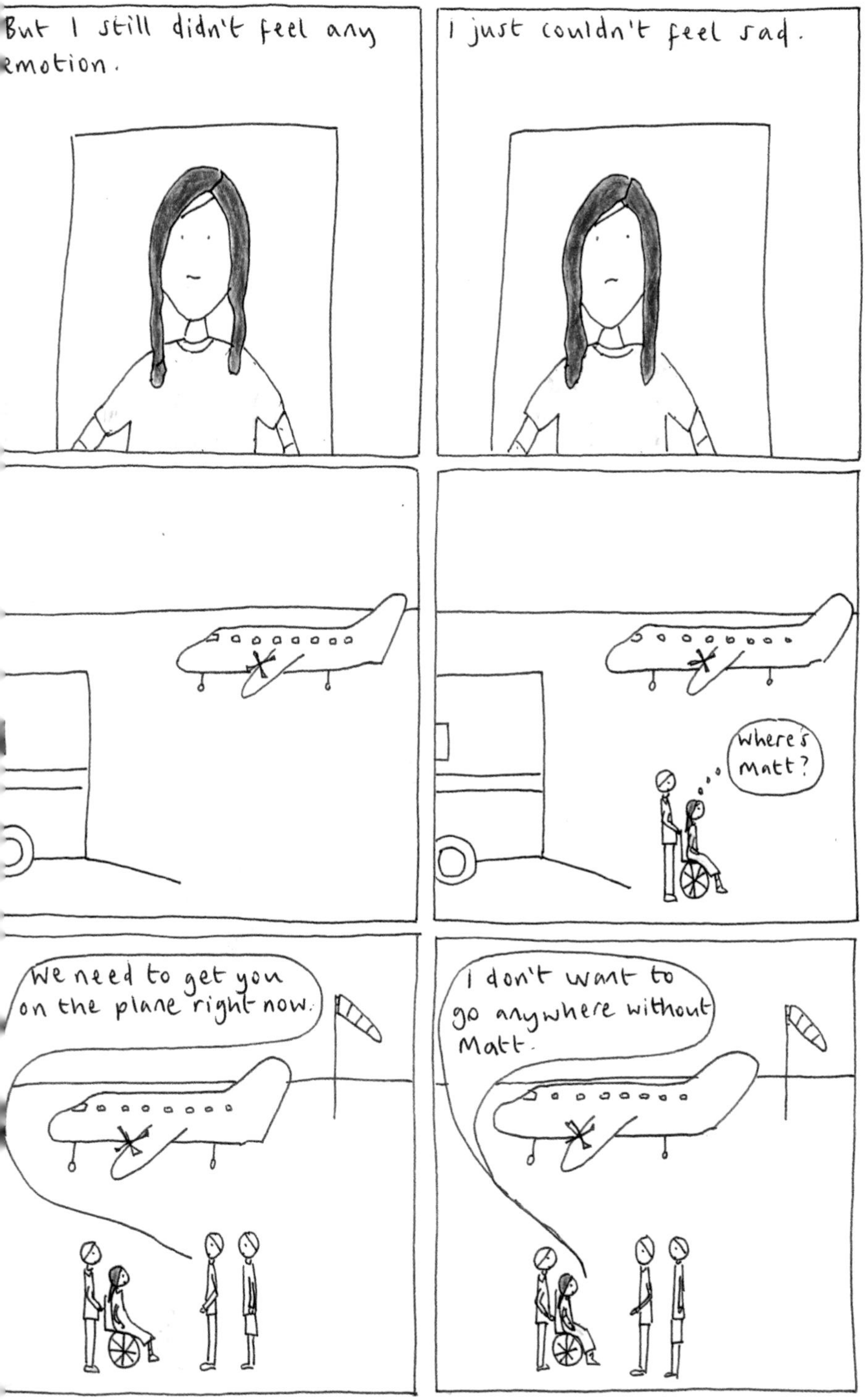
But I still didn't feel any emotion.
I just couldn't feel sad.
Where's Matt?
We need to get you on the plane right now.
I don't want to go anywhere without Matt.

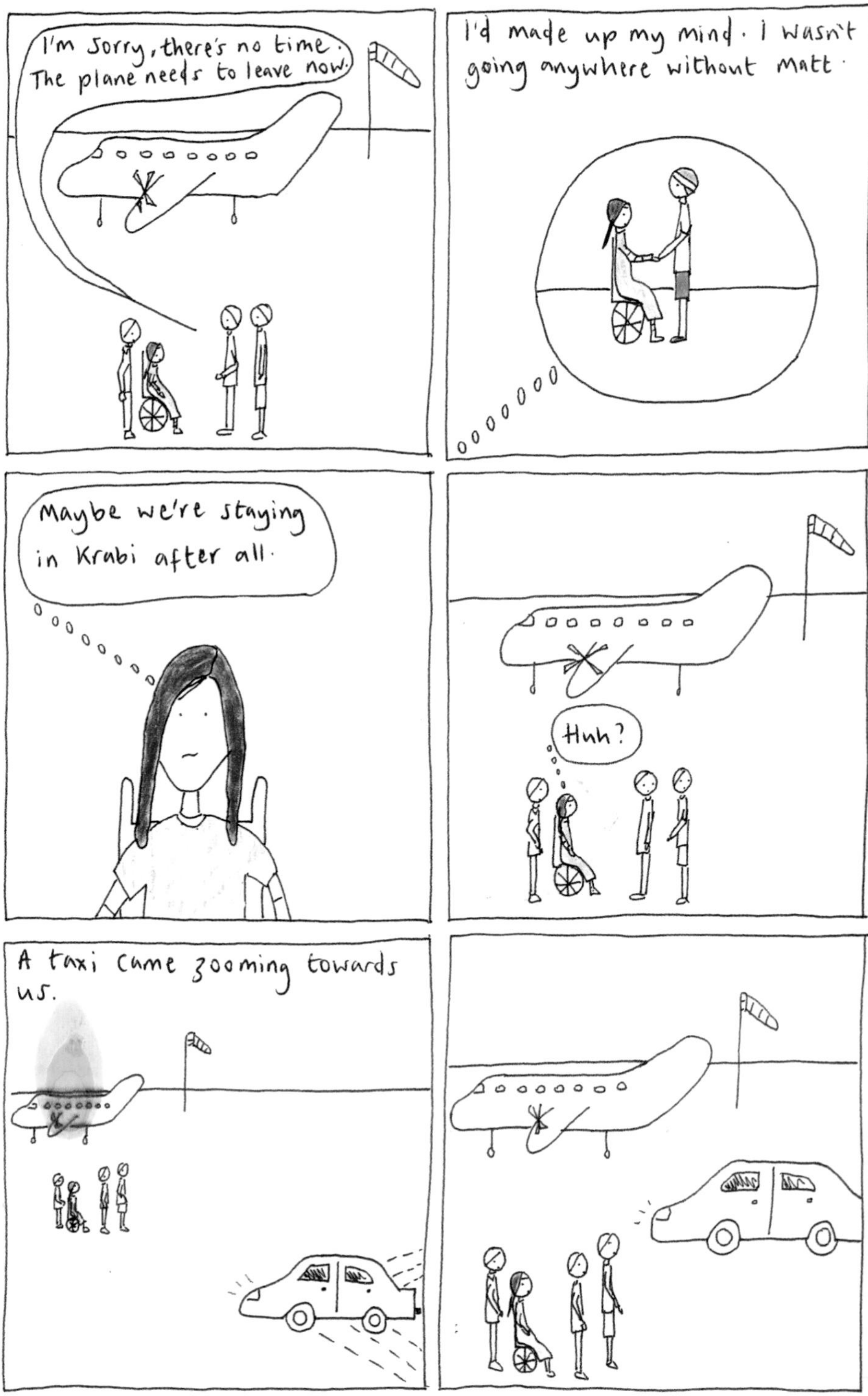
I'm sorry, there's no time. The plane needs to leave now.
I'd made up my mind. I wasn't going anywhere without Matt.
Maybe we're staying in Krabi after all.
Huh?
A taxi came zooming towards us.

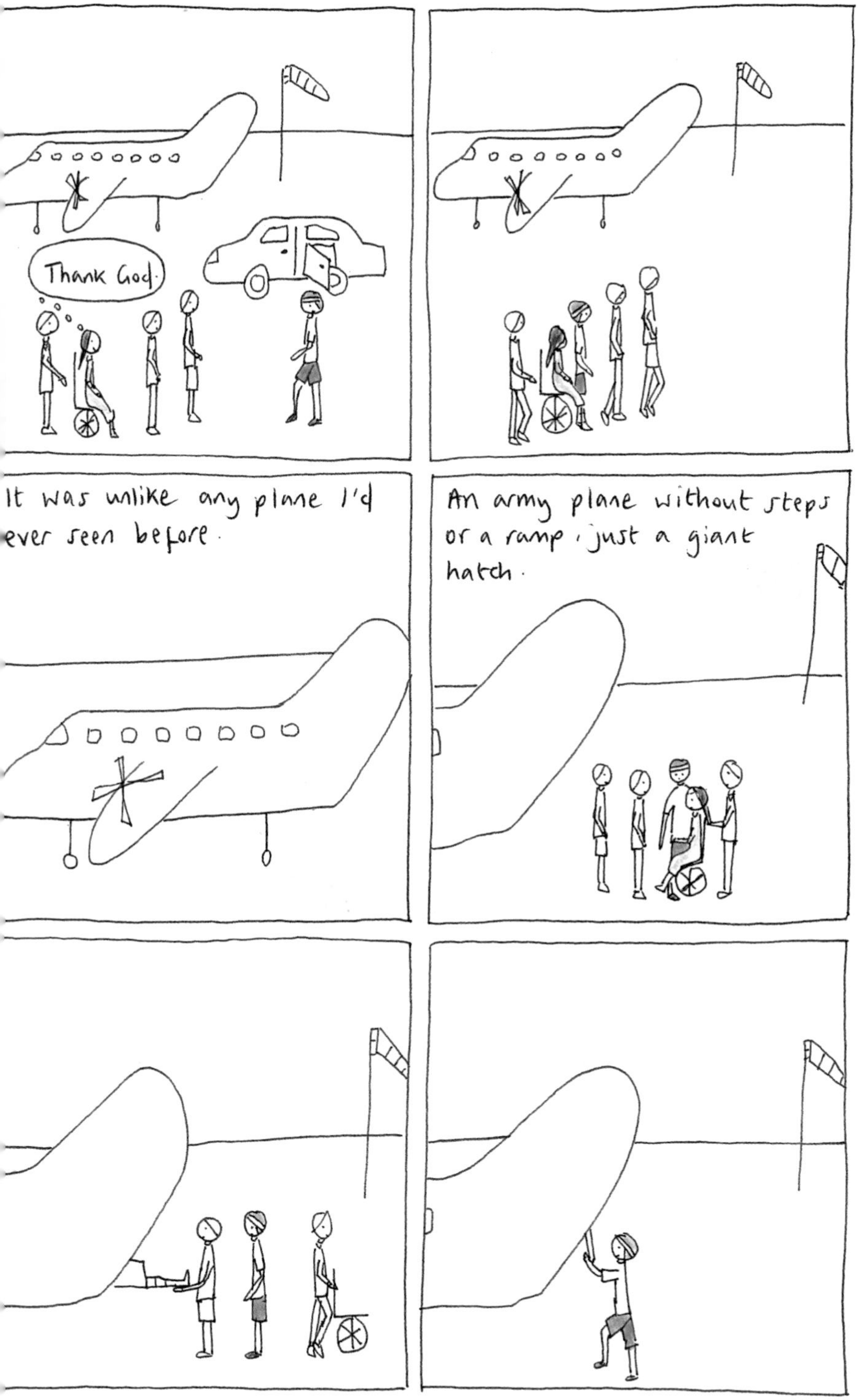
Thank God.
It was unlike any plane I'd ever seen before.
An army plane without steps or a ramp, just a giant hatch.

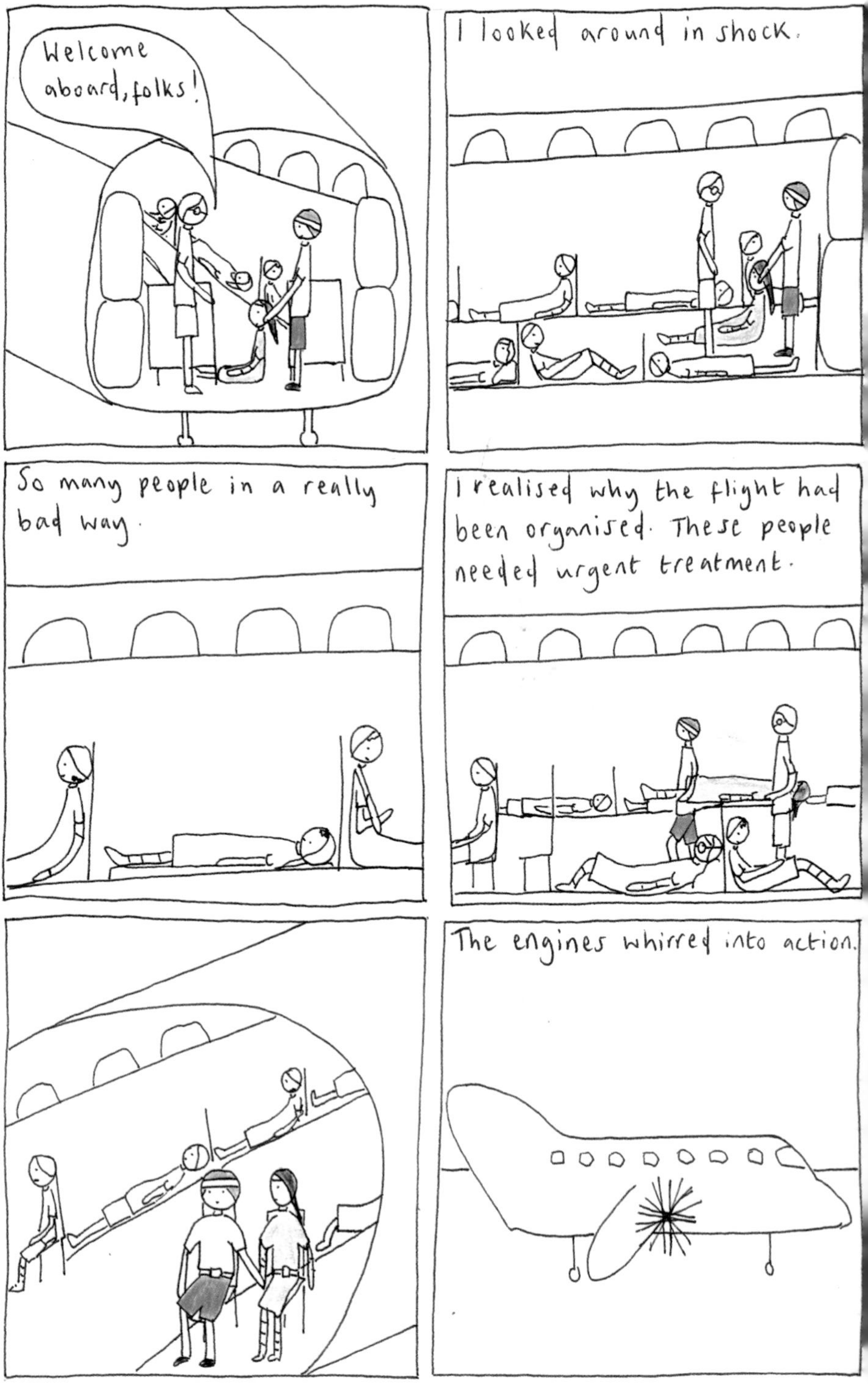
Welcome aboard, folks!
I looked around in shock.
So many people in a really bad way.
I realised why the flight had been organised. These people needed urgent treatment.
The engines whirred into action.

And without the usual details of flight route, catering and in-flight entertainment, we were off.

I was in a lot of pain.

And my fear of flying surged to a new level.

Panic

My mum had always assured me that there was no need to worry about flying, it was simple physics.

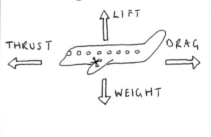

LIFT

THRUST

DRAG

WEIGHT

But after what happened, that reasoning no longer worked for me.

I was petrified that something bad was going to happen.

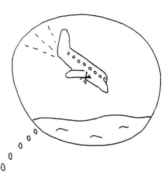

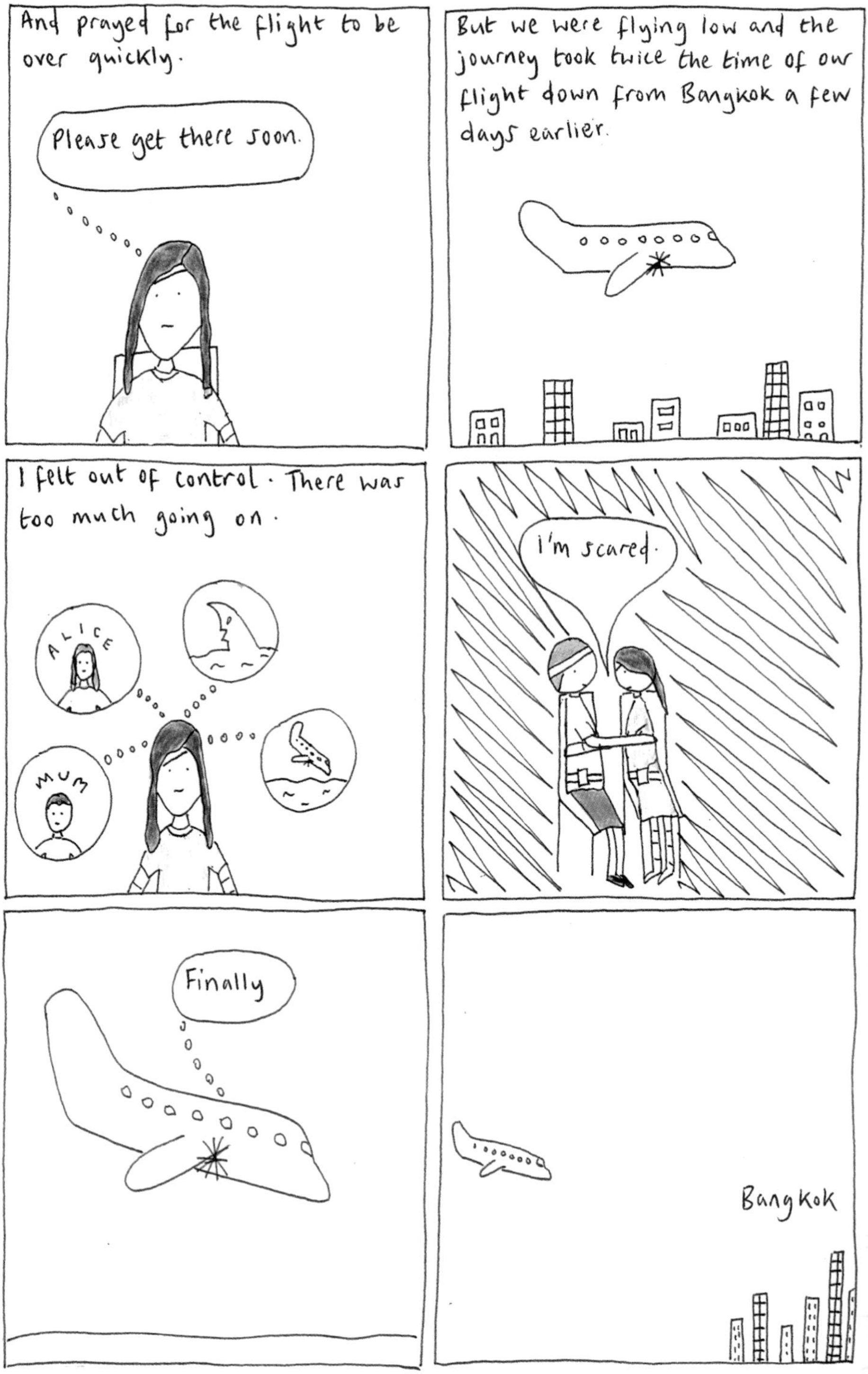
And prayed for the flight to be over quickly.
Please get there soon.
But we were flying low and the journey took twice the time of our flight down from Bangkok a few days earlier.
I felt out of control. There was too much going on.
ALICE
MUM
I'm scared.
Finally
Bangkok

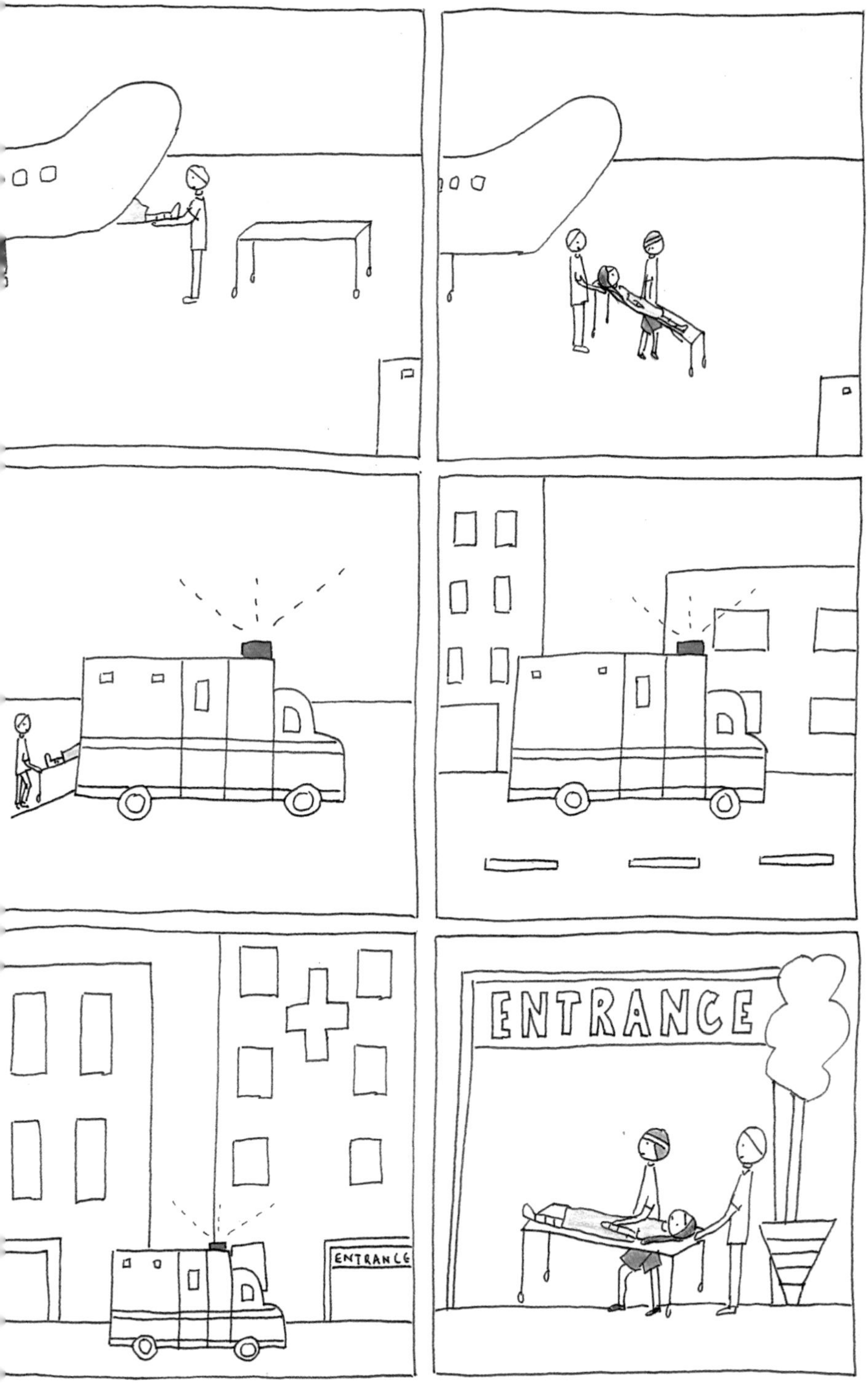
ENTRANCE
ENTRANCE

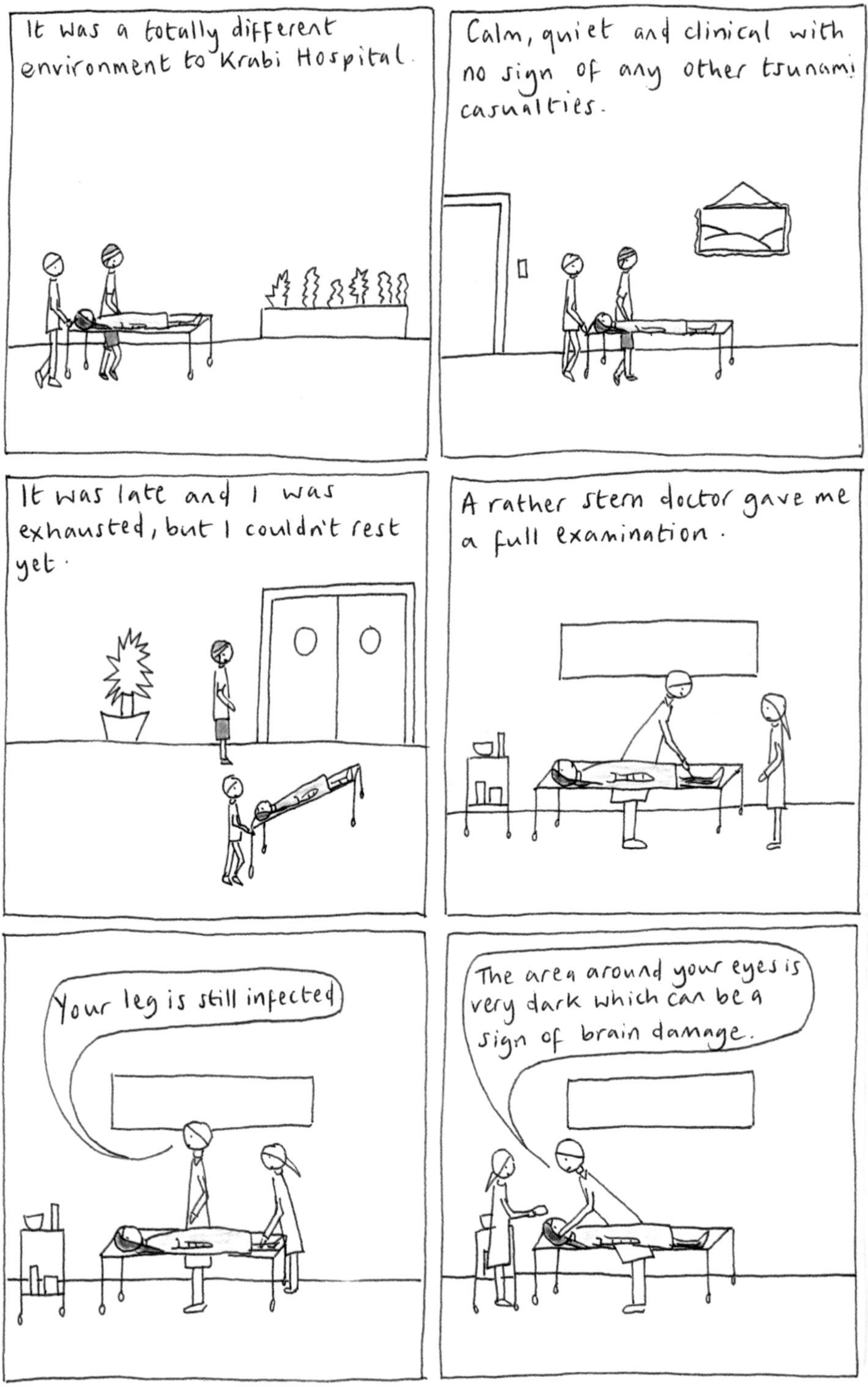
It was a totally different environment to Krabi Hospital.
Calm, quiet and clinical with no sign of any other tsunami casualties.
It was late and I was exhausted, but I couldn't rest yet.
A rather stern doctor gave me a full examination.
Your leg is still infected
The area around your eyes is very dark which can be a sign of brain damage.

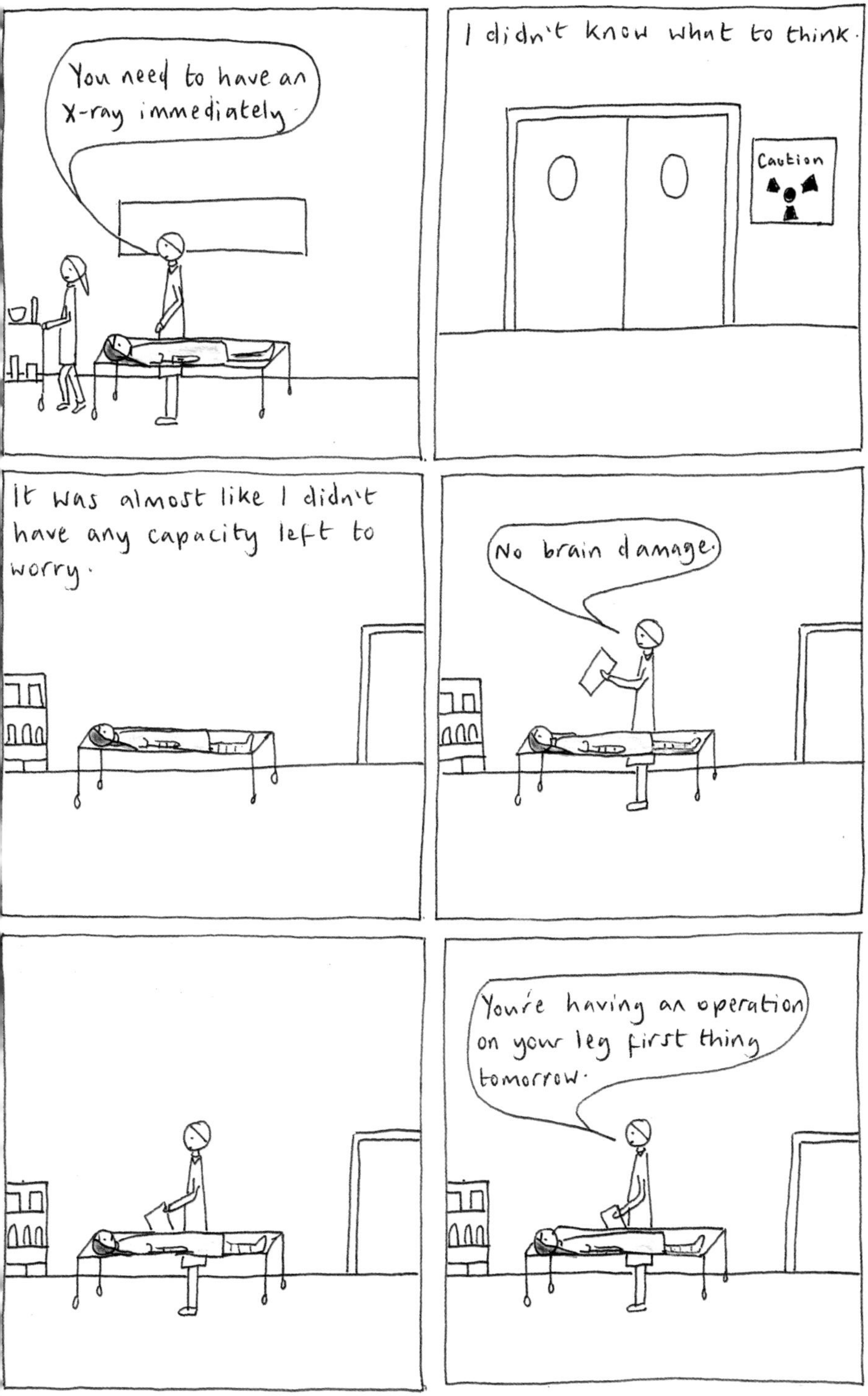
You need to have an X-ray immediately.
I didn't know what to think.
Caution
It was almost like I didn't have any capacity left to worry.
No brain damage.
You're having an operation on your leg first thing tomorrow.

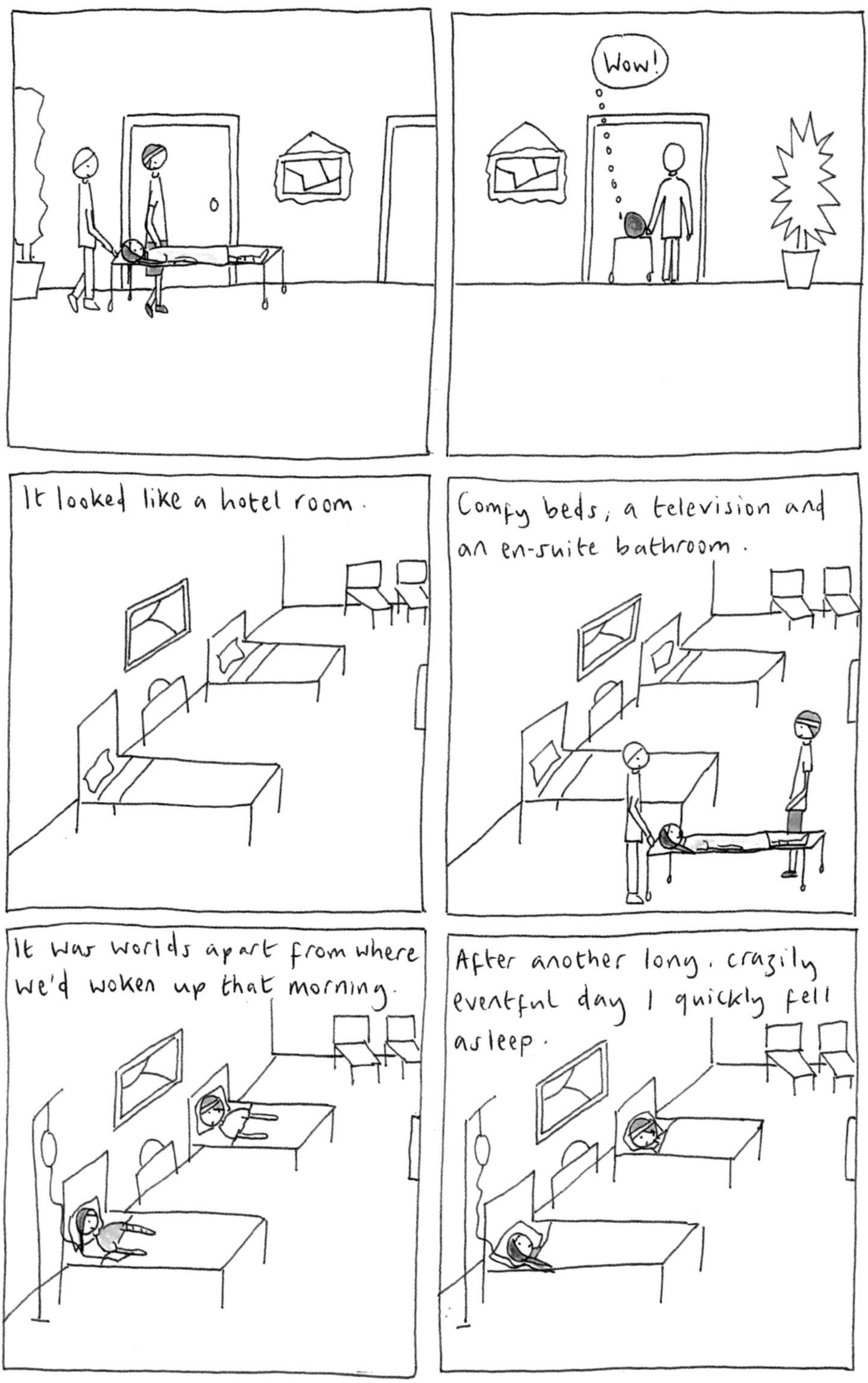
Wow!
It looked like a hotel room.
Comfy beds, a television and an en-suite bathroom.
It was worlds apart from where we'd woken up that morning.
After another long, crazily eventful day I quickly fell asleep.

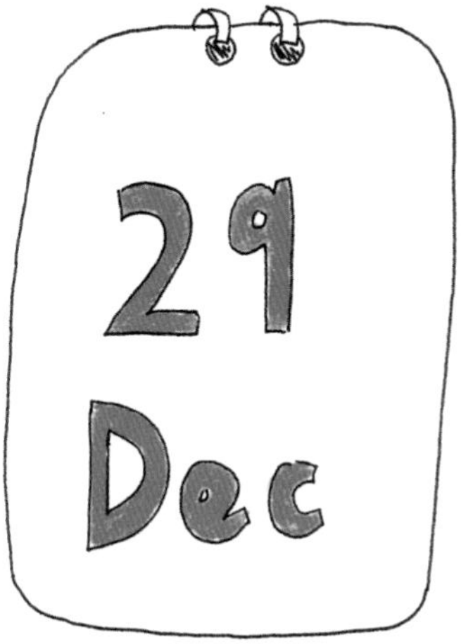
29
Dec

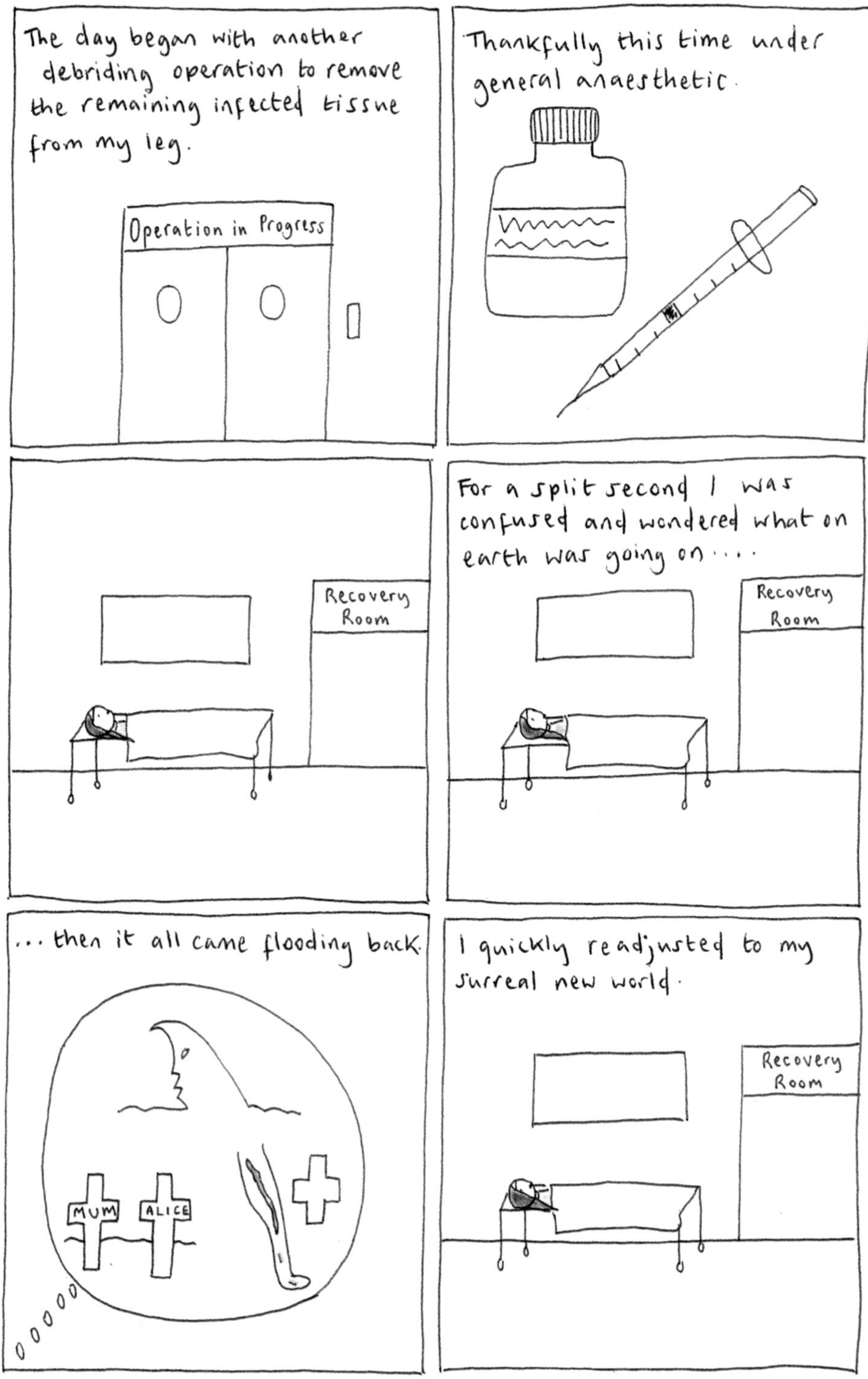
The day began with another debriding operation to remove the remaining infected tissue from my leg.
Operation in Progress
Thankfully this time under general anaesthetic.
Recovery Room
For a split second I was confused and wondered what on earth was going on....
Recovery Room
... then it all came flooding back.
MUM
ALICE
I quickly readjusted to my surreal new world.
Recovery Room

Back in our room...

Knock knock

FOOD!

A delicious cooked breakfast, coffee and juice.

t was perfect and made me realise how little I'd eaten over the last few days.

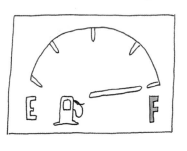

International TV channels and newspapers were part of the 4☆ service.

The News

Tsunami

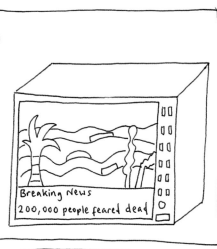

Breaking News
200,000 people feared dead

I couldn't believe the scale of it

Devastation in Indonesia,
Thailand, Maldives, Sri Lanka

In the confines of our luxury
hospital room I felt detached
from the images on the screen.

We were part of it,

but I was beginning to feel
quite disconnected.

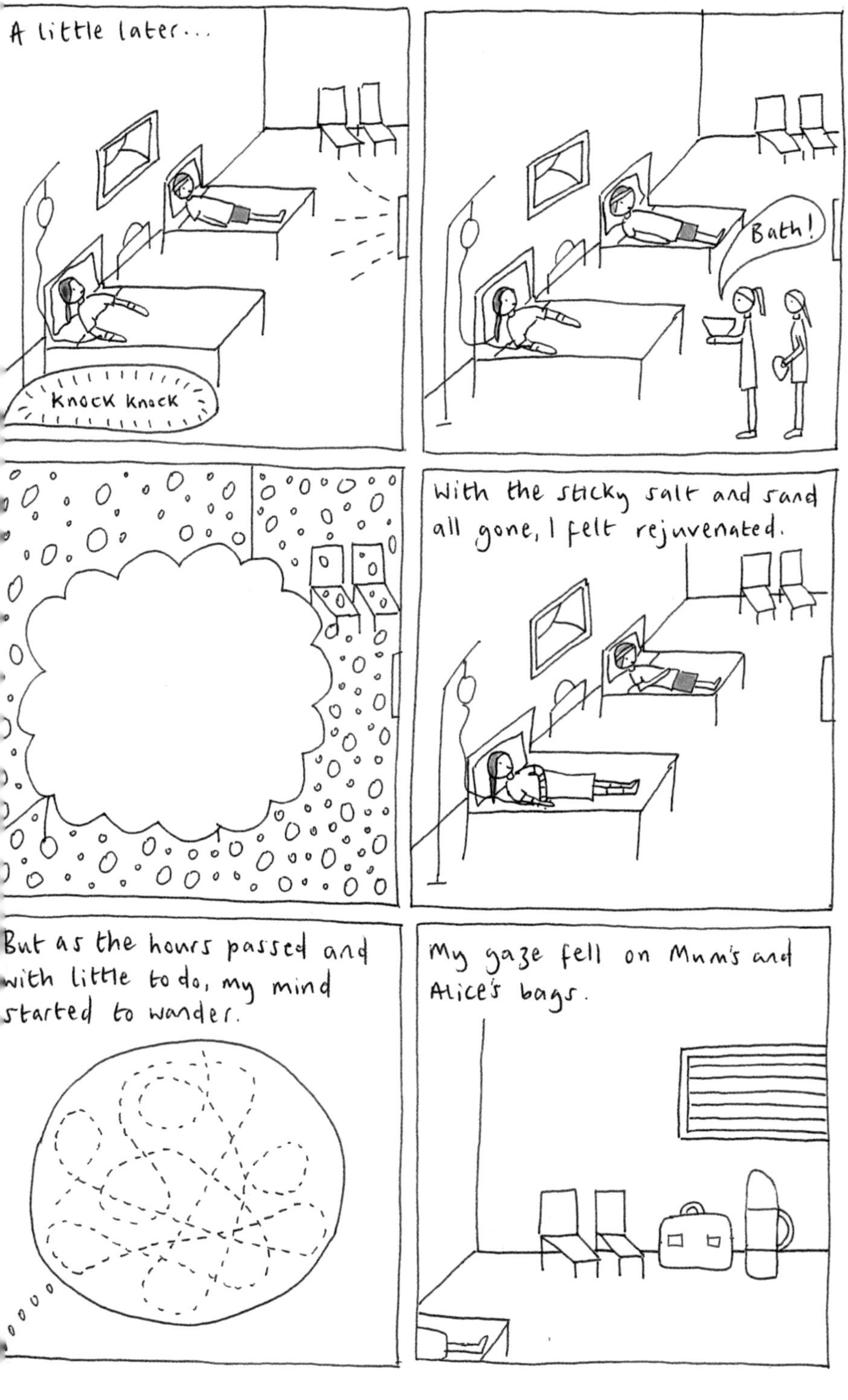
A little later...
Knock knock
Bath!
With the sticky salt and sand all gone, I felt rejuvenated.
But as the hours passed and with little to do, my mind started to wander.
My gaze fell on Mum's and Alice's bags.

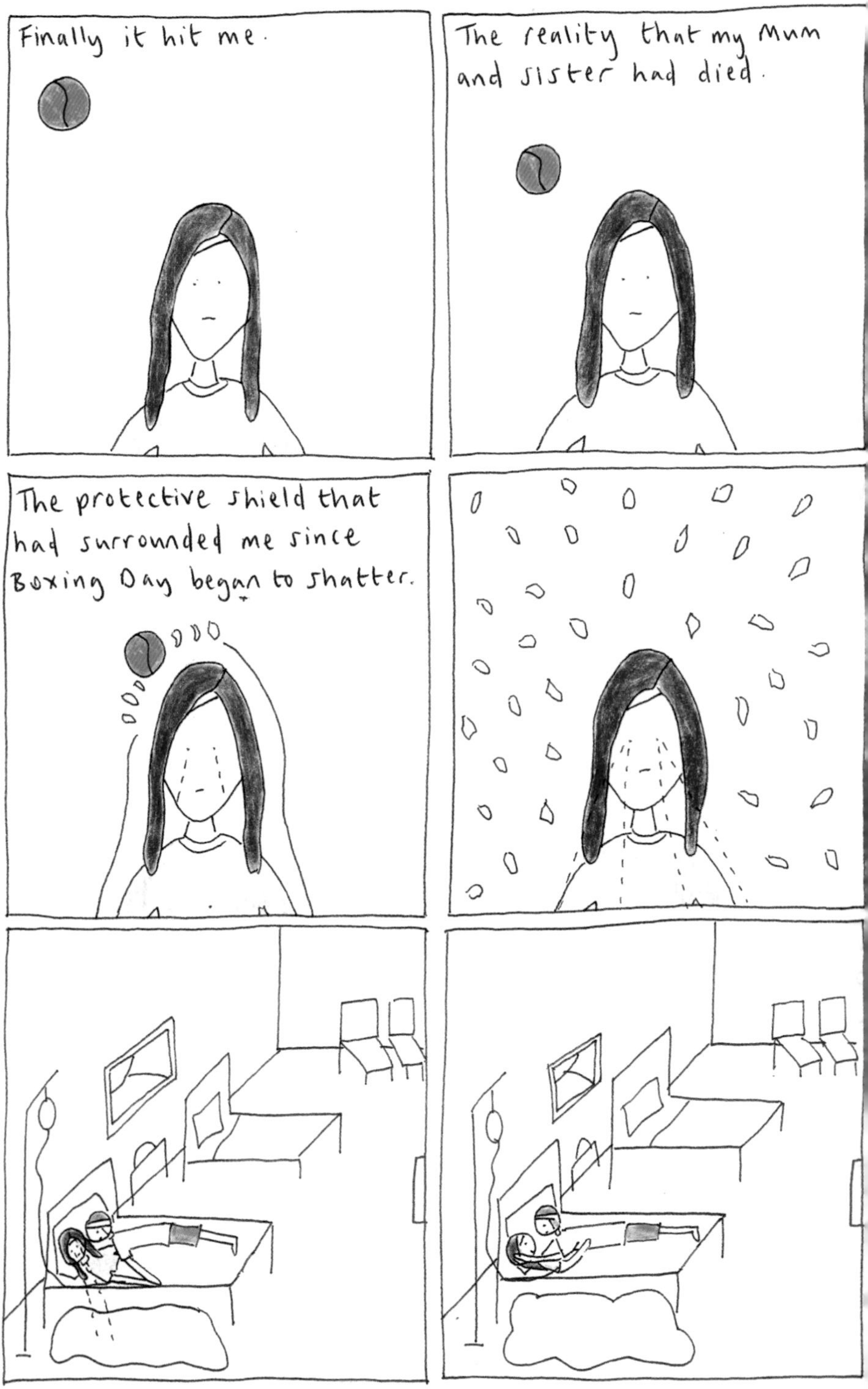
Finally it hit me.
The reality that my Mum and sister had died.
The protective shield that had surrounded me since Boxing Day began to shatter.

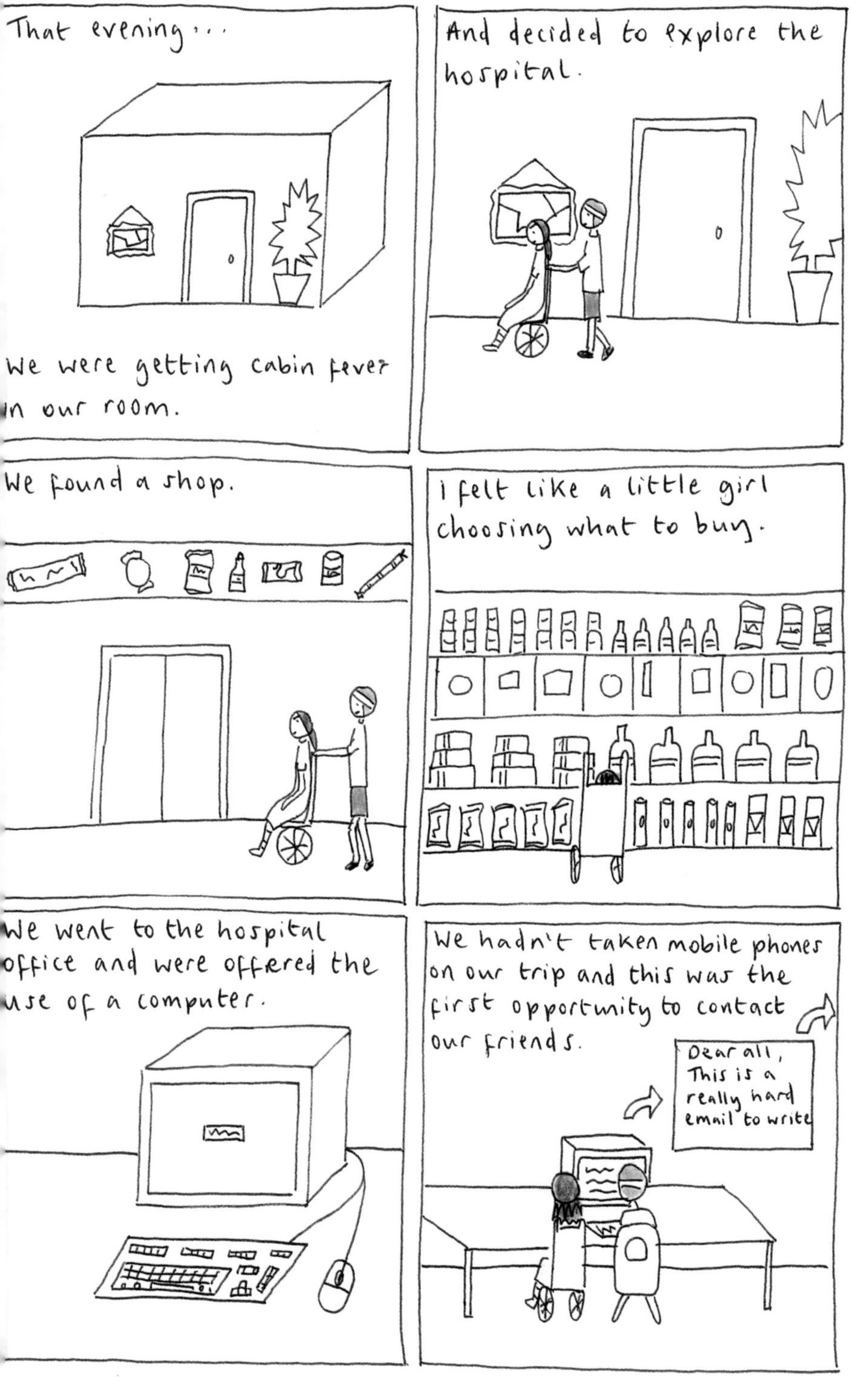

That evening...
We were getting cabin fever in our room.
And decided to explore the hospital.
We found a shop.
I felt like a little girl choosing what to buy.
We went to the hospital office and were offered the use of a computer.
We hadn't taken mobile phones on our trip and this was the first opportunity to contact our friends.
Dear all, This is a really hard email to write

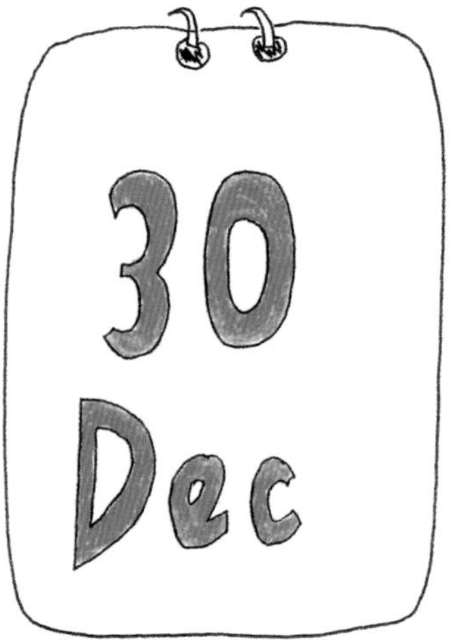
30
Dec

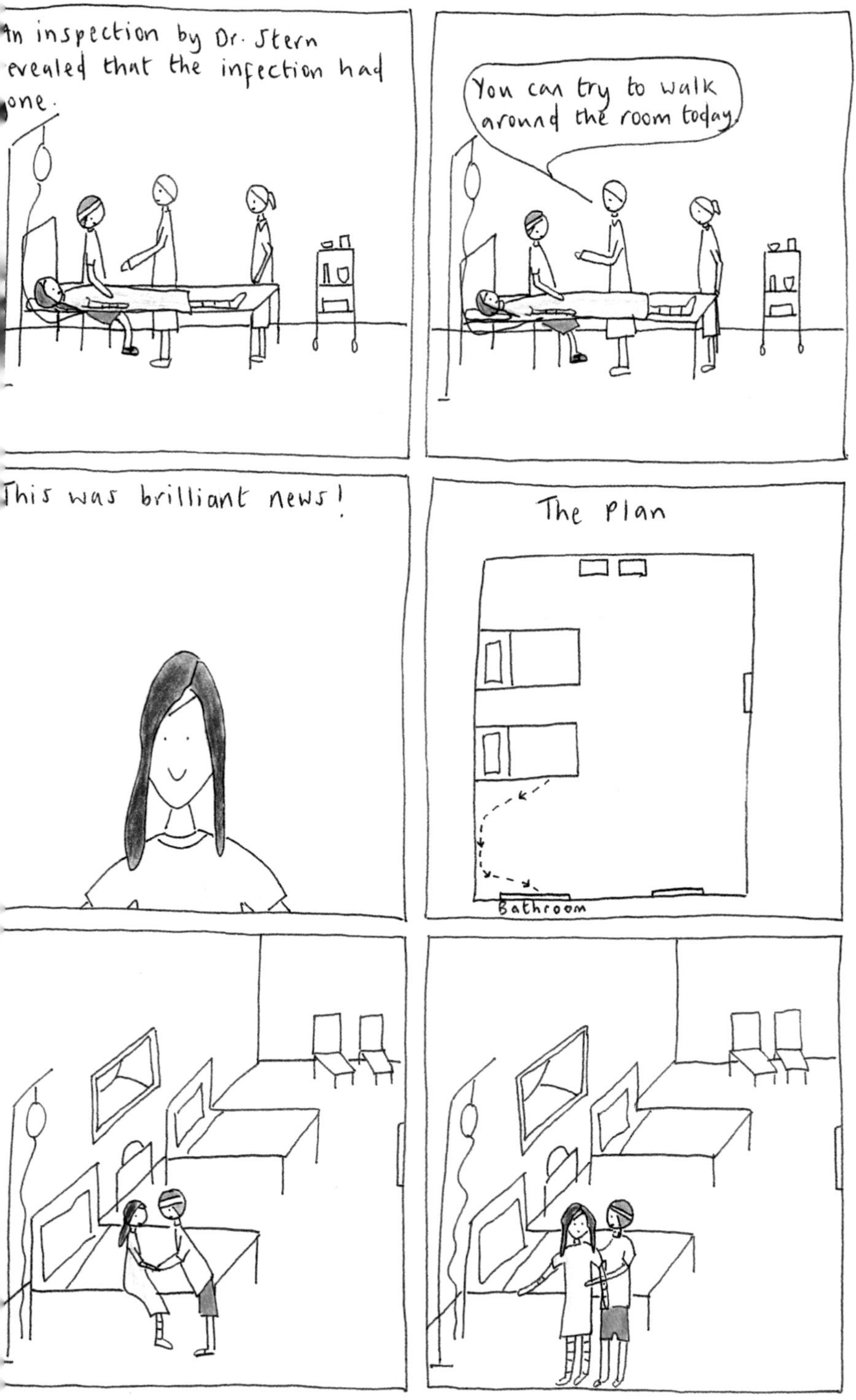
An inspection by Dr. Stern
revealed that the infection had
gone.
You can try to walk around the room today.
This was brilliant news!
The Plan
Bathroom

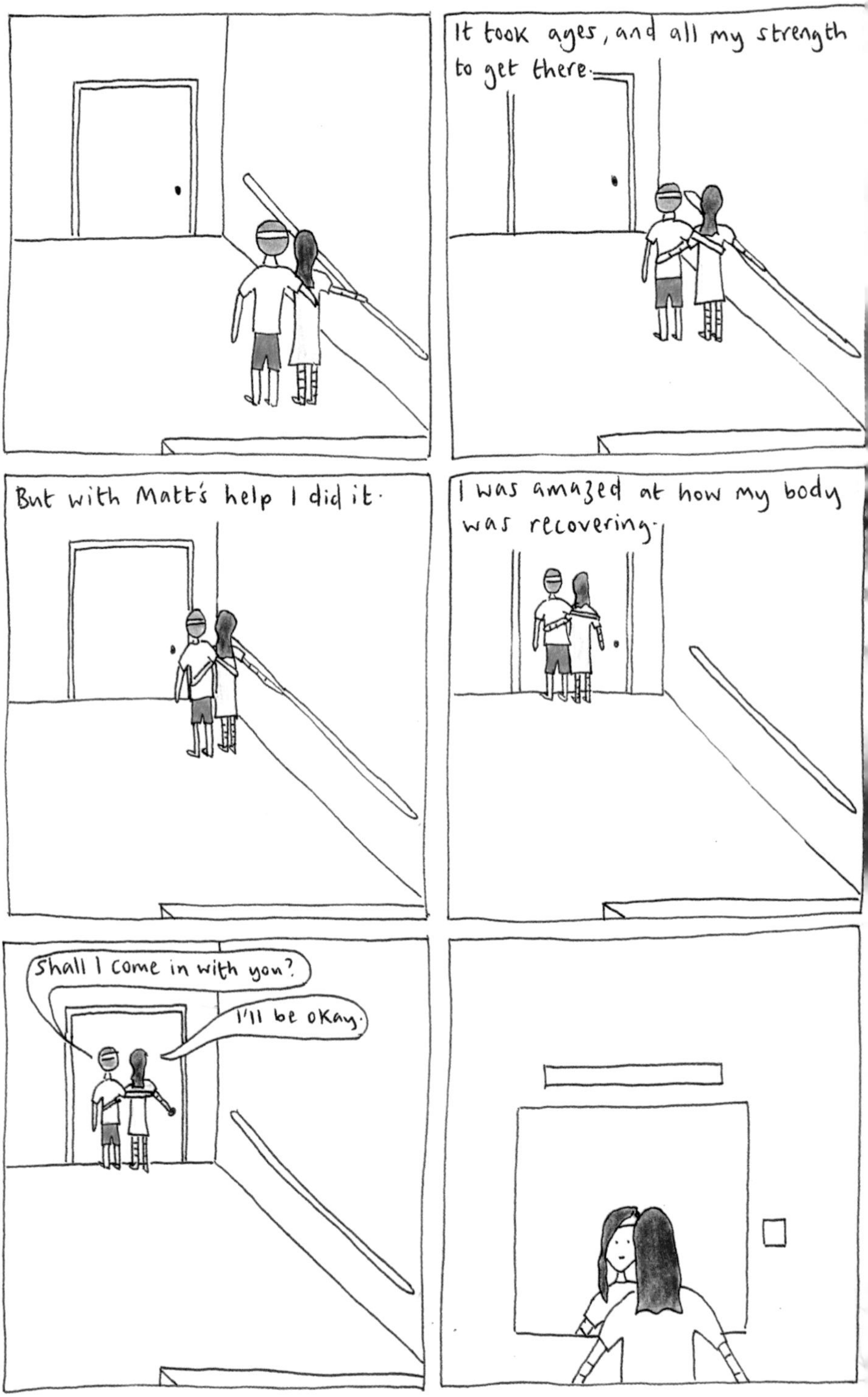
It took ages, and all my strength to get there.
But with Matt's help I did it.
I was amazed at how my body was recovering.
Shall I come in with you?
I'll be okay.

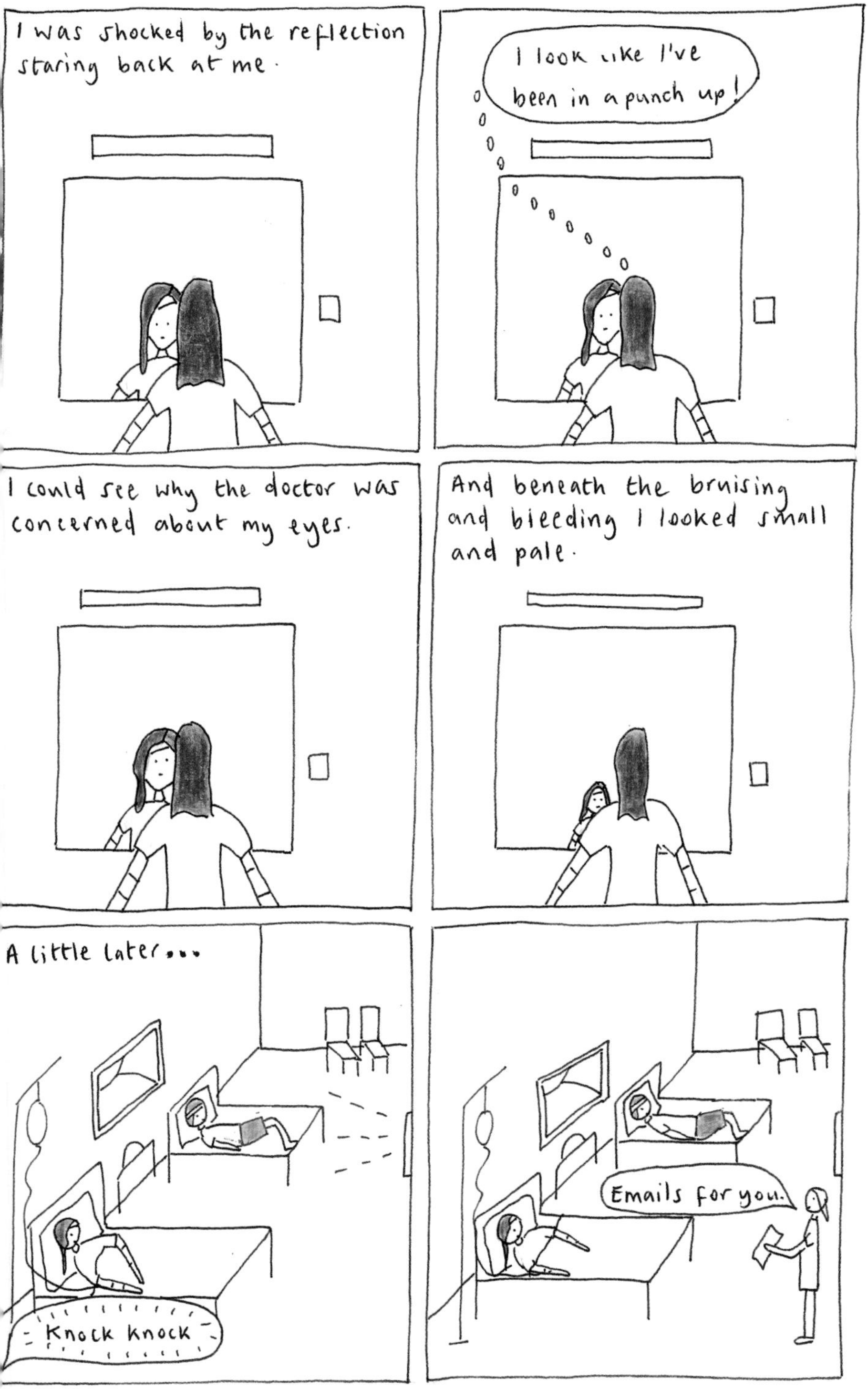
I was shocked by the reflection staring back at me.
I look like I've been in a punch up!
I could see why the doctor was concerned about my eyes.
And beneath the bruising and bleeding I looked small and pale.
A little later...
Knock knock
Emails for you.

Dearest Ede and Matt,

I love you both so much. I can't imagine what you have been through over the past few days but all I can do is send you the biggest hug I possibly can. Everyone has been thinking about you all loads and they send their love and support. There are no words that I can write to tell you how sad I am...

Love Beccy

Dear Ede and Matt,

I'm in utter shock at hearing this awful news and I don't even know where to start and what I want to say. I cannot imagine what you've been through in the past few days and are continuing to endure, it's been reeling through my head since I found out yesterday...

All my love, Lindsay

Dearest Ede and Matt,

I have been thinking of you both since the 26th and am so relieved that you are now both safe. Ede I cannot imagine the horror and pain you are going through. I just want you to know that you are constantly in the thoughts of me and my family and we are praying for you...

All my love to both of you, Amanda

Dear Ede and Matt,

I hope you get this message. I'm overwhelmingly glad that you are both safe and are being cared for in the hospital It hurts me so much to think about how this has affected you both and Ede, I am so sorry. Words must be no comfort. Your mum and Alice are such dear people to you...

All my love, Rae & Jesse x

Matt, Ede

I'm so shocked that this has happened. It's awful. Absolute shite.

I'm so sorry for the both of you. If there is anything that I can do then please don't hesitate to ask...

Condolences, best wishes and all my love to the both of you and your families.

James

Dearest Ede and Matty,

There's so much I want to say, but somehow words don't quite cut it.

I'm sure you're struggling to come to terms with everything you're concentrating on and getting Ede up and about... I love you both very much, you are very special to us all.

Sara

Dear Ede and Matt,

... I am devastated for you and I am so sorry that I can only send my love through an email. I wish I could be there with you. I never thought that my relief that you two are both ⁻ safe would be mixed with such sadness for you... I love you very much and will be here for you.   ●

Anna

Matt and Edie,

I can't even begin to imagine what you've both been through and are going through, but I'm sending you all my love and prayers, and thinking of you both every moment. Ede - it's so horribly sad to hear about you mum and I am continually praying that Alice will be found...

Polly

Dear Matt and Ede,

I'm so sorry to hear your news. I can't begin to think what you are going through at the moment and my thoughts and prayers are with you both and with Alice for safe recovery if she is still alive. I'm not sure what else to say as I suspect no words can bring much comfort to you at the moment...

Andrew

Dear Matt and Ede

... and you are both in the middle of it all, suffering the most enormous pain, both physically and mentally, slowly attempting to come to grips with the reality that will sadly haunt you for the rest of your lives. Your experiences are something that none of us can even begin to comprehend...

Beth

Dearest Ede and Matt,

I just don't know what to say. Thank God you are both okay, and I am so so sorry to hear about you mum Ede. I just hope and pray that Alice will be found safe and well I can't wait to give you both a massive hug... I'm still in shock...

Claire

Hi guys,

We are so desperately sorry. We are also thankful that you two are alive.

We are glad that you are together and looking after each other. There are plenty of people who love you both and will do anything they can to help... Our thoughts are with you.

All our love, Liz and Will

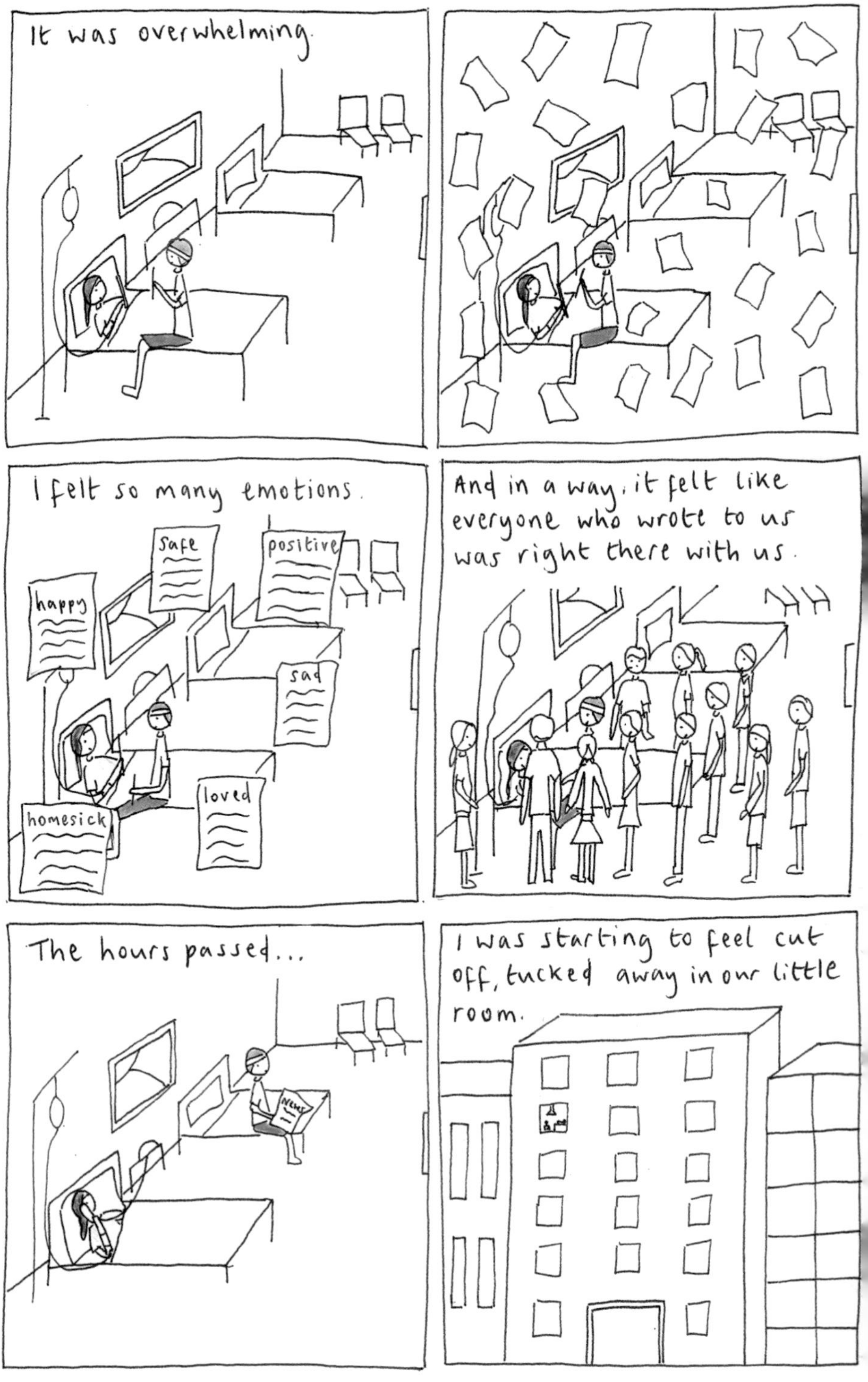

It was overwhelming.
I felt so many emotions.
happy
safe
positive
sad
homesick
loved
And in a way, it felt like everyone who wrote to us was right there with us.
The hours passed...
NEWS
I was starting to feel cut off, tucked away in our little room.

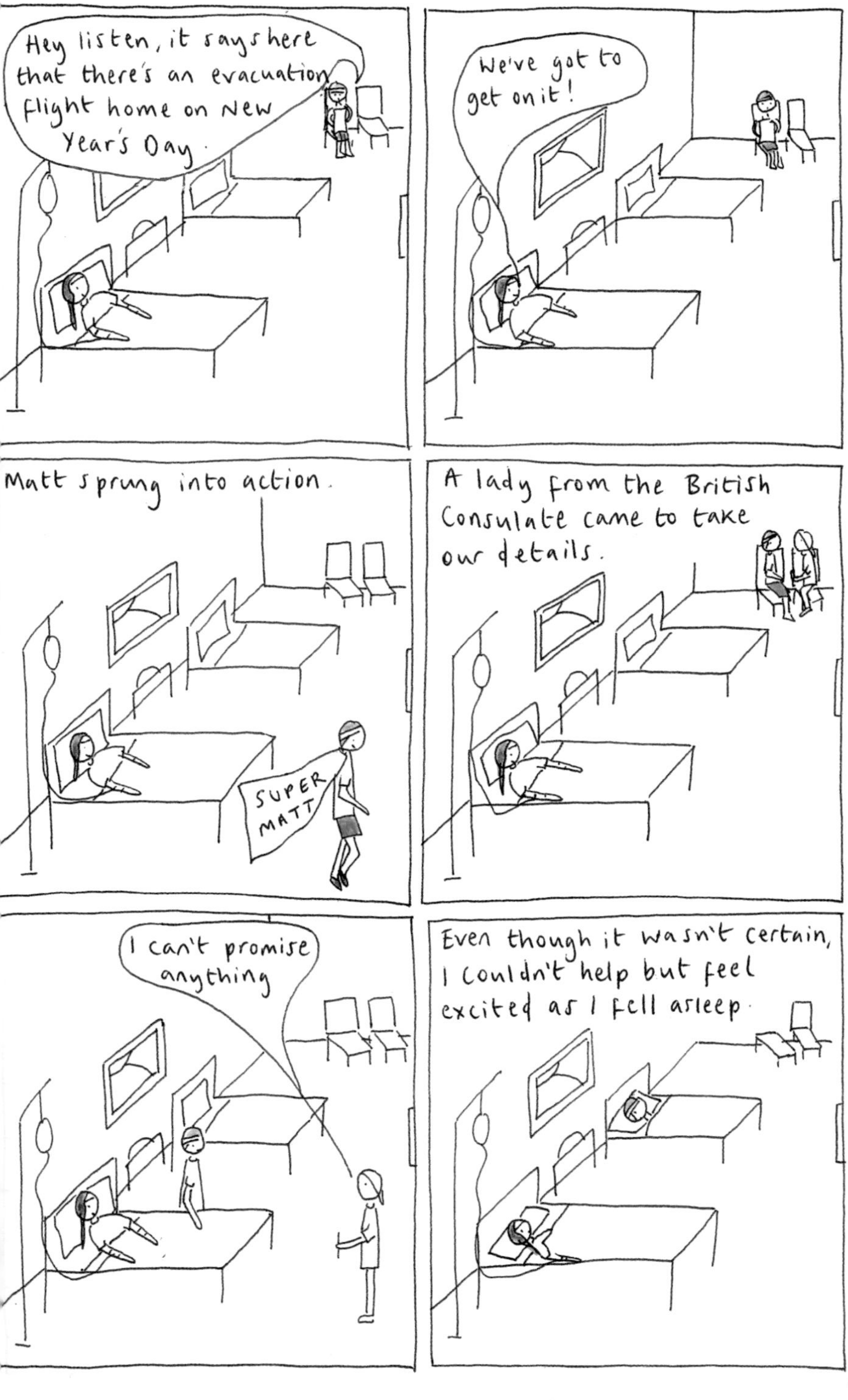
Hey listen, it says here that there's an evacuation flight home on New Year's Day.
We've got to get on it!
Matt sprung into action.
SUPER MATT
A lady from the British Consulate came to take our details.
I can't promise anything
Even though it wasn't certain, I couldn't help but feel excited as I fell asleep.

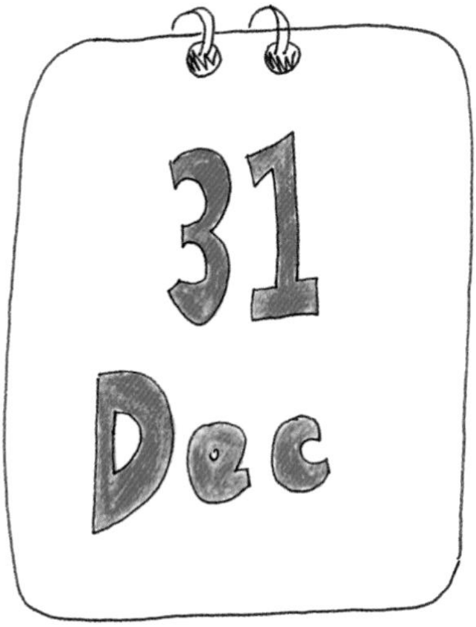
31
Dec

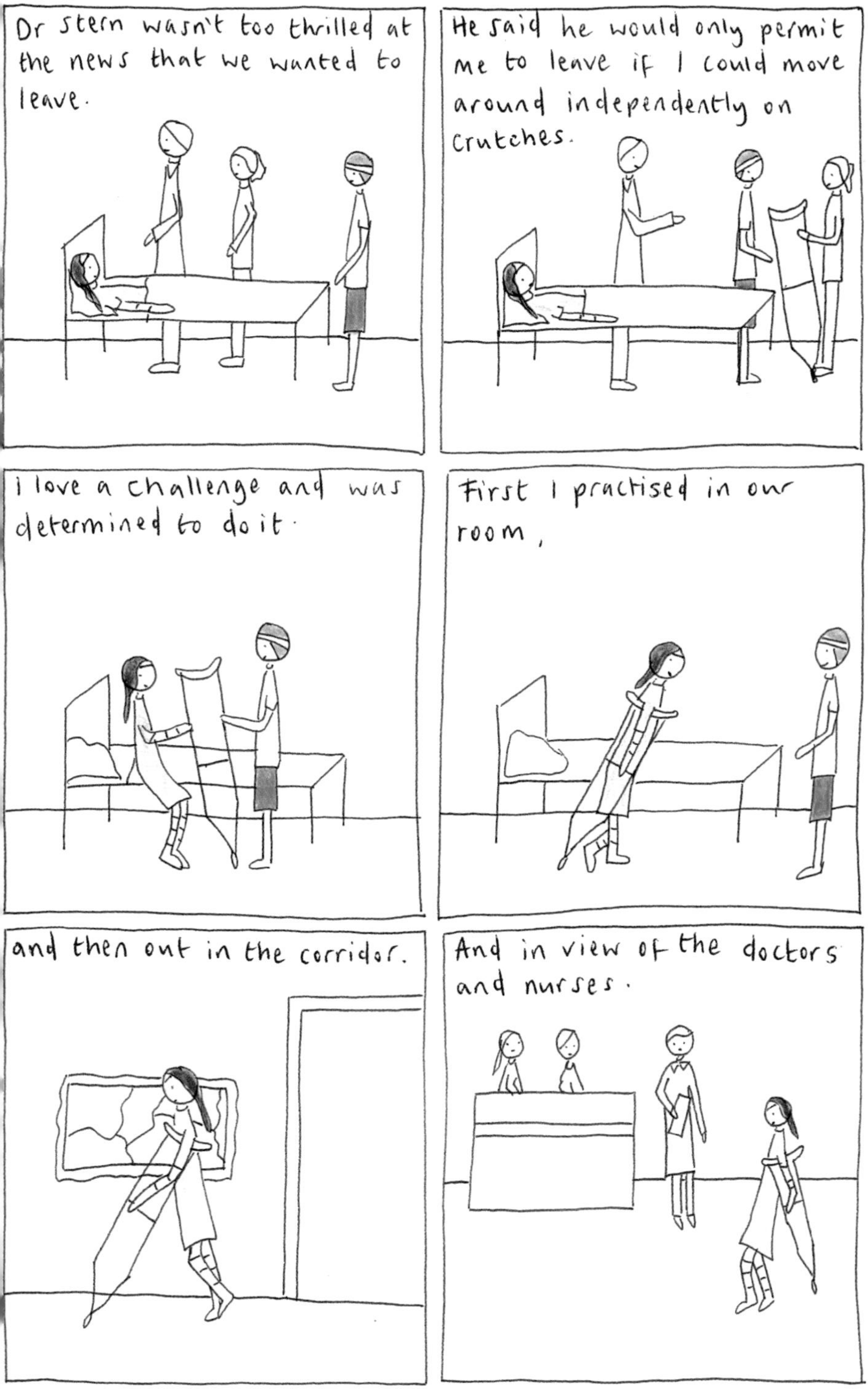
Dr Stern wasn't too thrilled at the news that we wanted to leave.
He said he would only permit me to leave if I could move around independently on crutches.
I love a challenge and was determined to do it.
First I practised in our room,
and then out in the corridor.
And in view of the doctors and nurses.

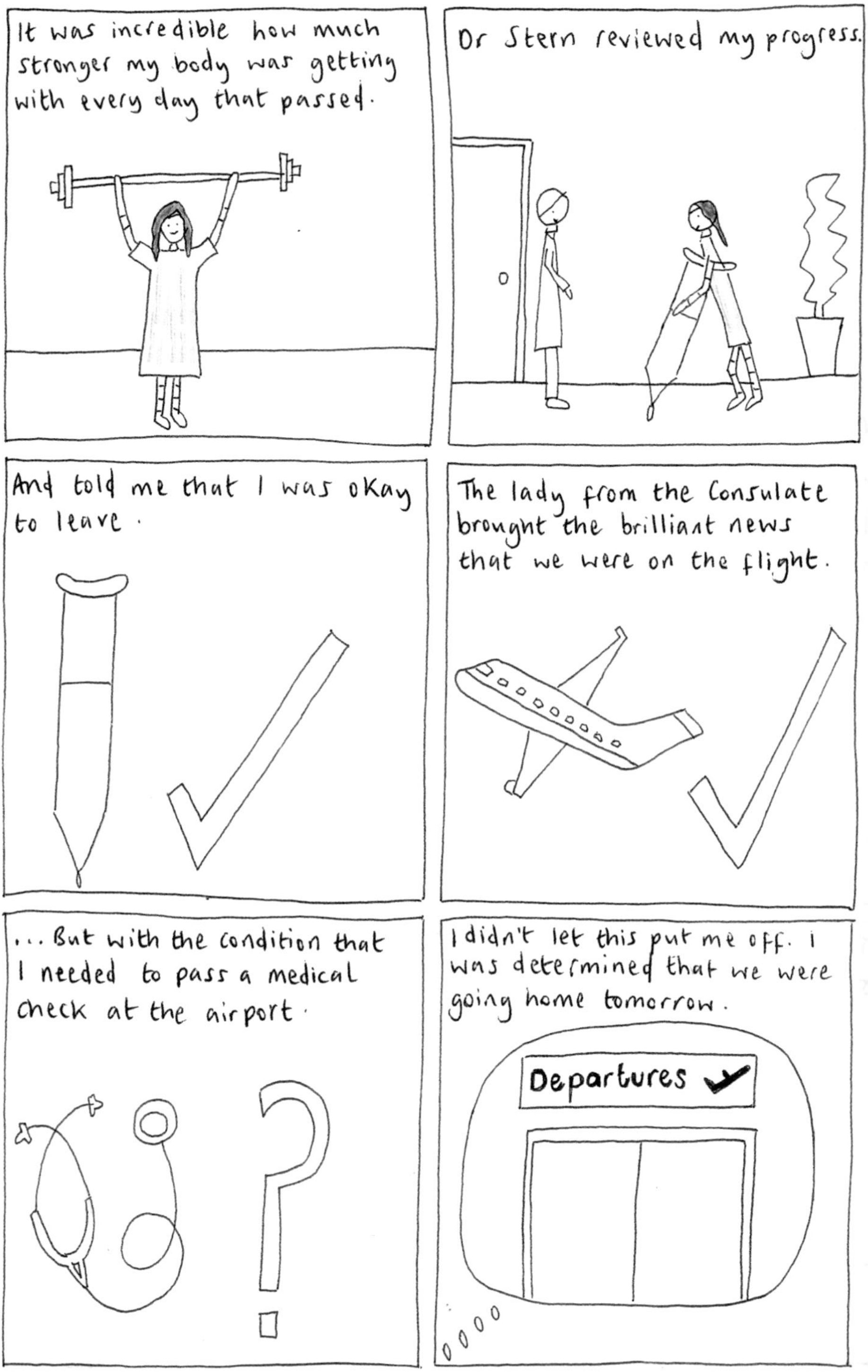
It was incredible how much stronger my body was getting with every day that passed.
Dr Stern reviewed my progress.
And told me that I was okay to leave.
The lady from the Consulate brought the brilliant news that we were on the flight.
... But with the condition that I needed to pass a medical check at the airport.
I didn't let this put me off. I was determined that we were going home tomorrow.
Departures

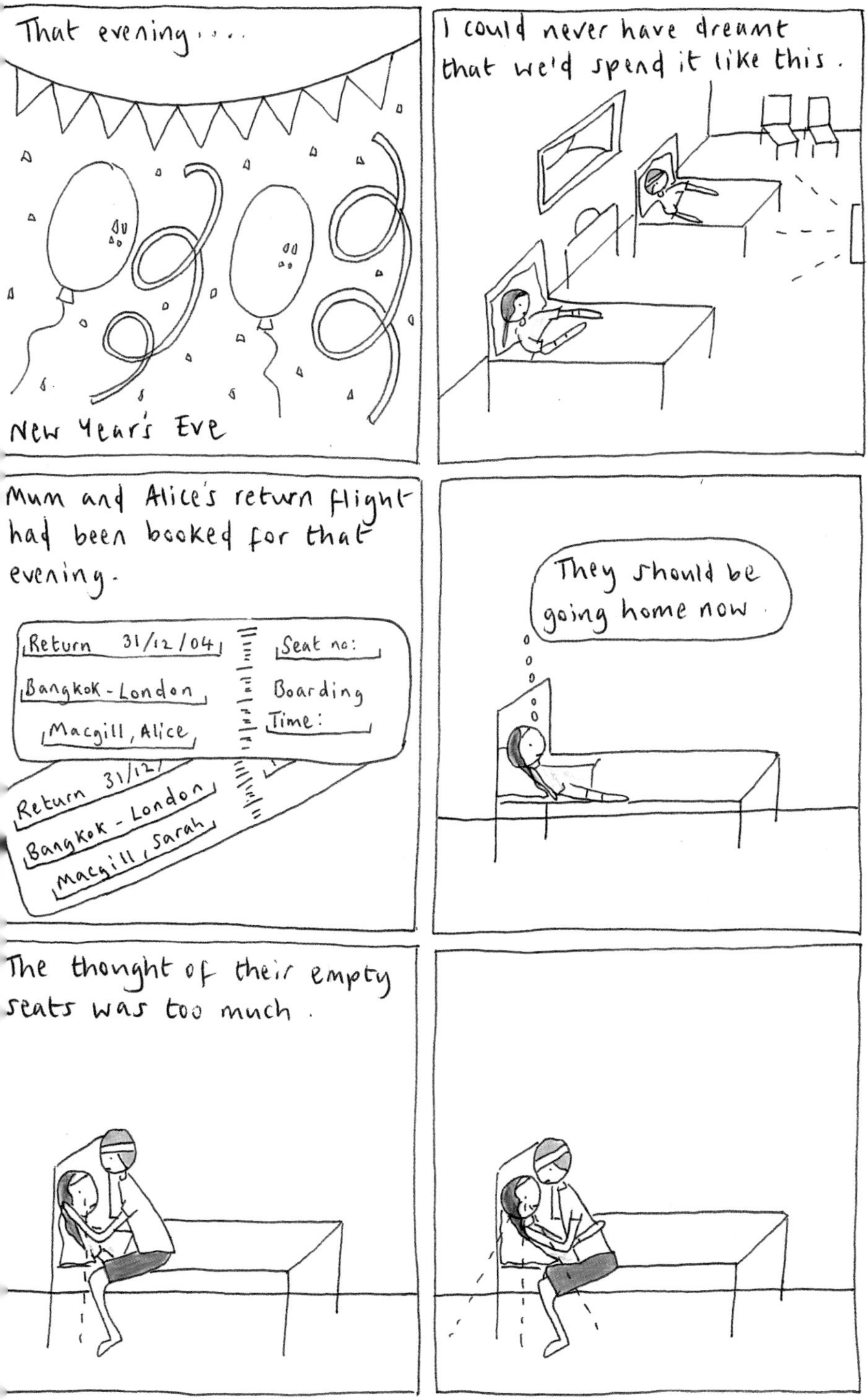
That evening....
New Year's Eve
I could never have dreamt that we'd spend it like this.
Mum and Alice's return flight had been booked for that evening.
Return 31/12/04
Bangkok - London
Macgill, Alice
Seat no:
Boarding Time:
Return 31/12/
Bangkok - London
Macgill, Sarah
They should be going home now.
The thought of their empty seats was too much.

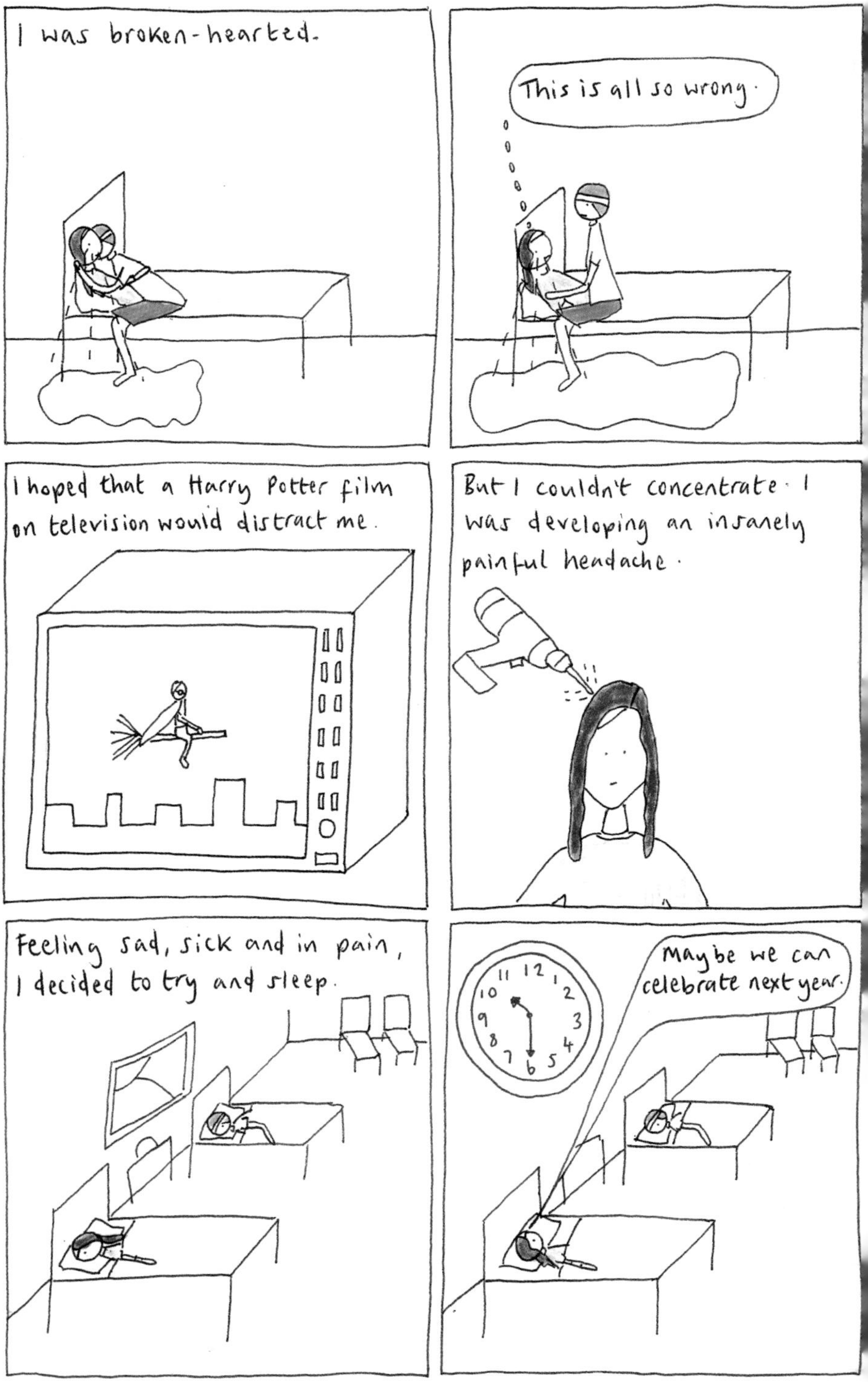
I was broken-hearted.
This is all so wrong.
I hoped that a Harry Potter film on television would distract me.
But I couldn't concentrate. I was developing an insanely painful headache.
Feeling sad, sick and in pain, I decided to try and sleep.
Maybe we can celebrate next year.

I woke up in the middle of the night in agony.
Press for Assistance
Uhh, I'll get the doctor.
Aarrgghh

You have maggots in your head.

MAGGOTS?!

It was a million miles away from what I was expecting to hear.

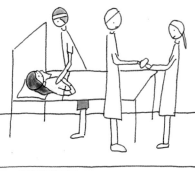

Or Stern removed the maggots that he could get to in the puncture wound on my forehead.

And gave me some super strength painkillers,

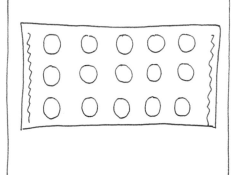

Which knocked me out in an instant.

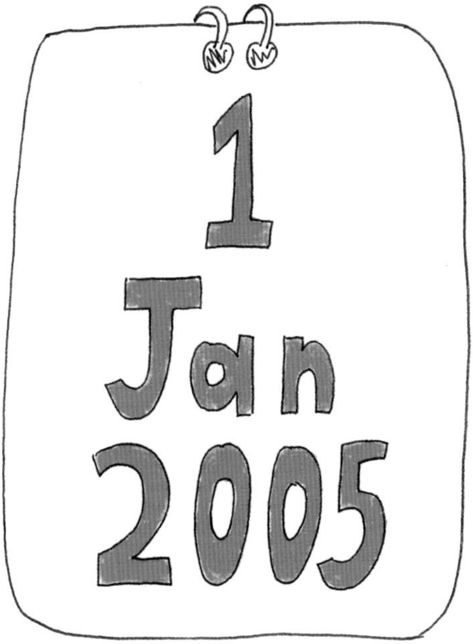
1
Jan
2005

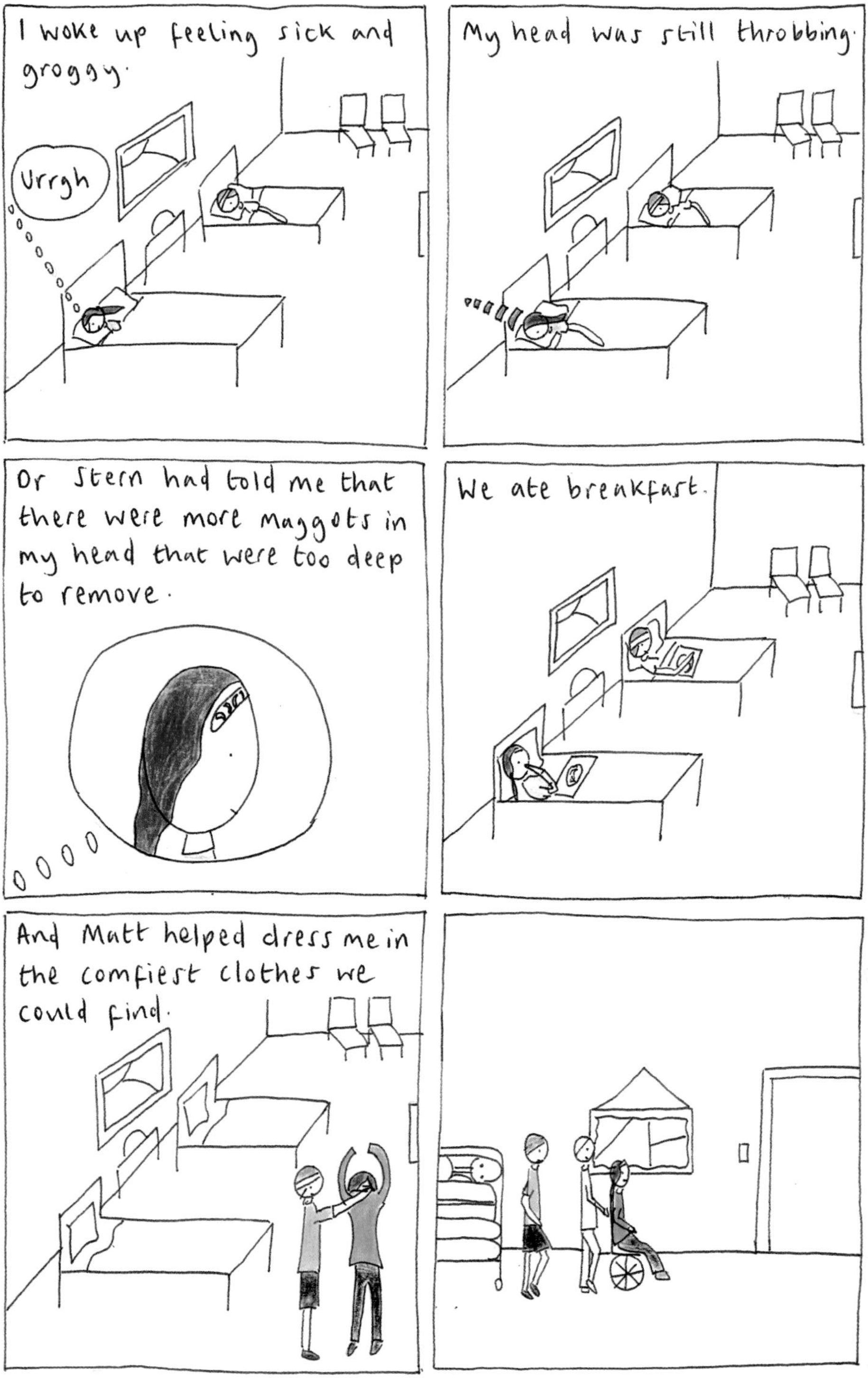
I woke up feeling sick and groggy.
Urrgh
My head was still throbbing.
Dr Stern had told me that there were more maggots in my head that were too deep to remove.
We ate breakfast.
And Matt helped dress me in the comfiest clothes we could find.

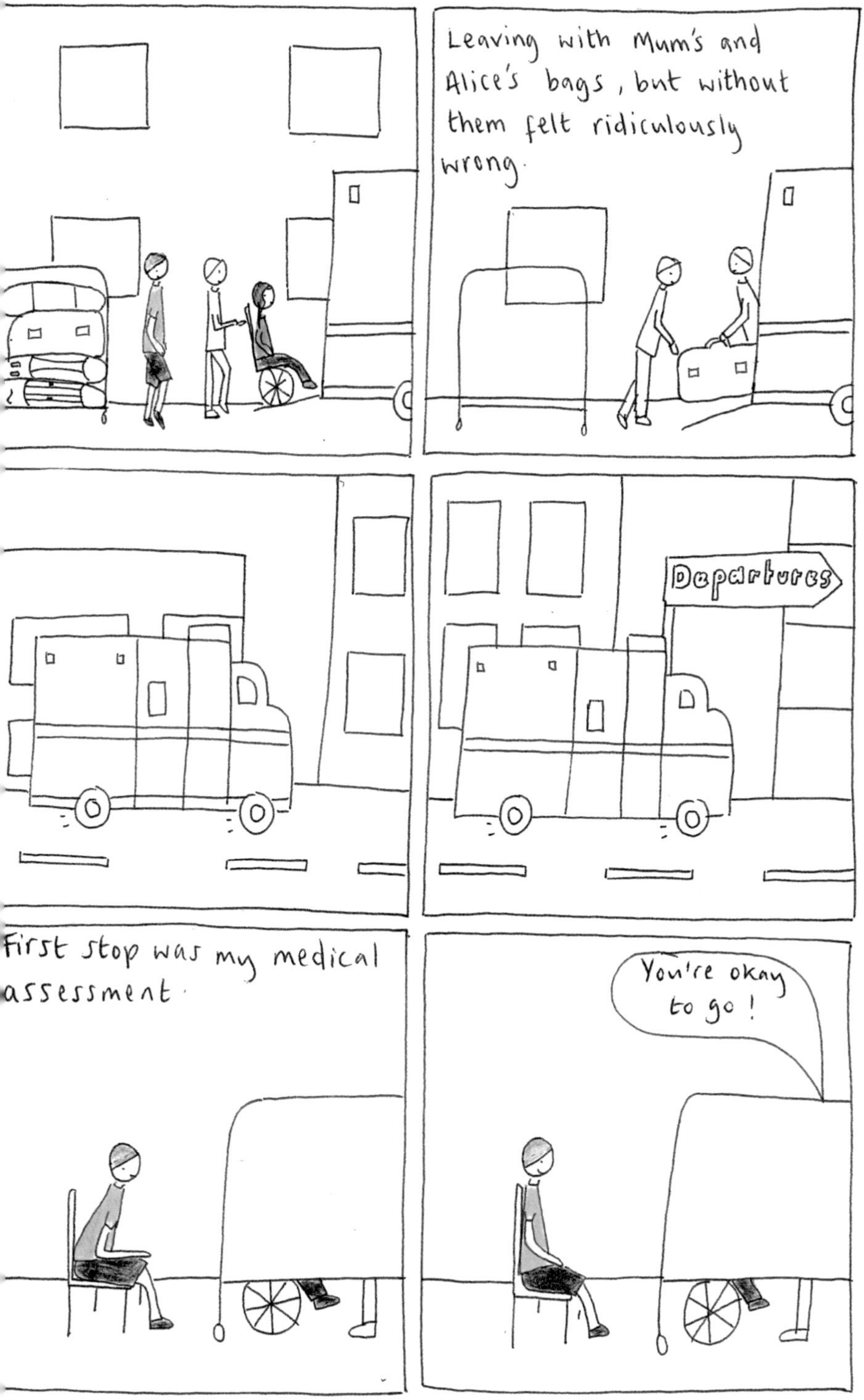

Leaving with Mum's and Alice's bags, but without them felt ridiculously wrong.
Departures
First stop was my medical assessment.
You're okay to go!

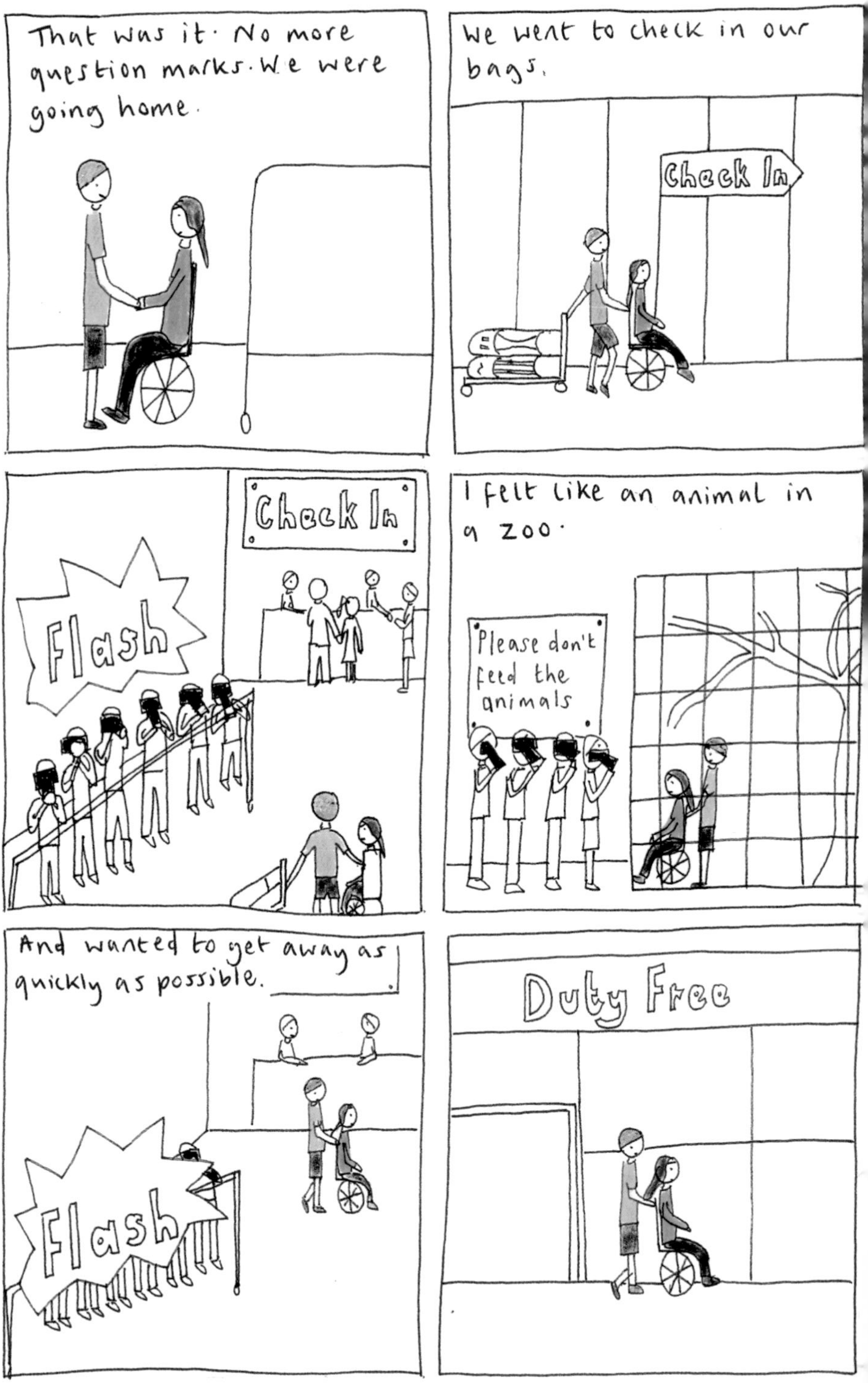
That was it. No more question marks. We were going home.
We went to check in our bags.
Check In
Check In
Flash
I felt like an animal in a zoo.
Please don't feed the animals
And wanted to get away as quickly as possible.
Flash
Duty Free

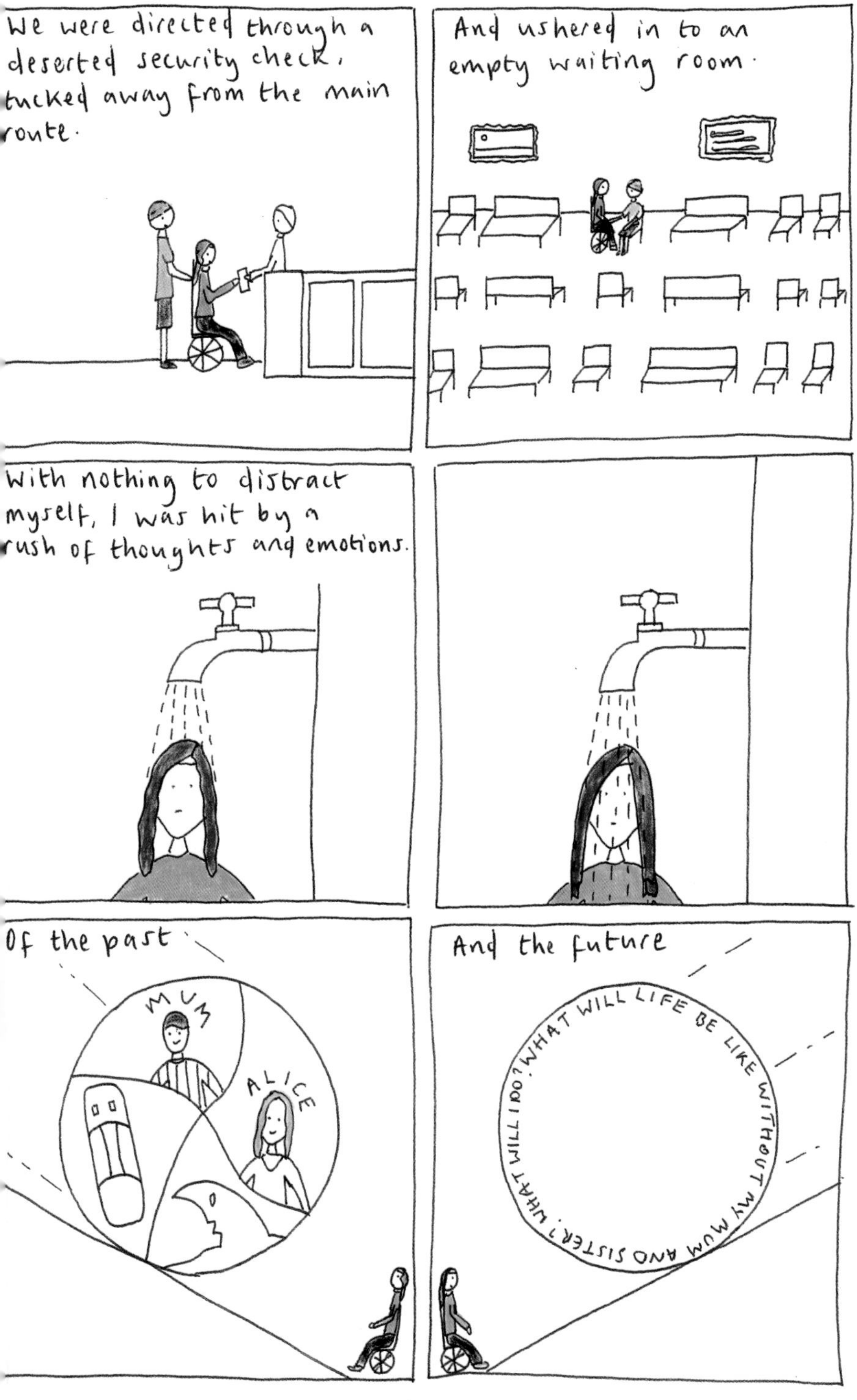
We were directed through a deserted security check, tucked away from the main route.
And ushered in to an empty waiting room.
With nothing to distract myself, I was hit by a rush of thoughts and emotions.
Of the past
MUM
ALICE
And the future
WHAT WILL LIFE BE LIKE WITHOUT MY MUM AND SISTER? WHAT WILL I DO?

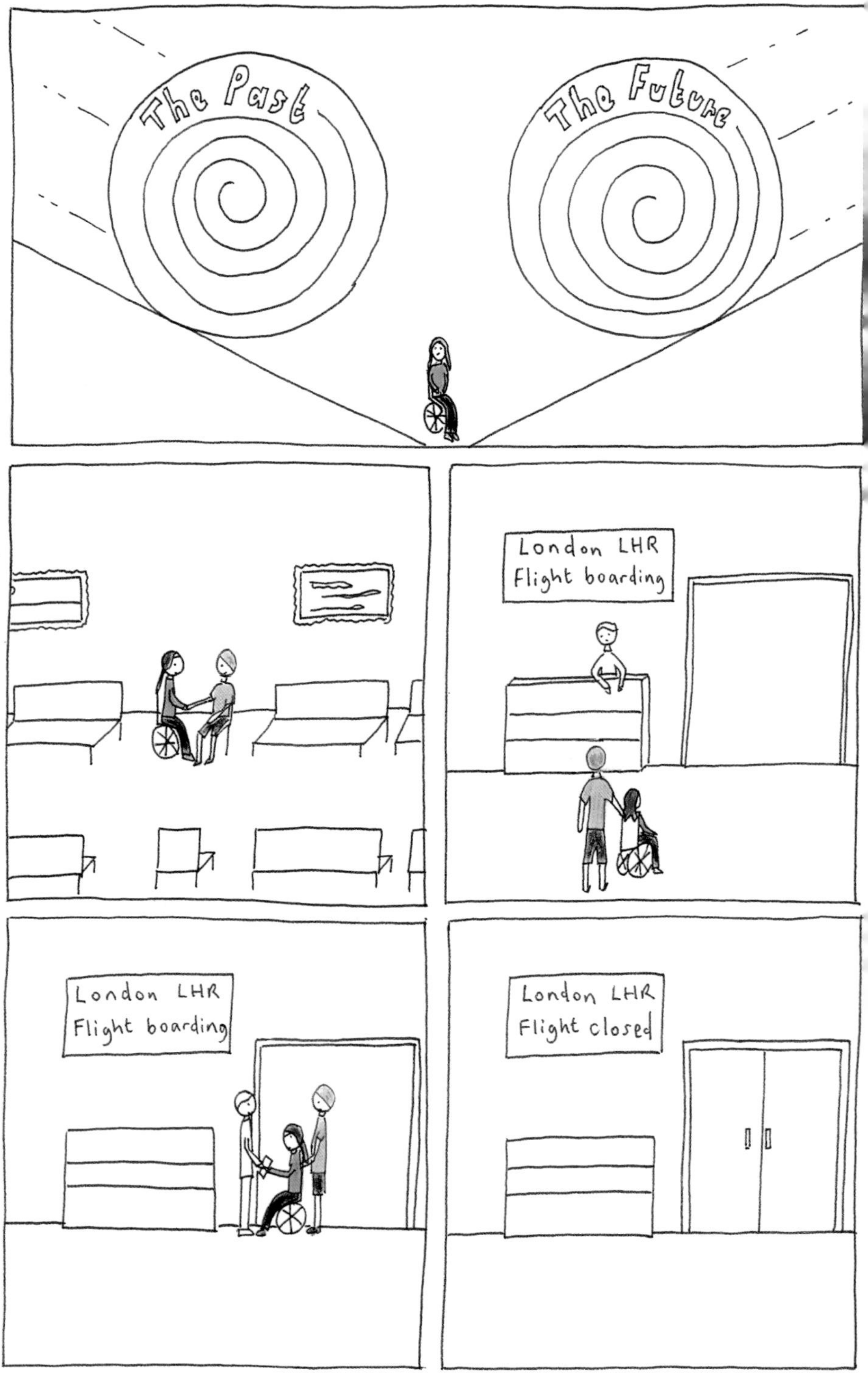
The Past
The Future
London LHR
Flight boarding
London LHR
Flight boarding
London LHR
Flight closed

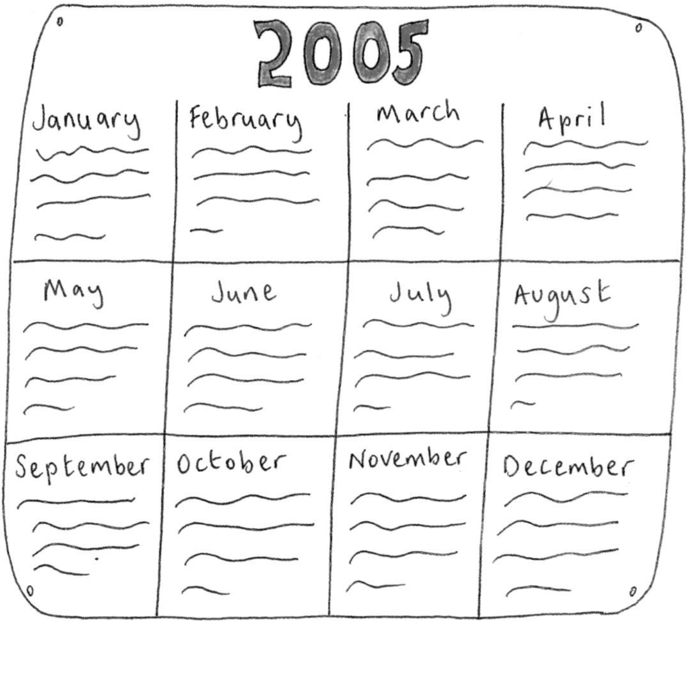
2005
January
February
March
April
May
June
July
August
September
October
November
December

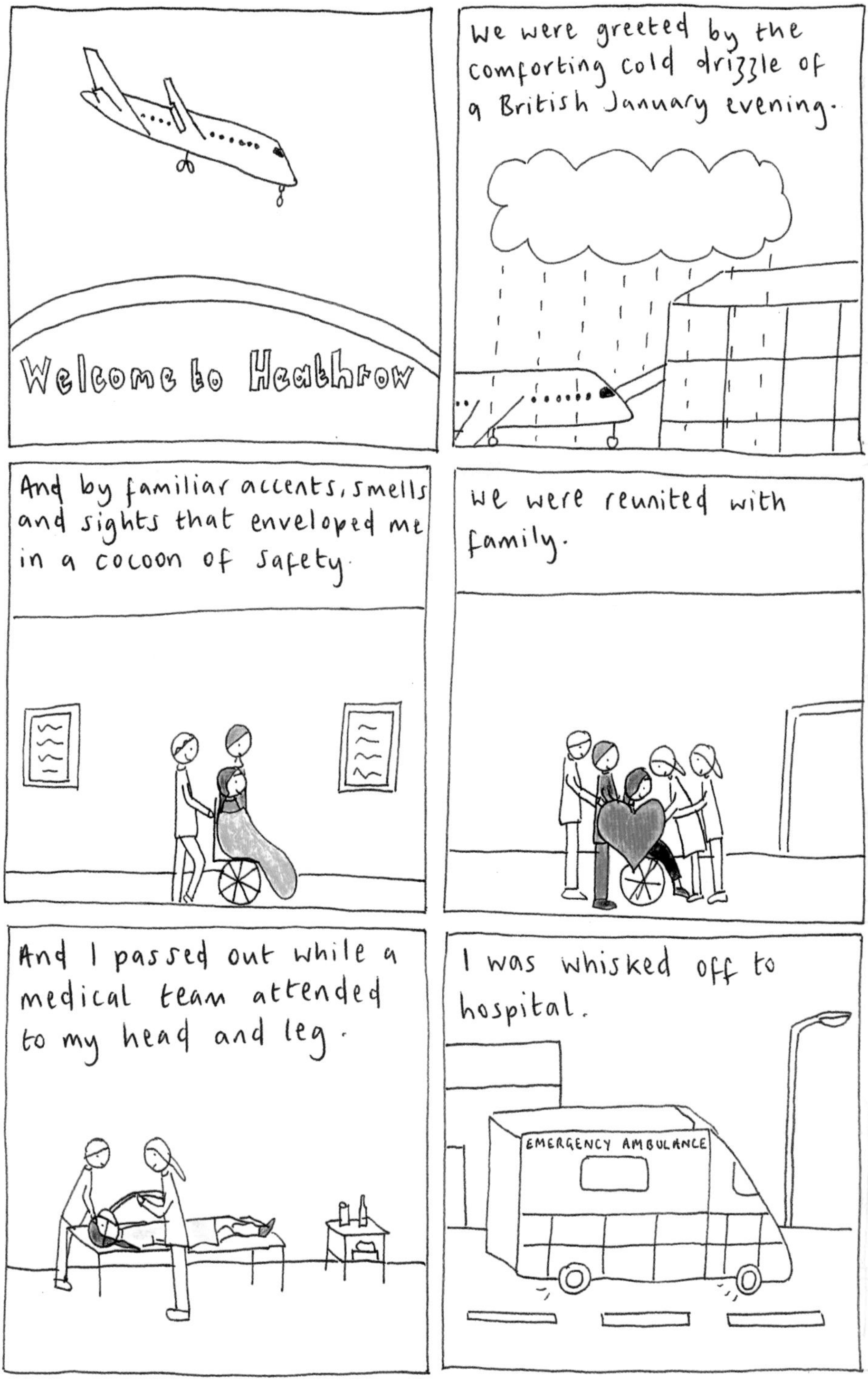
Welcome to Heathrow
We were greeted by the comforting cold drizzle of a British January evening.
And by familiar accents, smells and sights that enveloped me in a cocoon of safety.
We were reunited with family.
And I passed out while a medical team attended to my head and leg.
I was whisked off to hospital.
EMERGENCY AMBULANCE

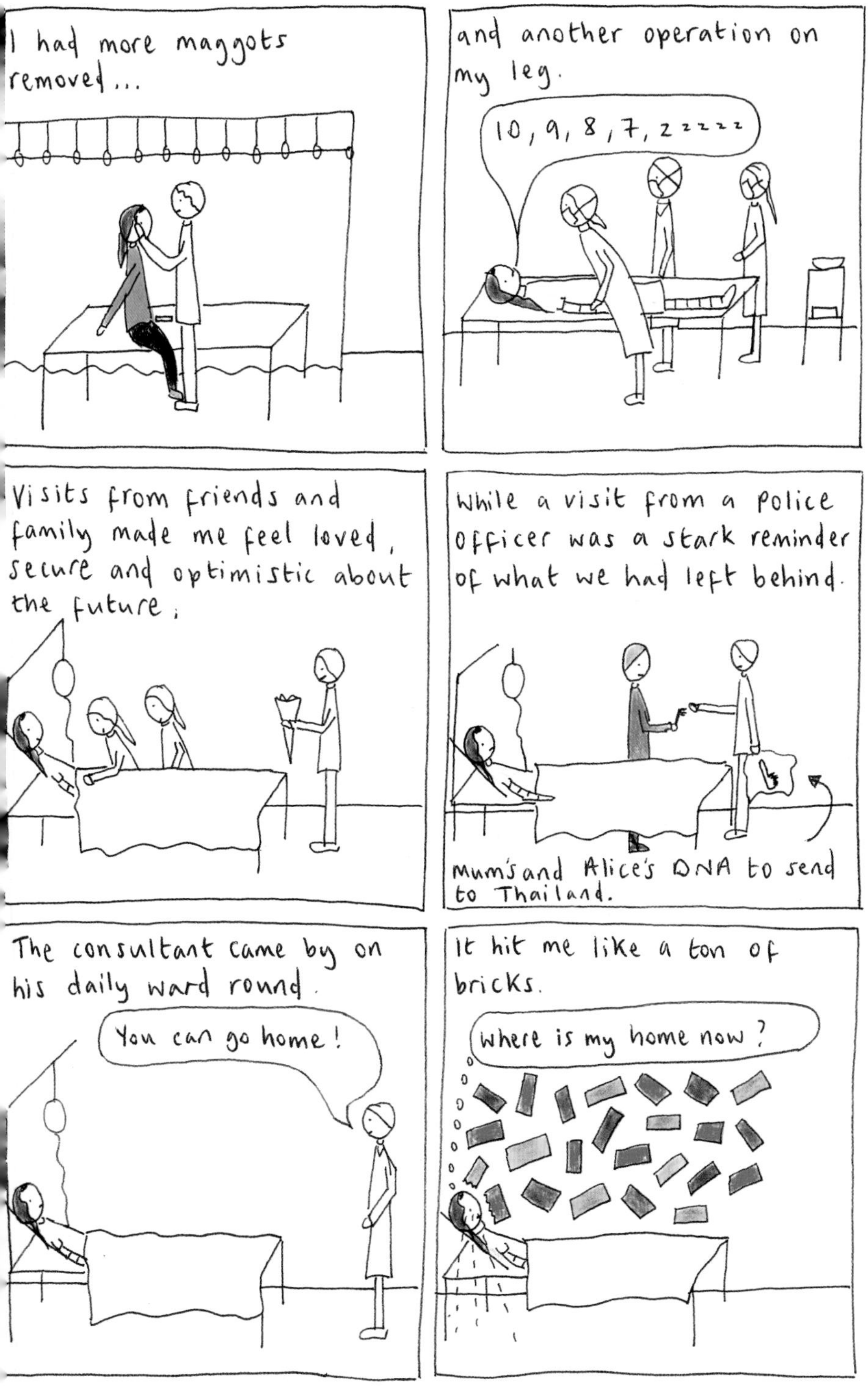
I had more maggots removed...
and another operation on my leg.
10, 9, 8, 7, zzzzz
Visits from friends and family made me feel loved, secure and optimistic about the future;
while a visit from a police officer was a stark reminder of what we had left behind.
Mum's and Alice's DNA to send to Thailand.
The consultant came by on his daily ward round.
You can go home!
It hit me like a ton of bricks.
Where is my home now?

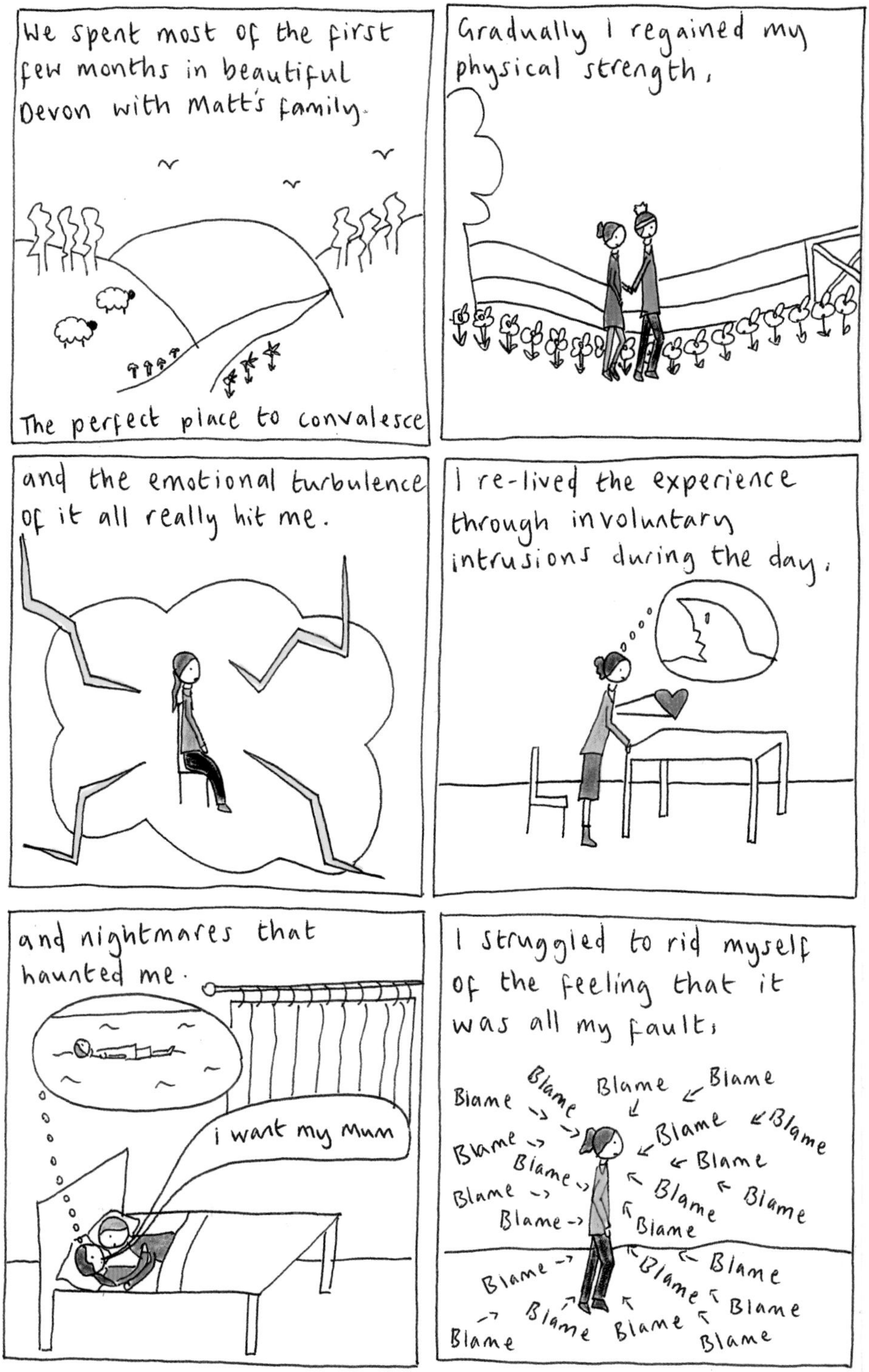
We spent most of the first few months in beautiful Devon with Matt's family.
The perfect place to convalesce
Gradually I regained my physical strength,
and the emotional turbulence of it all really hit me.
I re-lived the experience through involuntary intrusions during the day,
and nightmares that haunted me.
i want my Mum
I struggled to rid myself of the feeling that it was all my fault,
Blame Blame

and with the reality that I no longer had a mother or sister.

I would never ever see them again.

No more walks on Ilkley Moor on Christmas Day.

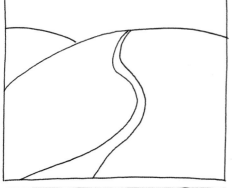

No more sound of them playing music together.

No more laughing around the kitchen table.

Their birthdays replaced by an uncomfortable emptiness.

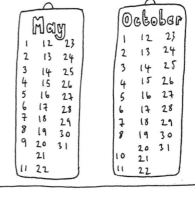

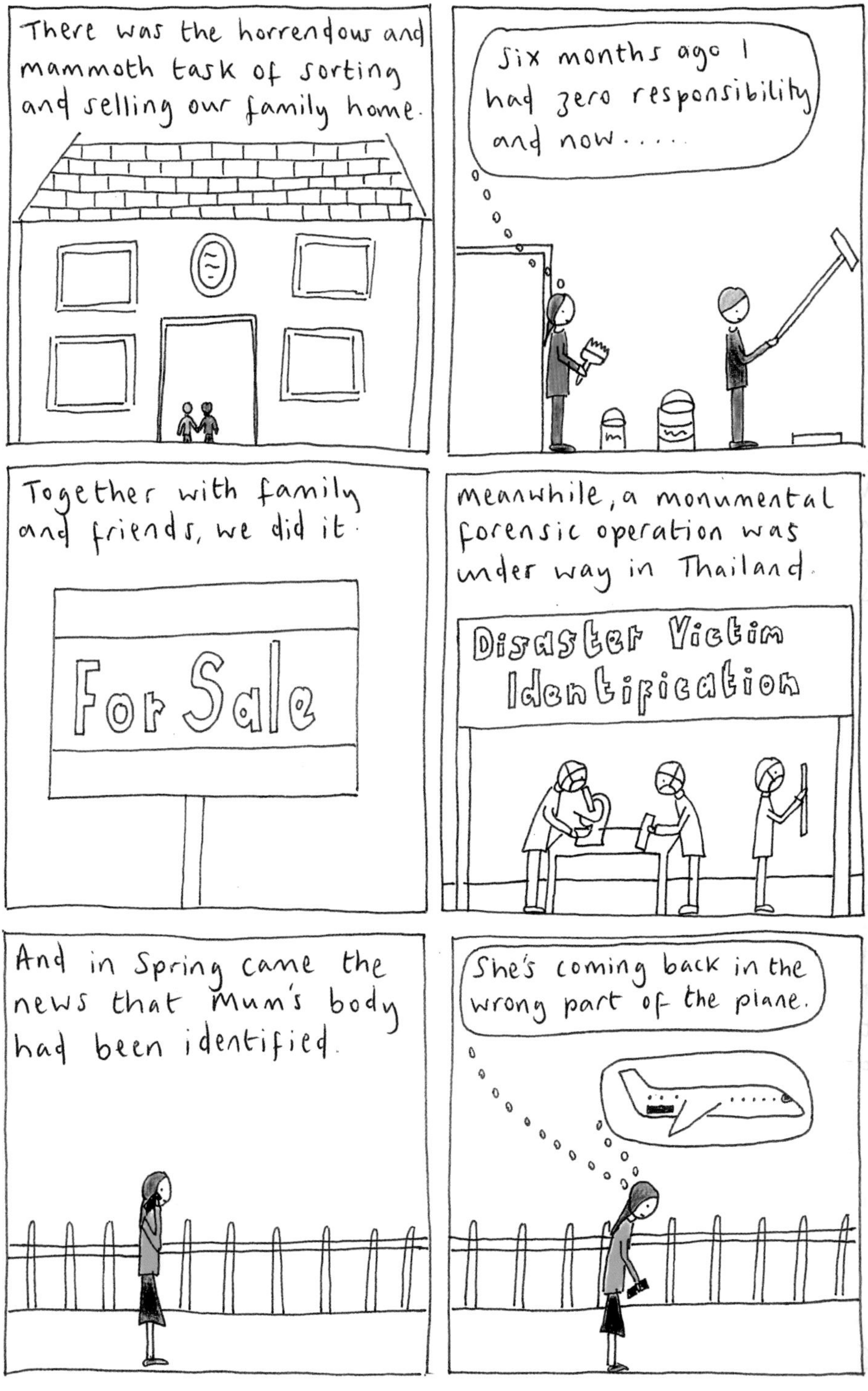

There was the horrendous and mammoth task of sorting and selling our family home.
Six months ago I had zero responsibility and now....
Together with family and friends, we did it.
For Sale
Meanwhile, a monumental forensic operation was under way in Thailand.
Disaster Victim Identification
And in Spring came the news that Mum's body had been identified.
She's coming back in the wrong part of the plane.

We attended a string of memorial events.

In memory
of
Sally Macgill

UNIVERSITY OF LEEDS

Concerts by Mum's and Alice's orchestras with pieces dedicated to them,

where I struggled to breathe hearing such beautiful music, but without them up on stage playing it.

A high profile service at St Paul's Cathedral.

where thousands and thousands of petals fell to represent everyone who died.

And we were surrounded by hundreds of people, each with their own painful story to tell of that horrible day.

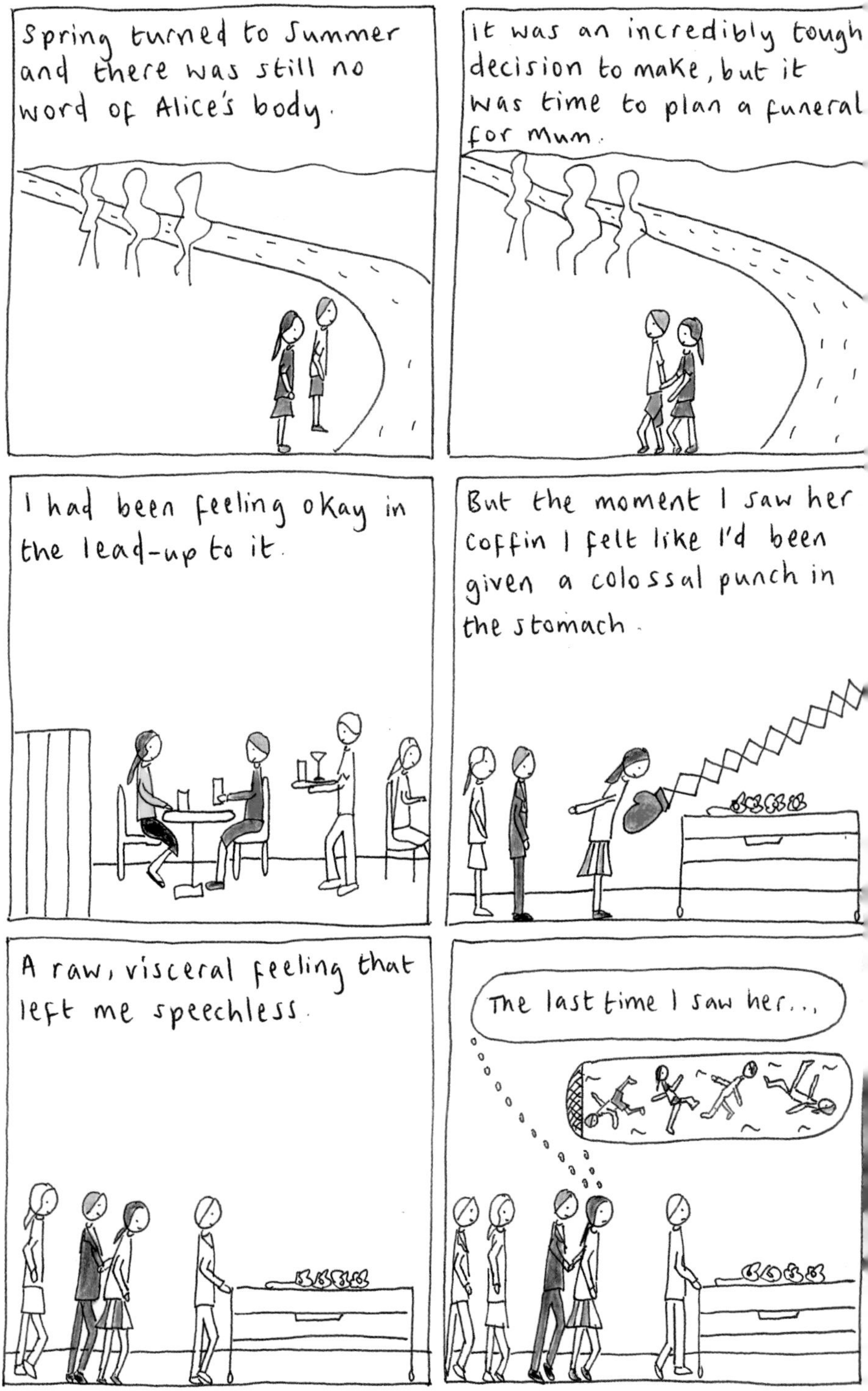

Spring turned to Summer and there was still no word of Alice's body.
It was an incredibly tough decision to make, but it was time to plan a funeral for Mum.
I had been feeling okay in the lead-up to it.
But the moment I saw her coffin I felt like I'd been given a colossal punch in the stomach.
A raw, visceral feeling that left me speechless.
The last time I saw her...

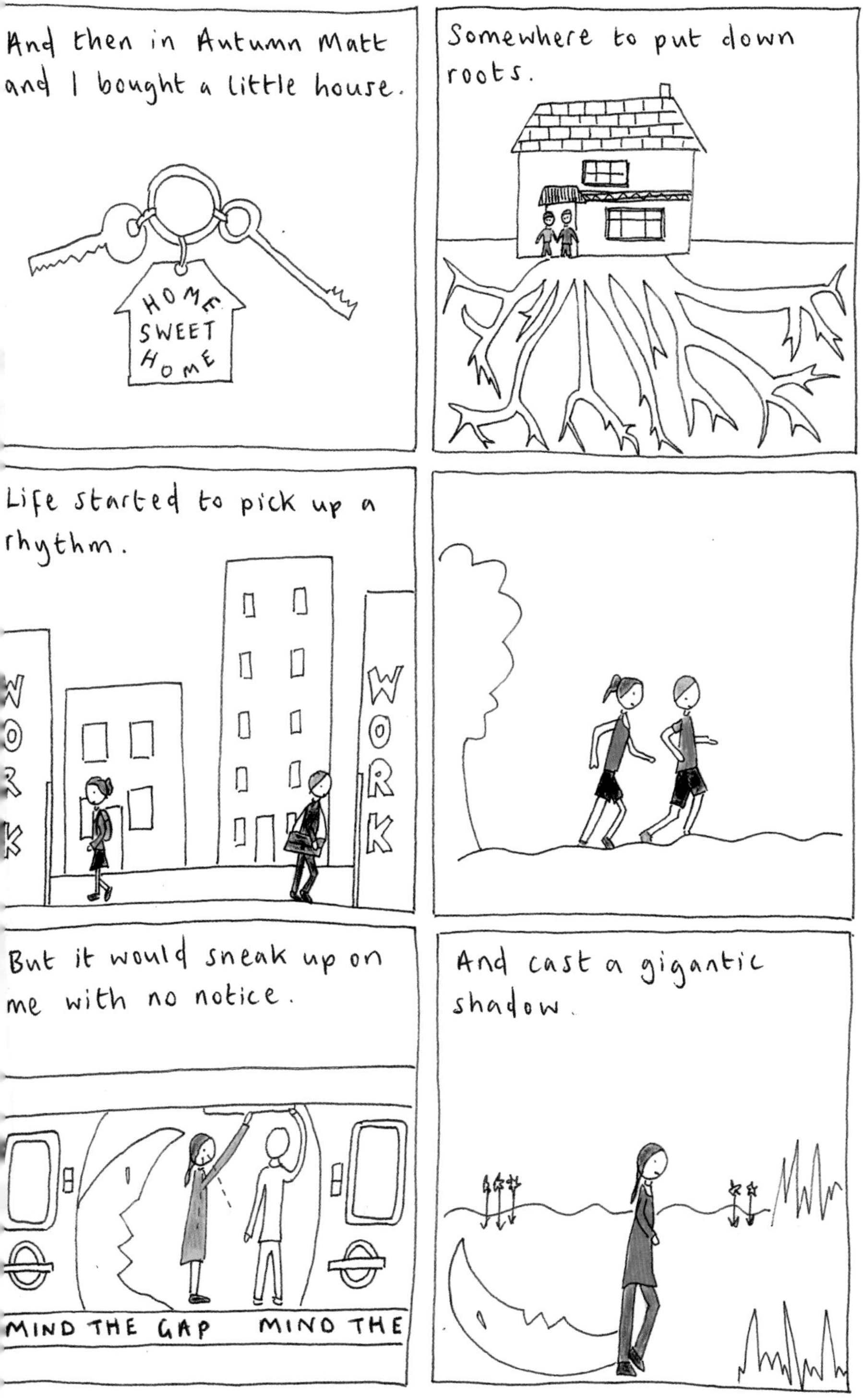
And then in Autumn Matt and I bought a little house.
HOME SWEET HOME
Somewhere to put down roots.
Life started to pick up a rhythm.
WORK
WORK
But it would sneak up on me with no notice.
MIND THE GAP MIND THE
And cast a gigantic shadow.

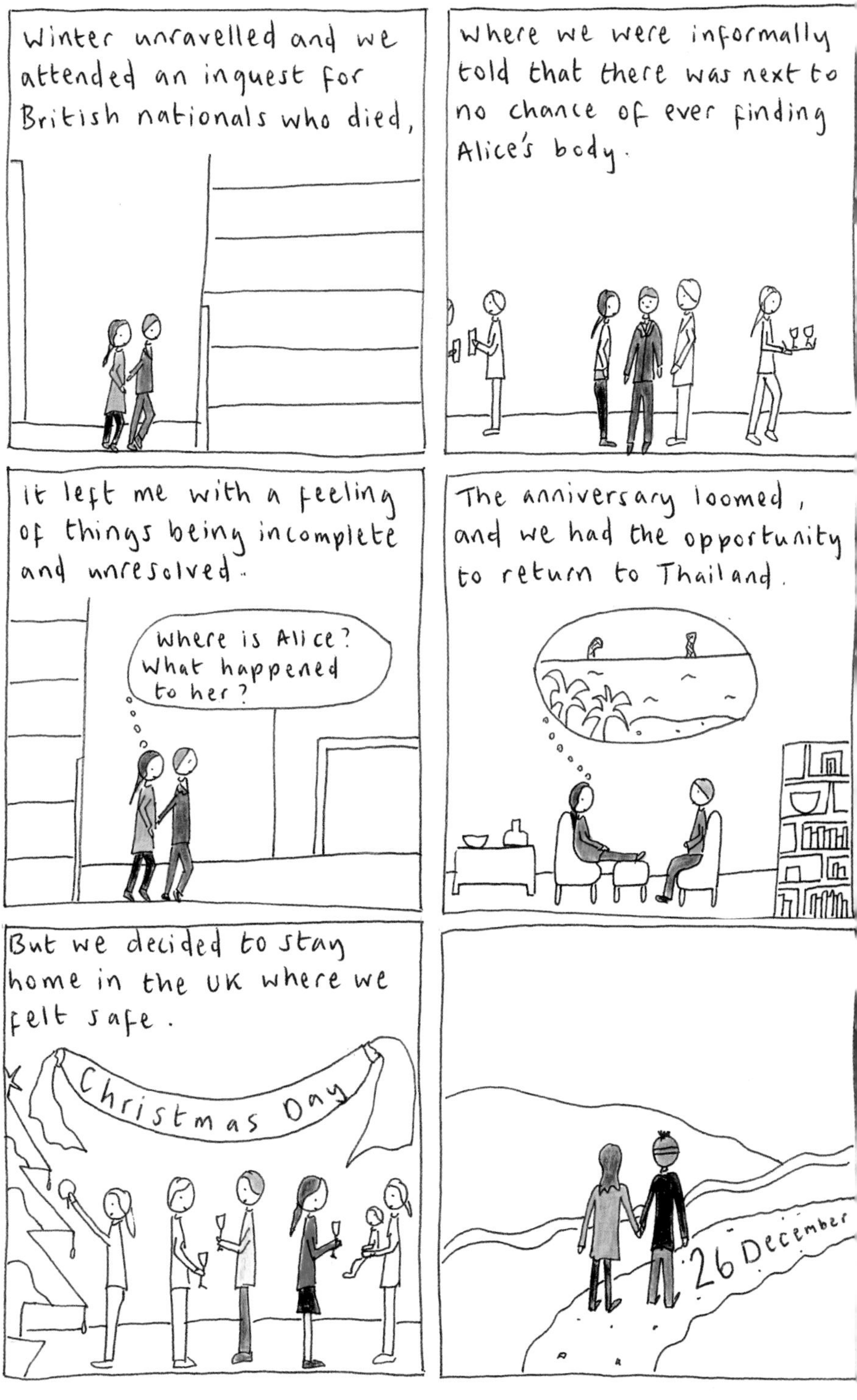

Winter unravelled and we attended an inquest for British nationals who died,
where we were informally told that there was next to no chance of ever finding Alice's body.
It left me with a feeling of things being incomplete and unresolved.
Where is Alice? What happened to her?
The anniversary loomed, and we had the opportunity to return to Thailand.
But we decided to stay home in the UK where we felt safe.
Christmas Day
26 December

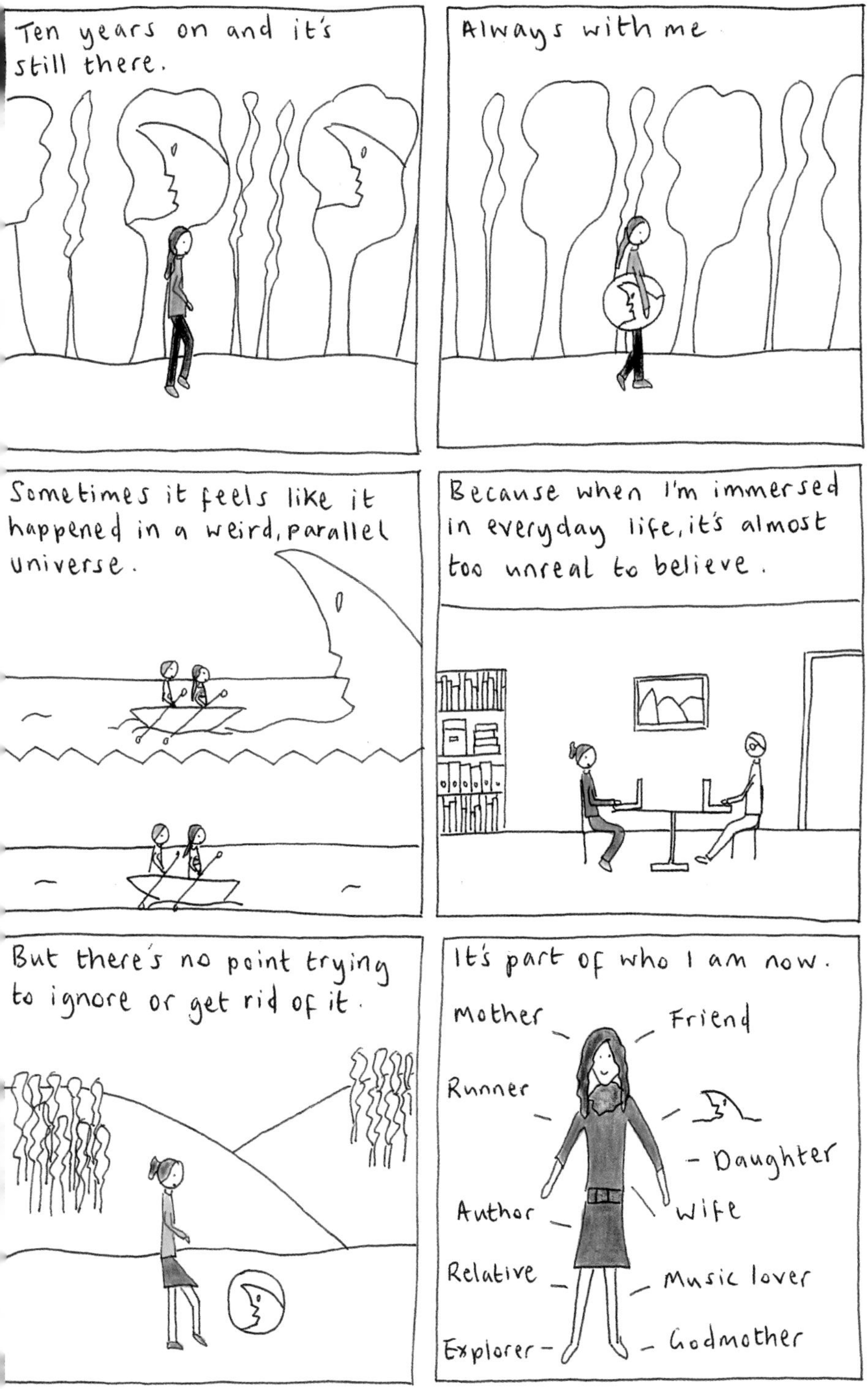
Ten years on and it's still there.
Always with me
Sometimes it feels like it happened in a weird, parallel universe.
Because when I'm immersed in everyday life, it's almost too unreal to believe.
But there's no point trying to ignore or get rid of it.
It's part of who I am now.
Mother
Friend
Runner
Daughter
Author
Wife
Relative
Music lover
Explorer
Godmother

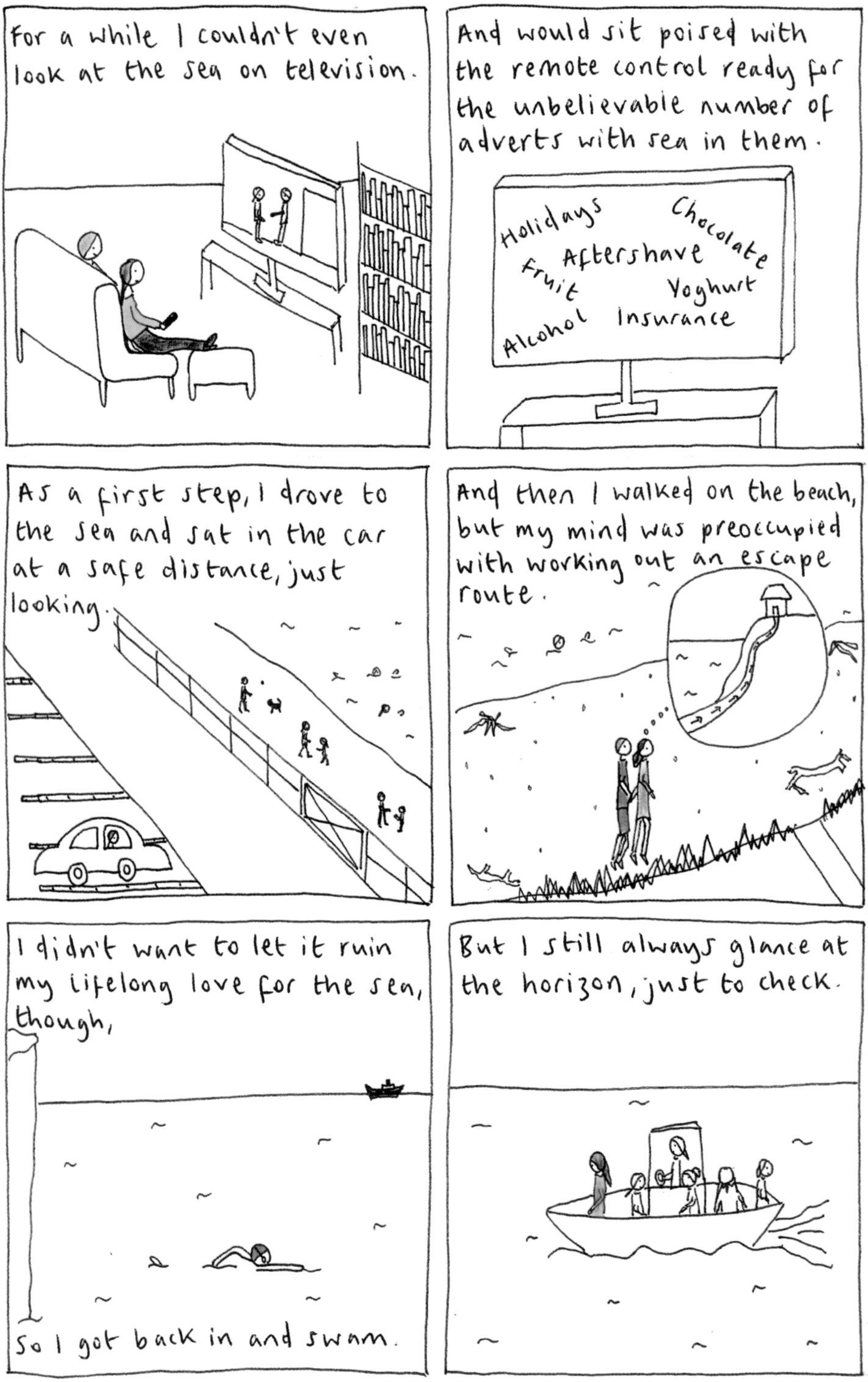
For a while I couldn't even look at the sea on television.
And would sit poised with the remote control ready for the unbelievable number of adverts with sea in them.
Holidays
Chocolate
Aftershave
Fruit
Yoghurt
Alcohol
Insurance
As a first step, I drove to the sea and sat in the car at a safe distance, just looking.
And then I walked on the beach, but my mind was preoccupied with working out an escape route.
I didn't want to let it ruin my lifelong love for the sea, though,
So I got back in and swam.
But I still always glance at the horizon, just to check.

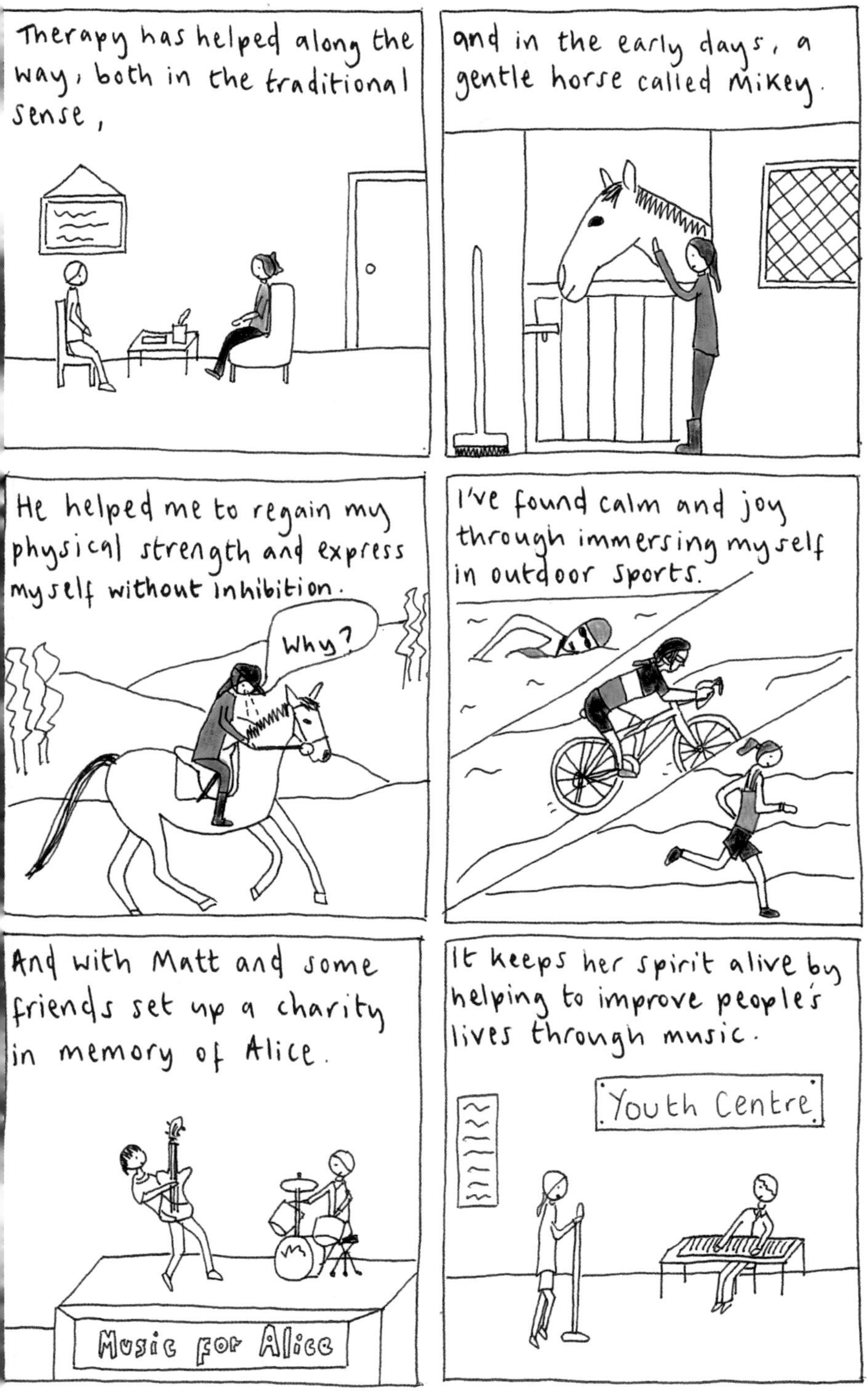
Therapy has helped along the way, both in the traditional sense,
and in the early days, a gentle horse called Mikey.
He helped me to regain my physical strength and express myself without inhibition.
Why?
I've found calm and joy through immersing myself in outdoor sports.
And with Matt and some friends set up a charity in memory of Alice.
Music for Alice
It keeps her spirit alive by helping to improve people's lives through music.
Youth Centre

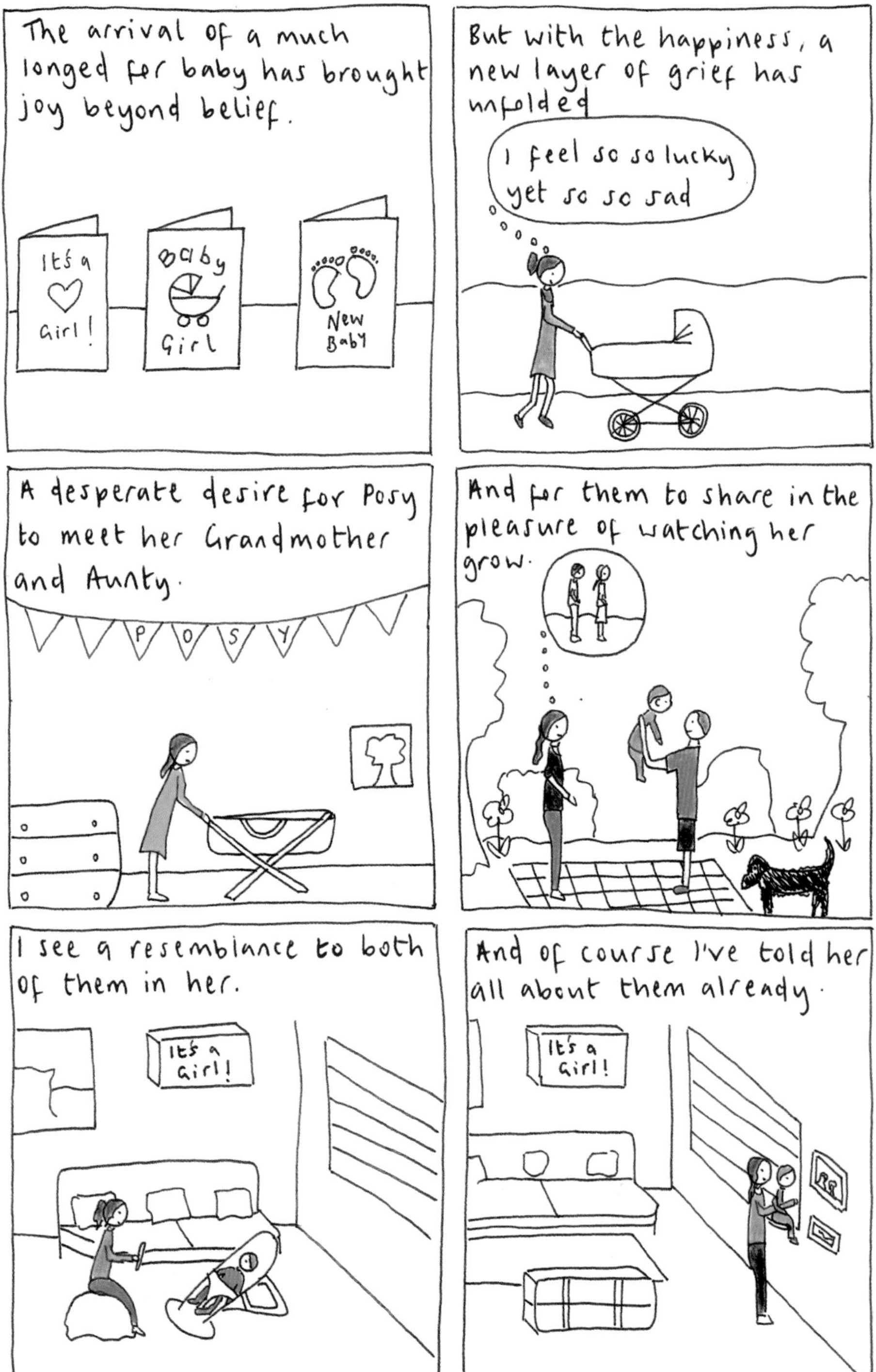
The arrival of a much longed for baby has brought joy beyond belief.
It's a Girl!
Baby Girl
New Baby
But with the happiness, a new layer of grief has unfolded
I feel so so lucky yet so so sad
A desperate desire for Posy to meet her Grandmother and Aunty.
POSY
And for them to share in the pleasure of watching her grow.
I see a resemblance to both of them in her.
It's a Girl!
And of course I've told her all about them already.
It's a Girl!

I'll always experience some things differently now.

I see a plane trail across a bright blue sky as a dangerous wave.

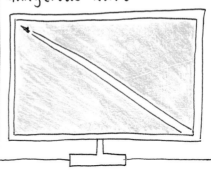

And an unidentified rumble at the theatre sends my heart rate soaring.

EXIT

I always stumble when I'm asked if I have brothers or sisters. There's no short answer.

Urrr

I don't think I'll ever get used to explaining how Alice died.

WHAT?

And that her body was never found.

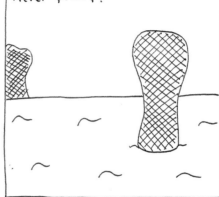

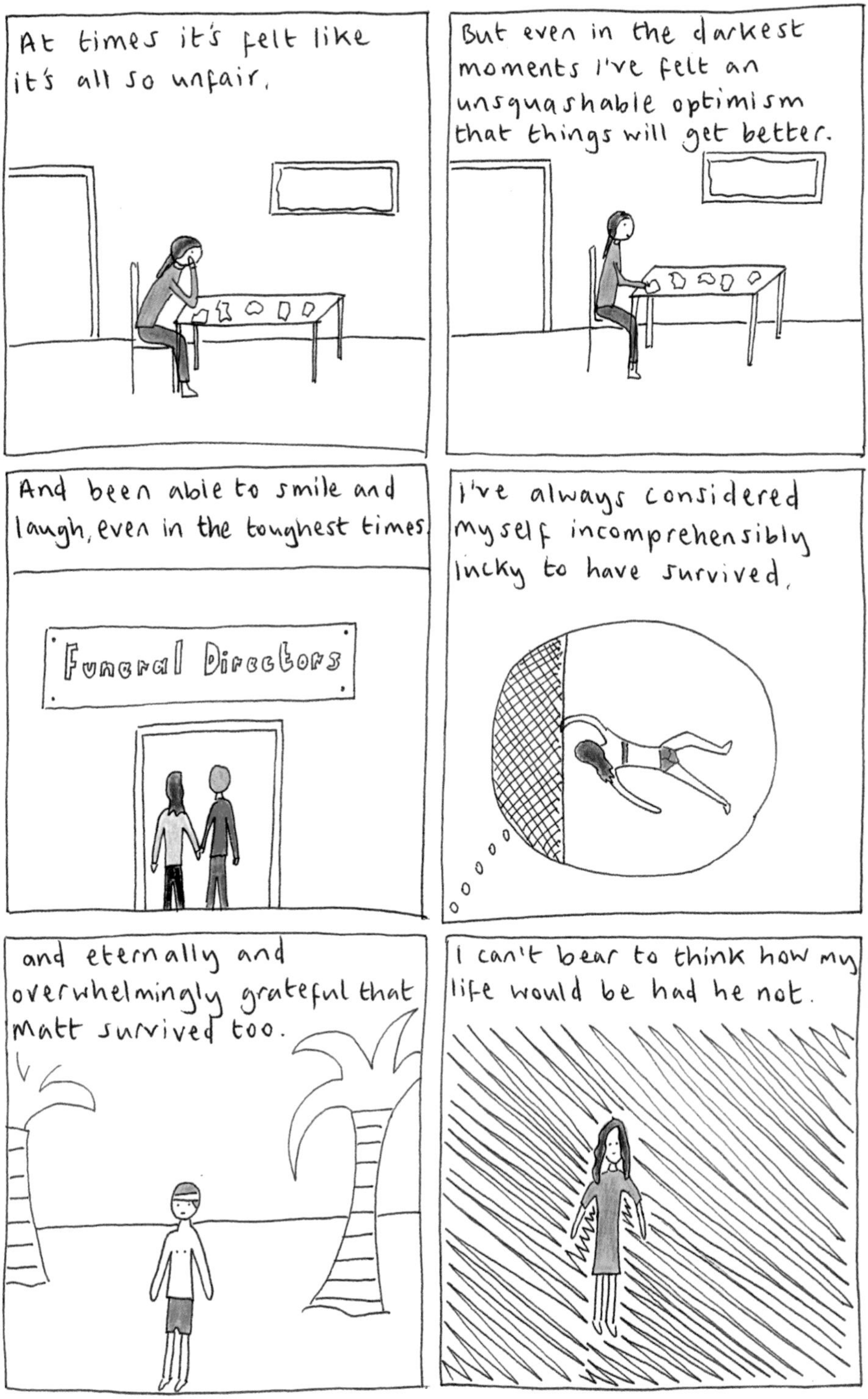
At times it's felt like it's all so unfair.
But even in the darkest moments I've felt an unsquashable optimism that things will get better.
And been able to smile and laugh, even in the toughest times.
Funeral Directors
I've always considered myself incomprehensibly lucky to have survived,
and eternally and overwhelmingly grateful that Matt survived too.
I can't bear to think how my life would be had he not.

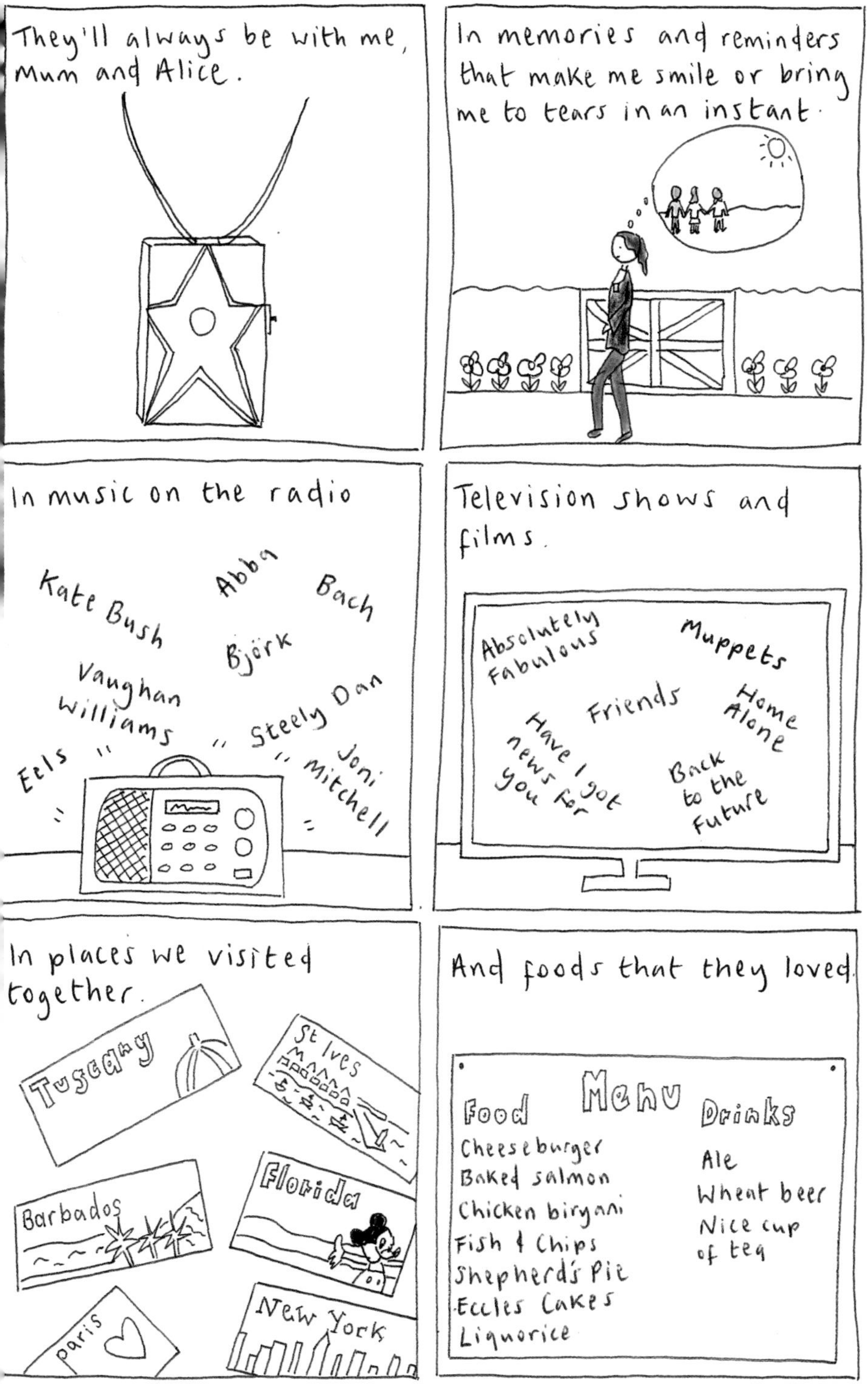
They'll always be with me, Mum and Alice.
In memories and reminders that make me smile or bring me to tears in an instant.
In music on the radio
Kate Bush
Abba
Bach
Björk
Vaughan Williams
Steely Dan
Eels
Joni Mitchell
Television shows and films.
Absolutely Fabulous
Muppets
Friends
Home Alone
Have I got news for you
Back to the Future
In places we visited together.
Tuscany
St Ives
Barbados
Florida
Paris
New York
And foods that they loved.
Menu
Food
Cheeseburger
Baked salmon
Chicken biryani
Fish & Chips
Shepherd's Pie
Eccles Cakes
Liquorice
Drinks
Ale
Wheat beer
Nice cup of tea

Sally, my incredible Mum - Inspirational, modest, fair
She excelled in academia, music and sport, but most of
all in being THE most loving and supportive mother.

And my beautiful sister Alice - Hilarious, caring, serene
She brought joy and laughter wherever she went and
left a cavernous hole in the lives of her family,
friends and the students that she never got to teach.

They don't need to worry about me. I'm in the safe hands of my unsnappable web of friends and family,

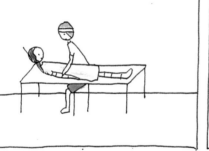

Who cried when I couldn't, and love me unconditionally.

And then there's Matt, who has always been by my side.

Calmly and quietly loving me and always, always putting my needs before his.

It was our experience, and it has bonded us in a way that no words can describe.

The
End

Unbound is a new kind of publishing house. Our books are funded directly by readers. This was a very popular idea during the late eighteenth and early nineteenth centuries. Now we have revived it for the internet age. It allows authors to write the books they really want to write and readers to support the writing they would most like to see published.

The names listed below are of readers who have pledged their support and made this book happen. If you'd like to join them, visit www.unbound.co.uk.

Isabella Acklam-Foulet
Rachael Adam
Ronni Adams
Jillian Adie
Aki Alaraatikka
Victoria Allan
Sue Allen
Alessandro Andreotti
Kim Appelquist
Ferne Arfin
Christine Asbury
Shayne Atkinson
Christina Baarda
Sohail Baig
David and Sue Baker
Jason Ballinger
Emily Bart-Smith
Mary Ann Barton
Pat Beaumont
Belle Benfield
Dorian Benson
Theodore Bentley
Sally Best
Joe Bickerstaff
Naomi Billington
Julian Birch
Marion Birch
Alison Blagdon
Nathan Bloomfield
Caroline Blott
Adrian Blount
Jessica Boatwright
James Bolchover
Jonathan & Joyce Bolchover
Samantha Bond
Imogen Bowers
Sarah Boxford
Carrie Boysun
Jenny Bray
Catherine Breen
Wendy Brooke
Joanna Brown
Philip Browne
Andrew Bullock
Noa Burger
Paul Burger
Esther Burton
Louise Cairns
John Caley
Sara Calverley & Amy Yard
Rachel Campey
Julie Carmichael
Anna, Richard & Orly Carter
David Carter
Laurie Carter
Rick Challener
Caroline Chapman
Marisa Charosky
Ruth Chase
Lindsay Clappé
Heidi Clark
Alexandra Clarke
Emma Clyde & James Gore
Mike Collinson
Frank Cook
Jo Cook

Odile Cook
Monique Corless
Eleanor Coulber
Imogene Coyne
Caroline Craig
John Crawford
Emma Critchley
Ross Crombie
Jenny Crossthwaite
Kate Crossthwaite
Kathy Crossthwaite
Hannah Cullen
Emma Darwish
Alison Davenport-Latif
Jesse Davies
Steve Davies
Joanne Dawes
Richard Deacon
Charlotte Dewhirst
Joachim Dietz
Pamela Dixon
Susannah Donnelly
Alan Dooney
Hannah Doughty
Simon Downs
Keith Dunbar
Fernanda Dutra
Charlie Easton
Tamsin Ede
Juliet Edwards
Stephen Edwards
Ronnie Elazary
Lynsey Ellard
El Etherington
Karen Etherington

Andrew Evans
Joe Evans
James Fassnidge
Kye Fassnidge
Matt Fassnidge
Nick Fassnidge
Tessa Fassnidge
Tom Fassnidge
Virginia Fassnidge
Harriet Fear Davies
Patrick Finnegan
James Fisher
Angela Fountain
Sam Gardner
Lisa Garvey-Williams
Stephanie Gaydon
Paul Geil
Julie Gibbon
James & Ruth Gibbs
Karen Gilchrist
The Giliker Family
Grainne Gilsenan
Sonia Ginty
Ali Glew
Paul Goodison
Giles Goodland
Kate Gosling
Joshua Grace
Tracey Grantham
Gregor Haddow
Christoph Haerringer
Louise Hake
Polly Haley
The Hall Family
Emma Halliday
Julia Haltrecht

Helena Hammock
Ed Hancox
Ellis Harrop
Joy Harrop
Lori Haugen
Leti Hawthorn
Gill Heath
Linda Hepper
Mareike Hermes
Rick Hewett
Alex Hickman
Nicole Hielscher & Tom Evans
Caroline Hildrew
Katie Hill
Amy Hillier
Rebecca Hillier
Natasha Hines
Polly Hobbs
Trish Hobson
Martijn Hoogerwerf
Bec Hopkins
Jacob Howe
Sandra Howles
George Hoyle
Amy Irvine
Worakarn Isaratham
Johari Ismail
Biliby Iwai
Dominic Jackson
Jordana Jackson
Margaret Jackson
Leigh James
Simon James
Lucy Jaques
Faysal Jhetam

Gabrielle Johnson
Amanda Jones
Lucy Jones
Nolan Jones
Paulene Jones
Marie Kamal
Rehan Kamal
Eileen & Peter Kellett
Janine Kellett
Stephen Kellett
Peter Kessler
Dan Kieran
Claire Kirkby
Doron Klemer
Catherine Kontz
Kerrie-Anne Langendoen
Aileen Laurance
Paul Lawrence
W Tom Lawrie
Jimmy Leach
Susan Leach
Sophie Lee
Luke Lennox
Kristi Ley
Mary & Jerry Ley
Kran Lin
Joan Luck
Richard Luck
Wendy Lunn
David Macgill
Jamie Macgill
Roger & Brenda Macgill
Catriona Mahoney
Amanda Malsbury
Kelly Mara
Anne Marshall

Simon Marshall
Carol Marston
John Mitchinson
Linnet Mattey
Emily Matthews
Jo Maxwell
Nicola Maxwell-Gumbleton
Lyndsay McAteer
Laura Walker McDonald
Katie McDowell
Martin Mcgarry
Carole McIntosh
Dan McKeown
Jody Mellor
Luka Melon
Frances Millhouse
John Mitchinson
Jay Modhwadia
Helena Monds
John Monds
Christine Morris
Helen Morris
Nancy Morris
Claire Morton
Courtney Murphy
Laura Murphy
Markus Naegele
Carlo Navato
Tracy Neal
Jean Neale
Liz Neale
Lenny Neale-Krommenhoek
Laura Needham
Louise Nevison
Christine Newall

Nick & Yona
Kate Novak
Gem Novis
Rebecca Nunn
Karen Nurse
Katharine Nurse
Tracey O'Brien
Georgia Odd
David Pack
Amy Parker
Victoria Parkin
Lisa Pember
Anna Penney
Rose Phillips
Harriet Pilkington
Luisa Plaja
Justin Pollard
Laura Popazzi
Adele Poskitt
Ollie Pound
Nicky Pratt
Charlotte Pritchard-Jo
Dan Pryce
Natasha Putnins
Alistair Ramsay
Erica Ramsay
Helen Ranner
Rosaleen Rashley
Lily Richards
Nina Ricks
Michelle Ritson
Colette Roberts
Jackie Roberts
Janet & Trevor Roberts
Jen & Richard Roberts
Rose Roberts

Lucy Robinson
Sophie Robinson
Ben Rogers
Lucy Rose
Chris Roughsedge
Tracey Rowe
Hannah Russell
Sue Rust
Claire Salvetti
Edward Samuel
Christoph Sander
Susie Sanders
Christina Sartori
Benjamin Schoo
Beth Scott
Tony Scott
Carrie Scuffell
Lynsey Searle
Markku Segerstedt
Andrew, Sarita, Mahi
    & Ishan Selman
Jo Sheppard
Adrian Sherwen
Sarah Shinn
Catherine Shutt
Heather Shutt
Ian Shutt
Natalie Sillwood
Louise Simmons
Jonal Smith
Verity Smith
Andrea Speed
Liz Spice
Jill Spice
Jonna Spinks
Harriet St Johnston

Julia Stevens
Nyola Stewart
Nicola Strand
Fi Sweetman
Isabel Tabraham
Jenny Thompson
Laura Thornton
Stephen Trickett
Matilda Tristram
Atsuko Tsujita
Kim Tuffield
Eve Turner-Lee
Alane Urban
Marianne Velmans
Emma Visick
Richard Visick
Octavia Waley-Cohen
Ben Walker
Emma Waterton
Phil Waymonth
Jules Weall
Cristal Webb
Nick Webb of Webb's Wonders
Clair Whitefield
Miranda Whiting
Linda Wickström
Angela Wiggan
Gareth Wilce
Nicky Wilce
Dorothy Wilkinson
Julie Williams
Richard Williams
Ruth Williams
Scott Williams
James Wilson

Rebecca Winder
Ian Wolf
Moya Wood
Flavia Woodwark
Jamie Woolley
Yeehwan Yeoh
Yvonne & Christoph

Edith Fassnidge grew up in Yorkshire. After university and some time working, studying and travelling abroad, she moved to London where she lives with her family.

She loves being active in the outdoors and has cycled the length of Great Britain, swum with a relay team across the English Channel and competed for the Great Britain Age-Group triathlon team.

Her career so far includes teaching, corporate responsibility and personal training. With her husband Matt, and two friends, she set up Music for Alice, a charity in memory of the sister she lost in the tsunami.

Rinse, Spin, Repeat is her first book, and 10% of her profits will go towards Music for Alice.

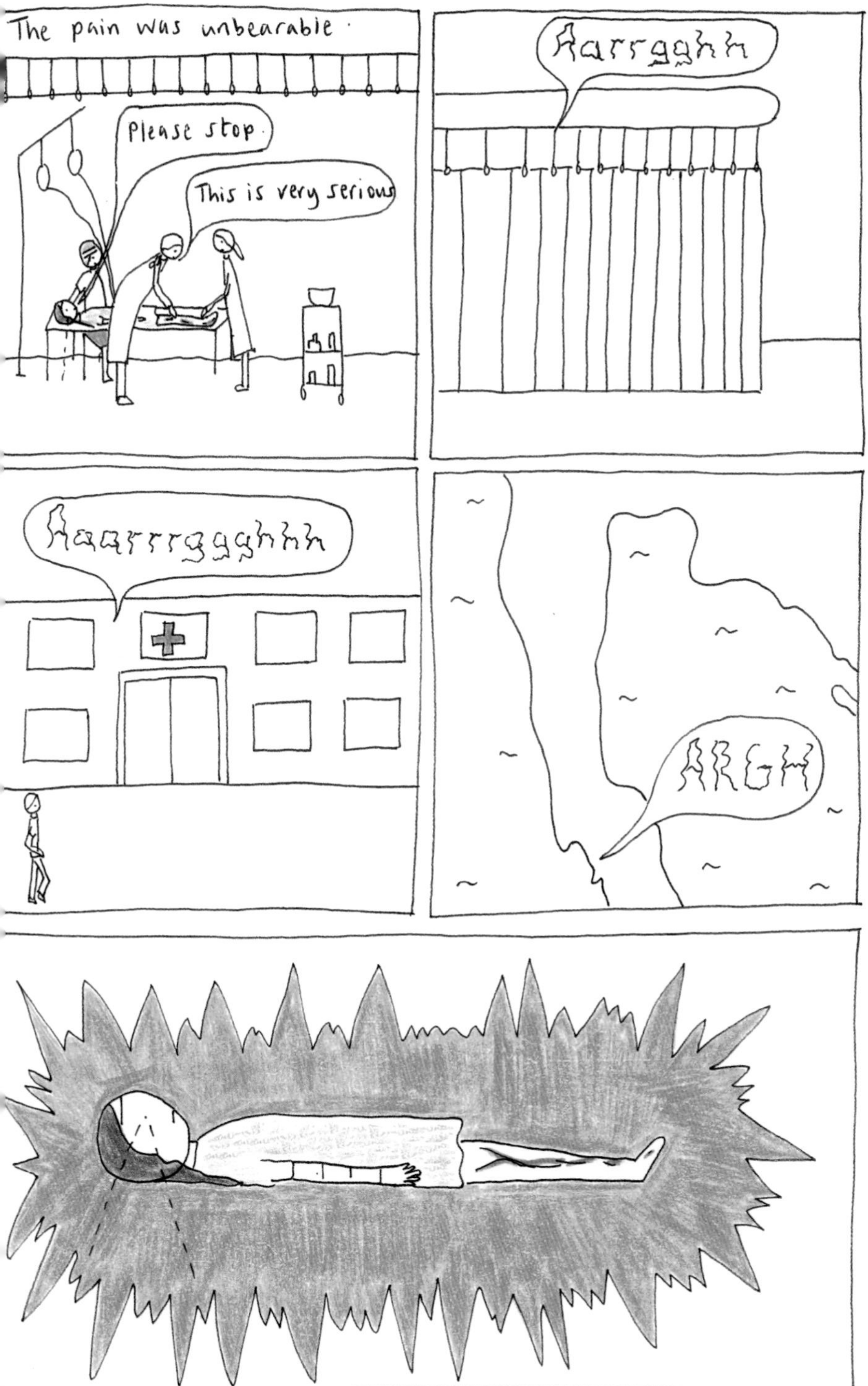
The pain was unbearable.
Please stop.
This is very serious
Aarrgghh
Aaarrrggghhh
ARGH

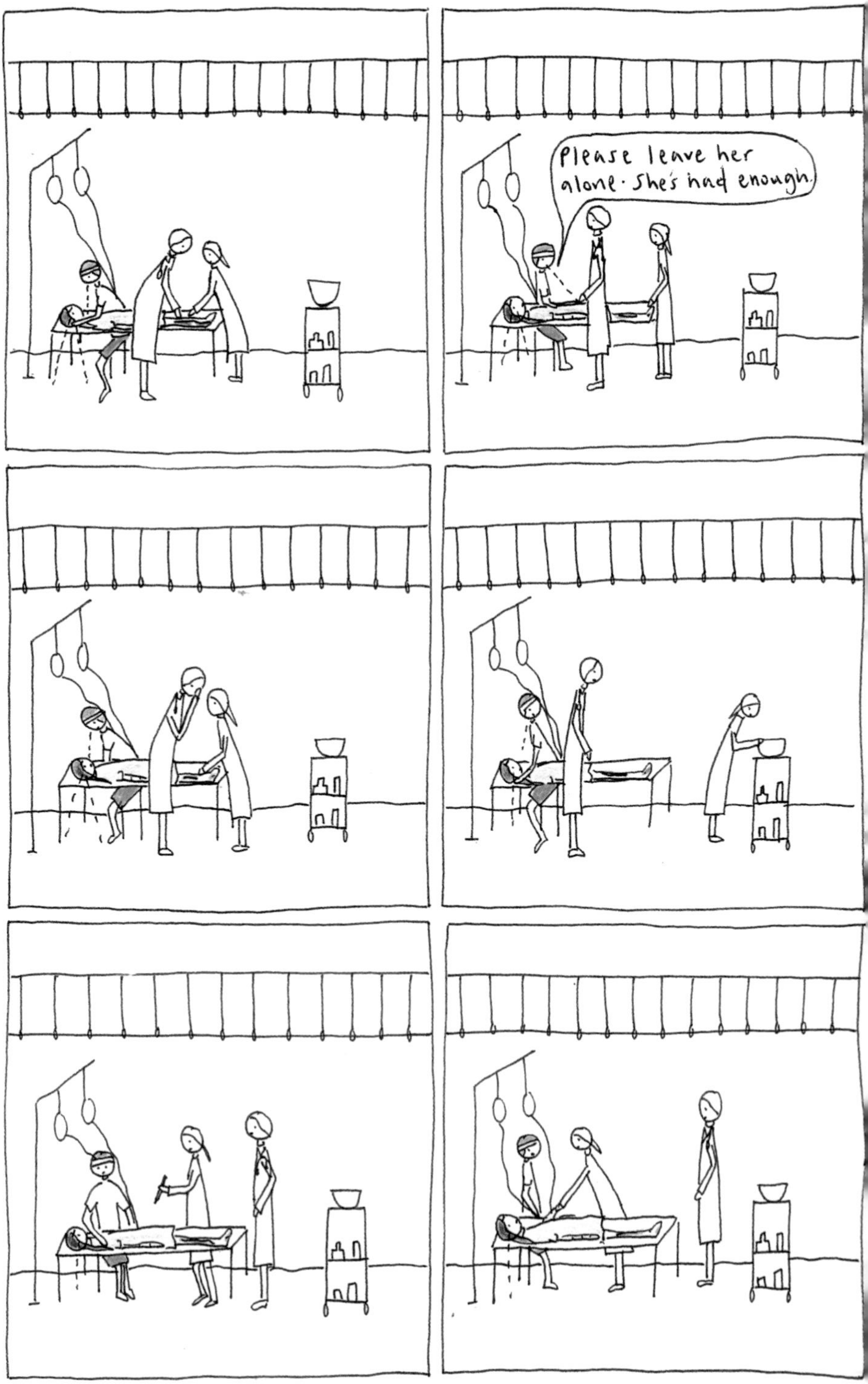
Please leave her alone. She's had enough.

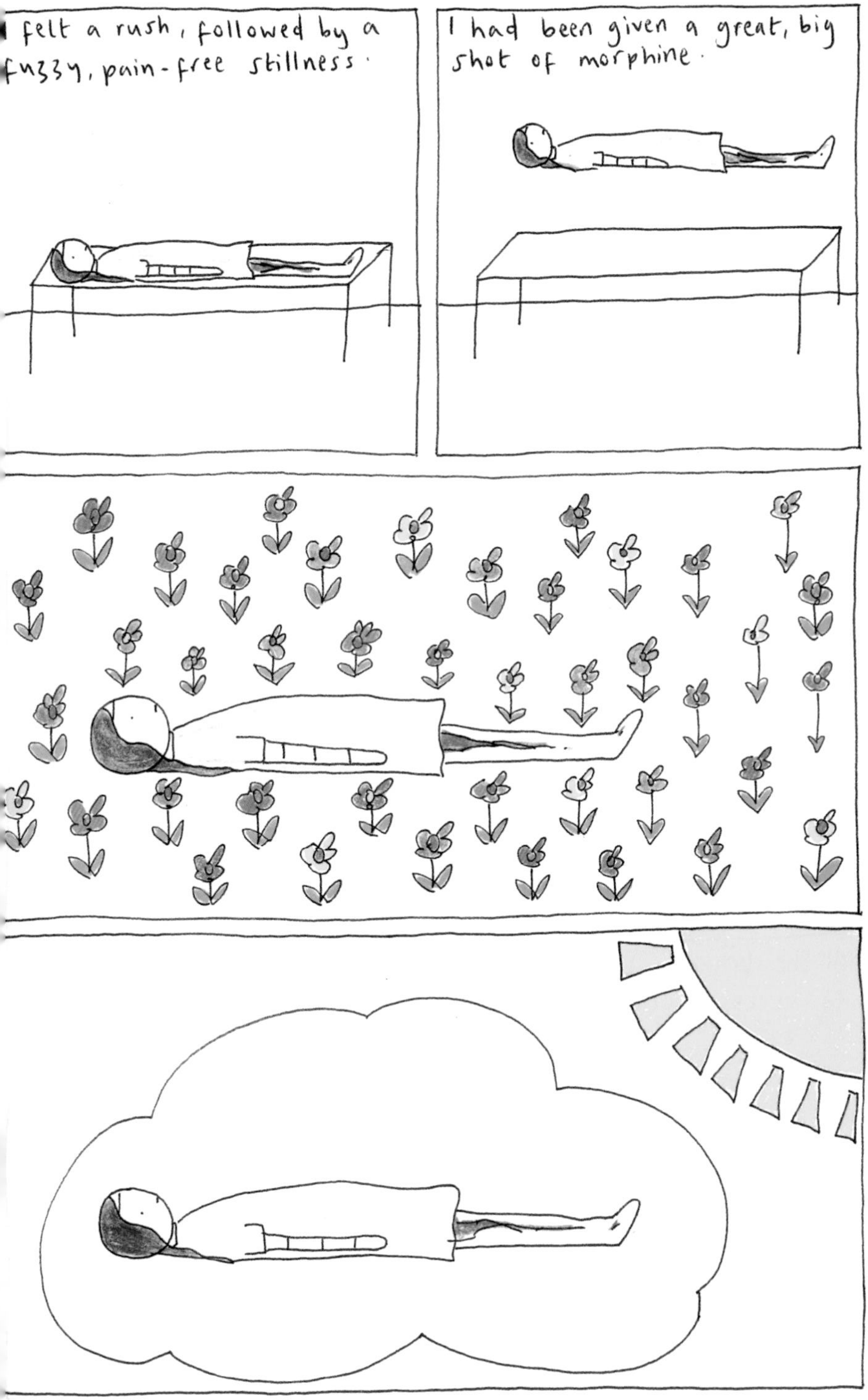
I felt a rush, followed by a fuzzy, pain-free stillness.
I had been given a great, big shot of morphine.

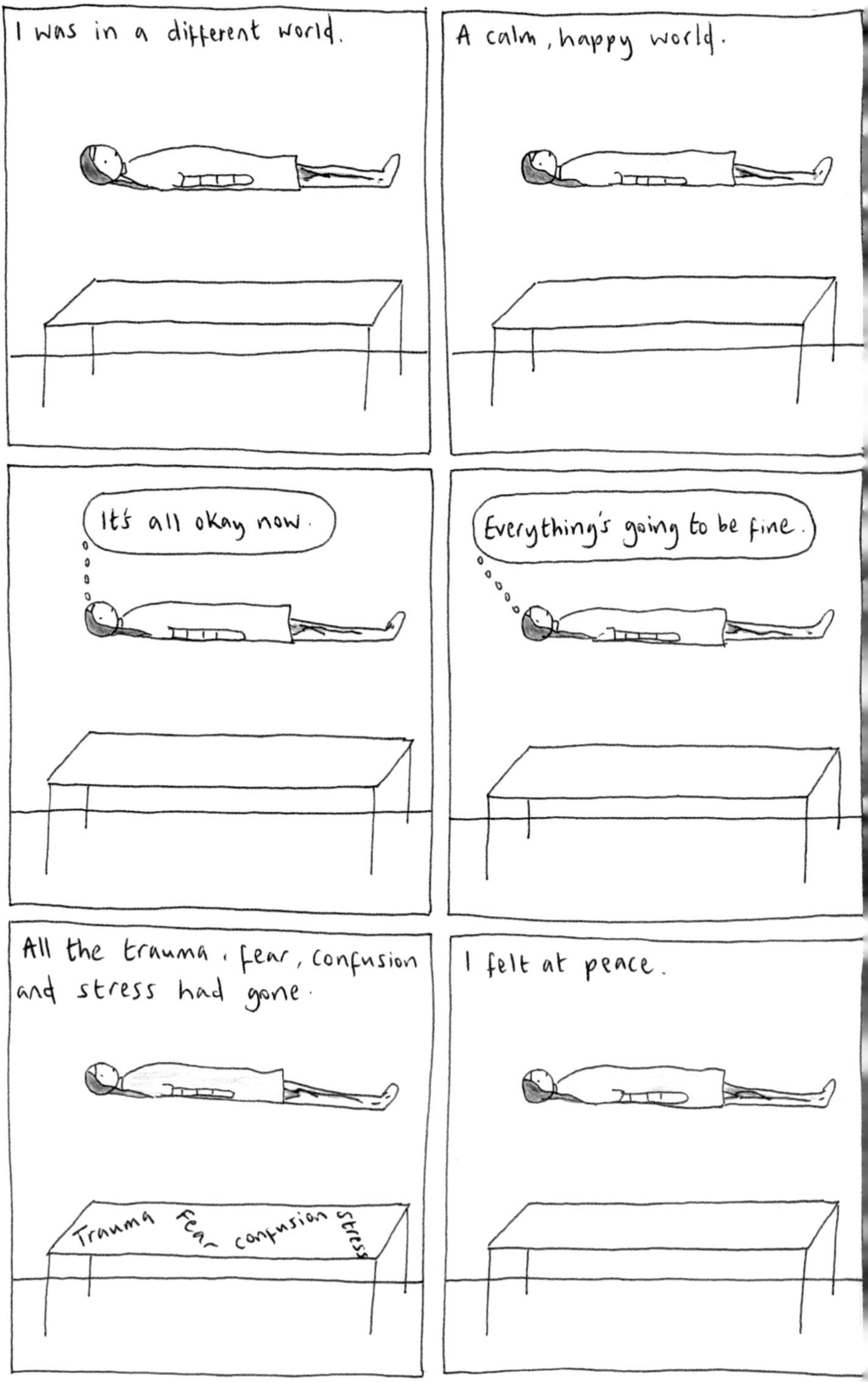
I was in a different world.
A calm, happy world.
It's all okay now.
Everything's going to be fine.
All the trauma, fear, confusion and stress had gone.
Trauma
Fear
confusion
stress
I felt at peace.